Duncan Rogers was born in the Midlands. After graduating with a degree in history from the University of Warwick in 1995 he took up a career in bookselling and publishing. He has been reading, writing and researching military history for as long as he can remember, having inherited his father's strong interest in the subject. He is currently engaged in the translation of a book about *Panzerkorps Großdeutschland* from the original German, and the co-writing of a major study of the First World War French Army due out in 2006, the 90th anniversary of Verdun.

Sarah Williams was brought up in Wales. She studied modern European history at the University of Warwick. From 1996 she pursued postgraduate studies in medieval history at the Centre for Medieval Studies, York, and was awarded a doctorate in 2002. For the past four years Sarah has been working as a general revision editor at the Oxford English Dictionary.

On the Bloody Road to Berlin

ON THE BLOODY ROAD TO BERLIN

Frontline Accounts from North-West Europe and the Eastern Front 1944-45

Edited by

Duncan Rogers and Sarah Williams

Helion & Company Ltd
in association with
The Military & Aviation Book Club

Helion & Company Limited
26 Willow Road
Solihull
West Midlands
B91 1UE
England
Tel. 0121 705 3393
Fax 0121 711 4075
Email: publishing@helion.co.uk
Website: www.helion.co.uk

Published by Helion & Company Limited in association with the Military & Aviation Book
Club 2005

Designed and typeset by Helion & Company Ltd, Solihull, West Midlands
Cover and maps designed by Bookcraft Limited, Stroud, Gloucestershire
Printed by Mackays of Chatham plc

ISBN 1 874622 08 6

British Library Cataloguing-in-Publication Data.
A catalogue record for this book is available from the British Library.

For details of other military history titles published by Helion & Company Limited contact
the above address, or visit our website: http://www.helion.co.uk.

We always welcome receiving book proposals from prospective authors.

Contents

List of Maps 8

Acknowledgements. 9

Introduction 11

The Eyewitnesses 13

Timeline 27

Glossary 35

I   NORTH-WEST EUROPE

      D-Day and Normandy (June-August 1944) 39

II   EASTERN FRONT

      The Soviet Summer Offensives (June-August 1944) 63

III   NORTH-WEST EUROPE

      Southern France, Arnhem and the drive towards the *Reich*

      (August-September 1944) 81

IV   EASTERN FRONT

      Withdrawal and regrouping (August-December 1944) 107

V   NORTH-WEST EUROPE

      The *Reich* border, the Ardennes and Alsace (December 1944-

      January 1945) 131

VI   EASTERN FRONT

      The Soviet drive through Europe (January-March 1945) 157

VII NORTH-WEST EUROPE

      The final push to the River Elbe (February-May 1945) 201

VIII EASTERN FRONT

      The last months (March-May 1945) 227

Further reading 273

Index 277

List of Maps

Map 1   Combat paths of the eyewitnesses: North-West Europe 23

Map 2   Combat paths of the eyewitnesses: Eastern Front 24

Map 3   North-West Europe: D-Day and Normandy 52

Map 4   Eastern Front: Soviet summer offensives 1944 64

Map 5   North-West Europe: Drive into the *Reich* 1944 132

Map 6   Eastern Front: Soviet drive through Europe 1944-45 158

Map 7   North-West Europe: Final push to the River Elbe 202

Map 8   Eastern Front: Berlin Offensive and final Soviet operations
in the southern sector of the front 229

Acknowledgements

O*n the Bloody Road to Berlin* has been a team effort requiring the assistance of a large number of people and organisations. Without the help of each and every one of them, publication would not have been possible.

The editors would like to thank David Hughes and Phil Sidnell at The Military & Aviation Book Club for making the whole project possible; Bob Baumer, who responded magnificently to our appeals for help; Kit and Patti Bonn at the Aberjona Press, whose help throughout has been invaluable; John Button at Bookcraft Ltd for his excellent maps; Artem Drabkin, whose assistance with the Russian accounts and photographs has been superb; Richard and Gwyneth Fairbank for their transcription skills; Paula Hurst at Pen & Sword Books Ltd; the staff at the Department of Photographs, Imperial War Museum; John Lowles, at the Worcestershire Regiment Museum Trust; Erik Norling; Marc Rikmenspoel, and finally, Louis Scully, for laying at our disposal his comprehensive knowledge of the 1st Battalion Worcester Regiment, as well as his collection of photographs.

For the use of copyright material the following are gratefully acknowledged:

- The accounts by Zoya Alexandrova and Vsevolod Olimpiev were both translated by Vladimir Kroupnik and edited by John Armstrong. Publication was made possible by the 'I Remember' website http://www.iremember.ru/index_e.htm and its director, Artem Drabkin.
- Robert Boscawen's account has been reprinted from *Armoured Guardsmen: A War Diary June 1944-April 1945* and appears courtesy of Pen & Sword Books Ltd. © Robert Boscawen, 2001.
- Sam Carter's reminiscences appear courtesy of Sam Carter, Bob Baumer, and the Aberjona Press. © Sam Carter.
- Denis Edwards' account has been reprinted from *The Devil'sOwn Luck: Pegasus Bridge to the Baltic 1944-45*, and appears courtesy of Pen & Sword Books Ltd. © Denis Edwards 1999 and 2001.
- Georg Grossjohann's account has been reprinted from *Five Years, Four Fronts: The War Years of Georg Grossjohann*, and appears courtesy of the Aberjona Press. Translation was by Ulrich Abele. © 1999 by Edeltraud Grossjohann.
- Franklin L. Gurley's account has been reprinted from *Into the Mountains Dark: A WWII Odyssey from Harvard Crimson to Infantry Blue*, and appear courtesy of the Aberjona Press. © 2000 by Franklin L. Gurley.
- Peter Hall's account appears courtesy of Peter Hall and Louis Scully. © Peter Hall.
- Dmitriy Loza's account has been reprinted from *Commanding the Red Army's Sherman Tanks: the WWII Memoirs of Hero of the Soviet Union Dmitriy Loza*, translated by James F. Gebhardt, and appears courtesy of the University of Nebraska Press. Copyright © 1996 by the University of Nebraska Press.

- Armin Scheiderbauer's account has been reprinted from *Adventures in my Youth: A German soldier on the Eastern Front 1941-45* and appears courtesy of Frau Scheiderbauer and Helion & Company Ltd. The English translation is by Christopher Colton. © 2003 by Helion & Company Ltd.
- Johann Voss' reminiscences have been reprinted from *Black Edelweiss: A Memoir of Combat and Conscience by a Soldier of the Waffen-SS*, and appear courtesy of the Aberjona Press. © 2002 by Johann Voss.
- Erik Wallin's account has been reprinted from *Twilight of the Gods: A Swedish Waffen-SS Volunteer's Experiences with the 11th SS-Panzergrenadier Division 'Nordland', Eastern Front 1944-45*, and appears courtesy of Thorolf Hillblad and Helion & Company Ltd. It was translated from the Swedish by Jackie Logan with the assistance of Thorolf Hillblad. English translation © 2002 by Thorolf Hillblad.

See the Eyewitnesses section for full citations of sources for the reminiscences listed above.

Credits for all photographs used appear alongside their captions. The editors and publishers are grateful for the permission of the various copyright holders for allowing us to reproduce them.

Introduction

One would imagine that two such titanic military campaigns as those in North-West Europe and on the Eastern Front between June 1944 and May 1945 would leave in their wake a vast swathe of personal accounts, making the job of editors such as ourselves rather straightforward. In fact, on approaching this project we found that the sheer quantity of material presented problems, as did the imbalance between the availability of accounts covering North-West Europe (many) and the Eastern Front (few and far between).

Our brief was to show war 'at the sharp end' on these two fronts during the final twelve months of World War II. In due deference to the other theatres of war, including Italy and the Far East, and the sacrifices of the soldiers who fought on these fronts, we wished to concentrate entirely on North-West Europe and the Eastern Front, what could be described as the 'central axis' of the war, and the combat path to Berlin from east and west.

Whilst we wished to base our book around eyewitness accounts, we sought to avoid using a large number of participants. Apart from the practical problems of finding a sufficient quantity of accounts, specifically with regard to the Eastern Front, the idea behind this book was to focus upon a small number of servicemen and women and probe their experiences of the last twelve months of the war in greater detail than is normally encountered in books relying heavily upon personal anecdotes. Likewise, we have taken the approach of providing only the minimum quantity of introductory and linking text between quotes - the reason for this book's existence is due to a desire to let the eyewitnesses speak directly to the reader.

As we began to uncover material, it rapidly became apparent that we were faced with two choices when it came to selecting material - attempt to print accounts all of a similarly equal length, or take the possibly bolder approach of deliberately reproducing accounts of varying lengths, depending on how we felt they fitted into the overall framework we were constructing. For instance, the fact that parts VI and VIII describing the Eastern Front from January 1945 occupy greater space than their chronological counterparts for North-West Europe reflects the quantity of outstanding material we felt we had for the former that deserved to make it into print.

A number of the accounts have also allowed us the opportunity to explore some of the lesser-known campaigns and battles fought during this final stage of the war. Whilst most readers will doubtless be familiar with the Ardennes offensive or 'the Battle of the Bulge', we have also included material covering the far less well-known German offensive launched in Alsace in early 1945, Operation *Nordwind*. Similarly, the earlier fighting in southern France - Operation Dragoon - receives attention. Apart from the Battle of Berlin, it appears individual campaigns on the Eastern Front during this period are even less well-known. Within these pages, the reader will be able to find out more about Operation Bagration and the other Soviet summer offensives of 1944, as well as the fighting in Hungary, Poland and eastern Germany in late 1944 and 1945.

Those readers encouraged to seek out, where available, the full texts of those quoted will find their complete bibliographic details in the section 'The Eyewitnesses'. It only remains for us to direct the inquisitively-minded to the 'Further Reading' section, which provides details of more specialist studies relating to these two climactic campaigns.

Duncan Rogers & Sarah Williams, March 2005

The Eyewitnesses

American

Sam Carter, 1st Infantry Division ('Big Red One')

Sam Carter in 1943. (Sam Carter)

Sam Carter is originally from Alabama and was a 1st Lieutenant in Company D when the 18th Infantry Regiment of the 1st Infantry Division was conducting training exercises at Fort Devens Massachusetts in 1940. By the time Pearl Harbor was bombed, he had become the commanding officer of the company and had received a promotion to Captain. Carter remained in command of Company D, which was comprised of two machine gun platoons and an 81mm. mortar platoon, through the fighting in North Africa and Sicily. In Europe, he landed with the company in the early afternoon of D-Day in Normandy and remained in command until reaching Caumont.

In July 1944, Carter was promoted to Major and transferred to the 18th Infantry Regiment's 3rd Battalion where he became its Executive Officer. He served in this capacity until early 1945 and was then assigned to the regimental staff where he became the Regiment's Intelligence Officer (S-2), a duty assignment he remained in until the war ended.

Sam Carter retired from the United States Army following the war as a Lieutenant-Colonel. He and his wife Norma have been married for over 60 years and live happily and independently at their home in Bradenton, Florida.

Sam's experiences of his time in North-West Europe with 1st Infantry Division were transcribed from his taped recollections. The transcript is on file with the 1st Division Cantigny Research Center, Wheaton, Illinois. Much related material can be found in the book *American Iliad: The 18th Infantry Regiment in WWII* by Bob Baumer, published by the Aberjona Press (ISBN 0-9717650-5-7).

Franklin L. Gurley, 100th Infantry Division

Frank Gurley was born in 1925 and grew up in several locations in the north-eastern United States before entering Harvard University in the summer of 1943. A rising star on the cross-country team and a reporter for the Harvard University newspaper the *Crimson*, he dropped out to enlist in the US Army. Initially assigned to the Army's intellectually elite Army Specialized Training Program (ASTP), upon the disbandment of that program, he was reassigned to the 100th Infantry Division as an infantryman. Frank deployed with the Century Division and fought his way through the rugged Vosges Mountains during the campaign that saw history's first penetration of that previously impregnable barrier. He focuses in

Franklin L. Gurley. (Frank Gurley)

revealing detail on his and his unit's bloody and unsentimentally inspirational two week baptism of fire in November 1944 during the penetration of the German Winter Line in the High Vosges, which Allied and German high-ranking officers expected would hold until at least the spring of 1945.

Surviving the entire six months of his unit's combat service, Frank eventually went on to earn his bachelor's and *juris* doctor degrees at Harvard by 1952. Through a 31-year law career, he served in a wide variety of positions with government agencies and private practices, eventually rising to serve as senior vice president and general counsel for a major international food firm headquartered in Europe. He resided in Switzerland for the last several decades of his life, and passed away there in 2004.

Franklin Gurley's experiences of the fierce fighting in the Vosges were published as *Into the Mountains Dark: A WWII Odyssey from Harvard Crimson to Infantry Blue* by the Aberjona Press in 2000 (ISBN 0-9666389-4-8).

British

Robert Boscawen, 1st (Armoured) Battalion, Coldstream Guards, Guards Armoured Division

Born in 1923, Robert Boscawen was educated at Eton and Trinity College, Cambridge before joining the Army in 1941. He was commissioned into the Coldstream Guards, following in the footsteps of his grandfather, father, uncle and two brothers, and posted to the 1st (Armoured) Battalion with whom he served in England and North-West Europe until being seriously wounded during the last month of the war. He was awarded the Military Cross.

Following a long convalescence, he joined a major oil company before taking up the call of a parliamentary career. After two unsuccessful attempts he was elected as Member of Parliament for Wells and later Somerton-Frome in which role he served from 1970 until 1992. He was a Government Whip throughout Margaret Thatcher's premiership and is a Privy Counsellor. Now retired, he and his wife live in Somerset on the edge of his former constituency.

Robert Boscawen's complete war diaries for the campaign in North-West Europe 1944-45 were published as *Armoured Guardsmen: A War Diary, June 1944-April 1945* by Pen & Sword Books Ltd in 2001 (ISBN 0-85052-748-1).

Denis Edwards, 2nd (Glider-borne) Battalion, Oxfordshire & Buckinghamshire Light Infantry, 6th Airborne Division

Denis Edwards was born near Sevenoaks, Kent in 1924. Seventeen years old (less four months!) he joined the 10th Oxfordshire and Buckinghamshire Light Infantry Young Soldiers Battalion. He was transferred to the glider-borne 2nd

Denis Edwards in 1942, aged 18.
(Denis Edwards)

Battalion, part of the 6th Airborne Division. After service in Normandy, the Ardennes and Germany (all related in this book), he was sent to India ahead of the Division, which never arrived, being diverted to Palestine. He rejoined the Division after hitch-hiking back to the Middle East. He ended his service in the Parachute Regiment. On demobilisation he pursued a career in estate agency around the Worthing area. Now retired he is actively involved with the Shoreham-by-Sea D-Day Aviation Museum and acts as correspondent to the survivors of the late Major Howard's Pegasus Bridge *coup de main* force.

Denis Edwards' experiences are drawn from his fascinating recollections *The Devil's Own Luck: Pegasus Bridge to the Baltic 1944-45*, published in 1999 by Pen & Sword Books Ltd (ISBN 0-85052-869-0).

Peter Hall, 1st Battalion Worcestershire Regiment, 43rd Wessex Infantry Division

Born into a middle-class Anglo-Irish family in 1919 in Weston-super-Mare Peter Hall was educated at Clifton College, Bristol. As a keen sportsman Peter excelled in cricket and hockey, representing Ireland in the latter. At the outbreak of the Second World War he attended Officer Cadet Training at the Royal Military Academy at Sandhurst.

At the age of 21, he was commissioned as a 2nd Lieutenant into the 11th Battalion Worcestershire Regiment and his first duty as a platoon commander was to guard a three-mile stretch of coastline north of Great Yarmouth. After the amalgamation of the 11th Battalion with the 1st Battalion Worcestershire Regiment in January 1943, he became the battalion Weapons Training Officer.

In June 1944, he landed in Normandy with the 1st Battalion. During the first major attack on enemy positions at the village of Mouen, whilst leading his platoon, he was badly wounded. He stayed with his men until the action was completed and was eventually evacuated back to a hospital in England. After treatment he rejoined his regiment back in France and was quickly promoted to Temporary Major in command of an infantry company.

During the later stages of the Second World War he was awarded the DSO for gallantry during fierce fighting, resisting an enemy attack of greater strength. Shortly afterwards he was wounded, this time by shrapnel from a German land mine, evacuated to hospital and had minor plastic surgery. After treatment he rejoined his regiment back in Germany just 2 weeks before the war ended.

His next posting was to the newly formed Rhine Army Training Centre at Sennelager as a Tactical Instructor, where he was to spend the next 3 years. Then followed a period as General Staff Officer (GSO 2) at the Royal Air Force HQ in Germany. By 1950 he found himself back with the 1st Battalion Worcesters who

Peter Hall receiving his DSO award from Field Marshal Montgomery at an investiture
held in the Parish Church at Celle, Germany on 24 June 1945.
(Imperial War Museum BU8273)

were now fighting the communist terrorists in Malaya, and was mentioned in
despatches for his leadership under enemy fire. By 1953 he found himself posted to
the 2nd battalion Malaya Regiment, followed by a period as Brigade Major in the
1st Malay Brigade.

During the Suez crisis in 1956 he was once again a staff officer (GSO 2) and
spent time in Cyprus. On his return to England he was posted as a Teaching
Officer at the Officer Cadet Schools at Chester and then Aldershot for a period of
time before rejoining the 1st Battalion Worcesters, this time as second-in-
command on service in the Caribbean.

In 1961 Peter Hall was promoted to the rank of Lieutenant Colonel and
commanded the 1st Battalion at their headquarters Norton Barracks, Worcester
then at Minden, Germany and finally in British Honduras (now Belize). A year
later he was posted back to Malaya but this time as Commandant of the British
Jungle Warfare School and was involved in the conflict in Borneo.

In 1967 after 27 years of eventful professional soldering Colonel Peter Hall
D.S.O. finally retired from the army and took up a management training position
in the insurance industry.

Peter's memoirs of his time in North-West Europe 1944-45 are drawn from
his unpublished recollections, *Tales of a Disorderly Officer*.

German

Georg Grossjohann, 198th Infantry Division

George Grossjohann was the youngest son of a landed family in East Prussia. Born
in 1911, he enlisted in the *Reichswehr*, the armed forces of the Weimar Republic, in
1928 as an infantryman for the minimum 12-year enlistment required by the
Treaty of Versailles. At the outset of WWII, he was an experienced senior non-
commissioned officer, and, like so many pre-war professionals, was quickly

commissioned to lead in the wartime *Wehrmacht*. During the course of the war, he commanded infantry units from the platoon through regimental levels in combat in Poland, France (1940), the Soviet Union (1941-44), and France again (1944), where he fought both elements of the American Seventh Army and colonial units of the French First Army in southern France and the Vosges Mountains.

Georg Grossjohann earned the Wounds Badge in Silver (for multiple wounds sustained in combat), both classes of the Iron Cross, the German Cross in Gold, and the Knight's Cross of the Iron Cross. He surrendered to American forces in Bavaria after the war's conclusion, and was released not long thereafter. Unable to return to his East Prussian homeland, which was under Soviet occupation and would eventually be reallocated, partly to Poland and partly (around Königsberg) to the USSR, Grossjohann settled near Stuttgart, in south-western Germany, where he founded his own business as a *couturier*, primarily serving US Army officers' wives. He eventually retired to the Taunus Mountains, where he passed away in 1992.

Major Georg Grossjohann poses for a portrait whilst on leave in early 1945. His decorations include the Knight's Cross, German Cross in Gold and Silver Wound Badge. (Georg

Georg Grossjohann's memoirs were published under the title *Five Years, Four Fronts: The War Years of Georg Grossjohann* by the Aberjona Press in 1999 (ISBN 0-9666389-3-X).

Armin Scheiderbauer, 252nd Infantry Division

Armin Scheiderbauer was born in 1924, the son of an evangelical pastor. After attending schools in Thuringia, and Stockerau, he was called up in August 1941. He served with distinction on the Eastern Front until 1945, with 252nd Infantry Division, reached the rank of *Oberleutnant*, was wounded numerous times, and was awarded the Iron Cross 1st Class and close combat clasp. He was wounded and captured by the Red Army in March 1945, returning home in September 1947. In the post-war years he became a senior lawyer in Vienna, and continued his close associations with the evangelical church. He married a doctor, and has one daughter, also a doctor. He now lives in Salzburg, Austria.

Armin Scheiderbauer's full account has been published as *Adventures in my Youth: A German soldier on the Eastern Front 1941-45*, by Helion & Company Ltd, 2003 (ISBN 1-874622-06-X).

Johann Voss, 6th SS Mountain Division 'Nord'

Johann Voss was born in 1925 to an upper middle class family from Brunswick, Germany. While his father, a WWI combat veteran, was strictly apolitical in his opinions, and his mother rather circumspect in hers, various members of his family held views that ranged from staunchly National Socialist to distinctly broad-minded and cosmopolitan. Coming of age when the war was on and after much self-examination of his beliefs and patriotic obligations, Voss terminated his enrolment in an academic high school and enlisted in the Waffen-SS. He served as a machine gunner in SS Mountain Infantry Regiment 11 of the 6th SS-Mountain Division 'Nord' for about 18 months in combat against the Red Army near the Arctic Circle, and about two months against elements of the United States Seventh and Third Armies along the border of the *Reich.* He was captured in early March 1945 after a fierce firefight with soldiers of the American 94th Infantry Division south of Trier, and spent 21 months in American captivity in France and Germany.

Armin Scheiderbauer as *Leutnant* in 1943, now wearing the ribbon of the Iron Cross 2nd Class and the *Infanteriesturmabzeichen* in silver. (Armin Scheiderbauer)

After the war, Voss resumed his studies and ultimately earned a *juris* degree from one of Germany's—and the world's—greatest universities. He went on to achieve a highly distinguished record as a lawyer and environmental adviser for a major association of the German energy industry at national and international levels.

Johann Voss's complete memoirs were published as *Black Edelweiss: A Memoir of Combat and Conscience by a Soldier of the Waffen-SS* by the Aberjona Press in 2002 (ISBN 0-9666389-8-0).

Johann Voss while in *Gebirgsjäger* training, Bavaria, early 1943. (Johann Voss)

Erik Wallin, 11th SS Panzer Aufklärungs Abteilung, 11th SS Panzergrenadier Division 'Nordland' (as told to Thorolf Hillblad)

Thorolf Hillblad writes:

At the end of World War II, the Nuremberg war tribunal sentenced the Waffen SS, possibly the finest fighting force the world has seen since Leonidas and his Spartans at Thermopylae, the bravest of the brave, collectively as war criminals. As an ex-Waffen SS volunteer, well aware of the strong discipline and high morale of these exceptional warriors, originally all volunteers, I decided to write down the experiences of some Swedish SS comrades in the fight against the Red Army.

Erik 'Jerka' Wallin, born 2 August 1921. He served with the *Panzer Aufklärungs-Abteilung* of the 11th SS 'Nordland' Division right up until the end of the war, fighting in the streets of Berlin. His life after 1945 was almost as eventful! (Erik Norling)

My first interviewee was Erik (Jerka) Wallin from Stockholm. In late 1945 he had just been released from a Swedish prison where he had served a few months for the 'theft' of his Swedish army uniform. Before crossing the border to join the Waffen SS he had wrapped it in a neat parcel, which somehow had gone astray. During the war it was no crime in Sweden to join the German or Finnish forces against the Soviet Union. After the war, however, the Swedish authorities felt embarrassed about their past neutrality and became anxious to establish good terms with Sweden's large neighbour in the east. So 'Jerka' had to go to jail as an expression of Sweden's new-found friendliness with the Soviet Union.

Erik's neighbours in prison were hard-boiled violent repeat criminals. Being 'politically correct' criminals, it was hard for them to tolerate this disgusting war criminal in their cosy Swedish prison, equipped with all modern conveniences. Erik had been quite a good amateur boxer, but he hadn't a chance when they made it a habit to collectively beat him up, with the wardens as onlookers.

He had been through the war up to the fall of Berlin, with a very short stint as a Red Army POW before he managed to escape to the British zone. It turned out that his experiences gave enough material for an entire book, so I forgot about further interviews. He visited me every evening, and between cups of coffee and cigarettes he talked 'til late in the night, while I took down the details.

As a marked man - after the war Sweden was no longer neutral - I was jobless, so in daytime I typed what he had told me the night before. I was in a bit of a hurry, because the profit from the sale of the book was to cover the debts of our weekly paper *Den Svenske*, the finances of which were in terrible shape. In two weeks the job was finished. We printed only one edition, which was sold out within a few weeks. It did not occur to us to print a second edition, because the first one had already solved our financial problems. In 1947 a German translation was published in Argentina where thousands of SS men - Dutch, French, Belgian, Scandinavian, and of course German - had sought refuge. In the mid 1990's - after 50 years! - pirate editions started appearing in Scandinavia and Germany.

Erik Wallin continued his eventful life in various countries - like many comrades, he became restless - some rather exotic, such as Morocco and Afghanistan. He met many interesting people and even became friendly with the last (or latest?) King of Afghanistan, Zahir Shah, who has lately enjoyed some publicity with his return to Kabul. Zahir Shah liked to listen to Jerka's war escapades.

Among other notables Erik met was Ilya' Ehrenburg, Stalins court jester, one of the few intimates of the Red Tsar to survive Stalin's 'clear-outs'. Ilya and Jerka must have had some interesting things to tell each other ... In later years, Erik and I used to meet in Stockholm for a few days once a year, reminiscing over bratwurst, sauerkraut,'Kommisbrot and beer. By then I had lived in Argentina for almost fifty years, a very, very different country. Erik's 'light' went out one evening at a get-together of Division Nordland veterans in Germany. It happened fast, as so many things in his life did!

Coeur d' Alene, Idaho, 2002
Thorolf Nilsson Hillblad

Thorolf Hillblad's full account of Erik Wallin's experiences has been published as *Twilight of the Gods: A Swedish Waffen-SS Volunteer's Experiences with the 11th SS Panzergrenadier Division 'Nordland', Eastern Front 1944-45*, by Helion & Company Ltd, 2004 (ISBN 1-874622-16-7).

Soviet

Zoya Alexandrova, 65th Tank Brigade, 11th Tank Corps

Zoya Nikifororvna Alexandrova was born in the village of Molodino, Moskovskaya *Oblast* (Province) in 1922. She moved to Moscow before the war and became an accounting clerk at a plant. She volunteered to go to the front in 1941. She served as a medical orderly, a nurse and from the end of 1944 as a scout in a tank brigade. After demobilisation in the summer of 1945 she lived in Germany with her husband. In 1951 the Alexandrovas returned to the USSR. Zoya finished a course in accounting and began work at a factory. She retired in 1987, and currently lives in Moscow.

Zoya Nikiforovna Alexandrova, 1945.
(Zoya Alexandrova)

Her memoirs of wartime service are previously unpublished. They were translated by Vladimir Kroupnik and edited by John Armstrong. Publication was made possible by the 'I Remember' website (http://www.iremember.ru/index_e.htm) and its director, Artem Drabkin.

Dmitriy Fedorovich Loza, 233rd Tank Brigade, 5th Mechanized Corps (later redesignated 46th Guards Tank Brigade, 9th Guards Mechanized Corps)

Dmitriy Loza was born in 1922, in a village in the Kharkov region. Upon leaving school he joined the Red Army in 1940, graduating from the Saratov Armour School in 1942. He served as chief of staff, deputy commander and battalion commander in the 233rd Tank Brigade, 5th Mechanized Corps – redesignated in

Battalion Commander and Hero of the Soviet Union Dmitriy Loza in 1945. On his right chest he wears the Orders of the Red Star and Patriotic War, as well as the Order of Alexander Nevsky. Commanders who displayed abilities in military leadership were awarded with the later.
(Dmitriy Loza Archive)

September 1944 as the 46th Guards Tank Brigade, 9th Guards Mechanized Corps – fighting against the Germans from 1942 until April 1945, before being transferred to the Far East to fight the Japanese in August and September of that year.

During the war he was identified as an *inomarochnik* in his personal files and documents, an official Red Army designation that was designed to ensure that officers such as Loza, who had experience using foreign-manufactured equipment (such as his unit's US-made Sherman tanks), would always be assigned to units employing such materiél. He was seriously wounded twice, the first time in September 1943, the second time on 19 April 1945 during tank-to-tank combat in Austria.

Just over a year after the war in Europe ended, on 15 May 1946, Loza was awarded the Soviet Union's highest military decoration, Hero of the Soviet Union, for his actions during the taking of Vienna in April 1945 (described in Part IX of this book). In the course of his military career he was also awarded the Order of Lenin, the Order of the Red Banner, the Order of Alexander Nevskiy, the Order of the Patriotic Wars (1st and 2nd classes), and two Orders of the Red Star.

Remaining in the Red Army at the end of the war, he graduated from the Frunze Military Academy in 1956, becoming an instructor there before retiring eleven years later as a colonel. He then worked as a senior military researcher and lecturer at a Moscow institute, producing a series of influential and acclaimed texts. In 1982 he received the Frunze Prize for his contribution to *Taktika v boyevykh primerakh* ('Tactics in combat examples').

Dmitriy Fedorovich Loza died recently.

Dmitriy Loza's memoirs of his service during the Great Patriotic War, focusing on the years 1944 and 1945, were translated and edited by James F. Gebhardt and published as *Commanding the Red Army's Sherman Tanks: The World War II Memoirs of Hero of the Soviet Union Dmitriy Loza* (University of Nebraska Press, 1996, ISBN 0-8032-2920-8). A further volume by Loza, more thematic and less chronological, was also translated and edited by Gebhardt and published by the University of Nebraska Press in 1998: *Fighting for the Soviet Motherland: Recollections from the Eastern Front* (ISBN 0-8032-2929-1).

Vsevolod Olimpiev, 143rd Guards Anti-Tank Artillery Regiment, 1st Guards Cavalry Corps

Vsevolod Ivanovich Olimpiev was born on 4 March 1922 in the town of Novo-Troitskoye, Donetskaya *Oblast* (Province), Ukraine. In 1939 he graduated with distinction from a school in Donetsk and joined the Shipbuilding Institute in Leningrad, from where he was drafted to the Red Army in 1940. He was at the Soviet-German front through the whole war. He fought as a Signals Section Commander in an Air Force Division, in infantry, anti-tank artillery and armoured forces on the Western, South-Western and 1st Ukrainian fronts. He finished the war beyond the Elbe.

Vsevolod Olimpiev.
(Vsevolod Olimpiev)

He was three times wounded, and was awarded a number of combat orders and medals. After being demobilised in October 1945 he returned to his Institute, from which he graduated with distinction in 1950. From 1953 till the end of his life he worked in Leningrad in the Central Boiler-Turbine Institute named after Polzunov. He was a PhD and professor in his field. In 1962 he organised and became the head of the Laboratory of Vibration, which successfully resolved technical problems related to work of thermo-electric and nuclear power stations, gas-turbine and compressor installations. V.I. Olimpiev died on 4 October 2001.

His experiences of the war on the Eastern Front 1944-45 are previously unpublished. They were translated by Vladimir Kroupnik and edited by John Armstrong. Publication was made possible by the 'I Remember' website (http://www.iremember.ru/index_e.htm) and its director, Artem Drabkin.

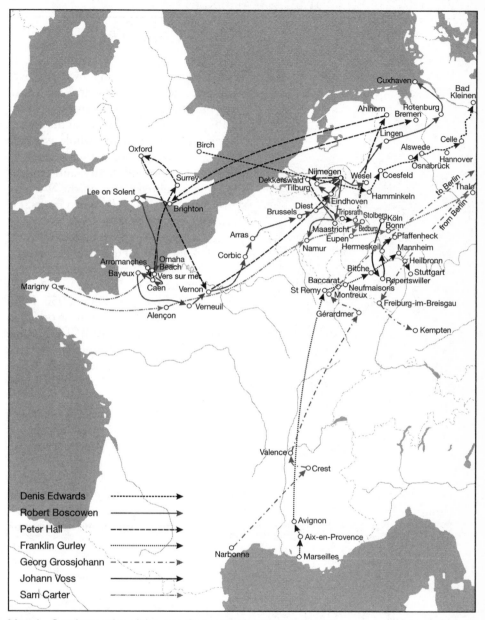

Map 1   Combat paths of the eyewitnesses: North-West Europe

Map 2   Combat paths of the eyewitnesses: Eastern Front

Timeline

Timeline

North-West Europe	Date	Eastern Front
	June 1944	
D-Day landings begin	6	
	9	Soviets launch major offensive against Finland
	22	Red Army launches Operation 'Bagration', its huge summer offensive against Army Group Centre
British launch Operation Epsom, aimed at penetrating the German defences around Caen	25	
US troops capture Cherbourg, British capture Hill 112	27	
Operation Epsom halted by fierce German resistance	28	
Hill 112 recaptured by the Germans		
	July 1944	
	3	Soviets recapture Minsk, 100,000 Germans encircled to the east of the city
	4	Soviet 1st Baltic Front launches an offensive towards Riga
US attacks in the Carentan area stopped by Germans	7	
Operation Charnwood launched by British aimed at capturing Caen	8	Germans have now lost 300,000 men during Operation Bagration
British troops enter Caen	9	Soviets launch offensive aimed at cutting off Army Group North
US troops reach St Lô	18	
British and Canadian attempt to breakthrough south of Caen, code-named Operation Goodwood, fails (launched on 18 July)	20	
US troops launch Operation Cobra, the breakout west of St Lô	25	
Operation Cobra successful	28	Brest-Litovsk falls to the Soviets
	29	Red Army reaches the Baltic coast
Operation Bluecoat launched by British, an assault towards the River Vire	31	

August 1944

US troops reach Avranches; Patton's 3rd Army begins its speedy advance into Brittany	1	Polish Home Army uprising begins in Warsaw
	2	Polish troops serving with the Red Army gain a bridgehead over the Vistula
German counter-offensive against US 3rd Army fails	7	Soviet troops enter the foothills of the Carpathian mountains
Operation Totalize – Allied troops complete encirclement of German troops in Falaise Pocket	8-20	
	14	Soviets launch offensive aimed at enlarging their Vistula bridgeheads
The Allied invasion of southern France, Operation Dragoon, begins	15	
	17	Soviet troops reach the East Prussian border
Uprising in Paris	19	
	20	Huge Soviet offensive launched in Romania
	23	Romania changes sides and joins the Allies
	24	Soviets encircle major concentration of German troops in Romania
Free French troops enter Paris	25	
	29	Slovak uprising begins; Ploesti oilfields in Romania captured by the Soviets
	31	Bucharest falls to the Red Army

September 1944

Allies enter Belgium	2	
Brussels liberated	3	
Antwerp liberated	4	Finland agrees a ceasefire with the Soviets
First Allied patrols enter Germany	10	
Dutch border crossed by British troops	11	
	14	Major Soviet offensive against Army Group North, Baltic states
US troops reach the Siegfried Line	15	
Operation Market Garden begins	17	
Nijmegen bridge captured intact	20	
	24	Soviet offensive against Army Group North ceases

Last British paratroops evacuated from Arnhem, failure of Operation Market Garden	25	

October 1944

	2	Polish Home Army in Warsaw surrenders
	5	Soviet 1st Baltic Front launches further offensive against Army Group North
	10	German Army Group North now cut off in Kurland for duration of war. Slovakian uprising fails
Rommel commits suicide	14	
	15	Hungary's attempt to change sides thwarted by the Germans, a new pro-Axis government is announced
	16	Soviet troops enter East Prussia in strength
Aachen falls, the first German city to be captured in NW Europe	21	
	23-30	Fierce tank battles in Hungary continue
	28	Strong German resistance halts Soviet incursions into East Prussia

November 1944

	2	Soviets enter suburbs of Budapest
1st Free French Armoured Division reaches the Rhine	19	
Strasbourg liberated	24	
	29	Soviets cross the Danube into southwest Hungary

December 1944

	8	Soviets begin major offensive aimed at capturing Budapest
Massive German offensive launched in the Ardennes (the 'Battle of the Bulge')	16	
Bastogne relieved by Patton	26	
Operation *Nordwind* launched by Germans in Alsace	31	

January 1945

German withdrawal from the Ardennes begins	1	
Operation *Nordwind* offensive halted	12	Soviets launch huge Vistula-Oder offensive

	17	Soviets capture Warsaw and continue to make huge advances towards Germany
	18	Germans launch offensive aimed at relieving Budapest
	23	Soviet troops reach the Oder in Silesia
Ardennes salient erased, failure of German offensive	28	
	31	Soviets establish a bridgehead over the Oder, now only 40 miles east of Berlin

February 1945

Belgium free of German troops	4	
Allied offensive into the Reichswald launched	8	
	10	German and Hungarian troops defending Budapest attempt to break out but almost all are killed or captured
	13	Soviets capture Budapest
British and Canadian troops reach the Rhine	14	
	15	Germans launch limited offensive in Pomerania, Operation *Sonnenwende*
US 3rd Army launches new offensive into Germany	17	
	18	Soviet resistance halts German progress in Operation *Sonnenwende*
	20-26	Heavy Soviet attacks against Army Group North falter
US 9th Army launches offensive from Roer river, towards the Hürtgen Forest	23	
	24	Soviet bridgehead over the Danube at Hron in Hungary eliminated

March 1945

	6	Operation Spring Awakening launched by the Germans to protect Hungarian oil fields
Cologne captured, Remagen Bridge over the Rhine captured	7	
	14	Operation Spring Awakening halted by fierce Soviet defence
	15	Soviets launch fresh offensive in Upper Silesia
Expansion of US bridgehead at Remagen continues	22	
British and Canadians launch assault across the Rhine	23	

British 2nd Army begins a drive towards the Elbe	28	
	29	Germany's last oil fields in Hungary captured by the Soviets
	30	Danzig captured by the Red Army

April 1945

Large concentration of German troops encircled in the Ruhr Pocket	1	
Clearance of Ruhr Pocket begins	5	
	13	Vienna captured by Soviets
	16	Red Army launches its final offensive on Berlin
Germans surrender in the Ruhr Pocket	18	
British 2nd Army reaches the Elbe	19	Soviets achieve a breakthrough on the Seelow Heights towards Berlin
	22	Outskirts of Berlin reached by the Red Army
US and Soviet troops meet at the Elbe	25	Berlin now completely surrounded
	30	Adolf Hitler commits suicide

May 1945

	2	Berlin surrenders
	5	Uprising in Prague
Unconditional surrender of all German troops	7	Unconditional surrender of all German troops
VE Day	8	
	11-13	Final pockets of German resistance in Czechoslovakia crushed

Glossary

Glossary

A Echelon	1st line petrol and ammunition trucks, fitters, stores etc. (B)
Abteilung	Battalion/Section/Detachment dependent upon context (G)
AP	Armour Piercing round (B)
AQMG	Assistant Quartermaster-General (B)
Armeekorps	Corps (G)
Aufklärungs	Reconnaissance (G)
Autobahn	Motorway (G)
B Echelon	Stores, cookers and officers' mess trucks (B)
Bataillon	Battalion (G)
Desantniki	See *tankodesantniki*
Efreitor	Lance-Corporal (R)
Emcha	Soviet nickname for the Sherman tank. Derives from the first letter and number of its alpha-numeric designation – M4 in Russian being *M-Chetyrye* (R)
Emchisti	Nickname for the men crewing the Lend-Lease Sherman tanks in the Red Army (R)
Fallschirmjäger	Parachute troops (G)
Feldgendarmerie	Field Police (G)
Feldwebel	Sergeant (G)
Festung	Fortress (G)
Füsilier	Fusilier (G)
GAD	Guards Armoured Division (B)
Gvardeytsi	Guardsmen (R)
Hauptfeldwebel	Senior Sergeant (G)
Hauptmann	Captain (G)
Heer	The regular German Army (G)
Heldenklau	Slang term applied to units who swept behind the frontlines, rounding up stragglers and rear-area personnel and sent them to the front line (lit. 'hero snatchers') (G)
Hilfswilliger	Auxiliary (G)
Hitlerjugend	Hitler Youth (G)
Hoheitsträger	Senior Nazi Party official (G)
Ia	First General Staff Officer (Operations) (G)
Jabos	Fighter bombers (G)
Katyusha	Nickname for a multiple-barrel rocket launcher (R)
Kriegsverdienstkreuz	War Service Cross (G)
Kübelwagen	Jeep, command car (G)
Landser	Nickname for German soldiers, equivalent to the British 'Tommy' or US 'G.I.'
Leutnant	Lieutenant (G)
LOB	Officer left out of battle, usually in A or B echelons (B)
Mahorka	Russian tobacco (R)
MC	Military Cross (B)
Micks	Slang for the Irish Guards (B)

NAAFI	Navy Army & Air Force Institute, usually used to refer to bars or canteens run by the NAAFI, a non-profit retailing organisation created in 1921 to service the needs of the Armed Forces (B)
Nase	Salient (G)
Nebelwerfer	Multiple-barrel rocket launcher (G)
Oberfeldwebel	Master Sergeant (G)
Obergefreiter	Corporal (G)
Oberleutnant	First Lieutenant (G)
Oberst	Colonel (G)
Ofenrohr	Anti-tank bazooka, lit. 'Stovepipe', also known as *Panzerschreck* (G)
Organisation Todt	German construction organisation (G)
Panzer	Tank/Armour (G)
Panzerabwehr/PAK	Anti-tank (G)
Panzerfaust	Single-shot disposable anti-tank weapon utilising a shaped charge (G)
Panzergrenadier	Armoured infantry (G)
Panzerjäger	Tank hunter (G)
Panzerschreck	Anti-tank rocket launcher, the German equivalent of the bazooka (G)
PIAT	Projector, Infantry, Anti-tank, spring-launched anti-tank weapon (B)
Pionier	Engineer (G)
Ratas	Soviet fighter aircraft (R)
Ratschbum	Slang for the Soviet 76.2mm gun (G)
RE	Royal Engineers (B)
S4	Battalion supply/logistics officer (US)
Schmeisser	German MP40 machine-pistol, named after its designer (G)
SS-Obergruppenführer	SS General (G)
SS-Oberscharführer	SS Senior Sergeant (G)
SS-Obersturmführer	SS Senior or First Lieutenant (G)
SS-Rottenführer	SS Senior Lance-Corporal (G)
SS-Sturmbannführer	SS Major (G)
SS-Unterscharführer	SS Corporal (G)
SS-Untersturmführer	SS Second Lieutenant (G)
Stavka	Soviet High Command (R)
Stellungsbaumeister	CO, trench construction (G)
Stonk	Slang term for shelling (B)
Strippenzieher	Nickname for signals troops (G)
Sturmgewehr	Assault rifle, the forerunner of the modern AK47 (G)
Tankodesantniki	Soviet infantrymen who rode into battle mounted on tanks, dismounting when in action against the enemy (R)
Typhies	Slang for Typhoons, fighter-bomber aircraft (B)
Unteroffizier	NCO/Sergeant (G)
VMI	Virginia Military Institute (US)
Volkssturm	German civil defence forces of Home Guard (G)
Wehrmacht	Armed Forces (G)

The letter in brackets after each term indicates the army to which the phrase refers to. (B) - British; (G) = German; (R) = Soviet; (US) = American.

Part I

North-West Europe

D-Day and Normandy
(June-August 1944)

Part I

North-West Europe

D-Day and Normandy
(June-August 1944)

*E*ngland, June 1944. Four years had passed since the British Army last exerted a direct military influence on the course of the war in North-West Europe. Since Dunkirk, British society had been on a total war footing, and had contributed materiél to the Soviet war effort in the East. For several years, however, Churchill had resisted Stalin's demands for a "second front". In the spring of 1943, however, the decision was finally made to launch a cross-Channel attack in the first half of the following year. In January 1944 Allied bombardment of bridges, military and industrial targets began, in preparation for the invasion. At the same time a deception operation was initiated, to persuade the Germans that Allied landings would take place in the Pas de Calais. To guard the time and place of the landings, the troops who were involved were kept in strict isolation from the civilian population. Peter Hall, then a twenty-five year old second lieutenant in the 1st Battalion of the Worcestershire Regiment, remembers the strange atmosphere:

Towards the end of May, the whole Division was consigned to a number of Battalion 'sealed camps' near Newhaven. A sealed camp meant that no-one, but no-one, was allowed out - in case someone, unintentionally, gave away the plans of the Allied commanders. A series of briefings at officer level took place. It became increasingly obvious where our initial landings would be. Normandy!

The sealed camp complex was essential to security but it was psychologically uncomfortable for the internees. It was rather like a prolonged stay in the dentist's waiting room, anticipating having all one's teeth out, with only a few ancient copies of the *Tatler* and *The Illustrated London News* to distract ones mind from the coming ordeal. Tempers frayed. Long established friends quarrelled - sometimes violently and physically. It was a difficult time. It was under these conditions that I truly learned that anticipation of an impending ordeal demands more courage than when 'the whistle blows' and the action starts. (Perhaps that's not quite true. The anticipation of a school caning was not worse than its execution!)

An additional irritation to all of us in 'internment' was the rigorous censoring of letters to families and other loved ones - in retrospect, a very necessary precaution.

After the war, my mother showed me a letter which I had written to her during this period. It consisted of three pages of my, not very decipherable, scrawl. The only news she received was as follows:-

'My dearest Mother ...' then three pages of heavily blacked-out script, ending 'but don't worry. I feel fine. Fondest love to you and Father, Peter'

The effect on her of those censored sentences can well be imagined. She had a strong maternal instinct and a vivid Celtic imagination. (In fact I had only griped about the food and boredom. I also mentioned that I had recently met some friends from Weston-super-Mare.) All highly explosive material if it had fallen into the hands of German intelligence, no doubt! It was a relief to everyone when our orders were received to embark on the great enterprise. THE LIBERATION OF EUROPE.

The first stage of the invasion began shortly after midnight on 6 June – D-Day – with the landing of British and US airborne troops on the flanks of the beaches which were to be the focus of the amphibious invasion later in the day. On the right flank, between Ste Mère Eglise and Carentan, 82nd and 101st US airborne divisions were to stage their landings. British airborne forces were to land on the left flank, east of the River Orne. The nineteen-year-old Denis Edwards, a glider-borne soldier of the 2nd Battalion of the Oxfordshire and Buckinghamshire Light Infantry, was destined to be in their midst. It was a fact of which he was to remain unaware until the very eve of the operation.

It was 4 June, 1944, and something was definitely about to happen, but what?

For some time we had been cooped up in the camp, one of the many high-security tented camps behind guarded barbed-wire fences in Southern England and, in our case, near an airfield. We had been transported from Bulford Camp on Salisbury Plain in covered lorries, and when we arrived at our new location I had no idea where we were. Years later I was to learn that it was Tarrant Rushton in Dorset, which, like many of the temporary wartime airfields, no longer exists.

A day or so after our arrival we were ordered from our Section tents, told to 'Fall In' and marched to an inner guarded and wired-off enclosure in the heart of the camp. A notice at the entrance read 'Secret – keep out unless on duty'.

We entered a large tent and received a briefing from Major Howard. Later, by platoons, each consisting of about twenty-eight men, we went to smaller tents for more detailed briefings from our platoon commanders.

The initial briefing had given us the general outline of the special mission that lay ahead of us. The invasion forces of the Allied armies were at last about to land along the Normandy beaches. As soon as weather conditions permitted – and favourable weather was expected within the next two days – they would start rescuing continental Europe from the grip of Hitler's Germany.

The British 6th Airborne Division had been allocated the task of landing from the sky on to the left flank of the British sea-borne forces. Two American airborne divisions would be carrying out a similar landing on the right flank of their sea-borne armies.

The sea-borne forces were to land, capture and secure the ground along the coastline to form a bridgehead. It would be expanded, move inland for several miles, then pivot in an anti-clockwise direction and thrust eastwards on a wide front.

Our Division had to capture and hold a large area on the left flank and prevent any attempt by the enemy to rush reinforcements along the coast from the east, where their main forces were located. It was mainly low-lying ground a short distance inland, much of it heavily wooded and with a large area – the valley of the

River Dives – flooded by the Germans as a counter-invasion measure. On the western boundary of our Divisional area the Caen Canal ran from the coast at Ouistreham down to Caen, eight miles inland, and parallel with it, 500 yards or so to its eastern side, was the River Orne. At a point about four miles inland, just on the eastern edge of the small village of Bénouville, both waterways are crossed by bridges, the road through Bénouville running eastwards by way of the two bridges.

It was the special task of 'D' Company (with two additional platoons from 'B' Company) of the 2nd Battalion Oxfordshire and Buckinghamshire Light Infantry (of the glider-borne 6th Airlanding Infantry Brigade) to gain both bridges intact, to enable the British Army to thrust eastwards with their tanks and other heavy vehicles. It was known through local French partisan sources that both bridges had been prepared for demolition and our specific task was to capture these bridges before they could be demolished.

The invasion plan required that several bridges were to be destroyed, to hinder the enemy, while others, such as those allocated to us, were to be captured intact to facilitate the Allied advance. Once the Germans realized where the invasion was really taking place they would wish to rush reinforcements from the east and, by denying them access over the bridges, they would be forced into a detour down to Caen. While we were capturing our two bridges, several parachute battalions would destroy five bridges over the River Dives, some eight miles to the east, and generally harass the Germans to the east of our inland airborne bridgehead. These operations would delay the enemy and buy the Allies the valuable time they needed to establish a firm bridgehead along the beaches during the first few vital days. Our party had been named 'The *Coup de Main* Force' by the Allied commanders.[1]

Various ways of carrying out a surprise attack for the capture of the bridges had been considered. Originally paratroops were to be used, but this idea was dropped due to the windy conditions that often prevailed in coastal regions, as there was a risk of the paratroops being scattered over a wide area. Subsequent events proved this to be a sound assumption as our back-up paratroops who were dropped to reinforce us shortly after we landed were badly scattered, many of them landing several miles from their intended dropping zones.

It was finally decided that the most effective method would be to use a compact force carried in six gliders – three to land by each bridge. They were to be crash-landed at night-time in a small strip of rough land between the canal and river.

Each glider was to be fitted with identical equipment and its passengers would include five Royal Engineers to deal with the demolition charges on the bridges. Because it was considered necessary to carry five engineers in every glider it meant that our infantry platoons – normally of twenty-eight men – would have to be reduced to twenty-three since the maximum glider load was twenty-eight plus two

---

1   The term *coup de main* is rather ambiguous in the French of today and may, have been so in 1944, but I have not been able to verify this. Nowadays, *coup de main* can be a blow struck with the hand - something like a punch or a slap, or it can mean 'a helping hand'. Our task force, therefore, can be thought of as the force that was to give a helping hand to the beach landings, or as one that would give the Germans an unwelcome and unexpected 'smack in the eye'. I don't suppose it matters too much, as both meanings seem to work quite well.

glider pilots. The airborne engineers and the glider pilots were fully trained to fight alongside the infantry.

Each one of the gliders had to be prepared to land in any sequence, and each team had to be ready to carry out any one of the six tasks in connection with the capture of the bridges. In any other circumstances we might have spent weeks learning our various tasks and practising them. Now we had no time left and we needed to learn and understand our individual responsibilities in just a day. The intense concentration helped to keep us from contemplating the implications of the awesome task that lay ahead of us.

Studying the different tasks of each platoon occupied us for several hours. We now understood the significance of the exercise we had carried out in May. Those bridges were indeed quite similar to the targets we were now about to tackle, but the Polish defenders of the Countess Weir bridges were basically 'friendly', while this time we could expect opposition that was decidedly unfriendly, and with much more to lose than just bridges.

My platoon, No. 25, was to fly in the first of the three gliders to go down on to the canal bridge. Each platoon was divided into sections, and the tasks of each seven-man section were considered. Finally, in cases where individuals had special tasks, these were also looked at in detail, since, working in darkness, it was essential that everyone knew what everyone else should be doing at any given time. If, for any reason, the detailed individual was not available to carry out the task, the others had to be aware of the requirements and able to carry it out.

The latest aerial photographs were very useful, as they showed the bridges and surrounding terrain in great detail. There was also a large-scale model and we were assured that every house, outbuilding, tree, bush, hedge, gateway, ditch and fortification had been meticulously recorded. Even if a pane of glass in one of the windows had been broken, we were assured, it would be shown!

Intelligence reports and aerial photographs said that within the past few days, probably as a result of a visit by Field Marshal Rommel, local people had been recruited to erect huge poles in the proposed landing zones. Such a pole could easily smash a troop-carrying glider, as the landing speed of a fully laden glider is between eighty and one hundred miles per hour and at such a speed it would only need the wing to touch a pole to reduce the flimsy craft to matchwood. Even landing on an airfield in daylight posed risks in such a lightly constructed machine, so landing on rough ground in darkness might be expected to pose a few additional hazards and the poles were something that we could well have done without.

For this special mission we were fortunate in having been allocated the best pilots that the Glider Pilot Regiment could produce. They were cool and efficient characters who informed us that although we may lose a wing or two, they were confident that they would be able to put us down close to our targets, and fully expected to finish the trip the right way up!

At 1700 hours we had tea and strolled over to a large tent to see a film show. There was little else to do because, now that our mission had been disclosed, the camp was sealed; no one could get in or out. Afterwards we rushed to the NAAFI tent where we queued for a glass of beer, but became fed up with the long wait, gave up and returned to our tent where we played cards, turning in eventually at around 2200 hours.

It was hot inside the small tent and I suspect that, like me, few of the others slept soundly. On my mind was the thought that the task that had been allocated to us seemed so great for so small a force. To be the only Allied unit in France, even if for only a short time, facing whatever German forces might be thrown at us, seemed a daunting prospect.

What if the Germans counter-attacked before the Paras came in to reinforce us? What if the sea-borne forces didn't break through the German defences in time to take over the positions we were holding? Although everything was planned down to the smallest detail, it was clear to us that there were so many possibilities for everything to go badly wrong.

I have never made a secret of the fact that I, like every one of my colleagues, thought that the whole scheme was little more than a suicide mission. A tiny force of around 180 men was to crash-land in gliders without heavy weapons or armoured vehicles, to capture a couple of bridges from the Nazis, with no guarantee of being relieved or supported for some hours at the very least. Even if we succeeded in taking the bridges – which was in itself quite possible as we had surprise on our side – the task of holding them until reinforcements got to us by air or fought their way through from the beaches seemed like a pipedream.

I smoked a great many cigarettes on the night after the first briefing, just about the longest night I can ever remember, and as such the most appropriate, if uncomfortable, start to D-Day, – later to be dubbed "The Longest Day".

Conditions on 5 June were far from ideal for an airborne operation, but apparently if there were further delays the sea-borne forces would have run into difficulties because of the height of the tides, and there were many more of the sea-borne troops than there were of us. We were told therefore that, weather permitting, we were to take off that evening, and we all knew that it was going to happen, whatever the weather.

We had an easy day, checking equipment and carrying out final briefings. Everyone was keyed up and the air felt charged with tension. Latest intelligence reports informed us that within the past few days the 12th SS *Panzer* Division and 21st *Panzer* Division (30,000 men with 300 tanks) had both moved into the area around Caen, some five miles from our targets. 12th SS *Panzer* Division 'Hitlerjugend' were the elite of the zealous Hitler Youth Movement and Nazi fanatics every one. Upon hearing this un-welcome news, the general feeling was expressed by one and all as "Just our bloody luck!"

After an early tea we saw another film, then rushed to the NAAFI tent for a final pint of beer but all too soon came the strident and unsympathetic command, "Get Dressed".

Fully equipped, we looked like pack mules. Everything that we would need during the next few days we had to carry ourselves. The glider pilots had warned Major Howard about the dangers of over-loading, and he ordered that we should all be weighed in our fully loaded condition. The average weight was then calculated – for our glider it was 231 pounds – but most of us subsequently took on extra loads, such as pouches of Mills grenades and bandoliers of .303 ammunition, so the exercise of weighing everyone earlier was really something of a farce. Later, when the glider pilots were debriefed, every one of them said that they were hopelessly overloaded.

Nonetheless, we clambered on to trucks that took us on the short ride to the airfield where we sorted ourselves into sections and platoons, drank hot tea and sat around on the edge of the runway smoking heavily and cracking corny jokes. The gliders were already in position behind their Halifax bombers, which were to be our glider tugs.

Nervously we waited to clamber aboard. We kept busy, smearing our recently issued multi-coloured grease paint on our hands, necks and faces so that our white skin would not show up in the dark. Then, at 2200 hours, the order rang out "emplane" and we clambered aboard the gliders, wishing each other good luck, singing and joking. Once aboard the jokes continued, and on the surface there was an air of good humour but it did not cover the strong undercurrent of tension.

As I strapped myself into my seat I became aware that I was becoming increasingly scared. Both Major John Howard, commanding the *Coup de Main* force, and our Platoon Commander, Lieutenant Den Brotheridge, were travelling in our glider. As they came aboard, having said their farewells to the 'Top Brass' who were standing around on the edge of the runway, they wished us all "Good Luck" and we responded in our various ways. Then, to let the Top Brass know that they had made a good choice in selecting us for this special mission, we sang for all we were worth.

At 2256 hours the steady hum of the bomber engines suddenly increased to a deafening roar. My muscles tightened, a cold shiver ran up my spine, I went hot and cold, and sang all the louder to stop my teeth from chattering. Suddenly there was a violent jerk and a loud 'twang' as our tug plane took up the slack on the 125-foot towrope. The glider rolled slowly forward and my muscles tightened as the flying plywood box gathered speed, momentarily left the ground, then set down again with a heavy thump and, finally, a jerk as with a loud roaring of the bomber's engines we became airborne. The other five gliders were to follow at one-minute intervals.

I experienced an interesting psychological change in the few minutes before and immediately after take off.

As I had climbed aboard and strapped myself into my seat I felt tense, strange and extremely frightened, much as I imagined a condemned man must feel on his last morning when he is being led from the condemned cell to the gallows. It was as if I were in a fantasy dream world and I thought that at any moment I would wake up from this unreality and find that I was back in the barrack room at Bulford Camp.

Laughing and singing, each one of us attempted to show the others that we were not frightened, but personally I knew that I was scared half to death. The idea of carrying out a night-time airborne landing of such a small force into the midst of the German army seemed to me to be a sure way of getting killed, yet at the moment that the glider parted company with the ground I experienced an inexplicable change. The feeling of terror vanished and was replaced by exhilaration. I felt as if I were on top of the world. The hand of destiny had guided me to this point in my life and I remember thinking, "You've had it, chum. It's no good worrying any more .. the die is cast; what will be will be, and there is nothing that you can do about it", and so I sat back to enjoy my first trip to continental Europe.

It was many years later that I understood for the first time that we did not head south as soon as we were airborne. To avoid clashing with the two American airborne divisions, who were to carry out missions parallel with ours, we first flew some seventy miles eastwards on leaving Tarrant Rushton. At an assembly area in West Sussex, between Worthing and Bognor Regis, we crossed the coast and headed for France.

To disguise our mission, our six gliders were towed over the coast in the midst of a large bomber force. It was hoped that, as, one by one, we were cast-off, those down below would assume that we were bombers that had been hit. The towing Halifax bomber and the Horsa glider are much the same size and in the darkness, and at such a height, it was unlikely that anyone would notice the difference.

It was about an hour after take-off when the glider pilots announced that we were approaching the French coast. Not that we needed telling since the reception committee was self-evident; to the front of us the sky was lit by a great carpet of flak. Numerous multi-coloured flashes of anti-aircraft shells, streams of coloured tracer and other missiles were exploding like an enormous fireworks display.

The time was just coming up to midnight and, although the full invasion would not start for several hours, for us 'D-Day' had already arrived.

As we drew level with the thickest of the flak and were beginning to make out the coastline, there came the familiar 'twang', and jerk of the tow-rope, followed by almost total silence which, from past experience, told us that we had parted company from the towing bomber.

While in tow there had been a continuous high-pitched scream of wind forcing its way through the cracks and crevices in the thin fabric covering of the wooden fuselage. The noise was increased by the fact that the door had been opened to facilitate rapid exit once we landed.

As we approached the coast the order was given to keep quiet. Hardly a sound could be heard as the bombers flew onwards on a diversionary inland bombing mission.

Once a fully laden Horsa glider is released by its tow plane it has just one way to go – downwards. Unlike the small sport gliders that can soar upwards on the slightest current of air, a fully-laden Horsa just keeps plummeting earthwards and I have the greatest respect and admiration for the glider pilots who have to make an immediate decision. If they misjudge their approach, unlike the pilots of the powered plane, they cannot go around again for another try. Theirs is a one-off decision as they swoop towards the ground at a speed approaching one hundred miles per hour.

Immediately after cast-off we had gone into a steep dive, a manoeuvre that had more than one purpose. Firstly of course the pilots knew exactly where we were and exactly the point we had to reach. Having no alternative to descent, they had to lose height at a rate which would allow us to arrive at the landing zone alongside the bridges with no further height to lose. To arrive at the landing zone while still too high, and then circling around to lose height is not a good idea when you are being shot at. Secondly, the German flak was ranged at the bomber formation, and rapid descent took us away from the immediate danger of flak damage. Thirdly, it was hoped that observers on the ground would assume that the rapidly descending glider was a crippled bomber on its way down.

From around 6000 feet we plummeted earthwards at what felt to us like break-neck speed until we were within 1000 feet of the ground, where we levelled out to glide more slowly down and take two sweeping right-hand turns to position ourselves for the run-in to the landing zone.

Now our pilot had seen his destination and turned and settled into his final approach. We seemed for an instant to be suspended in space, and then we were on the way down.

With our bodies tensed and weapons tightly gripped, the Senior Pilot, Staff Sergeant Jim Wallwork, yelled, "Link Arms", and we knew that at any moment we would touch down. The time was 0015 hours as we all held tight and braced ourselves for touchdown.

There was the usual slight bump, a small jerk and a much heavier thump, as the glider made contact with the ground, but only for a moment. It jerked again, shuddered, left the ground for a second or two, bumped over the rough surface and lurched forward like a bucking bronco.

We sped forward, bouncing up and down on our hard wooden seats as the vehicle lost contact with the ground, then came down again with another heavy thump, a tug and a jerk. For a few moments it appeared that we were in for a comparatively smooth landing, but just as that thought flashed through my mind the darkness suddenly filled with a stream of brilliant sparks as the glider lost its wheels and the skid hit some stony ground. There followed a sound like a giant canvas sheet being viciously ripped apart, then a mighty crash like a clap of thunder and my body seemed to be moving in several directions at once. Moments later the crippled glider skidded and bounced over the uneven ground to slide finally to a juddering halt, whereupon I found myself perched in a very strange position at an uneven angle.

I peered into a misty blue and greyish haze. From somewhere out in endless space there zoomed towards me a long tracer-like stream of multi-coloured lights, like a host of shooting stars that moved towards me at high speed. I realized after a moment that I was not being shot at. I was simply concussed and seeing stars!

The noise from the landing had ceased very suddenly and was replaced by an ominous silence. No one stirred, nothing moved. My immediate thought was "God help me – we must all be dead". The peace, after all the din and commotion, was unexpected and eerie. Then some of the others began to stir and the realization that we were not all dead came quickly as bodies began unstrapping themselves and moving around in the darkness of the glider's shattered interior.

If the pilots had done a good job – which they had, although we did not yet know it – we were now in the remains of a very flimsy vehicle adjacent to a bridge held by armed Germans. I thought that this was probably not the healthiest place to be sitting around day-dreaming, and the same idea obviously occurred to the others at just about the same instant. The whole interior of the glider erupted into a hive of furious activity as everyone sought their various weapons and equipment.

The exit door had been right beside my seat. Now there was only a mass of twisted wood and fabric across the doorway and we had to use the butts of our rifles to smash our way out.

When it was my turn, I clambered out and dropped to the ground. I glanced around from beneath the glider's tilted wing and saw the canal bridge's massive steel superstructure towering above me. The pilots had done a fantastic job in bringing the slithering, bouncing and crippled glider to a halt with its nose buried into the canal bank and within seventy-five yards of the bridge.

As I moved forward I glanced back towards the glider and saw that the entire front had been smashed inwards – almost back to the wing. There had been some twenty feet of structure forward of my seat, which was just below the front edge of the wing. Now there was a twisted mass of wreckage. I had been very lucky, but I thought that those who were forward of me must have been badly smashed up or killed. There was no time to think about this, however. The medics would take care of the injured. The job of my twenty-one-man platoon, together with Major Howard, his Wireless Operator and the five Royal Engineers, was to fight our way across to the west side of the bridge as quickly as possible.

The tall superstructure appeared to shimmer in the moonlight. A few of the lads were already up ahead and, not wishing to be left behind in this exposed place, I made haste to join them. Major Howard was already on the approach to the bridge and shouted, "Come on, boys. This is it!"

Charging forward, we reached the wide steel bridge, letting fly with rifles and automatics, and threw grenades, shouting at the top of our voices to frighten the German defenders and to boost our own morale.

An enemy machine gun on the far side of the bridge chattered into life. We returned fire and kept going, with our Platoon Commander Lieutenant Brotheridge, leading the way. The machine gun was firing long bursts as we charged, and Brotheridge, who was at the very front of the charge, was hit and fell to the ground mortally wounded.[2]

Later, when we learned what had happened, every one of us was really distressed that Lieutenant Brotheridge should have been killed in that way and at the very start of our mission. He was a man for whom we all had the greatest respect. Like all our Airborne officers, he had never asked us to do anything that he would not do himself. It was typical of him to have been ahead of the rest of us in the flat-out charge across the bridge.

As we neared the far side of the bridge, still shouting, firing our weapons and lobbing hand grenades, the Germans jumped to their feet and ran for their lives,

---

2   Lieutenant Denholm Brotheridge is officially recognized as the first Allied casualty to be killed directly by enemy action on 'D' Day, although Lance Corporal Greenhalgh was the first casualty - drowned accidentally after being trapped in the flooded wreckage of Glider No 3. He was later buried some miles away near Sword Beach, his death recorded in the official roll as having occurred on 7 June 1944, but that is clearly an official error. Den Brotheridge was cut down by machine-gun fire as he led the charge across the canal bridge. In one account of his death which I have heard, he died following a wounding by a grenade fragment. However, Major Jacob-Vaughan has been able to give first-hand evidence. 'Doc' Jacob-Vaughan volunteered to fly in with us as our MO, despite the paratroopers' distrust of gliders, which he shared. Doc set up a medical post about halfway between the two bridges, soon after the gliders landed. Brotheridge, mortally wounded, was brought to him, and 'Doc' remembers very clearly that he had a bullet hole through the neck. Den is buried in Ranville churchyard rather than in the adjacent war cemetery. Ranville war cemetery is the resting place for the majority of our Airborne casualties killed in action in those first few days, as well as for over a thousand others of numerous regiments who died in the area during the three months that the Germans managed to contain our bridgehead.

scattering in all directions. Relief, exhilaration, incredulity – I experienced all these feelings upon realizing that we had taken the bridge.

The first part of our mission had been accomplished and now we had to hold on to what we had gained until reinforcements arrived, the first of whom, the Paras, were expected to join us within the hour.

The three gliders allocated to the canal bridge landed within minutes of each other and with almost pin-point accuracy, although one broke in half by a small pond in which unfortunately one of the lads was drowned, having become trapped within the wreckage. Only minutes after landing the canal bridge was in our hands and we were keen to know what was happening at the river bridge. In due course, to our immense relief and pleasure, a runner came over and reported that, although only two of their three gliders had landed, they had also captured their bridge.

By thirty minutes past midnight we had taken both bridges and our Company Commander was able to transmit the coded wireless signal 'Ham and Jam' to tell High Command that both of the bridges had been captured intact.

Now began our anxious wait for the arrival of reinforcements, the wait that we all knew would be the most nerve-racking aspect of the operation. Pathfinder parachutists were scheduled to jump more or less as our gliders were landing, and their task was to set up marker lights nearby to guide in the reinforcements, 7th Parachute Battalion, who were due to jump about thirty minutes later.

We expected the Paras to reach us within an hour and, with the bridges now in our hands, we had to defend them against whatever counter-attack might be made. Still operating to the detailed plan rehearsed at the briefings before our departure, we took up our prearranged defensive positions. Our seven-man section moved a short distance down to the west side of the canal and took up positions astride a single-track railway that ran from Ouistreham to Caen along the top of the embankment.

We removed our heavy equipment and unstrapped our small lightweight entrenching tools. These had a short wooden shaft, with a metal head having a small pick and spade. The pickhead was about one and half inches wide and the spade about eight inches. This was our only digging implement – not the most effective tool, but just about the maximum that we could carry on top of everything else. They were not very useful on hard ground and even in soft soil they could lift little more than a handful of earth. They did, however, enable us to scrape shallow indentations in the ballast stones of the railway track to a depth sufficient to place our prone bodies below ground level. This offered us some protection against an enemy counter-attack, which we were sure would soon be launched.

Apart from the scraping and chinking noise of our entrenching tools against the ballast stones all was surprisingly quiet until the peace was suddenly interrupted by the sound of powerful engines from the west, somewhere around Bénouville. The accompanying clanking, rattling and squealing noises heralded the movement of tanks, and very obviously they were coming our way.

For tanks to arrive so quickly was terrifying and we stopped digging as they drew nearer. Our main concern was their size, as we had nothing to stop larger tanks. No doubt the guards who had fled from the bridge had been able to warn a nearby unit of our arrival and the tanks were sent to investigate. By now they were less than fifty yards to my rear and moving towards the bridge.

Suddenly I heard the familiar crack as one of the lads by the bridge fired a PIAT (Projector, Infantry, Anti-Tank) weapon. This was never a popular weapon with us, as we considered it rather ineffective. It stood on a short bipod and fired a fat missile which was not very accurate beyond fifty to seventy-five yards – and, at that range, if you fired and missed the target there was insufficient time to reload before the tank fired back at you. We had all been trained to use these weapons and, frankly, we were thoroughly sceptical about their effectiveness against real tanks. To our utter amazement, however, within a second or so of the PIAT being fired there was a mighty explosion quickly followed by shouts and screams, and it was obvious that an effective hit had been scored on the leading tank.

I learned later that this timely feat had been performed by Sergeant 'Wagger' Thornton, who had landed in glider number six, next to the Orne river bridge. Because of the light opposition over there he had come with a platoon of reinforcements to us at the canal bridge. The main enemy forces were known to be located at Bénouville and Le Port, and they would have to cross the canal bridge to get to the river bridge, and so it was clearly most important to hold the canal bridge.

The tank that was hit was a light machine, fortunately for us all, but still it burned very nicely, illuminating the bridge structure with a huge blaze of orange, red and yellow. There followed the sound of exploding ammunition as the tank 'brewed up'.

The following tanks were obviously not keen to chance their luck, so with much revving of engines and general commotion they withdrew in disorder. This was not really surprising, because an hour before they had been simply a unit in a largely unopposed army of occupation, and now, suddenly, they were having their tanks blown up and they could not have had any idea about what they were up against. As far as they could tell our force could have been anything from just a handful of paratroops to something much more formidable.

This uncertainty on the part of the enemy was to buy us valuable time. It is very probable that the Germans could have over-run our positions at the time of the attack by the tanks if they had realized how few in number we were. Our night arrival undoubtedly led to confusion in the German ranks – as intended – and bought us the valuable time we needed. 'Wagger' Thornton's successful attack on the enemy tank would certainly lead the enemy to assume that we had a significant anti-tank capability, which would have reinforced their caution about launching an all-out attack on a force whose strength they could not assess accurately until daybreak. If the Paras could get to us in time, although equipped much as we were, with not much other than small arms and a few additional PIATs, we stood a chance of holding out until the seaborne forces got through to us from the beaches.

While Denis Edwards and his fellow soldiers waited anxiously to be relieved, preparations for the main invasion were underway. From 0630 onwards an amphibious assault force of five divisions set out for the coast of France. Their targets were beaches between Ouistreham and Ste Mère Eglise, codenamed Utah, Omaha, Gold, Juno, and Sword. Peter Hall recalls the impressive scene:

The act of embarkation was an awesome and exhilarating experience for all of us. There were more ships in the Solent than I had ever seen before - or expect to see again. There were Royal and US Navy cruisers. There was a multitude of troop transports from the British and US merchant navies. All of the troop transports and most of the cruisers were suspending barrage balloons attached to hawsers from their main decks. This made them look like children going to a birthday party. Around this formidable armada, US and Royal Navy destroyers dashed around as if foraging foxhounds; sounding sirens which went 'Whoop! Whoop!' and flashing signals at the placid transporters embarking the men of the Division. This reminded me of my disastrous motorcycle days with the 9th Armoured Division. I must confess, though, that the young destroyer captains handled their ships with much greater skill than I had my bike. None of them crashed into anything!

Eventually, this mighty convoy was on its way. We were off to war! We crossed the Channel with no interference from the *Luftwaffe*. It was comforting to have a cloud of fighter cover in the otherwise clear blue June sky. We did, however, see one example of skilful and courageous flying. The Germans had just developed and put into service the V1 - the 'Doodle-Bug', a pilotless winged bomb - timed to cut out over its target and explode on contact. This was not a rocket, as was the V2, but powered by a jet engine. One of those weapons was chugging, menacingly, over our convoy, when an RAF fighter swooped down on it, flew alongside and then tipped its wing, thus changing its direction. The pilot repeated this remarkable manoeuvre twice more. The 'Doodle-Bug' was, now, heading back in the direction from which it had come! We soldiers on the transport all cheered like crazy. The pilot did a victory roll and then disappeared "into the wide blue yonder" My Platoon Sergeant, who was watching this astonishing incident by my side, muttered, "And many f....... happy returns to you, Fritz!" It was a great morale booster.

Unlike the assault divisions, we of the Wessex following up, landed in Normandy dry shod. This was because of a remarkable artificial harbour called The Mulberry. This inspired piece of military engineering had been put together in England - rather like a giant Meccano set. It was floated across the Channel and secured at Arromanche on the Normandy coast. It provided an instant deep water port - from which essential supplies and reinforcements could be landed into the Allied bridgehead. This would not have been possible had not the RAF and the USAAF achieved complete air superiority. Without the Mulberry, the great invasion would have foundered within a week of the initial landings. It was a daring and imaginative example of military staff planning and engineering, and was only made possible because of superb naval and air support.

We, the Worcestershires, moved through the sandy dunes of the Arromanche beach. We went through minefields, skilfully cleared and marked by the sappers of the assault divisions. Like so many military reinforcements in history - we marched towards the sound of guns!

As Hall's account suggests, the Allied invasion caught the Germans by surprise, and troops had little difficulty in securing a foothold at four of the five beaches. However, at Omaha, the target of one of the US assault divisions, problems were encountered. A German division had recently moved to the area, and it was not until the early evening of 6 June that the beach was in Allied hands. The US soldier Sam Carter, who was destined for this beach, realized his good fortune in making a safe landing:

Officers of the 1st Worcesters at Harrow, 1 January 1943. That day marked the reformation of the Battalion by merging 11th Battalion with the cadre of 1st Battalion who had evaded capture at Tobruk. Peter Hall (then a Lieutenant) is in the middle row, third from right. (Louis M. Scully)

The 1st Battalion, 18th Infantry, was to land on Omaha Easy Red Beach at 10.00 hours, 6th June 1944. B Company, 18th Infantry, commanded by myself was on the Landing Craft Infantry as our LCI came under artillery fire and was ordered to take the alternate plan, as one LCI had already been destroyed. The Company LCI moved back further from the shore, and we loaded on to Landing Craft Vehicle personnel. As this was taking place, a destroyer moved from the west to the east, so close to the shore I thought it would sure run aground. It was firing every gun it had at the crest of the bluff above the beach.

As soon as the destroyer cleared our area, we landed just east of the knocked-out LCI without opposition. All German OPs on the crest of the bluff had been destroyed by the fire of the destroyer. To this day, I thank the Lord for that destroyer and its wonderful crew.

Once off the beaches, Allied forces were able to make steady progress inland. Lieutenant Peter Hall was soon to face his first battle:

Shortly after our landing, the Division took the role of spearhead to exploit the initial success of the assault divisions.

This is a traditional military ploy. I liken it to the tactics on a rugby field. The forwards (the assault infantry) have the first clash and trial of strength with the opposition. This is in two stages - the scrum and the loose maul. The loose maul carried on by the back row forwards (the follow-up infantry). When a sufficient dent has been made into the opposition, the ball is released to the speedy backs (the armoured divisions) who go for the line.

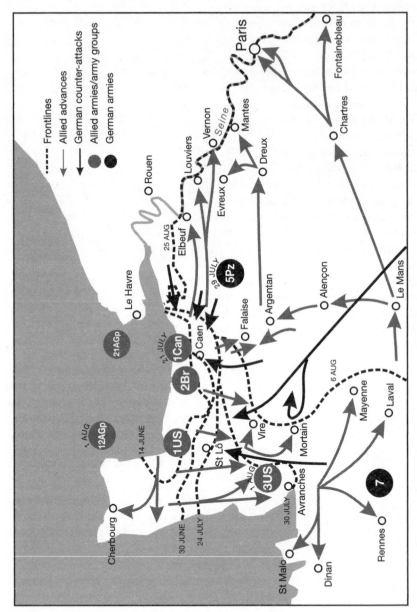

Map 3 North-West Europe: D-Day and Normandy

The forwards (the infantry) then re-forms - in case the attack breaks down - and to prevent counter-attacks. The forwards have to close down the situation to allow the backs to re-group for a further attack.

The 43rd Wessex Division were the back row forwards - supporting the initial thrust of the 15th Scottish Division (the front row scrum). We passed through 15th Scottish and were directed eastward to the first major objective of 21st Army Group. The capital city of Normandy - Caen! Under these circumstances, I experienced my first major battle.

The first objective, north-east of Bayeux (which had been captured by 15th Scottish), was a small village called Mouen. Not until many years later did I learn that a furious argument took place between the Divisional Commander (Thomas) and our Brigade Commander (Essame), as to whether there should be a day or a night attack. In the end there was a compromise between these two senior commanders. The result was a brilliant success.

The plan was that the Worcestershires should attack Mouen by daylight - but under cover of an intense artillery smoke screen, mixed with artillery high explosive fire on located forward enemy positions in the hedgerows just west of the village. From the start line to our first objective we had to move for about 800 yards through a cornfield that afforded little or no cover from enemy small arms fire and machine guns. These enemy positions were situated on a small ridge - dominating our line of advance.

Without the smoke - or without the cover of darkness - our assault troops would have been mown down, incurring horrendous casualties. One of the many problems of attacking a strongly defended position at night is that Verey lights can be fired by the defenders which illuminate the attackers. In a whirl of smoke these lights are far less effective. One has only to drive at night - or through dense fog to draw the same conclusions. The car headlights at night enable the driver to see. The fog, however, causes this light to bounce back at the driver and visibility is severely restricted.

The original plan of attack was in a diamond formation. The company to which I belonged was allocated to spearhead the attack. The platoon that I commanded was allocated to spearhead the company. My company commander (the late Major Johnny Gutch MC) and I discussed our tactics for this attack. We agreed that we should keep as close behind the artillery barrage as possible - perhaps risking casualties from our own guns. The advantage could be that we would descend upon the enemy whilst they were still stunned by the weight of artillery shells which had descended upon them. This tactic paid off handsomely. The only casualty which we had in my platoon was me! Suddenly there was an almighty crash - about 20 yards to my left. I felt a great smack on my left arm, buttock and shoulder. It was rather like the experience I had frequently had on a pre-war hockey field. A big wham, and then no pain. The adrenaline was flowing and we stormed on. We were going to capture our first objective! Some close quarter fighting took place. I am, now, confused about the details. All of us were on a 'high'.

We took a number of prisoners - who we discovered were remarkably like us. They were not the 'bogeyman' that our propaganda had depicted that we should encounter. We were not the despicable, degenerate lackeys of democracy that they had been educated to hate. We were all young male humans, rather frightened. We

The farmhouse at Mouen, Normandy, where Peter Hall and his comrades discovered a
dead baby. The baby was wrapped in a linen cloth and buried in the garden, under a
cross that read 'To a baby. RIP little fellow'. Moments later Peter was badly wounded by
shell fragments. (Louis M. Scully)

were all determined to do our duty - as we saw it. Having been through the enemy
front line, I judged it necessary that my platoon should exploit for about another
100 yards beyond our initial objective. This to enable the two reserve platoons of
the company to advance further into Mouen - supported by a solid firm base - us.

This plan necessitated my platoon's occupation of a derelict farmhouse on the
reverse slope of the original German position. Occupation of this building would
give covering fire for my company commander to deploy his two remaining platoons down the reverse slope to secure the total company's objective. I, with one of
my sections in support, cautiously investigated this farmhouse. We found a most
pathetic sight which I shall never forget - or can ever explain. Lying in the middle of
the kitchen table was a dead male baby, about 6 weeks old. He was naked - but the
table was covered by a linen cloth on which he lay. There were no marks on his
body to show how he died. He was a beautiful and well-formed little chap; blue
eyes open and a toothless smile on his face. We wrapped him in the linen cloth and
buried him in the garden. We put up a cross for him and a sign that read: "To a
baby. RIP little fellow" and the date. It was not much, but we had done our best. I
hope that, subsequently, those who had loved him would have returned to the farm
and given him a proper burial.

Some moments later ... two things happened. One: my company commander
arrived on the scene. Two: the enemy reacted with heavy artillery and mortar fire.
We both dived for cover in a German slit trench, one on top of the other. What I

think happened next was that my company commander looked at my left arm and said, "Peter, your left side is a bloody mess. I'll get you evacuated!" I think I answered, "Sod you, Johnny!" I then passed out. I cannot recall what happened after that. Except that I, eventually, found myself in a hospital 'somewhere in Surrey'.

The first phase of the Allied invasion had proved a great success. The German forces had been taken by surprise, with the result that many D-Day objectives were achieved quickly, and with fewer casualties than had been expected. July was prove a more difficult month, however, as the Allies struggled to break out of Normandy. For the Allies, the most difficult fighting was in the bocage, areas of meadows enclosed by banked hedgerows. These conditions restricted the use of tanks and air support, creating difficult fighting conditions, almost reminiscent of First World War trench warfare. This phase finally came to an end on 18 July with the capture of St Lô, followed by the seizure of Avranches on 30 July. The latter was of vital strategic importance, as it opened the way to Brittany in the west, the Loire to the south, and the Seine to the east.

For the British and Canadian forces, the focus of fighting was the cathedral city of Caen, which was strongly defended by the SS. The city, which had been a D-Day objective, was finally captured on 9 July, after heavy losses on both sides. Eleven days later Operation Goodwood was launched, with the aim of breaking out south of Caen, and towards Falaise. Robert Boscawen, then a twenty-one year old officer in the Coldstream Guards, had only recently arrived in Normandy. This was to be his first battle, and he and his fellow soldiers looked forward to it with excitement.

Saturday, 15 July. All officers were summoned before the 'Commander'. From that moment we knew our ordeal had started.

"Well," he began, "the great day has come at last. On Tuesday we go into our first battle. It is going to be a big show and ought to be a very good party."

Lieut-Colonel Ririd Myddleton; under him the battalion had trained in armour. A shy man, he was well liked and trusted by all ranks. He then gave us the plan.

The position was that rather a deadlock had taken place all along the front. Caen had been taken, but the American advance in the west had made little progress. So in order to draw the German armour away from the Americans, to enlarge the bridgehead and to place us in a good position 'for further operations', the British were to put in an attack in the east.

30 and 12 Corps, both infantry, were to attack on Sunday and Monday respectively west of Caen, to draw the enemy away from the main attack. On Tuesday 18th, preceded by a terrific artillery barrage and the 'heaviest aerial bombardment of the war', 8 Corps, consisting of the Guards Armoured Division, 11th Armoured Division, 7th Armoured Division and 3rd Infantry Division, were to attack south from the new direction east of Caen. The Canadians were to occupy the suburbs of Caen east of the Orne and 51st Highland Division were to take Troarn on our eastern flank.

The plan was that after the barrage 11th Armoured Division would advance almost regardless of loss due south as far as the main Paris railway at Cagny some five miles, the furthest limit of the bombing, and then turn due west to take the high ground on the right flank near Bourgeubus. John Rodney, a fluent French-speaking officer, raised a good laugh when asked by the commander to put us right on the pronunciation. The G.A.D. were to follow led by 2nd Grenadiers, followed by 1st Coldstream and 2nd Irish, to reach the railway at Cagny and then turn east to take high ground by Vimont, and so protect the east flank. The 7th Armoured were to follow us and continue south as far as they could get, directed on Falaise. The armour was to smash straight through without its infantry, and this was to follow by lorry in rear; 'flail' tanks and flamethrowers would be in support.

All the towns and villages as far as Cagny were to be plastered by the heavy bombing, and our route was to be covered with fragmentation bombs from the 'Mediums'. The opposition was expected to be feeble after the bombing. A few tanks, we were gaily told, and the only thing in Vimont was the 'tailor's shop of 21st *Panzer*'.

It sounded a big plan and excited us all a lot. To us then it seemed as if it might be the big offensive towards Paris, but little did we realize what wishful thinking that was. We left that little barn where our orders were given anticipating great things.

On Sunday all officers in the Division went to listen to the Divisional commander, Major-General Allan Adair. We learnt of the wonderful tank country beyond Caen, flat and open cornfields; and that we had 700 tanks to be let loose on the enemy's possible 30. He was impressive and cheering. He told us the plan and encouraged us with his dramatic voice to shoot straight. Good straight cool shooting, he bawled out. Exactly the thing one expects a General to say before battle.

The Brigadier, Norman Gwatkin, spoke to all the men in the evening, a very short speech and to the point, but much as everyone else had said. In the evening we had a short church service in the corner of the field, where we sang the troops favourite hymns followed by a good little sermon from Tony.

Monday was spent feverishly preparing for the battle. Yesterday and today we listened to a continuous rumbling of artillery in the distance that showed us 30 and 12 Corps were attacking. The weather had suddenly turned good, though the early morning was misty, a perfect excuse for the Royal 'Advertising' Force to call off their bombing tomorrow. We spent the afternoon folding maps, studying aerial photographs, receiving and giving orders, and cleaning our guns. For this occasion George would not be with us, he had the disappointment to be the officer left out of battle, or 'L.o.b.', in the echelons. It was a day of anticipation and I was glad when we set off for a night drive north of Caen. With a slight feeling of regret we left our old field and trundled out down the road.

It was an awful approach march, cross-country on a very dark night with only tail lamps, and, worst of all, a thick cloud of dust everywhere. The dust was appalling. I had made my co-drivers drive as I thought it would rest the first drivers, but this turned out to be a mistake. The visibility was so bad that it needed the best possible driving to keep going without running into everything. Because of this I lost one of my tanks, 'Cobra', which went into the ditch, and Brough was not seen again until after the battle.

'Cougar', Sergeant Emmerson's tank with the 17-pounder, also broke down due to dust in the petrol filter. This disappointed me a lot. My own tank, being driven by Liddle, the co-driver, hit something, but no damage was done. Eventually we arrived at about one in the morning drawn up in a long column in a field west of the bridge over the Orne and a few miles north of Caen. We filled up with petrol, shook the dust off and got down under a blanket for a few hours' sleep.

Many people have written about one's feelings before one's first day under fire; baptism of fire and other such rubbish, they call it. But I must admit that evening I had no real reaction at all. Tomorrow was going to be just another day and I did not think it could be anything other than rather disagreeable. A clear starry night. I lay gazing at Orion the Hunter for a time before going to sleep.

The operation opened with a heavy bombardment, and things began well, with the remaining parts of Caen secured, and a five kilometre advance achieved towards Falaise. From the first day of the offensive, however, the British encountered fierce resistance, both in the form of 88 mm guns, and German Panther and Tiger tanlss, for which the Sherman tanks of the British were no match. Losses of both soldiers and tanks were extremely heavy. As early as the second day of the offensive, the breakthrough to Falaise already seemed unlikely. Soon adverse weather conditions would add to the considerable problems faced by the troops on the ground:

Wednesday, 19 July. A short and noisy night. During it one stonk of *Nebelwerfer* landed amongst us. I was anxious that night, only lying under my tank there was not much protection. Not above two hours' sleep. Around five we were woken by the guard to move our tanks out of close laager into a defensive position. We moved out to a very nasty place on the forward slope, overlooked by the enemy, a few hundred yards from where we slept. However, nothing happened, and when it got light we cooked some breakfast, the inevitable 'swanks' and tea.

We were reserve battalion during the day, so hoped for a reasonably quiet time, but after yesterday's disaster to 11th Armoured nobody was inclined to push on to our original objectives, and court another armoured débâcle. Shelled intermittently, we lost a few men wounded in Battalion H.Q., including No.3 Squadron's Sergeant-Major. We passed the morning in the same place until we had an order to move to a defensive position as enemy tanks were reported behind. We moved only to be told to come back again. Yet a second time we moved back to this position, followed immediately by being sent to the north of Cagny behind the 2nd Irish Guards in case of a counter-attack. I met Nigel on the way; he merely repeated the rhyme about the young lady of Spain who it was 'changed not once but again, and again and again, and...'. When belting along between these positions, I suddenly saw an aeroplane engine lying hidden in the corn in front. Had we hit it we would have overturned at that speed. I shouted "Right" at Jepson, who swerved just in time and ran into the next tank on my right. It was Bill's. Luckily we only hit a glancing blow and did no damage. He swore voluminously at me above the roar of battle. I heard something about two horses colliding out hunting.

A shocking position. We ended up on a forward slope in view of the enemy, as usual. Suddenly an M10 tank in front of us was shot by a Panther and it brewed up at once in a cloud of smoke. I saw some of its crew running away in the corn so I hope they all got out. It was disheartening to see these tanks burn up so quickly. The Germans called our Shermans 'Tommy Cookers', a fitting name. The generals and senior officers were angry if one called them this, and we were not meant to know what the Germans thought of Shermans. They were definitely no good for the job of attacking tanks. We needed a heavily armoured tank with a big gun like the German Tiger to do any good.

The rest of the day we spent sitting uncomfortably on the slope inside the tanks. Shelled all day, we could not get out. I managed to get hold of the bulldozing tank to dig in my 17-pounder, or 'Charlie' tank, 'Cougar', in a good dug-in position. Orders had come to the leading troops following this brew-up in front of us to protect our main weapons, but it was an unsatisfactory and difficult job to push up a mound of earth on a receding slope and I am not surprised it was never suggested we did it again.

No.1 Squadron tried to advance a little in a wood on the left. To our right there was a large amount of stonking and smoke as our infantry went forward to capture Frénouville. From time to time the 'moaning minnies' or *Nebelwerfer* rockets shrieked into the air. An abandoned battery of the six-barrelled launchers for these horrors lay beside my troop's position here and I had a good look. Still loaded, their shells were an alarming 5-inch calibre at least.

It could be called a fairly typical day in the line. We were fast beginning to learn how to live under these conditions of shelling. With headphones on and the wireless crackling all the time, we talked little. I shaved precariously on the floor of the turret and Liddle cooked, or rather 'did' a meal, in the front seat. We felt unsafe all day and were glad to move back in the evening.

I learnt how dangerous small mistakes in war can become. This evening I had a short but unpleasant experience. We moved back to the spot where we spent last night, but David's and mine were sent forward as protective troops well in front of the battalion. David was on watch first. Nothing much happened, so I left one man on sentry on the tank and the rest got out to cook, while I sat on the floor of the turret and tried to read.

We were sent to a forward slope overlooked by the enemy, I thought. After a time I had an uncomfortable feeling. The Boche could easily waddle up an 88mm and pot us. I walked back and told Bill, but he assured me all the Grenadiers were in front of me and I was not overlooked. He came up to have a look as I was far from reassured. The open ground, more or less level for about a mile to the railway embankment, rose up gently beyond to some wooded country held by the enemy around Borguébus.

Bill climbed on my tank with his telescope. Just then there was a loud bang. I thought at first we had been hit, but then realized Corporal Arnold, my gunner, had pressed the firing pedal and let the '75' off. Dreadfully easy to do, when all guns had to stay loaded in the line, but it had an after-effect.

While we were still looking through our glasses about thirty planes appeared flying low and quite slowly across our front. They seemed a bit odd for a moment until I saw the black crosses. Bill jumped down under my tank and lay flat, and I jumped on to the 'point 5' AA gun. One plane was a lovely shot but the something gun would not fire. It had become clogged by the dust. I made frantic efforts to get it going to no effect apart from single shots, and gave it up. I saw the planes circle round and come towards me. All was well. They were halfhearted when the flak of the other tanks went up, and did no damage. As the planes flew away I did another stupid thing.

Bill was walking back to Squadron HQ after assuring me my position was OK. I stood on the turret of my tank and tried to wrestle with the AA gun; I was facing the wrong way too. Suddenly I heard the sickening whizz and saw the tracer of an AP shot bounding away behind me. It must have passed close, luckily too high. It went near Bill and I heard him shouting at me to come back.

Whittle, my operator, caught the enemy gun-flash through his periscope two thousand yards away. He tried to put us on to it, but it was too vague. The 'overs' were bouncing in Battalion HQ, so frantic calls for smoke were sent out by them which amused me. Luckily I wasn't hit, so put out smoke, a good screen fortunately (to the consternation of the Grenadiers ahead) and withdrew behind a small ridge.

In the middle of the firing an extraordinary thing happened as a Guardsman, on foot, completely oblivious of the battle and missiles, threw some earth at me in my tank to attract my attention, and said, "Will you take the squadron mail sir and the bread ration?" I almost burst out laughing. Rather shaken, I was handed a welcome letter from my brother George, serving with 2nd Coldstream in Italy. He thought the war would end by October. It cheered me up a lot.

Ian Jardine got a Panther today. He was sent to lie in wait for it at dawn, a lucky chance.

We dug in under our tanks and spent a noisy but not too bad a night. Anyhow I was too tired to worry. I took my turn on guard, slept well and remembered nothing.

Thursday, 20 July. Quite quiet. By now it was obvious that the much vaunted breakthrough had completely fizzled out. We spent the day in the same place sitting in our tanks. I dug a slit trench outside mine and sat there reading, amongst other things, Hugo's *Tatlers*. My crew were dubious about my digging, until we had a heavy 'plastering' at one moment. In the afternoon the rain started. It poured and poured, and soon there was a quagmire. We moved back to where we spent the night and I put my tank over the same, now waterlogged, trench.

I soon went to sleep only to be woken by a great tragedy. About 1.30 I was woken by Nigel who told me simply that David had been shot. I did not quite take it in properly and asked him if he was bad. Nigel replied, "Yes, I'm afraid so". I then realized he was dead, but it did not come at all as a shock yet. It was too sudden to comprehend. I got up quickly and found Nigel who showed me what had happened. At first I was more concerned whether the Germans were still about until Nigel told me that David was shot by a sentry of Nigel's tank. I remembered then I had heard two shots in my sleep. Nigel had done well and was brave and calm about it. He had had a very unpleasant few minutes as David did not die at once. He was lying out in the open, so we carried him back close to the line of tanks. He and I then woke up Bill and told him; he was very calm and sorry. I sent Nigel back to bed and remained myself on guard for the next hour. It was then I began to understand and feel. I thought of my brother Evelyn in 1940. How frightened I felt standing near David's body in the rain seeing the telltale blanket lying over him. He was a great friend, and I had known him since I first went to Eton.

It was the most dreadful hour I had experienced. Total darkness and incessant rain added their dismal worst, with sporadic firing going on all round. David had been coming across the open ground in the laager between the lines of tanks to wake me for my turn on guard. The sentry fired two shots with his pistol. When the hour was up I was greatly relieved and woke Val, the next officer on sentry. He was taken aback. I went to bed and thank goodness was too tired to think any more.

Friday, 21 July. It continued to pour with rain. The papers gave the rain as the excuse for holding up the so-called breakthrough, but this was rubbish; it had been stopped two days before. The place had turned into a swamp nearly, a tank leaked like a sieve, and we were all soaking. We rigged up sheets, buckets and mugs to no avail. It was a most depressing day. David was buried in the morning, but I did not attend. It was at Battalion HQ and we had had to move out at daybreak to take up a defensive position. I did not really want to, and seeing it going on in the distance made us upset. I felt better as the day wore on and, though we were shelled a bit, I went and talked to Nigel and we managed to laugh over something which was a tremendous relief.

During the afternoon we were ordered to move out of the Caen plain to the suburbs of the town for a few days' rest and regrouping. With difficulty the squadron started to pull out, for the rain had found its way into several engines and some were disinclined to work.

I was very pleased to leave that horrible plain. Bleak, grim, dreary, soaking with no cover, like all battlefields, it was a horrible place to those who fought there. The attack had succeeded in bringing the enemy armour over to the eastern flank and had contained the enemy's main forces, so, as it turned out, it wasn't wasted. Now we would have to keep them here by displaying ourselves as far as possible in range of the enemy, we were yet to discover.

We went into a field at Faubourg de Vaucelles, the SE suburb of Caen. When we arrived it was still mined and a fifteen-hundredweight truck blew up on one just in front of us. It caused a complete wreck of the truck and it surprised me how much damage. The whole of the back was smashed and the people in the back were badly hurt, one lost a leg. It sickened me, but luckily an ambulance column was passing at the time, so saved their lives.

We dug in deep, the rain stopped and all felt much happier. Ian came round to say how sorry he was about David. He told me then about his Panther which had pleased him a lot.

The rum ration was issued that evening and we had a good meal. Then Val and I attacked a bottle of whisky. It did us a lot of good and we cheered up. I had a really good sleep, the first for several nights. Thank God the battle of Caen was over.

Operation Goodwood did not achieve its objectives. However, the long period of stalemate in Normandy was finally coming to an end. The initiation of operation Cobra, on 25 July, was to begin a new, and from the Allied point of view rather happier, chapter in the campaign.

Part II

The Eastern Front

The Soviet Summer Offensives
(June-August 1944)

Part II

The Eastern Front

The Soviet Summer Offensives
(June-August 1944)

More than almost any other month during the war, June 1944 demonstrated the impossible strategic situation in which Hitler's Germany found itself. Following D-Day on 6 June, the bulk of German reserves should naturally have been sent to France to throw the Allies back into the sea. Yet the German High Command knew that Stalin's Red Army was planning a continuation of its major offensives that had recaptured so much territory in the southern part of the USSR during the preceding winter and spring. Such inter-theatre strategic considerations go a long way towards explaining why German offensive power during the last twelve months of the war was so limited.

Whilst D-Day and the Battle for Normandy are rightly regarded as landmark events in the defeat of the Third *Reich*, the concurrent Soviet efforts on the Eastern Front, notably Operation Bagration, remain virtually unknown in the West. Despite this, their results heralded a huge success to the Allies, dealing the German armies on the Eastern Front a mortal wound from which they would never recover.

In a masterly plan of deception, the Red Army's high command or *Stavka* misled the Germans into thinking that their main offensive would continue efforts in the southern part of the Eastern Front. In actual fact, the Soviet forces in the south had suffered considerable losses during the winter and spring months of 1943/44, and the major thrust for the summer would come against Army Group Centre in Byelorussia.

By this stage of the war, the Soviets had learned a great deal from their past errors, and the Red Army was an adept instrument of war, not merely the 'sledgehammer' it is so often portrayed as. Conversely, German tactical flexibility was becoming more limited, particularly after Hitler decreed key locations as *Fester Plätze* or 'fortified places', to be held onto at all costs and thus limiting the ability of the commanders on the spot to respond to situations with their initiative.

The Red Army opened Operation Bagration on 22 June 1944, three years to the day since Operation Barbarossa had begun.[1] Despite stiff resistance, the Soviets punched through the German main line of resistance and in a series of titanic engagements encircled and annihilated Army Group Centre. A chronic weakness in tanks and virtual absence of air support combined with astute Soviet planning condemned it to defeat. On 4 July Minsk fell. In the days following scattered German remnants were hunted down and destroyed. The defeat was nothing short of cata-

---

1 Although this was actually by chance, due to railway congestion behind the Soviet lines, rather than for propaganda purposes.

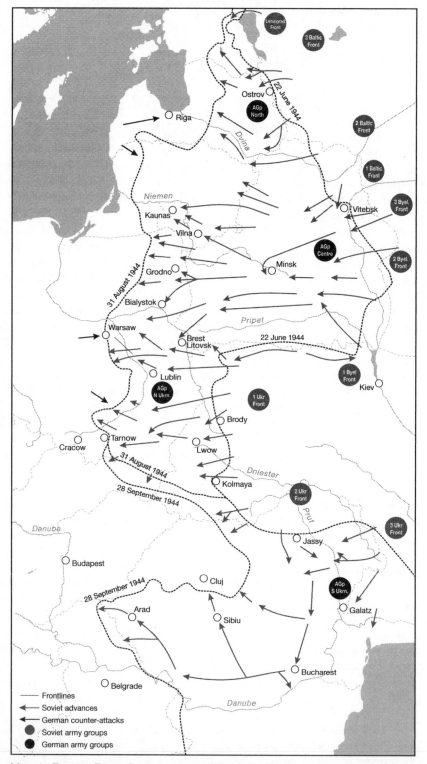

Map 4   Eastern Front: Soviet summer offensives 1944

strophic to Germany, which had lost nearly 20 divisions completely destroyed, and approximately 350,000 men – more than at Stalingrad.

Further Soviet offensives in the north achieved major gains in the Baltic states. On 13 July, 1st Ukrainian Front unleashed its own offensive against Army Group North Ukraine – the Lvov-Sandomierz Operation. Although less spectacular than in the centre, considerable gains were made into Poland.

A further success, albeit on a smaller scale than against Army Group Centre, was scored in Romania. The Jassy-Kishinev Operation was launched against Army Group South Ukraine on 20 August. Aided by Romania's defection to the USSR three days later, the majority of the German 6th and 8th Armies were destroyed. Further gains were made when Bulgaria also changed sides, whilst 2nd Ukrainian Front began penetrating into Hungary. By the autumn of 1944 only Hitler and his most sycophantic supporters could believe that they could still wrest the strategic initiative from the Red Army.

Although aged only twenty in June 1944, Armin Scheiderbauer had every reason to consider himself a veteran. He had joined his unit, the 252nd Infantry Division of the regular German Army or Heer, at the front in spring 1943, serving as a platoon commander in the 10th Company, 7th Grenadier Regiment. During the coming months he received his baptism of fire, becoming a company commander at the age of nineteen, and surviving – albeit with a wound – the Soviet winter offensive. Following a period of convalescence, he was sent on an officers' course, before returning to the front during the first days of June. Upon his arrival he was appointed Adjutant to the 2nd Battalion, 472nd Grenadier Regiment. This Regiment, and indeed the whole 252nd Infantry Division², was typical of the majority of the German units facing the Soviets in June 1944 – reliable and solid infantry formations containing many experienced soldiers who have been overlooked in a post-war literature that has instead chosen to focus on the far less numerous Panzer formations.

First-hand German accounts of the inferno that was Operation Bagration are rare – simply because so many men involved became casualties. Armin Scheiderbauer's description is doubly fascinating for its thoughtful and honest approach, pulling no punches at times about the fragile willingness to fight of men pushed to the extremes of human endurance.

Our 252nd *Infanteriedivision,* the *Eichenlaub* or 'Oak leaf' Division, was the division located at the point of connection between army groups Centre and North. That meant particular danger, because a preferred target for attack was at those points of connection, where areas of command were separated. The enemy knew that there it would be harder to re-establish connections once they had been broken than it would within a single area of command.

The Soviet summer offensive was imminent. We were greeted with that announcement. So for formation and training, for getting to know one's way about, there only remained days, or at most weeks. On 15 June the *Füsilier* battalion under Major von Garn, deployed in the main line of resistance, had succeeded in

---

2   Part of IX Corps, 3rd *Panzer* Army. It is worth noting that this formation was a *Panzer* Army in name only, since all the divisions under its command were infantry.

Armin Scheiderbauer as a recruit in 1942. (Armin Scheiderbauer)

shooting down a Soviet reconnaissance aircraft. Its passengers had been general staff officers, who wanted to view from as close as possible the terrain over which their troops would attack.

The battalion was welded together 'in a flash', so to speak. The work as adjutant was exciting and reconciled me with the fact that for the time being I could not be with my Regiment 7. I was responsible for the preparation of battalion orders, correspondence and personnel matters. But above all, the fact that I was leader of the battalion staff with the orderly officer, the signals staff and the runners, was a new experience for me.

On 18 June an exercise involving the whole battalion took place, in which *Hauptmann* Muller and I participated on our horses. My Army-issue horse, the white horse Hans, was a wilful chap. It was difficult to keep him within the prescribed distance of half a horse's length behind the commander's horse. He had also well and truly stripped me of a waist belt against a wall. In order not to get trapped by my left leg, I had to jump off at the last moment. With that battalion exercise, my life as a 'cavalryman', so to speak, came to an end. From then on there was no more opportunity for riding. On 20 June the battalion was moved up to the village of Lowsha along the Vitebsk-Polozk railway line. Then there was no more doubt that the Soviets would begin their offensive on 22 June, the third anniversary of the beginning of that campaign. On the evening of the 21st the commander, *Hauptmann* Muller, invited all his officers to celebrate the start of their new posts. For many, it would at the same time be a farewell.

To the north of Vitebsk, where we were, the Soviets began their offensive in the early morning of 22 June. On a front extending 64 kilometres, the IX *Armeekorps* with Corps Detachment D and the 252nd Infantry Division were conducting the defence. There, eight divisions of the Soviet 43rd Army attacked. To those were soon added the first division of the 6th Guards Army. It was intended to achieve a breakthrough some 25 kilometres wide. Along with the offensive divisions of the Red Army there rolled two armoured brigades into the focal-point of the breakthrough area. The two offensive wedges encountered the right-hand and central sectors of the 252nd Infantry Division. In the course of the night of 21 June and in the early hours of 22 June, the Soviets pushed up nearer and nearer to our position. At 4am the enemy's heavy barrage began and at 4.20am they attacked on a wide front. Breakthroughs were made in the sector of the 1st Battalion *Grenadierregiment 7* and the Division's *Füsilier* battalion.

As I recall, the hurricane broke at 3.05am, on the dot, just as it had in 1941. The fire was concentrated mainly on the main line of resistance. Only isolated heavy-calibre shells dropped in the village. We had long since left our quarters in houses, and were waiting in the cover trenches beside them. I had been woken by the crash of bursting shells after just an hour's sleep. That action began for me with a thundering within my skull, weakened by schnapps and tiredness. Towards 5am the battalion received orders to move into the second line, that is, the trench that was planned for that purpose. It was good news, because as soon as the enemy attacked up front, we could expect the fire to be moved to the rear. Then it would be mostly the firing positions, villages, and roads, the position of which had been long established by enemy reconnaissance, that would be under fire.

We moved forward, the bombardment ahead of us and the impacts of heavy-calibre shells behind us. In the event, the Division was divided into two halves. Under its command remained *Infanterieregiment* 7, the divisional *Füsilier* battalion, and our 2nd Battalion 472. But of these, the 5th Company deployed on the left, the 1st Battalion, the regimental staff and the whole of Regiment 461 were pushed north-westwards. Even on the next day there was no news whatsoever of the 5th Company. In the meantime the second line had become the main line of resistance and the gap that had opened on the left urgently needed to be blocked off.

Visiting our main line of resistance, *Hauptmann* Müller and I found an 8.8cm Army anti-tank gun, commanding the road to Lowsha from a clearing in the woods, on which the Soviets were bringing up tanks. A T-34 passed by; one shot, and it was in flames. The second followed straight behind it. The next shot hit it, it stopped and from the turret an oil-smeared figure twisted itself out. A third tank came up and drove slowly past its comrades. The number one gunner of our anti-tank gun watched with a tense expression and once again pressed the firing button. Once again the shot scored a direct hit and from the tank the whole turret blew into the air. High flames shot up.

After a short rest of only one hour on the night of the 22nd, and no sleep the next night, on the night of the 23rd and 24th I still did not get a wink of sleep. Our command post was located in a leafy shelter, probably the construction shelter of the *Stellungsbaumeister*, when the second trench was constructed. In the morning we were still holding on. Then towards noon, as ordered, we withdrew behind the Vitebsk-Polozk railway line. The enemy was pushing up behind us, the railway installations were under fire. Beside the station, where just 14 days before I had alighted from the train, the remaining part of the battalion crossed the line. At the Lowsha station a goods train was waiting with steam up to set off to Polozk. Like a magnet it attracted the *Landsers* to it. Müller and I, with a great deal of shouting, tried to counteract the signs of disintegration. We just about managed to hold together the remnants of our battalion.

However, many did not think, but saw an opportunity to get away and wanted to use it. They climbed up and bombarded the engine-driver with appeals to leave. When the train had at last drawn up, our battalion was already in order and had withdrawn behind the railway line. The train had not gone 100 metres when it came under fire from an enemy anti-tank gun. A direct hit in the locomotive's boiler abruptly ended the journey. The passengers leapt out again and rushed on along the tracks.

As dusk was falling I received orders to undertake a counter-attack. With the men of my staff I put the Soviets to flight from the houses of the village of Werbali. Since there were not many of them and since we roared like mad, the operation was fairly easy for us. In the evening a 'V-man' from the Division was brought forward. He was an Armenian in Soviet uniform. During the night he had to scout around in the enemy lines and then return. Meanwhile, it was announced that the gap to the left was becoming wider and wider. There were no German troops within miles.

As Army Group Centre began to fracture under the pressure of the Red Army's offensive, the remnants of Armin Scheiderbauer's Division fell back over the Düna river. After several narrow escapes, Armin and his comrades were posted five miles upstream from their crossing point, adjacent to the junction between 252nd Infantry Division and its neighbour, Corps Detachment D, an ad-hoc formation. The junction rested on the village of Labeiki, which rapidly fell into Soviet hands.

Müller brought the order to retake the village of Labeiki. To me he did not seem to be in his right mind, he was speaking incoherently and was not steady on his legs. He must have drunk too much *schnapps* at the regiment or, more probably, a small quantity of it had overcome him, since he was just as exhausted as I. But, perhaps he had a premonition that the time of his death was near. 'We're off, Scheiderbauer', was the first thing he said. Then he gave the details. The entire battalion staff had to take part in the attack. Labeiki was to be attacked from the north and south along the Düna, and had to be taken. We had to do it without artillery, without assault guns, or any other heavy weapons to support us, without even adequate information concerning the strength of the enemy, but with only 'Hurrah' and the 'moral' support of the night.

When dusk had fallen we moved forward. The night was no use at all to us. When the Soviets noticed that an attack was underway, they fired flares and deployed anti-tank guns and mortars that they had already brought across the Düna. In a small pine wood, at close range, the attack ground to a halt. It seemed impossible to overcome the enemy's wall of fire. Anti-tank shells exploded against the trees. Ricochets and explosive shells whizzed, crashed and exploded in between. It was a noise that could not be drowned out by men's voices. The darkness of the wood was lit briefly and spectrally by tracer ammunition. When the magnesium glow of flares had gone out, the blackness of the wood by night surrounded us all the more profoundly.

Müller did not seem to me to be in his right mind. Gesticulating with his pistol he cried 'Hurrah', but that did not get the attack any further. Finally he sent me to the left flank, where I looked for *Leutnant* Kistner, the commander of the 7th Company. Seeking cover behind pine trunks, I went forward step by step and so drew near to the main trenches on the bank of the Düna. Instead of *Leutnant* Kistner I found a couple of helpless men waiting for orders. The Soviets were still firing with everything they had got. Suddenly there was calm and you could hear the 'Hurrah' from the direction of the enemy, coming closer and closer. Briefly we thought that it was the attack of the neighbouring unit to the east of us. Nothing had been heard of them until that moment.

But the attackers approached surprisingly quickly and by their throaty voices we could recognise that they were Soviets. They counted on us being more afraid of our 'Hurrah' than of the Soviet 'Urray'. Because they seemed to be making their assault along the trench, I ordered the men to get out of the trench and to take cover to the side of it. In that way we could have let the Soviets charge past us into the trench and throw in hand-grenades after them. The men leapt to the right out of the trench. While the threatening 'Hurrah' shook me almost physically, I turned to the left out of the trench, crept quickly into a bush and lost the ground from under my feet. 'A steep bank' was my only thought. I could not feel the ground under me. I was slipping and rolling downwards. I fell and went head over heels, until my fall came to an end in the soft sand of the bank of the Düna. I must have slipped down almost 20 metres. I had not taken into account of the gradient of the bank in relation to the higher level of the village of Labeiki.

I found myself alone. It seemed, in the almost complete silence of a dawning summer morning, that there was nothing else for me to do but try somehow to get back to my men. For almost 200 metres I went downriver along the steep bank, until I found a place where I could clamber up. Everything was calm, but I did not know where or if I would find *Hauptmann* Müller and the other members of my staff. They would doubtless have withdrawn from the pine wood.

The counter-attack on Labeiki was a failure. Armin managed to rapidly locate his comrades, discovering that Hauptmann *Müller had been killed. With the battalion now under the command of* Oberleutnant *Mallwitz, a second counter-attack was successfully conducted the following night, the unit capturing 40 Red Army soldiers and a quantity of equipment. Unfortunately, pressure elsewhere along the defensive lines necessitated a further withdrawal, Labeiki being abandoned within hours of its recapture. All German units in the near vicinity were now making for the village of Ulla, and its bridge leading west.*

We waited, concerned, for the order to withdraw. When it was finally given by wireless it was, to all appearances, too late. As the battalion, widely separated, moved back into the Ulla valley, on the road there were already scenes of a wild flight. I saw baggage wagons with galloping horses, motorised vehicles of all kinds, and among them soldiers rushing on foot. The vehicles were loaded with men and material. Obviously behind them Soviet tanks were coming. The rumbling reached our ears. Those who were fleeing were driven before them. The picture of the flight, the approaching enemy tanks, firing their cannons and machine-guns, swept the remnants of the battalion along in the panic.

No commander was able to hold his unit back any longer. *Oberleutnant* Mallwitz had suddenly disappeared. I ordered the men from my little staff group, who were still around me, to cross the Ulla somewhere and to assemble on the other side. It was obviously out of the question that we would be able to reach the bridge at Ulla. In the ditch by the side of the road I suddenly found myself alone again with two enemy T-34 tanks driving past me at full speed. Both were loaded up with infantrymen, riding on them. The fantastic situation surprised me so much that I never thought of firing after them. With no cover I just watched the scene. The next rational thought caused me to jump across the road in order to reach the riverbank.

Completely calm again, I looked for a lump of wood in order to make the crossing easier. I found a veritable beam. Then a medic joined me. It was the red-haired Beuleke from my staff. I knew him from the Asorowa cemetery the previous autumn. Beuleke had stripped off down to his vest and underpants and said that he was not a good swimmer. I carried the beam, about the size of a railway sleeper, to the water. Then I told Beuleke to sit down on it, in front of me, and it would carry us both safely. Beuleke clung frantically to the wood. It was better after I had told him to stretch out his arms sideways, flat along the surface of the water. I had sat down on the beam in full uniform behind Beuleke. It sank about half a metre under our weight, so that we were submerged half way up our chests.

The little river was getting on for 20 metres wide and should have been crossed easily and quickly. My hastily conceived plan, however, intended to make use of the current and to go down river. I intended to connect up to a larger group and also to get to the opposite bank. On the right hand bank soldiers of all ranks were discarding their weapons, equipment and clothing. I shouted as loud as I could that they should find themselves lumps of wood. But many had been seized by panic and swimmers and non-swimmers alike were throwing themselves into the river.

Meanwhile, I steered my beam with the help of my hands, taking care that my machine-pistol did not get wet. Before getting on the beam I had tied it round my neck on a quite short strap so that, in spite of our being half submerged, it was protected from the water. As we were moving round a bend of the almost rushing river, bursts of machine-gun fire lashed the surface of the water. I struggled to look round to see if the firing just chanced to hit the river or whether we were observed by the enemy. In moving I unwittingly lost my right rubber boot. It had filled up to the top with water. The water had simply dragged it off. Angrily, I let my left boot follow it. It slid off just as easily.

After a kilometre of that memorable journey on the water I found Major von Garn standing on the left bank putting on his boots. He had swum alone across the river and, careful man that he was, had taken his boots off before doing so. I steered towards him and we climbed on to the bank.

The Divisional history (page 205) records those events as follows:

On 26 July the enemy crossed the Ulla in several places and there rolled up the weakly manned positions from the rear, mostly from two sides. The combat weary troops - they had been in combat without a break since 22 June - had had no sleep and only a little food. They were trying, after their ammunition had run out, to make a fighting withdrawal over the rushing Ulla. Without bridges, without boats, under fire from the enemy the few survivors were trying to reach the opposite bank. Men who could not swim were hanging like grapes on men who could and dragging them down into the depths. Swimmers were pulling wounded men across the river and trying that several times until their strength was exhausted. Watery death reaped a rich but cruel harvest. On the morning of the next day on the road there appeared individual naked men, who were carrying nothing but a weapon. Everything was done to get these men fresh clothes, if only so that they could join in the fighting again.

With Major von Garn, Beuleke and I went to the road leading southwards from Ulla, an unparalleled road of retreat. Beuleke, who the previous year had escaped with me at Asorowa, left us in order somehow to find the baggage-train and to get hold of a uniform again. He was not the only one. Down the road were coming *Landsers* of all ranks. They were still rushing, many without uniform or only

dressed in their underwear, without weapons and without equipment. Running towards them with just bare feet I was almost fully dressed. Von Garn said that the
regimental orderly officer, *Oberleutnant* Kruger, had stretched a cable across the
river at the regimental command post, by means of which 15 non-swimmers were
able to pull themselves across. *Oberfeldwebel* Miller, the man in our battalion who
held the Knight's Cross, was a non-swimmer. He said he had got himself across the
river in his vest, with his service cap on his head in which he had wrapped his
Knight's Cross. To protect the congested traffic on the bridge, an anti-tank gun
had been positioned there. Its clear-headed crew were shooting up, one after the
other, the tanks that had broken through.

Still barefooted I supported the Major in assembling the returning men, insofar
as they belonged to our units. But a *Leutnant* from the *Panzerjäger*, like me without
boots, was among them. The hot midday sun soon dried our clothing. The fact that I
had no boots and was not responsible for losing them was to me of little consolation.
But I had rescued weapons, ammunition, map case, and uniform. I was glad that the
Major did not blame me for the loss, but I was tormented by the undignified picture
that I presented as a barefoot officer! We quickly gathered together the remnants of
Regiment 7. The remnants of my battalion we used for topping-up.

In the small baggage-train at the regimental staff there was so-called 'light gas
clothing'. Other reserves of uniform and footwear were with the baggage-train said
to be 80 kilometres behind us. Until the *Hauptfeldwebel* of the regimental Staff
could get hold of a pair of decent boots, perhaps from a wounded man, I had to
content myself with the famous *Schuhwerk*. They consisted of a rigid sole and an as-
bestos cover coming from the sole and reaching to the knees, normally tied over the
boot under the knee. They were never used in the Second World War. With such a
temporary arrangement, that did not allow you to walk properly, I began my duties
as second orderly officer in the staff of Grenadier Regiment 7.

For the next six weeks, the 252nd Infantry Division was involved in a virtual
race westwards, trying to outpace the Soviet units advancing as fast as their logistics
would allow them. The Division travelled nearly 500 kilometres, moving from the
Vitebsk area all the way to the borders of the *Reich* itself. During these withdrawals,
gaps of up to 70 kilometres opened up between units from Army Groups Centre
and North.

For the IX *Armeekorps*, in which the 252nd *Infanteriedivision* was fighting, the
six weeks that followed 22 June developed into a memorable race. It stretched over
some 500 kilometres from the area of Vitebsk in a generally westerly direction almost as far as the western border of the *Reich* in East Prussia. The wedges that the
Soviets had driven into Army Group Centre to destroy it, caused the *Armeekorps* to
lose its connection with its right hand neighbour. Principally, it caused a gap of
varying widths of up to 70 kilometres to open up between the Division and Army
Group North, to which a considerable number of the Divisional units had been attached. Under the command of the IX *Armeekorps* were the remnants of the 252nd
Division and of Corps Detachment D. Into them had been gathered remnants of
other divisions which themselves had been shattered. Our Division had Regiment
7, the *Füsilier* battalion, and the remnants of my battalion that had been absorbed
into Regiment 7. After the Düna position had been surrendered the regiment had

again been under the command of Corps Detachment D. Only on 30 June had it returned to the command of its own Division.

On the evening of 22 July it was announced that an assassination attempt had been made on the *Führer* on 20 July. Among us there was more surprise than fury. We had no time to comment on the event and scarcely had any time to reflect on it. I thought to myself, it was doubtless a kind of treachery that had taken place. But, I went on to think, men with names like Yorck, Stauffenberg, Witzleben, and Moltke would not be likely to betray Germany, nor would they be likely to betray what the German Fatherland meant to them. I wondered if perhaps they had acted for Germany and not against her.

On the night of 30 July, once again after having become completely exhausted, I slept through a surprise attack. I had lain down in the back of the *Kübelwagen* to get some sleep during the withdrawal. During the journey through a wooded district, partisans or members of the Red Army who had already outflanked us, had thrown hand-grenades into the column and fired off shots. I must have been sleeping like the dead, because I had heard nothing of the whole 'business'. As my batman Walter told me, they could not get me to wake up. The *Hauptmann* was said to have been lost for what to do, and instead of giving a sensible order he had tried personally to shake me awake. However, he failed.

At about noon on 3 August we reached the little town of Raseinen. I quote from the Divisional history concerning the fighting around Raseinen:

> The enemy pushed into the town of Raseinen with tanks. By a counter-attack carried out by the 252nd *Infanteriedivision* Raseinen was snatched back from the enemy again. Despite sending in the 7th *Panzerdivision* and *Gruppe* von Werthern, on 9 August Raseinen was lost once again. But the enemy contented themselves with their success and did not push any further forward. Deployed along the slope and at the edges of the town were: Divisional *Füsilierbataillon* 252, *Grenadierregiment* 7, *Grenadierregiment* 472, supported by *Artillerieregiment* 252, *Panzer-Jägerabteilung* 252 and *Pionierbataillon* 252. With the deployment of all the available forces of our Division and the 7th *Panzerdivision*, in exemplary co-operation, the town of Raseinen and the old positions were taken again on 15 August. In heavy fighting that lasted for several days, the positions were held.
>
> In that fighting in the sector of the 252nd *Infanteriedivision*, in addition to the units already mentioned, there were also involved a reconnaissance battalion, the SS *Fallschirmjäger* Battalion 500, 2 assault gun brigades, army artillery units, and several 8.8 cm self-propelled guns. The Division was mentioned on 15 August in the *Wehrmacht* report. In July/August the enemy had sent in against the IX *Armeekorps*, and thereby also the 252nd *Infanteriedivision*, their 5th Guards Tank Army with the 3rd Guard Tank Corps and the 29th Tank Corps. Their forces too seemed to be exhausted. The Lithuanian people were particularly friendly and ready to help the German troops. The time in positions that then began was used to reorganise the troops and to re-fill the command posts.
>
> Finally the remnants, or rather the ruins, of *Grenadierregiment* 461, the 3rd Battalion, *Artillerieabteilung* 252 and the 2nd *Pionierkompanie* arrived back with the Division. With the newly arrived replacements came *Oberst* Dorn, recovered again from his wounds, who took over the command of *Grenadierregiment* 7. Major von Garn took over command of *Grenadierregiment* 461 and Major

Herzog took over command of *Grenadierregiment* 472. In magnificent summer weather the unit was welded together again. By combing through all units to the rear, by lightening the load on vehicles, and reducing the amount the men carried, the unit was made mobile.

On 5 August the Soviets, with strong infantry and tank forces, took possession of half the town, including the raised Osthügel with the hospital, visible from afar, and the convent. They also commanded the low ground adjoining it to the south and the high ground beyond it. From my command post there was played out before my eyes the enemy tank attack across the lower ground. The tanks approached the firing positions of our artillery on the western edge of the low ground, where, well camouflaged in bushes, the howitzers stood in position. From my window I observed how seven tanks were destroyed by the gunners' direct fire. They were firing with impact fuses. The last tank had approached to within 50 metres of them.

Our command post in the sawmill no longer proved to be ideal. Again and again individual artillery shells were exploding in the vicinity. Finally eight tank or anti-tank shells smashed through two walls of the room above my head. So the transfer of the command post 300 metres further westwards to a little house on the road to Vidukle was indicated. But even there we were not secure. For the first time since the previous June, we received getting on for 100 replacements for the battalion. They were 18 and 19 years old *Kölsche Jungs*. During the time in which they were being allocated the Soviets dropped some shells on the road in front of that house. Most of the poor young lads did not even take cover they were so shocked. Three of them were killed instantly. Two others were wounded. The others were shivering with shock for a long time, while we old and experienced men, as if by nature, it seemed to me, got up unscathed.

During the night the Soviets had dropped leaflets over the town, most likely from a slow-flying biplane, one of which I had found on my way to the regimental command post. It was a safe transit for deserters and concerned itself with the events of the 20 July. 'Hitler called on the hangman Himmler and ordered him to ruthlessly annihilate the German generals and officers who spoke out against Hitler. Hitler is also pushing experienced generals to one side and putting in their place crooks and adventurers from the SS, with no talent. Leave the front, get back to Germany, and you, too, take part in the fight against Hitler and his bloody clique! Up and to it!' Then came a personal note, 'To our comrades in Regiment 7', with a description of the casualties of the 11th Company which mentioned the names of men killed and wounded. 'Why do you want to be killed or to be shot up and crippled at the last minute? Just to prolong the existence of the doomed adventurers like Hitler and his clique?' The situation was not as simple as the leaflet made out. Nobody thought that it was simply a matter of the survival of 'Hitler's clique'.

On 14 August the counter-attack began to re-take Raseinen. Regiment 7 and the units under its command, with the addition of a Tiger and Panther *Abteilung*, two mortar regiments, and two Army artillery units supported the attack. *Oberst* Garn was back in command. His Adjutant was *Hauptmann* Nicolai, my friend from the spring in Schweidnitz. Major von Garn, promoted to *Oberstleutnant*, had to hand over the command and temporarily lead the *Panzergrenadier* regiment in a counter-attack on Schaulen. I was sorry that he was not allowed to command the attack on Raseinen. It would have been a worthy conclusion to his career as a regimental commander in the '7th'.

The supporting units had been brought up the previous night into the most forward trenches. The Tigers and Panthers, those excellent tanks, were assembling behind houses and ruins close to the main line of resistance. It is true that my confidence in the assault and fighting ability and versatility of the tanks was lessened when I saw that their crews consisted of young men. Thin little chaps with children's faces, in the midst of it all, they looked lost. They had not yet grown up together and not yet grown together with their vehicles and cannons. That was the impression given by the men of our old escort, the Swabian assault gun *Abteilung*.

The attack went according to plan and was successful. The Soviets were thrown out of the town with heavy casualties and moderate casualties on our side. Only the convent could not be taken. The 23 years old *Hauptmann* Ahlers from the *Füsilierbataillon* was indeed able to get into the church with a few men, but came under fire from the chancel and from behind the altar and had to get out again. Several T-34s were standing in the convent courtyard, protected by thick walls. All the same they were encircled and cut off.

On 15 August several enemy deserters were brought back. They were elderly men who came from Tschernovitz and the Bukovina that had been annexed to Russia in 1940. They had all taken part in the Great War and served in the Austrian Army. In itself, that was shocking.

Just like Armin Scheiderbauer, Dmitriy Fedorovich Loza had tasted combat on a number of occasions prior to the major offensives of summer 1944, initially serving with the Red Army's 233rd Tank Brigade, 5th Mechanized Corps as its chief of staff.

He had the unusual distinction of being one of those members of the Red Army who spent the majority of their war fighting in a unit equipped with US Lend-Lease equipment, specifically the M4 Sherman tank. Although the ubiquitous T-34 was the most common medium tank employed by the Red Army, over 4,000 M4 Shermans were nevertheless supplied to Stalin's USSR by the USA. After victory in 1945, and the onset of the Cold War, Soviet sources barely mentioned the existence of the Lend-Lease scheme, and the various British, US and Canadian-built vehicles, aircraft and equipment used in their thousands by its armed forces. Yet Dmitriy Loza's account makes it clear that those Red Army soldiers that were equipped with the Sherman regarded it with some degree of affection, nicknaming it the Emcha *from the first letter and number of its alphanumeric designation – M4 in Russian being* M-Chetyrye.

By the summer of 1944 his unit was poised to participate in the major Soviet offensive targeted at Army Group South Ukraine in Romania.

From 20 to 29 August 1944, units of the 5th Mechanized Corps of the 6th Tank Army participated in the Jassy-Kishinev offensive operation as part of the Second Ukrainian Front. During this time, the *Emchisti* covered a distance of 350 kilometres. The offensive developed with a tempo of from 35 to 75 kilometres per twenty-four-hour period. The gap between tank units and combined arms formations sometimes reached 60 to 80 kilometres.

In such rapidly unfolding and intense battles, the Sherman was subjected to an all-encompassing and severe trial, the likes of which it would never have experienced in the most thorough test environment. The experience was doubly hard on the crews. They bent, but they did not break. The situation forced all categories of officers to make exceptionally cogent and, on occasion, risky decisions.

The 233rd Tank Brigade, along with other corps units, was committed to the fight on the afternoon of 20 August. Overcoming stubborn enemy resistance, by the end of the day the forces had penetrated into the enemy's third defensive belt that passed along the Mare ridge. Fierce battles continued throughout the night. On the morning of the following day, brigade units began a rapid movement in the direction of Vaslui (fifty kilometres south of Jassy, Romania) and beyond to Birlad. During this time, a rather complex situation was developing in the rear of the attacking formations. A portion of the German-fascist forces that had been surrounded north-east of Khushi (twenty-five kilometres east of Vaslui) had broken out of the 'ring' and, moving in a south-westward direction, had cut all the roads leading to the front line. Several of our logistic facilities and headquarters had been destroyed. Troubling news reached us. We could not count on any timely resupply of fuel or ammunition! Meanwhile, the command was demanding that we increase the tempo of our own attack - there was an uprising in Bucharest. We had little ammunition for the infantry weapons, one-half of the specified norm of main gun rounds, and our diesel fuel was exhausted. In a word, the picture was bleak. The 233rd Brigade eliminated two infantry battalions on the approaches to Birlad that had the mission to set up a defence at a good position to cover the town from the north. We captured some good booty: weapons and food. Senior Lieutenant Ivan Yakushkin ordered each *tankodesantnik*[3] to arm himself with a German submachine gun, in addition to his own PpSh. Each soldier was also to take three hundred rounds for his German weapon and conserve his own ammunition.

This imaginative decision by the commander of the 1st Tank Company became known throughout the battalion and, in a brief time, in other brigade units as well. "A good idea spreads to the world!" It reflected the spirit of commanders of various ranks.

One vexing problem had been resolved. Another no less important issue remained - fuel. We searched for diesel fuel in Birlad. There was gasoline and some kerosene, but no diesel. The Shermans were draining the last litres from their fuel cells. Ivan Yakushkin made the following suggestion to Major Grigoriy Gorodilov, the battalion commander. He recommended we prepare a 'cocktail' for the *Emchas* from the available fuels, a measure of gasoline mixed with two measures of kerosene, and test it on one tank.

We filled the tank of Junior Lieutenant Konstantin Stepanov with such a mixture. The Sherman made a three-kilometre circle, with reassuring results. The motor overheated a bit, requiring more frequent stops during movement to cool the diesel motor.

---

3   The Red Army made extensive use of *tankodesantniki* or *desant* infantry during the mid- and later periods of the war. These were infantry that rode into battle mounted on the tanks, dismounting when in close contact with the enemy.

An appropriate order was issued. We all refuelled. When all the main fuel cells were topped off, we filled our auxiliary drums. Forward! Forward! On to Bucharest! The Romanian 'cocktail' did not let us down. Our tanks accomplished the assigned mission.

One of the most interesting aspects of the latter stages of the war highlighted by Soviet veterans is the continuing presence of the Luftwaffe *on the battlefield. Although numerically weaker and crippled by a shortage of fuel, spare parts and trained aircrew, the soldiers of the Red Army continued to treat it with respect, as demonstrated by this episode recalled by Dmitriy Loza.*

Immediately before the Jassy-Kishinev operation, we received a shipment of Shermans in the brigade that lacked large-calibre anti-aircraft machine guns. We sorely missed these weapons in the fierce August-September battles.

After Birlad, the tanks of the 233rd Brigade surged southward toward the 'Focsani gates' (mountains on the west, river on the east, 114 kilometres southwest of Vaslui). If it was at all possible, we had to get there in a hurry. The Germans understood our intentions well. They fell upon the brigade units with air strikes. We had nothing with which to ward off the aircraft.

It was the morning of 25 August and already the third air raid. Two tanks had been damaged and one wheeled vehicle set afire in Ivan Yakushkin's company. Ivan Ignat'evich was upset and pensive. He assembled his platoon and tank commanders and the commander of the *tankodesantniki*. They conducted a careful analysis of the actions of their subordinates during the enemy air attacks. It was noted that some crews halted their vehicles during an immediate threat of air attack. "This is a big mistake. It is more difficult for the enemy to hit a moving target." The issue was posed to everyone, "How can we avoid the bombs dropped by the enemy dive-bombers?" Lacking a response, the officers were silent.

Ivan Yakushkin suggested what at first glance seemed to be an improbable course of action for the crews in such a situation. He explained his idea in some detail and even gave a practical demonstration of how to execute it. "Let's try it. I think it'll work. Right now, I don't see any other solution," the company commander said.

Upon receipt of the warning signal "Air!" two members of the crew, the tank commander and driver-mechanic, had to combine all their will into a single, coordinated effort. They had to display nerves of steel. Even now, after many years have passed, I can't help but be astonished. How did this work?

The company column was moving along a road at maximum speed. The *tankodesantniki* were sitting atop the tank, the barrels of their trophy *Schmeissers* bristling to the right and left. They were prepared to unleash heavy fire at any moment. High corn was standing on both sides of the road. Be alert! The tank commanders were standing almost waist high in their hatches, warily searching the sky.

Several kilometres of road lay behind us. We heard a loud "Air!" on our headsets. Picking up speed, the Shermans acquired some distance between vehicles, not less than one hundred meters. Everyone outside the tank jumped into the turret. It was very crowded in the tank's crew compartment, but the *tankodesantniki* were protected from machine-gun fire and bomb fragments.

The tank commander kept his hatch half open in order to track the manoeuvres of the attacking aircraft. The tank intercom system passed communications only in one direction during these crucial moments - from the tank commander to the driver-mechanic.

The German bombers circled above. They had spotted a target on the ground. The decisive moment arrived. The tank commander spotted a bomb separating from the Ju 87 *Stuka* aircraft diving on his vehicle. The bomb grew larger with every second of its flight. The officer, calculating the trajectory of its flight, adjusted the subsequent movement of the Sherman. A spurt forward, and the bomb fell behind the tank; a rapid drop in speed or momentary halt, and the geyser of the explosion was in front of the tank. A rush forward, and the *Emcha* hurriedly abandoned the danger zone.

This, of course, was a dangerous 'game with death'. In a majority of cases, the foreign-vehicle tankers came out of it the winners. True, our fatigues and coveralls were sweat-soaked. There was time later to wring them out. The tank commander's exceptional eyesight, will, and courage and the driver-mechanic's masterly command of the vehicle defeated the efforts of the enemy pilots.

The 'Yakushkin method' (thus it was nicknamed in the brigade, a name that was carried to other corps units) was successfully employed to the end of the Great Patriotic War. All the phases of this 'suicide dance' were carefully polished. Thanks to this, scores of Shermans remained combat effective.

Part III

North-West Europe

Southern France, Arnhem and the drive towards the *Reich* (August-September 1944)

Part III

North-West Europe

Southern France, Arnhem and the drive towards the *Reich* (August-September 1944)

A s we have seen, in July 1944 events were reaching a bloody crescendo in Normandy. In the south of France, by contrast, the situation remained almost ominously quiet. In anticipation of an invasion, labourers of Organisation Todt were engaged in a rushed attempt to strengthen defences between Nice and Marseilles - constructing concrete casemates, installing gun emplacements, and laying hundreds of miles of barbed wire. When Georg Grossjohann, a thirty-three year old East Prussian major serving in the 198th Infantry Division, was moved to France's Mediterranean coast, he was far from sanguine about the future. At the same time, he was greatly relieved to have left the desperate conditions on the Eastern front far behind:

There was a well-known motto amongst we infantrymen, "Enjoy the war, peace will be terrible." Thus, we spent the few weeks that remained in radiant sunshine of the Mediterranean coast until the beginning of the invasion on the French Riviera. But all of us, especially those from the eastern part of the *Reich*, were concerned about what the future would bring!

On 20 August, following an intense barrage, ninety Russian divisions and forty tank brigades crossed the River Pruth and flooded Rumania.[1] Then, on 24 August, Rumania broke off relations with the *Reich* and the following day declared war on Germany! The break-off of Rumania created a desperate situation for the German Sixth and Eighth Armies. The new Sixth Army, re-established after Stalingrad, was completely annihilated, as was about half of the Eighth Army. Sixteen German divisions were lost, and the fate of 80,000 missing in action remained forever unaccountable! This made us realize what unimaginable good fortune our division was granted when we were shipped out of Rumania!

The 198th Infantry Division took over a huge section of the Mediterranean coast, reaching from the peak of the Pyrenees almost to the delta of the Rhône river. My regiment was assigned the southernmost part, the right wing of which ended directly at the Spanish border.

My colleague Majer resided in 'Chateau Valmy' near Perpignan, situated picturesquely against the impressive backdrop of the Pyrenees. My slightly more modest residence was 'Maison Rouge', near the road from Perpignan to Canet-Plage. In addition to the highly-touted Atlantic Wall, the Propaganda Ministry occasionally talked about a Mediterranean Wall. My little *Oberst* Newiger would probably have commented on that with "Well, if you want to call that a 'Wall'!" I am not aware of

---

1   The Jassy-Kishinev Operation.

Hauptmann Georg Grossjohann poses with his horses Susi (left) and Siegfried, Russia, autumn 1943. (Georg Grossjohann)

anything that was built that could legitimately could have been called 'fortification' in the sector of my regiment! Our predecessors had built dug-outs of the most primitive type, which would not even survive shelling from the lightest artillery. Personally, if I were under fire, I would rather have dug into the flat sand, instead of looking for shelter in such a dug-out. Some of them were constructed of brick, believe it or not, and plastered with cement, somewhat like a stucco house.

The *Organisation Todt (OT)* did actually exist in Perpignan and occasionally could be seen surveying something somewhere, but with that, their activity was exhausted. Sometimes I visited the *OT*-Bureau in Perpignan to discuss problems with the construction of positions. The only result was that I once invited a very attractive secretary for an excursion to Port-Bou on the Spanish side of the Pyrenees. As Spain remained neutral, it could happen that one was seated at the same table with English or Americans in a restaurant. We Germans in our uniforms were always treated especially nicely by the Spaniards. In any case, I could not spend one single *peseta* during my visit to Port Bou. Whatever my companion and I consumed was paid for by a nice Spaniard. Had I then known that at that time, a cousin of mine by marriage was the German Consul-General in Barcelona, I might have extended my trip to Spain. Because of its location at the border, Port Bou was presumably a preferred place for agents from both sides, who, after all, seemed to know each other. A young man came to my table and asked to talk to me for a moment. He stated that my companion was under observation by the Gestapo for suspicion of espionage. I considered this nonsense and a case of showing off. When he demanded that I return with the lady at once to France, I declared that I would re-

Hauptmann Georg Grossjohann poses for a formal portrait while stationed in France, 1943. (Georg Grossjohann)

turn in the evening, as planned, but not earlier. What a pity that at that time I did not know of the existence of my cousin in Barcelona! We exchanged our vital statistics, but I never again heard from this young man. After I reported the incident to my nice Bavarian *Oberst*, he called and gave hell to the local Gestapo *Obersturmführer* in charge of this agent . . . which the *Oberst* could well afford to do, being an intimate friend of Heinrich Himmler!

My companion later mentioned that she knew the boy, and that he repeatedly tried to score with her in Perpignan. So that's how it was!

Again our division was worked into shape, for the umpteenth time. Men and arms were replenished and small exercises were undertaken. Besides this, as mentioned earlier, we enjoyed the few pleasant weeks that remained.

As Grossjohann anticipated, however, this period of comparative tranquility was to be short-lived. On 15 August Operation Dragoon, the Allied invasion of southern France which had long been advocated by Eisenhower, was finally launched. Effective deception operations by the Allies concerning the focus of the invasion, combined with the comparative slowness of the Germans to strengthen coastal defences, meant that the invasion met with only weak resistance from the Germans. The 19th Army, of which Grossjohann's 198th Infantry Division formed a part, were forced into a desperate retreat up the Rhône valley, not only pursued by the US VI Corps, but also harried by French partisans, inspired by the success of the invasion force:

On 15 August 1944, the enemy succeeded in landing three American infantry divisions and an Allied airborne task force in southern France. The weak German units didn't have much to oppose them, and they were already badly decimated by the heavy fire from the Allied naval gunfire and by air attacks. The invading Allied units pushed forward in three directions. The strongest advance went towards

Toulon and Marseilles, to secure those two ports for subsequent use. The second group moved through Provence toward Grenoble, where no resistance at all was to be expected. The third finally headed for Nice, but it encountered heavy resistance near the French-Italian border and came to a halt. The American and French were supported everywhere by the French resistance movement. Twenty-four thousand resistance fighters were said to be in action at that time.

In my experience, these guerrillas only appeared where and when they could do so without great risk to themselves. Typically, they would liquidate small German rear guards or scattered groups, and then mostly from ambush. Even then, the German OKW allowed them the status of combatants if they complied with two conditions—to come forward as an integral military unit and to wear clearly visible armbands to identify themselves. Nevertheless, the French guerrillas would always avoid open confrontation. Instead, disguised as civilians and without any distinguishing mark, they would lurk in the shadows, waiting for a chance to strike in some clandestine way. During the battles of retreat up the Rhône, German soldiers disappeared again and again without a trace. The most common victims of French 'resistance' included lone messengers or communications people who were sent out in small parties to repair cables.

I remember one such case very clearly. I had sent a motorcycle messenger with a companion to the regimental command post. They had to drive through a small forest *en route*, but after a short while they returned without having reached their destination. They were fired on by civilians in the woods and one of them received a bullet wound in his thigh. Half an hour or so later, a young Frenchman walked by the isolated house that was my command post. First, we did not pay any attention to him, but then our motorcycle messenger jumped up and yelled, "Well, there is one of those 'brothers'!" Shortly after, the young man stood before me, pale as death, probably suspecting what was coming. When he was searched, we found a heavy American Colt .45 automatic pistol, a hand grenade, and finally, the white armband with the Cross of Lorraine insignia of the *Forces françaises de l'intèrieurs* (FFI). During his interrogation, he admitted shooting at Germans in the nearby wood within the last half hour. When captured, his mission had been to assess our strength here because his group wanted to finish us in the evening. Clearly, by posing as a civilian and concealing his membership in an organized military group, he forfeited the protection due a combatant. A court martial immediately awarded him the death sentence and he was executed by firing squad shortly thereafter. All in all, the French resistance was loath to expose themselves to a great amount of danger in battle and did not earn too much admiration from us.

Before the Americans and French landed in southern France, our regiment had already been moved to the area around the port city of Sète, presumably because our high command expected the Allied landings to take place in that vicinity. After the successful landing, we were pulled out and bussed eastward. We crossed the Rhône near Arles at least to slow down the advance of the Americans toward Toulon and Marseilles.

The division staff moved on to Aix-en-Provence. We were deployed for now in the areas to the southeast of it. The bridges across the Rhône had already been destroyed up to the north of Avignon before the landing, mostly by Allied air raids.

The strain of battle shows on the faces of the commander of Grenadier Regiment 308 (*Oberst* Gümbel, seated in the front passenger seat of his *Kubelwagen*), some of his staff, and of the commander of one of his battalions, Major Georg Grossjohann, second from left, August 1944. (Georg Grossjohann)

The two most battleworthy German units, the 11th *Panzer* Division, and the 198th Infantry Division, stood *exactly* on the wrong side of the Rhône, which may show, intentionally or not, what little effect the German defence had! There existed the danger for all rear echelon units in southern France and in Army Group G to become cut off from the Burgundian Gate, due to the forthcoming collapse of Army Group B in northern France. But nothing that I knew of was done at least to move out all unnecessary dead weight before the start of the battles in the area of the 19th Army. The only good road along the east bank of the Rhône was, therefore, totally blocked by retreating rear echelon units!

As commander of the 19th Army, I would not have worried about the rear echelon units' activities unless they were urgently needed to bring supplies to the front. I would have ordered them to get out of the way, to allow freedom of movement to the combat troops. Trying to stop the advance of the Americans and the allied French units towards Toulon and Marseilles ended in failure. Grenadier Regiment 305 fought only one or two days against the US 3rd Infantry Division. Our Grenadier Regiment 308 and the 198th Infantry Division's *Füsilier* battalion were fighting further north in the area of the small Durance River against the US 45th Infantry Division. Because the capacity of bridges and ferries was not sufficient, Grenadier Regiment 326 did not even cross the Rhône to get into the fight. Astonishingly, withdrawal to the Vosges was permitted by the highest Commander-in-Chief on 18 August.

During the period 20–22 August, Toulon and Marseilles were already encircled by the enemy who, on 23 August, reached Grenoble without encountering any resistance during the advance. The danger of the Nineteenth Army becoming cut off so far south was colossal. North of Montélimar, the wooded foothills of the French Alps reached directly into the Rhône valley. Here, and some twenty kilometres further north near the river Drôme, the opponent pushed forward to the Rhône.

I probably was not the only one who could not understand why the 19th Army was capricious enough to move its only two valuable divisions painstakingly to the east bank of the Rhône. There was no doubt that these would not have any chance against the overwhelming opponent, and therefore, three days later, we had to be pulled back northbound in forced marches.

Toulon and Marseilles fell on 28 August, with great loss of men and materiel to our side. But by 25 August, after a tremendous forced march, the 11th *Panzer* Division and our 198th Infantry Division already stood in readiness east of Montélimar to force out the Americans from their commanding position at the entrance to the Rhône valley.

Our attack failed, foiled by strong American artillery fire. My regiment fought near Sauzet, and our neighbor to the right, Grenadier Regiment 326, fought at Bonlieu at the Roubion River. Grenadier Regiment 305 secured the south from the enemy advancing in our direction.

It is interesting to consider an American report from this battle, cited by Graser:

> The Germans attacked the lines of the 36th Division along the Roubion at the weakest point—Bonlieu—and thrashed the combat engineers there. This attack also split the 141st and 142d Infantry Regiments. Attempts by the 1st Battalion, 141st Infantry Regiment and Task Force Butler to close off Route Nationale 7 near La Concourd, failed. Since the 141st Infantry Regiment is under constant pressure and is not capable of achieving control of the hills north and northeast of Montélimar, reinforcements will be moved toward Crest on the Drôme. Artillery and airstrikes will support the troops in blocking the enemy's withdrawal up the Rhône.[2]

As a directly involved battalion commander and eyewitness, I must say that this announcement by the American commander remains incomprehensible to me to this day. Who could have, on 25 August, imposed such great pressure upon the 141st Infantry Regiment, situated exactly opposite from me? Me, with my roughly one hundred men fit for combat? I agree only with the last sentence of the report: American artillery and a few dozen *Jabos* inflicted indeed disastrous losses on the retreating German supply columns and rearward units.

In my opinion, all the Americans would have had to do was to climb down from their secure heights above the Rhône north of Montélimar into the valley and to fight. They could have bagged us all. Thank heaven that our opponents there were not Russians!

I do not believe that there were noteworthy enemy forces in place at the west bank of the Rhône, other than elements of the *Maquis*. Even these guerrilla forces, however, would not have been a problem for two divisions (11th *Panzer* and our

---

2   Quoted in G. Graser, *Zwischen Kattegat und Kaukasus: Weg und Kämpfe der 198. Infanterie-Division* (Tübingen, 1961), p 312.

198th Infantry) to brush aside or move around them in an orderly manner. To this day I still don't know why we crossed over to the east bank of the Rhône. . . .

The success of the Allied landings in Normandy proved that Rommel's concept of defending at the beaches was not necessarily the most prudent. The opponent succeeded with the landing in spite of strong fortifications, large-scale laying of mines, and beach obstacles of all sorts, albeit with considerable losses. With our experiences from the Maginot Line in 1940, we should have known better about the value of fortifications, yet, the defensive conditions on the Mediterranean coast could never be realistically compared with those on the Atlantic. There was nothing set up behind the weak coastal defence at the Mediterranean. It was obvious that this line of defence would be overrun in the first attack. So why should one expose it right there to certain destruction? As things developed in northern France, the defence of southern France became meaningless in a short time anyway. After barely fourteen days, this was the result of the defensive actions of the Nineteenth Army versus the allied landing in southern France!

The coastal defence east of the Rhône was wiped out within a few hours. Tens of thousands of German soldiers were killed, wounded, or taken prisoner. Once more, tremendous amounts of irreplaceable materiel, such as arms and vehicles, were lost. Both so-called 'strongholds', Toulon and Marseilles, were finished. Two good battle-capable divisions were decimated, mainly for the purpose of securing the delayed flight to the homeland for rear echelon units, which actually succeeded only with limitations in any case.

If, at the time of the advance of the Allied landing fleet, we would have pulled back from the coast every battle-worthy fighting unit, free of the dead weight of rear echelon units, and then deployed them out of reach of the devastating effect of the heavy naval artillery, we could have established a flexible posture for battle. The invading enemy would then have run into empty terrain, and could later have been made to suffer considerable losses.

But for the last years of the war, it was probably true what General Hans Kissel said about the potential of the German leadership in general. It seemed as if these people had completely resigned and forgotten everything they had mastered so well at the beginning of the war. Certainly, at this point in time, there were few survivors of the first, or even the second, generation of fighting soldiers of the *Wehrmacht.*

Because the bulk of the 11th *Panzer* Division was badly needed by the 19th Army to keep the *Route Nationale* 7 open north of Montélimar, on 27 August, our Division stood alone as rearguard, fighting around Montélimar. By 28 August, we were compressed into an area that became smaller and smaller.

It may be worthwhile to mention an event from the days of battle around Montélimar. Early on the morning of 27 August, my aide-de-camp, a recipient of the Oak Leaves to the Knight's Cross, *Oberfeldwebel* (later *Leutnant*) Christian Braun, volunteered, as always, with a few men for patrol. In Russia he had perfected his personal recipe for taking prisoners by cutting field telephone wires in the enemy's rear, and then waiting for the repair party to show up. When they arrived, all Braun and his companions had to do was to welcome them to German captivity—it worked every time! After less than an hour, he and his men came back with a whole platoon of American infantrymen, including two officers, as prisoners. He told us that they were about to freshen up in the early morning hours in an isolated house. Braun had only to fire two rounds from his sub-machinegun into the front door and loudly bark commands to surrender. That was enough to convince the Americans to give up. The two young officers were especially surprised when they realized the simple trick that had bested them. In all, more than thirty American soldiers were captured by Braun and his small patrol.

When the patrol returned with the prisoners, I offered cigarettes and a glass of wine to the two officers, which they declined, as they were probably taught during their training. They had their own cigarettes and they may have assumed that we wanted to poison them with the wine. Or they may have simply been loath to partake in something which was not available to their men. They proved to be exemplary prisoners. They never left my side when we broke through to the north the next morning. Since I simply had no use for them, I gave them the choice to march a few hundred meters up the hill and return to their own people, but they refused the offer. "No, Sir," they said, "we are prisoners now!" All they asked for was quick transportation to more tranquil domains, a wish I could by no means fulfil.

During the many attacks by their own *Jabos* they ran in all directions, but afterwards I had all of them right back on my neck!

Only a nation that, based upon its tremendous material superiority and being so sure in the end to have the war's outcome in their favour, can afford to go to war with fighters like these. Of course, there were different experiences with Americans on other occasions.

In the morning of 28 August, I received the regimental order regarding the breakthrough to the north planned for the early morning of the 29th. North of the Drôme River, the Rhône valley widens again. Therefore, the most difficult part was to pass through the approximately twenty kilometres between Montélimar and that river. The order caused my battalion, with the support of some tanks, to advance through the high ground east of *Route Nationale 7*. The tanks would link up with me early in the morning. Right away, I raised concern, because in my opinion it made no sense to get involved in further fighting in the woods with the far better equipped Americans. What mattered was to reach the north bank of the Drôme, if possible, without any further losses. My *Oberst*, accustomed to similar situations from Russia, just like me, shared my opinion but stated, "Grandjean, this is an order from the General, so you can't do anything about it! He wants to march out the same way." Then I said, "Herr *Oberst*, I'll wait and see how the situation looks tomorrow morning and act accordingly." With this he agreed.

I ordered my company commanders to keep the greatest possible distance from the enemy in the early morning of the next day, and to assemble at my command post. Anyone who could not be there in time for any reason would have to get through on his own. The direction was known, and we would meet later north of the Drôme on *Route Nationale 7*. At the crack of dawn, everybody at my command post was ready to march off, hopefully without having to effect a fighting breakthrough, but waiting for the promised tanks as well as for the rest of their companies. Only part of my battalion was there at the determined time, the others were still involved in occasional skirmishes with the Americans. When the tanks still did not show up a half hour after the agreed upon time, I ordered the elements present to form up and move out. Our route of march took us not through the mountains, as I been directed to do, but directly along the bank of the Rhône, covered by high swamp grass and brush. I could imagine why the tanks did not appear. To deploy them on narrow mountain roads, through the woods with dense undergrowth on each side, where the enemy could lie in wait behind every bush, was especially dangerous for them.

In late afternoon, after we had crossed the Drôme almost untouched, I was not surprised to learn that during his attempted breakout, my Division Commander and many of his staff were captured, and right on the course that was meant for me, too!

Much later, we laid our hands on an old American newspaper in which his capture was described in detail—when a US soldier tried to get him out from behind a bush, he demanded to be taken prisoner by an officer. Of course, I could not judge if the US Army paper reported truthfully, but that he put great emphasis on good manners certainly sounded right. After all, this was the man who spent an entire evening toasting his subordinates at his own party!

In the days immediately following Richter's 'departure', our Ia, *Oberstleutnant Freiherr* von Finck, assumed command of the Division. It was not easy for our 1st Battalion, nor for the 1st Battalion of Grenadier Regiment 326. In the course of the late morning hours, the latter took back La Coucourde in heavy fighting, and opened up the important road for our retreat. *Hauptmann* Dresel, who was killed in action later, was awarded the Knight's Cross for this. Now, the remainder of the Division could escape across the Drôme, suffering relatively small losses. The total losses for the Division during the breakthrough were estimated to be close to 1,500, including our commanding general.

On 31 August, the Division went into position in a line of resistance on the River Isere. In Valence, we procured provisions from a huge warehouse owned by the *Wehrmacht*. The food we got there was of such good quality that we were only able to remember most of the items by name! Incidentally, the French civilian population was already waiting all around the depot for the last Germans to leave, so that they could help themselves. As always, we left this building intact.

On 2 September, we marched in close formation through Lyon, 140 kilometres to the north. Thousands of French people lined up along the road of our withdrawal, but I personally did not notice any hostile demonstrations.

North of Lyon, the retreat continued through the Saône valley, and after more strenuous marches we formed a new line of defense, northeast of Chalon-sur-Saône, at the Doubs, the western tributary of the Saône.

Oberst Otto Schiel, an older gentleman from the OKH, assumed command on 3 September. He was an energetic man, the sort who makes a successful businessman. On 1 October, he was, as usual, promoted to *Generalmajor*. *Major* i. G. Grauer became the new Ia of the division, replacing *Oberstleutnant Freiherr* von Finck, who, in the mean time, had had a bad accident.

The Americans followed us very carefully along the Rhône and in the Saône valley. To the west, between the rivers and the Swiss border, where the *Maquis* practically rolled out the red carpet for them, the Americans moved, by their standards, quite quickly ahead. During this, they occasionally attempted to push from the French Jura into the Doubs valley. My battalion marched further west, through the world-famous wine town Beaune, known to me quite well from spring 1943. There, I had a surprising encounter.

We stopped for a short break in the centre of the town and, together with a few of my men, I sat down on the terrace of a restaurant for a glass of wine. When I was seen by the French waitress who was serving, she was so stunned that she almost dropped her tray. The pretty young woman had been the girlfriend of a comrade of mine in nearby Dijon in 1943, and both she and her sister had been guests in my apartment several times. I understood her terrifying situation right away. At this point, of course, nobody in her hometown could learn that she was the girlfriend of a German officer. As I was paying my bill, she whispered to me that her German friend had been killed in Russia. A former comrade of his from Dijon had recently informed her of this.

Up to this time, when the German troops had to pull out of much of France, it was my experience that there had been more 'collaboration' than 'resistance' on the part of the average French citizen. There were in France, as well as in our country, before and after 1945, always disgruntled informers, who often for most abject reasons, denounced their fellow citizens to their own officials, or to the German occupation forces. This was one reason for collaboration. There were also numerous Frenchmen who despised Communism, and who perhaps foresaw what could happen to them if the Germans were defeated in the east. As far as the former lot are concerned, nobody was saddened by the fact that they later sometimes were punished, and even sentenced to death. For the second category, of course, harsh punishment was more than questionable.

Perhaps their judges believed in having to restore France's honour by sentencing collaborators to death or long imprisonment. Some of these people were actually guilty of little more than establishing a passable relationship with the occupying forces. They may even have, out of honest conviction, approved of enduring relations with the Germans, but still have remained French patriots. France did lose the war with the Germans in 1940, but not its national honour!

What was done to French girls was especially ugly; indeed, it was most crude and heartless how French girls, whose only crime was to fall in love with a German, were treated by the French mob. Typically, their hair was shaved or closely cropped, then they were humiliated and beaten as they were run out of their native villages or towns by a local mob, seething with hatred. For the French men who participated, this may have been an expression of primitive sexual jealousy and insulted arrogance.

Evidently, one has to put up with the fact that any major upheaval brings the lower side to the surface. We, too, had most evil denunciations, and not only after 1945.

Our division moved into its next position at the Doubs River. The front line of our Corps ran from Chalon-sur-Saône to Dole and on to Besançon. By 8 September, the front had to be shortened because of numerous penetrations by American tanks. The next morning, the line of resistance lay along the Ognon, five to twenty kilometers northwest of Doubs.

On 8 or 9 September, my colleague, *Major* Dr. Majer, together with his adjutant, was wounded by tank fire and captured by the pursuing Americans. Later, when he returned to his hometown of Stuttgart, Majer told me that he was brilliantly taken care of by the American nurses. Without penicillin, which at that time was not yet available to us, he would most likely not have survived his severe injury.

During the days of fighting in the first half of September, I had three experiences that were most significant. One was quite successful, one questionable, and one a little unusual.

I had positioned a few infantrymen equipped with *panzerfausts* at a railroad underpass—it could have been on the line southwest of Dole.35 Suddenly, a jeep with four US soldiers came rolling along toward our underpass, clearly unaware of any danger. It stopped hardly ten metres away and the occupants prepared to dismount. Two of my men had aimed their rocket launchers at the jeep already, when I whispered to them not to shoot at the vehicle, but beyond it. Seconds later, there were two terrible explosions and our four Americans froze in place. When we called on them to surrender, they came marching forward with their hands up. Later, they said they believed our lines to be much further to the north. This was why they did not expect *panzerfaust* fire from an ambush position, but rather perhaps artillery fire, at the most. We took them and their jeep to my command post.

The boss was a well-fed, redheaded major, apparently of Irish decent. He and his comrades were not as touchy as the two US lieutenants from Montélimar. Together we had a strong drink, and at that time I was even rich enough to offer a choice between whiskey or French cognac. "I prefer whiskey," the redhead said objectively. When we searched the vehicle, we found maps with the firing plans of the American artillery. Our major was no little fish, but obviously the artillery officer of the US division which opposed us. Of course, the American soldiers were allowed to keep anything that was personal property, but the maps were clearly a different story. Despite his entreaties to the contrary, I had to withhold them from him.

Years later, I met him on the street in Bad Tölz. We exchanged a few casual words, but I had the impression that our short encounter was not especially pleasant for him. Besides, it was shortly after war's end.

The event of questionable import was this. Later on, when we took some American prisoners, one of them asked to be able to speak to the German commanding officer. My English at that time was still somewhat bumpy, but it quickly became clear what concerned the GI. "Sir, I am Jewish!" he told me. I responded that, to me, he was just an American prisoner of war (PW). Besides, I was absolutely certain that no American PW would be sorted out in this respect. Antisemitism was not an issue for me. In my East Prussian homeland, my father did business with Jews when they showed up at our farm to buy animal pelts or scrap iron. My Aunt Helene worked for decades as a chief bookkeeper in a Danzig (Gdansk) cigarette factory. Privately, she was also involved in a friendship with the Jewish owner of their firm and his family. Presumably, part of the Christmas gifts she brought each year came from the Borg family. My first wife was an apprentice in a Jewish-owned warehouse before we were married.

The unusual experience of this time was of a different kind. I often saw how German 88mm *Flak*, tanks, self-propelled assault guns or antitank guns destroyed enemy tanks, and, of course, the other way around as well. This time, I was an eyewitness to playing the game in a way that was new to me. Immediately across from the position of our heavy infantry gun section, several American tanks suddenly appeared in the dense brush. The short-barrelled 150mm guns were basically used only for high-angle fire. The surprised gun crews had to find means for their own protection, so they aimed directly at two enemy tanks and fired. I don't know if anything like this had been practiced before. The distance amounted surely to not much more than fifty meters. The effect was horrible. The two tanks that were hit literally exploded, while the others behind them shifted at once into reverse, as one could clearly hear. Unfortunately, those "experiences of success" became more and more scarce.

Continuously fighting, on 15 September the division moved back to the western edge of the Vosges Mountains via Lure. To present an idea of what was left of people in the replenished division one month later, 1st Battalion of the Grenadier Regiment 308 consisted of only twenty-two men, including the two officers! One of the battalion commanders was seriously wounded and taken prisoner by the Americans, the second one was killed in action just three days later. The third battalion commander in a week, *Hauptmann* Bengel, a member of the division since the very first day of its formation, had only a few weeks left to live. On 6 October, during a counterattack, he was badly wounded and died shortly thereafter in a field hospital from an infection.

It is simply impossible to detail all that took place in the battles between Chalon-sur-Saône and our later deployment west of Gérardmer. One incident that is particularly vivid in my mind took place near Lure. My soldiers brought in a seriously wounded comrade whose abdominal wall was completely ripped open by a shell splinter. Since we had to pull back, we considered dragging him along. We emptied the rear seats of my jeep and loaded him in. The poor guy was fully conscious and suffered unbearable pain. Since the larger part of the battalion had already marched off, our physician could not be reached. The moment we started to drive, the wounded soldier continuously screamed in pain, so we carefully took him out of the car and laid him on the ground. While we stood around rather helplessly, a young French woman—I think she was the local teacher—came out of the neighbouring house. She made us understand that the soldier would die within a short time, so why torture him? She promised to stay with him to the end and she would see to it that he was buried in the town's cemetery. When we left, quite distressed, she was sitting on the ground with the boy's head in her lap.

By the end of September, our division was deployed around Gérardmer. Our opponents were the US 3rd and 36th Infantry Divisions, both of which were fully motorized and equipped with tanks. But shortly thereafter, my regiment was moved back to the area of Le Thillot, not far from where we had been just a short time before. There, my future opponent, the 3d Algerian Infantry Division, had just crossed the Moselle and approached the Cornimont-Remiremont road.

By the autumn of 1944, southern France was already secure in Allied hands; the port of Marseilles, which had been captured as early as 28 August, was to provide a vital source of materiél and troop reinforcements over the coming months. When the eighteen-year-old American Frank Gurley arrived in this port in October, straight out of Fort Benning training camp, he encountered a scene strikingly different from that described by Georg Grossjohann a mere three months earlier.

Friday, 20 October. Just two weeks out of New York, the coast of southern France finally came into view, a ridge of barren purple hills extending out of sight in both directions. We had imagined that the Riviera coast would be flat with sandy beaches and (we hoped) female bathers in skimpy suits. Rounding a promontory, we saw a sea of red tile rooftops shining in the sun. We had finally reached Marseilles. High above the city on a rocky hill escarpment stood the lofty basilica of Notre-Dame de la Garde.

The port facilities of Marseilles had been methodically blown up by the German occupiers before their withdrawal in August, and their remnants had been strewn all over the harbour as if by a posse of angry gods. Upside-down rusting hulls protruded from the water everywhere, systematically sunk in an effort to render the port unusable for Allied convoys. But despite all the enemy's efforts, a passageway had been opened through the cordon of sunken hulks and the battered port facilities were again operable. A screen of anti-*Luftwaffe* barrage balloons tied together with cables floated above the waterfront like school kids with linked hands dancing around the Maypole. The nearest German air bases were only thirty minutes away in northern Italy.

The familiar shipboard 'Voice of Authority' intoned over the loudspeaker, "All troops will return to their compartments immediately and prepare for debarkation." After some incredible confusion in saddling up our packs and other equipment in the confused troop quarters, we hauled our belongings up the steep companionway to the deck. We were each issued two K rations as our meals until next day. One by one our names were called to cross the gangway.

"Gurley," First Sergeant Thomas Mulligan read from his list.

"Franklin L." I replied and headed for the narrow gangplank. Major Barney Lentz, our beloved Battalion Executive Officer, stood beside the gangplank, monitoring our passage, arms folded in his usual Roman emperor's manner.

"Buckle your chinstrap, soldier!" he said. How could I have forgotten to buckle the damn thing? But even if I had forgotten, so what? I thought we had come over here to fight Germans, not to continue Barney's "cadence marching" and other parade ground nonsense.

I had been confident that everything would be different overseas and that Barney Lentz and the others would eliminate the chicken shit, if only as a means of ensuring their own health and longevity. But the Old World so far looked pretty much like our own country, and the Major's reprimand did not sound like an auspicious beginning.

Over the gangway, I found myself crossing the hull (!) of an upended white hospital ship. From there a second gangway led into a battered wharf. After sinking the ships in the Old Port, the Germans had blasted and wrecked the jetties, piers and berth spaces, and booby-trapped the ruins.

Then down many steps, through a bombed out warehouse and out onto the street, I staggered under my horseshoe-roll pack. German and Italian prisoners of war were sweeping and stacking rubble stones under the surveillance of carbine-wielding GIs.

"All right, column of ducks and shake it up!" Lieutenant Mueller shouted. When compliance was slow, the Lieutenant raised a whistle to his lips and sounded a shrill blast. Like Barney Lentz, the Lieutenant apparently hadn't got the message yet that the enlisted men were expecting more democratic treatment overseas, if the officers hoped to preserve their own good health.

"Where'd Junior get that whistle?" someone muttered. "My name ain't Fido."

"During our march to the new staging area," Lieutenant Mueller announced, "there will be no talking with the French population. Nor will any food items be accepted from the locals or given to them. Spies will be trying to learn everything possible about us."

"I thought we liberated these folks," someone said. "Ain't they supposed to be our friends?"

"Those are our orders," the Lieutenant replied. The Battalion moved out in a seemingly endless column of twos along the rough-surfaced street beside the port. It was Act I, Scene 1 of our 'Hike to the Reich', a stage production with a cast of thousands being put on in the European Theatre of Operations under General Eisenhower.

We passed clusters of troops from many nations standing in groups or reclining along the roadside. There were black colonial troops from Senegal wearing tall red fezzes, dusky-skinned Moroccans called 'Goums', and bearded Gurkhas from India wearing turbans. There were also lean, tanned GIs still wearing summer uniforms, who had parachuted into the country during Operation Dragoon, the August invasion of the Riviera. They were waiting to board the ships we from which we had just debarked.

Our route of march led us out of the waterfront district and upward through the city streets toward the range of purple hills that dominated the city. Charcoal-burning trucks and ancient autos chugged and coughed their way up steep cobblestone streets, pursued by bell-clanging, triple-unit trolleys loaded to overflowing with civilians and soldiery. Children flitted about the feet of our marching columns. "*Cigarette pour papa?! Chocolat pour mamma?!* Hey, Joe, you got any chunggum?" Robert E. Jones from my squad reached inside his BAR ammunition belt and produced some chocolate bars and chewing gum for the children.

"Hold it, Jones!" Lieutenant Mueller called.

"What's up?" Jones asked.

"Giving things to people is forbidden," the Lieutenant said.

"Hell, these ain't people, these are kids," Jones snorted, but put the gifts back in his ammo belt.

Short-skirted girls demurely observed our passage and the general populace along the road was warm and receptive. Many held out flowers, grapes, tomatoes, and bottles of wine to our still untested foot-sloggers. Lieutenant Mueller seemed as busy as a hockey goalie as he scooted about attempting to block these manifestations of welcome.

"Lieutenant, these folks act real glad to be liberated," someone in the column said. "They're just trying to say thanks."

"Nobody asked you," the Lieutenant said firmly.

The men began to complain of sore feet and overheating as they marched uphill through the sunny afternoon air under the seventy-pound weight of their horseshoe-roll packs.

"I been on that damn ship fifteen days," Robert E. Jones said, "and I ain't got my land legs back yet."

"Keep plugging," Sergeant Gardner said. "Maybe Red Gurley can spell you on the BAR a while."

"Sure," I said.

"Here, let me do it," said Ernie Emmons, Jones' regular assistant.

"No, that's okay," I said, slipping the BAR sling from Jones' broad right shoulder and handing him my M-1 rifle in exchange.

"Thanks, man," Jones drawled. "Now mebbe ah kin look at these French broads without raising my blood pressure and having me a stroke."

"I thought you was married," Ernie Emmons said, eyes blinking mischievously.

"Never said I wasn't," Jones replied.

"How about you, Hershberg?" Lieutenant Mueller said. "Would you like Hogberg to spell you on the BAR?"

"Naaaah," Lennie Hershberg said, laughing. "Hoggie's got bad feet already and will need somebody to carry him."

"That's no lie," Hoggie Hogberg replied. He was limping already and the march had practically just begun. "When do we take a chow break?" Hoggie asked rhetorically, licking his lips.

Despite the instructions about not accepting gifts or communicating with the French, we could sense that we were being treated like VIPs as the people along the road waved and cheered us. If the Camp Kilmer cadres had treated us like princes, the Marseilleans were treating us like kings. These French civilians seemed even more appreciative than our own people back home, many of whom considered the war to be practically won already.

"Take ten, men!" Captain Young called.

Our Assistant Squad Leader, Real Parenteau, wandered into a walled courtyard looking for a drink of water. There an attractive young French woman was delighted to discover that Parenteau spoke French. She had one '*petit*' at her feet and another 'on the way'. I heard her telling Parenteau that her husband was with General Leclerc's French 2nd Armoured Division. She disappeared into the house and moments later reappeared with a wine bottle and several small glasses. Members of our squad clustered joyfully around our French-speaking NCO and we were soon clinking glasses. After the long hot march, the wine quickly created a collective mood of euphoria. Just then a whistle blew and Lieutenant Mueller came striding into the courtyard clutching his carbine sling, a grim expression on his face.

"Sergeant Parenteau, you know there is to be no communication with the French population or receiving gifts from them. You are setting a bad example for your men. Get back out on the road immediately."

Real Parenteau's cheeks turned red and his eyes flashed defiance. After several moments of unresolved tension, he shrugged his shoulders and turned away. We glumly followed him out of the courtyard and back onto the road.

The road left the Marseilles suburbs behind and entered farm country. The road was bounded by stone fences and rows of wispy poplars that stood like tall question marks in the twilight. The column moved ever more slowly as soldiers limped, perspired, grumbled, cursed softly, or said nothing.

Pfc. Jack Ogden, the company Mail Clerk, collapsed quietly on the road as though he had been hit by a sniper. He was picked up by a truck put into service to transport those unable to move under their own power.

Farmers in blue denim clothing came forward in the gathering darkness to offer small tomatoes and large bunches of grapes to the marchers. Because of the limited visibility, Lieutenant Mueller was forced to give up trying to block all gifts. Thus we enjoyed the finest grapes from France's vineyards, whose reputation remained intact despite the German conquest of France.

After darkness fell, we heard a faint motor noise in the sky overhead. Captain Young said we were under surveillance by a German reconnaissance plane better known as 'Bedcheck Charley'. Ground searchlights fingered the dark clouds overhead and we could hear friendly ack-ack (antiaircraft) guns opening up.

"Talking to the local people is the quickest way to let the enemy know where we are," Lieutenant Mueller said, making plain that he felt vindicated by Bedcheck Charley's visit.

Bedcheck Charley's motor sound soon faded from the sky, but a few minutes later a stronger motor was heard, followed by the sound of explosions down the road behind us. Again our ack-ack guns were heard, sounding more determined than before. Word traveled along the column that Company D behind us had been the victims the enemy's first air attack on our newly debarked division.

Finally, after eleven or twelve miles of marching, the column was led off the road into a meadow near the village of Septêmes. We bedded down on the ground and were soon asleep.

While the infantry battalions were making the long trek from the port up into the hills that Friday afternoon, General Burress called together his principal officers at Marseilles' Grand Hotel. "Welcome to France, gentlemen," he said with a friendly twinkle. Then he became all business. "The front lines are beyond the Moselle River in the foothills of the Vosges Mountains. Our advance has slowed to a snail's pace. This has its good side in giving us what is called an old lady's sector of the front while our boys get used to the weather and the feel of combat. General Truscott plans to work our regiments in one at a time between his veteran divisions. This will allow our boys to break in alongside units who know all the enemy's tricks."

The divisional staff officers and senior commanders listened with attention. Apart from Bill Miller and Andy Tychsen, none of them had even been old enough to be in the Army during the First World War. "The big problem now," General Burress told his officers, "is removing the cosmoline from your jeeps and trucks and reassembling them for a rapid move of about 450 miles to the front. What do you say to that, gentlemen? How long will it take you?"

"We lack the necessary know-how, sir," said Colonel William Ellis, Commander of the 397th Infantry Regiment. "That's a specialized task for Ordnance."

"I expected a better answer than that from a VMI prof, Bill," General Burress told Ellis, whom he had brought to VMI to teach military science when Burress was serving as Commandant of Cadets there.

"Sorry, sir," Colonel Ellis said with a smile.

"What about you, Nelson?" General Burress asked Colonel Fooks, 398th Regimental CO. Fooks had been a Tactical Officer at West Point, where the cadets had called him (behind his back) "Foggy" Fooks.

"Same problem as Bill Ellis," Colonel Fooks replied. "No trained specialists available."

"Are you in the same boat they are, Chris?" General Burress asked Colonel Tychsen (whose middle name was Christian).

"No, sir!" Colonel Tychsen replied briskly. "My officers and men volunteered to go to a special school in the States to learn vehicular assembly and disassembly. We can do the job, and quickly."

"Good!" General Burress said. Bill Ellis and Nelson Fooks appeared startled. "Weren't you in the Vosges sector in the First War, Chris?" General Burress asked, knowing very well what Tychsen's answer would be.

"I commanded a machine-gun company there in the 88th Division," Colonel Tychsen replied with pride.

"All right, Chris. As soon as you get your vehicles in shape, your regiment will depart for the front. Yours will be the first regiment to meet the enemy."

"I'm looking forward to this," Colonel Tychsen responded. "I asked for a combat assignment nearly three years ago."

"I remember," General Burress said. "One more point. I want all ammo trucks to carry double the prescribed quantity of ammunition."

"But, sir," Tychsen said, "that's far in excess of the limits we were taught to adhere to in training."

"Don't worry, I can assure you the trucks will handle the increased weight easily," General Burress said firmly. "Besides, this is war and we've got to get on with it."

The General's tone of voice made clear that there would be no further debate on that issue. "One disquieting bit of information I just heard," General Burress went on. "The French dock workers won't unload our equipment from the ships during the weekend, and they may go on strike Monday."

"On strike?" Colonel Ellis asked. "Don't they know there's a war on?"

"Maybe they think it's over," General Burress replied. "Anyway, if they don't come to work on Monday I want all three regiments to send contingents down to that waterfront, and keep them there till every last jeep and truck are off those ships." Everyone nodded in agreement.

General Burress' aide came into the meeting and whispered something to him.

"Well, ah'll be dayamed!" General Burress exclaimed in his best Richmond drawl. "Gentlemen, we've been mentioned on the radio by the enemy, in fact by no less a luminary than Axis Sally. She welcomes the 100th Infantry Division to the European Theater and promises us a hot reception up at the Belfort Gap in the Vosges Mountains!"

There was a buzzing among the officers. General Burress went on. "Do you know what Axis Sally said next? Get this. She said she was gonna play 'General Burress' favorite song' on the radio."

"What was the song?" someone asked.

"There'll be Some Changes Made!" General Burress said, rolling his eyes and exploding with laughter. . . .

In the south of France, then, the story of the late summer and early autumn of 1944 was one of spectacular Allied success. In August, the campaign in Normandy also took a turn for the better. Although Operation Goodwood, on the eastern flank, had not brought the hoped-for breakthrough, it had been successful in drawing in German reserves. On the western flank, the US Operation Cobra was more produced the elusive breakout west of St Lô. At this point, Allied commanders made an important strategic decision. They saw that by swinging US 3rd Army back eastwards, towards the Seine, they might be able to form a link with the Anglo-Canadian and Polish troops driving southwards from Caen, and so encircle a large number of German troops in the Falaise pocket. This plan was initiated on 8 August. Although some hesitancy in the Allied advance allowed a substantial number of Germans troops to escape, by 20 August 50,000 had been taken prisoner.

In late August the Allies chased retreating German troops. While US divisions drove down the left bank of the Seine, British and Canadian troops continued the pursuit eastwards, towards Belgium. On 3 September Brussels was liberated, followed a day later by Antwerp. The Allies had now established a continuous front, running from the Swiss border south of Belfort in the south, right up to the English Channel in the north. At this point, it seemed possible that the war in Europe could be brought to a conclusion before the year's end. Yet things were about to take a negative turn for the Allies. The opening act in this new, more difficult period, was the British-led operation to open a bridgehead to the Ruhr, codenamed Market Garden.

The aim of this famous operation was to seize bridge across the Rhine at Arnhem, in Holland, thus opening a path into the Ruhr. The plan was to drop paratroopers at four points; near Eindhoven and Son; near the bridge at Nijmegen, and finally near Arnhem itself. The lightly armed paratroopers were to be relieved by the tanks of British XXX Corps, who were to proceed along the road connecting these points, beginning at the Meuse-Escaut Canal inside the Dutch-Belgian border, and ending at Arnhem. Hopes were high on the eve of the operation. On 10 September Robert Boscawen noted in his diary:

By a brilliant stroke of the 2nd and 3rd Irish and the Household Cavalry, the division had cut the Escaut Canal and captured the bridge across. Henceforth known as 'Joe's Bridge', it was the key to the next major obstacle across our front, the Meuse-Escaut, about fifteen miles north of the Albert Canal and only a mile or two short of the Dutch frontier. This was very good news and pleased the higher command a lot. In fact, they said it had shortened the war by making a bridgehead for the next operation.

On Tuesday, 12th, I moved over the Albert Canal and the camp was pitched just beyond Beringen. Next morning we moved on to a clearing in a large pinewood two or three miles north of Hechtel, beside the main road that led up to Joe's Bridge and on into Holland.

Humphrey Gascoigne, a Grenadier in charge of the Transit Camp, and I went to Brussels in the afternoon to see if we could find some captured German vehicles for our use. We were unsuccessful and returned after a long drive as Brussels was now seventy-five miles back. Every few yards the roadside was strewn with burnt-out Hun vehicles caught by the RAF. There were dozens and dozens. On the way back we stopped at a cafe and drank some excellent iced beer, while the barmaid insisted on playing that ill-fated corny old tune from 1940 over and over again at full blast on an ancient gramophone: "We're going to hang out the washing on the Siegfried Line, if the Siegfried Line's still there". I suppose she thought it might encourage us.

Thursday, 14 September. By now I was fully rested and getting bored with having nothing to do, so I went up to the battalion who had been resting for a few

After the 'Island'. Nijmegen. Oct. 1944.

No 2 Troop, 1st (Armoured) Battalion, Coldstream Guards, October 1944, outside billets in Hatert, Nijmegen. Top row: Guardsman Walker, L/Sergeant Palmer. Middle row: Guardsmen Gruchy, Thompson, Edwards. Front row: Guardsmen Meadows, Daniel W., Sergeant Shipley, Corporal Driscoll, Corporal Siddons, L/Sergeant Fawcett. Robert Boscawen is far right. (Robert Boscawen)

days just up the road. I saw Oliver first and he said they were still short of tanks, there was nothing for me to do, and it was much better to stay 'LOB' for a bit longer. Later I tackled Bill and he insisted on the same. This was very boring and I said so, and went back determined to get the best out of it. Michael Hamilton I saw up there too, but everyone seemed rather tired and suffering from colds. A crowd of reinforcements arrived at the camp this evening including David Kennard and Greville Chester, both Coldstreamers, so we tackled more than the usual amount of champagne.

Next day I escorted two German officers back to a POW cage, miserable specimens who all the time looked as if they thought they were going to be shot. Nobody wanted them and I had great trouble in finding anyone to take them off my hands. Most people laughed and said, "Why not throw them back?" Eventually Corps AQMG himself was the only person willing. I saw Dermot this afternoon. He has become a captain at brigade. I am very glad as he has had a poor deal.

Saturday, 16 September. Back to 'B' Echelon in Hechtel to see Michael and tackle some champagne before lunch. Somehow I had acquired a German Volkswagen off the RE, an amphibious one, a funny little open boat on wheels, painted black, with a propeller behind, a rotten car really, but it was just what I needed now.

All this time supplies, guns and men had been pouring up to the Escaut Canal ready for the breakout from the bridgehead. The plan is to take place tomorrow and the Guards Armoured Division are to lead. This evening I drove up to the battalion, harboured on a sandy heath, to the right of the main road about a mile or so behind the canal, near Overpelt. They were getting ready for tomorrow's attack. I had dinner with No.2 Squadron, John Baddeley appears to be there now, acting second-in-command, but there was rather a strained atmosphere. Nothing like the old carefree days in No.2. Afterwards I met Ian and spent some time talking to him of everything except the war and then drove home depressed at being left out of it.

Sunday, 17 September. The day broke dull and overcast, a morning much like any other without any extra noise than usual until after midday, when the attack opened. A moderately heavy barrage went down and then came the drone of aircraft, a heavy solid drone, which lasted all afternoon. It was uncanny to think that during that short time a whole army had been landed in Holland. At the same time the GAD, led by the Irish, advanced over the Escaut to meet them.

Later in the afternoon I went to Heppen in the Volkswagen to find where Brough was buried. I found his tank by the side of the road where it had been hit, but could not find his grave. After a good deal of incoherent signs and noises with some local natives, I gave it up. I had a look round and saw where the *Jagdpanther* had fired from. It was only fifty yards away. This was the first *Jagdpanther* we had encountered, and it was now to be seen knocked out by the Welsh Guards about to cross the main road west of Hechtel. One of the most formidable of all German vehicles, it had a long 88mm SP gun mounted on a heavily armoured Panther chassis. Hugh Griffiths managed to get it from behind and evidently pumped a number of AP shot into its backside.

Back for tea at considerable speed as the extraordinary machine certainly shifted, though it made an alarming clatter and did not have any brakes. Afterwards I went up to 'A' Echelon to see whether Billy Denbigh had any news of the attack. He had none since the battalion had not yet moved, so we attacked the 'Widow' instead. Everywhere one goes champagne is produced, one almost washes in it these days.

Monday, 18 September. I drove up to the battalion at lunchtime and saw them moving out over the Escaut Canal. On the way back the Volkswagen's front axle suddenly gave out and after a grinding crunch it skidded to a standstill. Slept all afternoon while hundreds more gliders and Dakotas flew over.

The next five days I had little to do and were very frustrating. Practically no news about the battle filtered back to us and all we saw were the slow-moving soft transport of the airborne divisions and 30 Corps going up towards Joe's Bridge...

Sunday, 24 September. Today I crossed into Holland. We left the Escaut area to go up to the division who were somewhere around Nijmegen in the Rear-Division convoy. Watty and I were travelling in the front of a couple of three-tonners. It was the slowest drive I've ever done. We crossed over the Escaut at Joe's Bridge and went on up to Eindhoven.

Nine brewed-up Irish Guards' tanks lay within a hundred yards near the Dutch frontier so they must have had some trouble. I heard later that these tanks were nearly all in the second squadron of the column and were caught by a Mark IV tank with a 50mm gun hidden in a house on the flank. The Micks said that the Typhoon support was magnificent. They were diving down and rocketing beside the tanks themselves, a new squadron taking the air every few minutes. I've always thought that this was the way to use them.

We went through the edge of Eindhoven and passed Philips Radio factory. The town had been badly bombed by the Germans in a spite raid last night. Despite this one could soon see the much higher living standard amongst the Dutch, as their houses were all well built, clean and attractive looking.

We reached Nijnsel that evening, a small village ten miles north of Eindhoven between Son and St Oedenrode in the dropping zone of the US 101 Airborne Division, to find the Germans had cut the centre line, the only road, a mile in front and had brewed up a hundred of our vehicles. So there we had to stay. Completely unprotected, not far from some three hundred SS paras, the road ahead suddenly appeared deserted. Tony Watkins, Henty Smith, Welsh Guards, and I set about making a defensive position in a small house. Henty I had not seen since he left school years ago. We shut the unfortunate inhabitants in the cellar and with the few Guardsmen available set about to man each window. They had rifles with little ammo, and I only had my revolver with six rounds. There was one 17 pounder anti-tank gun in the column we brought up, but it too had no ammo. There was little else we could do and we spent an anxious and uncomfortable, if not frightening, night awaiting the Germans, added to which it was pouring with rain. We were mortared and shelled, but never actually attacked. Two splendid Padres in a mobile Church of Scotland truck just outside invited Tony and me in but several times we had to jump out of it and throw ourselves into a soaking ditch.

During the night a lone jeep suddenly appeared at our position and the sentry on the road and I stopped it going any further. To our utmost astonishment the voice from the blackness said 'Corps Commander'. He was told the enemy had cut the road ahead so the driver turned about immediately and went back. He managed to get round the Germans in an armoured carrier and on up to the forward troops.

It was a relief when morning came and the American parachutists put in an attack. The attack, however, failed and the road was still cut. They did not seem to know what was happening, but the enemy were reported to have a brigade across the road by now. Supplies were reported running out further forward and ammo was badly needed. But the division had captured an enormous army food dump at Oss, over a million tins of food, so they certainly couldn't starve.

Meanwhile a few Sherman tanks of the Division's Forward Delivery Squadron had passed rapidly through us to put in a brave but disastrous attack with the Americans. The assorted enemy force from one of General Student's para divisions that had come across from the west was much stronger than expected and these tanks ran up immediately against some 88s in the woods beyond the next village. Not normally trained to fight as a unit, while some of the crews probably would not have been in action before, their attack ended in the tragic loss of several men and vehicles.

Unknown to us at the time, for the past two days the Grenadier and Coldstream Groups had been attacking south towards us a few miles further up the centre line. They had been ordered south from the Nijmegen area to reopen the centre line at Veghel which had been cut there by a force from the eastern flank.

The Coldstream Group had cleared the area to the east at Volkel and Boekel about five miles to the north-east of us, not without some casualties, I'm afraid. But no sooner had 30 Corps' only road, the famous Club Route, been opened there than the Germans had cut it again from the west near us, as we had found.

In the evening the 7th Armoured Division, who had been fighting their way slowly up on the left flank of 30 Corps, arrived and put in an attack on the gap. By midday next (the 26th) it was cleared and we moved on. Tony and Henty insisted on trying to watch the battle as they had only just come out from England. I did my best to persuade them they would see nothing and only get 'stonked', but we had to walk right up to the leading armoured battalion before they were satisfied. The little square in Nijnsel was a chaotic sight, full of vehicles of all kinds who had just escaped the gap. I saw Tony Leetham there from 5th Brigade H.Q., very indignant indeed as his jeep trailer's tyres had been punctured by mortar splinters. Further back we found Michael Fox, an occasion for more champers behind his jeep.

When we moved on through the gap the US airborne were still literally dug-in along the ditches on either side of the road prepared for further counter-attacks. The tangled wreckage of our supply vehicles was a sad spectacle, with one of our knocked out Delivery Squadron tanks upside down resting on the top of its turret in a field.

We crossed the Meuse or Maas at Grave and finally pitched camp at a wood near this river at Overasselt, where we spent a peaceful day. David Ryder, Irish Guards, had been sent back to the Transit Camp to rest, slightly 'bomb happy'. It was he and his platoon I had attempted to support at Sourdevalle. In the recent battle he had done well and had been recommended for an M.C., but had had an awful time.

The news came this evening, the 27th, that Arnhem had been evacuated and out of the 6,000 men landed only 1,200 had been brought back safe across the northern Rhine. It had been a very hard fight by the 1st Airborne Division against overwhelming odds, but they had held out for nearly nine days. They must have had a terrible time and it must go down as one of the hardest battles of the war. The bold plan had fallen at the last fence. Not in vain though. They had enabled 2nd Army to hold the Nijmegen bridge across the Waal or Lower Rhine. During the evening we had listened to one of the most moving broadcasts I have ever heard by Stanley Maxted, a Canadian War Correspondent, who was among those few who came back over the Rhine. After nine days fighting with 1st Airborne in Arnhem his description of the withdrawal of these gallant men brought us near to tears. In single file, holding on to the man in front, boots wrapped in blankets, he told us they had walked silently through the enemy lines under steady machine-gun and artillery fire to the little assault boats which ferried them back across the swift current of the Rhine.

Although undoubtedly a costly failure in many respects, Operation Market Garden did secure an important bridgehead for the Allied forces in Nijmegen. This was to be of strategic importance in the coming months, forming the jumping-off point for Operation Veritable. More significantly, Market Garden had taught the Western Allies a sobering lesson about their enemy. It was clear not only that the German army still possessed the will to resist, but also the logistical and organizational resources to do so. The Allies would not now have the opportunity to 'hang out the washing' on the Siegfried Line by Christmas, as the vainglorious marching song boasted. On the contrary, they were about the enter one of the most difficult phases of the campaign.

Part IV

Eastern Front

Withdrawal and regrouping (August-December 1944)

Part IV

Eastern Front

Withdrawal and regrouping (August-December 1944)

The summer offensives of 1944 conducted by the Red Army had enjoyed spectacular success, possibly even greater than that anticipated by Stalin and his commanders. Germany, on the other hand, had suffered grievous losses in men, material, and military prestige. On 17 July the Soviets had paraded over 50,000 prisoners captured during the defeat of Army Group Centre through the streets of Moscow, pointedly hosing the streets clean in their wake. Finland had been knocked out of the war[1], and Romania and Bulgaria had switched sides and were now fighting their erstwhile allies. Yet the Soviets had suffered too, losing over one million men (killed, wounded and missing). Not only that, but their rapid advance had caused huge logistical problems as efforts were made to ensure supplies of fuel and ammunition continued to reach the forward mobile units.

By September 1944, the main Soviet thrust in the centre of the Eastern Front had expended itself. For the remainder of the year the frontline in this sector barely moved. Both sides needed time to regroup. Of course, such a statement disguises the fact that fighting – some of it very fierce – nevertheless continued as both sides jockeyed for position. The Red Army worked hard at consolidating its vital bridgeheads over the Vistula and Narev rivers, whilst the Germans attempted to eliminate them, and a limited Soviet incursion into East Prussia – the *Reich* itself – caused bloody fighting in mid- and late October.

Whilst the centre remained strategically dormant, the axis of Soviet offensive action shifted to the north and south.

In the north, links between Army Groups Centre and North had become increasingly tenuous following the collapse of the former. Attempting to seize the initiative, the Soviet 1st, 2nd and 3rd Baltic Fronts and Leningrad Front launched a series of major attacks during September in an effort to cut off Army Group North. Initially, these failed, partly due to the Germans skilful deployment of mobile armoured forces. However, further attempts succeeded, so that by the end of October Army Group North was bottled up in the Kurland peninsula, in western Latvia, isolated and with no land access to the *Reich*. It was to remain there until the end of the war – the debate regarding its strategic usefulness or otherwise to the German war effort rumbles on.

In territorial terms the Red Army and its allies gained most in the southern part of the front during this period. Army Group E conducted a withdrawal from

---

1   To be precise, Finland also switched sides and engaged German troops. However, compared to the fates of Bulgaria and particularly Romania, Finland's armistice was less stringent, and Finnish troops saw only limited action in ejecting German forces from specific locations.

Greece and much of Yugoslavia, harried by Tito's partisans throughout the latter. Belgrade was captured on 15 October. The fulcrum of the fighting in the autumn centred on Hungary, one of Germany's last remaining allies, albeit of doubtful loyalty. The Soviet 2nd and 4th Ukrainian Fronts mounted a series of attacks during October to force the Germans and Hungarians back towards Budapest. These were generally successful, and involved a major tank battle – virtually unknown in the West even today – around Debrecen.

In a political interlude, the Germans launched Operation *Panzerfaust* in Budapest on 15/16 October. In the days leading up to this, the Hungarian leader Admiral Horthy had reached agreement with the USSR for an armistice. Germany could not afford to lose Hungary, principally because of its vitally important oil fields. Consequently, Horthy was persuaded to request 'asylum' in Germany, whilst his closest allies were arrested by the Gestapo. His place as Hungarian head of state was taken by Ferenc Szalasi, leader of the Fascist Arrow Cross party. Hungary would remain a German ally until the end of the war.

In what remained of 1944, the Soviets focused their attention on trying to capture Budapest. In a series of fiercely-contested engagements involving 2nd and 3rd Ukrainian Fronts fought throughout late October, November and December, the Red Army pushed ever closer to the Hungarian capital. Nevertheless, it was not until 26 December that the city was encircled – an indication of the intensity of German and Hungarian resistance. Two days later the Soviets temporarily halted their offensive.

Following the collapse of Army Group Centre during the summer of 1944, Armin Scheiderbauer's unit had been positioned around Raseinen, Lithuania, helping to form a line blocking further Soviet advances. In late September, the 252nd Infantry Division was withdrawn, and relieved by the 95th Infantry Division. Its destination was near Nasielsk in Poland, where it came under the command of XX Armeekorps, part of the 2nd Army.

At the end of September the units of the Division went into assembly areas to the south-east of Nasielsk. The task of the Division was to eliminate a larger bridgehead that Soviet troops had formed across the Narev between Serock and Pultusk (Ostenburg). In the 2nd Army sector the enemy had formed several bridgeheads over the Narev. They could be considered as jumping-off points for a large-scale enemy attack, especially as they could be expected to expand them at any time. *Hauptmann* Schneider and I learned of the position at the regimental command post. It was clear to us that we were to come into a new future hotspot. We consoled ourselves with the assumption that sooner or later the 'old magic' would work again, even in Raseinen.

On 26 September the battalion was unloaded in Zichenau. A look at the map showed that we were behind the most southerly of the two bridgeheads on the Narev. The short journey through German East Prussia had, depressingly, made clear to us the extent to which we were already fighting 'along the inner line'. For parts of the way we travelled attached to a regular passenger train. Civilians got into the staff compartment, even a *Hoheitsträger* from the Party in his brown uniform. He did all the talking and expressed really confidently the simple message that 'the *Führer* will soon sort things out'.

In Deutsch-Eylau where the branch line led southward into Polish territory, there was a longer stop. In the orderly surroundings of that German railway station, that looked clean swept, the transports with our 'mob' presented a really strange picture. The companies were loaded by platoons into cattle trucks. Other wagons were loaded with horses and old vehicles from the baggage-train. Among it all straw was everywhere, there was baggage-train equipment, and even live cattle and pigs. There were also Soviet women with their headscarves, who worked as washerwomen and on other jobs for the baggage-train. We were there too in our shabby uniforms. I wore a pair of deep yellowish-brown Lithuanian riding breeches that Walter had found for me on the way, together with boots. The boots fitted well and saved my rubber boots. Yellow lice had first to be removed from the trousers before I could wear them. Then there was the disciplined yet free atmosphere. I addressed as *du* the staff runners, telephonists, and wireless operators of whom I had become fond. At the beginning of the sixth year of the war, it seemed that in our frontline units, all human relationships had been reduced to a certain essential core.

There followed a few days of complete quiet. In order to keep our forthcoming attack as secret as possible, no exercises of any kind were staged. The men tried to catch up on the sleep they had lost in the summer. They lay on their backs for days on end and when it was dark visited the front-line cinema that had been established in a neighbouring village. *Wien 1910* was showing there and it would have interested me because of the young Otto Wilhelm Fischer whom I liked very much. But I remained in my quarters in order to get a little peace and quiet. I was afraid too that I would be seized by homesickness for Vienna. But what I once more thoroughly enjoyed again in those days was riding. It was one last opportunity for it and only then was my life as a cavalryman to come to an end.

On the other hand, I denied myself another kind of pleasure. My batman Walter, always very concerned about my physical welfare, told me that Marja, a pretty and buxom washerwoman from the staff baggage-train, had fallen for me, and he offered to arrange a rendezvous. He could not understand and was almost hurt when I told him that I was not interested in anything like that. The fact that he had made the offer made further explanation seem superfluous.

On the night of 2 October the battalion was brought up to a point four kilometres behind the frontline. We were placed in houses that were still standing there. The order went out that, during the day, no movement must take place on account of enemy aerial reconnaissance. The attack was supposed to be a complete surprise. It was therefore impossible to take a walk. We could only leave the hovels to answer calls of nature.

In the afternoon came the regimental order for the next day. The Division had been given the task, together with the 3rd and 25th *Panzer* Divisions, of eliminating the bridgehead at Serock. After a concerted preparatory artillery barrage lasting 30 minutes, our Division was to move up between the two *Panzer* divisions. Within our Division it had been ordered that Regiment 461 would advance on the right, and Regiment 7 on the left, while Regiment 472 had to follow in the second wave. Most importantly, participating in the attack too were an assault gun brigade, two *Nebelwerfer* brigades, one heavy SS *Panzerabteilung* (Tiger), one *Heeresartillerieabteilung*, two mortar battalions and one flak regiment. The fact that we were to run up in reserve behind the two other regiments was almost a source of relief to me, since it showed me how highly General Meltzer valued the capability of the regiment and its commander. But it strengthened my resolve to return as soon as possible to my Regiment 7.

We spent the night of 3 October on straw in a hovel. We were lying pressed closely together, waking, dozing or sleeping. In the straw I found a small crucifix that I kept since it did not belong to anyone there. One of the people who had slept there before me or an inhabitant of the house must have lost it. I do not know what became of the crucifix. However, I lost it later when I was a prisoner. But there came to me the cheering promise of the *in hoc signo*, and I knew full well what victory that meant.

At 5am the half-hour heavy barrage began. We moved slowly forward between batteries of howling mortars and barking cannons. We had never before seen that kind of concentration of our own heavy weapons. We still had ammunition, we could still fire it, we could still attack and hopefully we could still gain the victory. Regiment 7 had already reached its target for the day at 10.30am. The attack had gone off smoothly and the enemy had fled. They had left behind few prisoners, but a lot of material. *Oberleutnant* Husenett and his company had taken an enemy mortar battery.

Half an hour after the attack began we had crossed the trenches. We looked with amazement at the American war matériel that had been left behind, from tinned meat to a motorcycle and sidecar and heavy Studebaker lorry. Some Soviet trenches smelled of perfume. By this and by the articles of clothing that had been left behind, it could be seen that women, perhaps women soldiers, had been there. The Soviets had not built bunkers, they simply had dugouts, each for two men, over which short thick tree trunks had been laid. They were an example of the admirable Soviet capability of combining improvisation with the greatest usefulness. Since the entrances to these small bunkers opened, from our point of view, on the side facing the enemy, for myself I preferred to spend the night in a simple one-man foxhole without a roof. I remembered Major Brauer and *Leutnant* Buksch who had met their deaths a year before, at Nevel, in such a dugout that faced towards the enemy.

On 5 October, the second day of the attack, the Division was once more successful and Regiment 7 had reached the Narev at 2.30pm. We, in 472, moved up behind them as reserve and at the same time as spectators. The high ground facing the river was shelled by our mortars and artillery and then stormed. I was able to observe it through the field glasses. On the way I saw a human torso that had been torn apart by massive force. It was lying beside a destroyed SS *Panzer* reconnaissance vehicle, burnt out, a relic of the heavy fighting at the time that the bridgehead was being formed. From that sight even the hardened among us turned away in horror.

After the southern half of the bridgehead had been pushed back and was again in German hands, on 8 October the attack on the northern half was to take place. On 6 October we were moved 10 kilometres to the north, into a village that on the map looked like a star made up of roads. At the centre was a crossing from which seven roads or lanes stretched out exactly following the points of the compass. The only problem was that there was no road leading south-westward. As such, the crossing formed an ideal target for heavy weapons and was constantly under fire. In spite of that the cellars of the surrounding houses were fitted out with command posts from all possible units. The frontline was not a kilometre away towards the east.

As the orders had said, quite generally, that units should take over the command posts of the units to be relieved, *Hauptmann* Schneider had insisted on moving into the cellar at the crossing. He remained impervious to my suggestions for us to take up position in a cellar away from the crossing, especially since the cellar roof, only some 10 centimetres thick, did not provide adequate protection. The constant impact of shells very close by was gruelling even before the attack. In addition, runners and all who wanted to get to us were exposed to the most serious danger. When finally the leader of the signal section and two men had been wounded, I went on my own initiative to look for a suitable command post. I found it 300 metres along the road leading westwards, in a considerably deeper and better-covered cellar. Without Schneider's approval, I asked the regiment whether we could move. It was approved and *Hauptmann* Schneider himself was afterwards pleased that we were away from the main impact area.

There were no good omens for the second part of the attack on the bridgeheads. With the rain, mist and badly softened ground it presented a very difficult task, to which situation the confused terrain was also a contributory factor. We had advanced only one kilometre. During previous days the Soviets had laid many mines, so that numerous tanks drove over them and were lost. In addition the preparatory fire was weaker than it had been on 4 October and we had not succeeded in destroying the underwater nets over the Narev. As they had done in Stalingrad over the Volga, the Soviets this time too laid nets under the surface of the water across the river, over which, with columns of carriers, they brought ammunition and above all mines.

The units had to dig in just where they were. The battalion command post was in the open behind a small rise in the ground that did not deserve the name of hill. Foxholes were lined with straw. The nights were already cold and we were freezing pitiably. Since 3 October no one had been able to wash. To add to that it began to rain continuously and the tarpaulins, after 24 hours, were almost completely porous. The Soviets were preparing a counter-attack. Every hour, low flying aircraft flew over our positions and fired on the roads, luckily mostly behind us. But an unmistakable sign that an attack was being prepared were the shells exploding in the air by means of which the enemy artillery registered their fire.

On 14 October the expected counter-attack took place. There was surprisingly little Soviet artillery preparation. Instead, there was a large-scale deployment of aircraft. With machine-guns, cannon and shrapnel bombs, the *Ratas* and IL 2s attacked everything that they thought to be German positions. Up to 20 aircraft circled in our immediate vicinity. We knew better than to stick our heads out of the ground. Whether casualties were too great or the men had been worn down by the air-raids, in any event they climbed out of their foxholes and came back. As they were struggling to get back to the rear across the wide field, I stood desperately on the battalion's hill, waited and shouted to them until they had got up to me. But my cries of *Stellung, Stellung* were in vain. They limped, rushed, and ran on, 50 or 100 metres ahead of the Soviets who were charging after them.

Finally I saw that I was alone, facing the brown wave of the attackers. To stay so long had been idiotic, but I had been gripped by resignation. Then, not 40 metres ahead of the Soviets, who were moving more slowly, I turned and ran. My map case under my arm, clearly recognisable as an officer, I ran on, weaving, in front of the Soviets. I am convinced that the only thing that saved me was that the fact that the Soviets were advancing at the run. Some were running ahead and their wave was fairly thick, but none of them wanted to stop and aim at me or the others. I ran and ran and after 200 metres I had reached the retreating line of our men. We reached the firing position of a battery that was ready to fire directly on the Soviets. I succeeded in bringing to a halt a handful of men, by which action a small amount of infantry cover would at least remain for the guns.

The enemy infantry assault halted facing the battery position. However, we were exposed there to the latest attacks of the enemy aircraft. In one such attack Walter, my batman, was wounded. He was able to limp and reported to me with tears in his eyes. He asked me to write to him and take him back when he was recovered.

Hope that the war would soon be at an end was something that I did not cherish even in secret. I also did not believe that a single one of my comrades shared it, because the alternative, namely what would become of Germany if the dams of the Eastern Front broke, was plainly unimaginable. In that sense, and not for the sake of Hitler and the Party, we had our duty to do and did it diligently, even if it was soon to be with the last strength we had.

Like Dmitriy Loza, Vsevolod Olimpiev was a veteran Red Army soldier by 1944, having served at the front since 1941. By the autumn of 1944 he was with a Guards anti-tank artillery regiment. The Guards formations were élite troops, usually designated as such due to their battlefield prowess. What is fascinating about these extracts from Vsevolod's account is the way in which they can be compared with Armin Scheiderbauer's experiences to build up a picture of the way in which both sides used these autumn and early winter months to prepare for the inevitable battle for the eastern part of the Reich *that all knew was coming.*

After four months of staying in hospitals in connection with my third wound I got an assignment not to a reserve regiment but straight to the 1st Guards Cavalry Corps where I had served from March 1942 to November 1943. In the beginning of September I was getting off a train in Kiev on the way to which I had to change trains several times. Here I spotted a Lieutenant with purple cavalry insignia. It turned out that he was from the 1st Corps as well. We decided to look for our unit together. We rode to Lvov on freight trains and spent one night on the roof of a sanitary train moving towards the front. The way from Lvov to the frontline was made in passing trucks, fairly well organised at that time. One had to come to a roadside checkpoint, show your documents and would then be placed on the first passing vehicle.

My travelling companion and I had to part several kilometres before the frontline at a routine checkpoint. I was lucky as only half an hour later an artillery sergeant whom I recognized - a familiar gun crew commander - pulled out of a stopped car. An hour later I was in the headquarters of my 143rd Guards Anti-

The commander of a Soviet 45mm gun crew observing the enemy. During the war these guns were positioned amongst the infantry lines, forming the core of battalion artillery and anti-tank units. This kind of positioning led to heavy losses among crewmen and led to the gun being nicknamed "Farewell to the Motherland" on the frontlines. (Artem Drabkin)

Tank Artillery Regiment positioned on the Dukla Pass, along which the border between Poland and Czechoslovakia ran. Shortly before that moment two divisions from the 1st Guards Cavalry Corps had broken through the frontline into eastern Slovakia with the aim of helping the Slovakian uprising. Nevertheless, the pass was quickly blocked by German tanks, so the regiments which had not made it through had to take up defensive positions right in the pass in unfavourable conditions. The enemy, situated on three sides around them, kept pounding our troops with constant fire. At times it was simply impossible to leave the trenches. We were suffering considerable losses, which led our soldiers to call the Dukla Pass the 'Valley of Death'. However our artillery was not backward about firing in retaliation. At one point a heavy anti-aircraft battery was placed near the Regimental headquarters, firing at ground targets with hardly a pause. Even seasoned soldiers could hardly bear the harsh reports of supersonic anti-aircraft shells

There were still quite a few of my old battle comrades in the Regiment but there were also many raw recruits. Although I had been absent for nine months I was remembered and immediately placed in my previous position as Deputy Commander of the Regimental HQ Platoon. Within two hours of my arrival telephone lines with the batteries were literally torn apart during a regular bout of shelling. The Regiment's Signals Commander ordered them restored immediately and if that couldn't be done, to collect remnants of the cable for subsequent repairs. It wouldn't be realistic to get such a job done under constant shelling without serious losses. But we did it with not a single man lost only due to an unexpected pause in the artillery duel. Nevertheless we failed to avoid losses of signalmen later on. I was especially upset by the death of my old comrade Sasha Vedeneev, who had gone out alone to fix up damaged cable. It was him who had helped me, then wounded, to get out of the Zhitomir pocket in November 1943.

Intense shelling dragged on for two weeks. At one stage the Germans began to use heavy rocket artillery (*Nebelwerfer*) and their explosions shook the ground like aviation bombs. Once an elderly soldier and I came under their fire during our work on a telephone line. There happened to be a slit trench, the soldier jumped into it and I followed on top of him. The situation was not comfortable as the shells were falling literally next to the trench. Then I heard him saying a prayer: "Almighty Lord in heaven..." I had to pretend I heard nothing as in that situation there was no other resort but a prayer!

In early October our Corps was pulled away from the front for regrouping. We spent the rest of the year in different towns in south-eastern Poland. The soldiers of the Regiment were billeted in private houses in the small town of Brzoszuw. Some other soldiers and I were allocated a room in a mansion owned by quite a rich man.

I remember an episode which happened in my presence in another apartment, where soldiers of the Control Platoon were placed. A poorly dressed man with a grey beard falling down to his waist knocked on the door and came in. In his words he was a Jew, the owner of that house which had been confiscated from him by the Fascists. A Polish family had been keeping the unfortunate wretch in a cellar for several years and saved his life.

We often did our marching exercises and sang ceremonial songs in the streets of Brzoszuw. One of them was Alexandrov's famous *Rise the great country, rise for the mortal battle against the Fascist dark force, against the accursed horde...* The locals liked this song. Perhaps there was something extraordinary in it and the tune in some unexplained way was reflecting the tragedy of our folk and determination to fight to the victorious end. The Poles who had survived five years of occupation could feel it.

The Regiment left Brzoszuw two weeks later and relocated to a Polish village. I must say that our soldiers didn't come across any hostility there either. Moreover, our contacts with Polish peasants were always friendly and mutually cordial. I can remember one occasion, which we laughed at for quite a while. The regimental signalmen were placed on a small farm owned by, in our opinion, a man of average means. He, his wife and adult daughter worked all week long from morning till night, walked barefoot, but on Sundays they would put on festive dress and go to church. Just at that time the Polish Government in Lublin had begun to conduct a land reform. Our host had abandoned his work and was spending his time at meetings of some sort. When asked by me he answered that land redistribution was underway in the village then. After one of those meetings he came back home upset and gloomy because he had been given a bad allotment. He declared that he would write a complaint not to Lublin but to Comrade Stalin in Moscow and asked me for a piece of paper for it. I gave him a double sheet torn away from a notepad. Next day the host came back in a good mood for he had received a better allotment. To achieve this it was enough to show a piece of paper obtained from the 'Mister Russian Sergeant' and announce the address he was intending to write it to!

From October to December 1944 the Regiment was busy with various kinds of drilling and especially in anti-tank combat training. We ourselves arranged a small firing range with a mobile wooden target shaped like a silhouette of a Tiger tank, which was towed by a vehicle on a long rope. All the gun crews of the Regiment went through artillery range training where the shooting was done not with blanks but live anti-tank shells.

In the second half of January 1945 the 1st Guards Cavalry Corps was relocated to the Sandomierz bridgehead beyond the Vistula River.

Whilst the central sector of the Eastern Front remained relatively quiet during this period, the same could not be said of the southern sector, where Soviet efforts focused on driving into Hungary towards Budapest.

Due to sterling work in the battles of 1943-44, Dmitriy Loza's parent unit – the 5th Mechanized Corps – including his 233rd Tank Brigade, had been awarded Guards status. His unit was now renamed the 46th Guards Tank Brigade, with 5th Mechanized Corps becoming the 9th Guards Mechanized Corps. However, such status also had its drawbacks, as it meant that they would be closely involved in the 2nd Ukrainian Front's offensive actions in Hungary in the run up to Christmas 1944/45.

On 5 December 1944, after a brief pause, the forces of the centre of the Second Ukrainian Front renewed the offensive from the area of Hatvan in a general northwest direction. The intent was to go around the east side of Budapest. The 6th Guards Tank Army was committed on the afternoon of that day. At first the tankers were unable to develop a rapid tempo of advance, but they surged forward on the night of 6 December. The 9th Guards Mechanized Corps reached the bulge at Galgaguta, and the 5th Guards Tank Corps captured Acsa (approximately thirty miles northeast of Budapest).

Overcoming stubborn enemy resistance, units of the 9th Mechanized Corps developed the attack into the depth of the enemy's defences, toward the town of Šahy (due north of Budapest on the Czech border). At the same time, the 5th Corps broke through toward the city of Vac. The result was a sort of "scissors". Between the two corps remained an enemy grouping, which at any moment could have consolidated its strength and struck a blow against the flanks of the attacking Soviet forces. Tactical intelligence became exceptionally important in these conditions.

On 12 December, the brigades of the mechanized corps, defeating enemy counterattacks, slowly moved toward Šahy and by the close of this day reached the outskirts of the town. The command of the 46th Guards Tank Brigade was interested in information on the enemy in the area southwest of Šahy. The mission was assigned to the brigade's scouts. The chief of staff of the 1st Battalion, Guards Captain Nikolay Bogdanov, was ordered to conduct a daring raid into the zone of Bernesebarat and Kemence. Captain Bogdanov chose to conduct this raid on a Sherman tank.

Two circumstances, Nikolay Nikolayevich asserted, would assist him in accomplishing this task. First, the enemy's defence in this sector had been created hurriedly. Only built-up areas along the roads had been prepared for defence. The terrain between them was considered impassable during this time of the year, even on foot. Hardly a thought had been given to armoured equipment. But this was exactly how Bogdanov planned to penetrate into the enemy rear - on a tank. The low ground pressure of the *Emcha* permitted him to engage in such a risky venture.

Second, the captain's excellent knowledge of German would play a decisive role in his accomplishment of the mission. The suggested scenario for Nikolay

Nikolayevich's actions went something like this. He and a driver-mechanic would dress in German uniforms. They would take with them an additional two crewmen - a gunner and a loader. These two personnel would remain inside the turret and not expose themselves. They would maintain the tank's weapons in constant readiness to open fire.

The brigade command, acknowledging the many favourable combat qualities of these *gvardeytsi*, gave their approval to this unusual tank reconnaissance, to be conducted on the night of 13 December. It was raining steadily, at times turning into snow. There is an old saying about this kind of weather: "A good master does not send his dog outside."

The commander of the 1st Battalion, Guards Captain Ivan Yakushkin, understood the risk that Bogdanov was taking. Ivan Ignat'evich felt it necessary to remind his chief of staff of already proven courses of action: during the approach to any objective in the enemy's rear, if the situation permitted, sneak up on one motor. The *Emcha* could crawl like a cat. Stay on the downwind side, and use the radio only in the most extreme emergency.

This advice was important. German radio intelligence constantly monitored our communications channels and quickly homed in on the position of the source of radio transmissions.

The Sherman's motors hummed quietly. It slipped off into the darkness at a slow speed. Bogdanov had in his hands a 1: 100,000 German topographic map. One centimetre equalled one kilometre. It was a good, detailed map. The Germans were very familiar with the territory of their Hungarian vassal. The tank proceeded along a woodline, in freshly fallen shallow snow, that extended along the western slopes of the Berzhen hills. Nikolay Nikolayevich had chosen this route for a reason - it was deserted. There were no villages along it, only fields and thickets. After moving ahead five kilometres, he turned the *Emcha* ninety degrees and drove westward, and later northward, to approach the target area from the rear. In this rapidly changing situation that frequently was obscure to the enemy, such an approach would perhaps bring success.

The weather worsened. The wind blew wet snow into their faces. It was coming out of the north, through the "tunnel" between the Gron River and the Berzhen hills. They maintained their course using the tank's gyrocompass. Soon they should come upon the highway that ran between Bernesebarat and Kemence. His watch was showing 2200 Moscow time. Finally, they reached the hardstand and increased speed. A little more than a mile down the road, Bogdanov spotted the dark silhouette of an enemy armoured vehicle on the road. He ordered his driver-mechanic, Guards Senior Sergeant Mikhail Bolotin, to stop. Bogdanov jumped down to the ground. Not hurrying, he approached the enemy machine. In an authoritative tone of voice, he called out to the crew. A hatch opened on the turret. One, then a second, head appeared. Bogdanov asked, "Where are the rest of the tanks?" They explained that only the two of them remained in the self-propelled gun. Their engine had broken down, and the commander and two other crewmen had gone to the headquarters in Kemence.

Nikolay Nikolayevich went around the left side of the self-propelled gun. His spirits soared. A week ago, a small advance guard of the brigade had suddenly attacked the village of Erdetarcha at night. The enemy was caught totally by surprise and offered no resistance to the attacking column. Two self-propelled guns were parked next to the church in the village, but they remained silent. The Germans had abandoned their equipment in flight for their own lives. The 1st Battalion passed through Erdetarcha in a rush, without a thought for these two self-propelled guns. They were to have been set afire later. This was an inexcusable mistake. For some reason, the brigade's following unit was delayed a bit. The enemy regained his senses, starting with the self-propelled gun crews. They returned to their recently abandoned machines and occupied their combat positions. And when the Shermans of the second echelon moved into the village, the Germans caught them in an ambush. Two *Emchas* were set ablaze. The enemy ambush was destroyed in a lopsided firefight. On this same day, one interesting detail was revealed: the self-propelled guns had something still unknown to us – a piece of equipment for precision firing during periods of darkness. Later it received the name "night vision sight". At that time, one of the least damaged vehicles was taken from Erdetarcha and sent directly to Moscow, to a tank scientific research institute of the Ministry of Defence of the USSR. The order went out to all tank armies to capture intact and preserve any armoured vehicle that was equipped with this apparatus.

The following recognition indicators were specified for these sights: an infrared searchlight, with a protective cover, was located on the upper portion of the gun of the tank or self- propelled gun. Attached to the order was a brief sketch of the night vision device and a full-frontal photograph of the self-propelled gun, in which the searchlight was clearly visible. This self-propelled gun was equipped in this way. This is why Bogdanov became so excited.

Such luck was rare! As scouts frequently said (in their own slang): "Capture a live prisoner, or capture a vital piece of equipment." And here, at one and the same time, was the possibility of capturing prisoners and experimental equipment. This was an exceptional opportunity.

The situation demanded lightning reflexes and instant, precisely considered actions. The more so because the enemy gun crewmen had begun to stare in uncertainty at the Sherman, barely recognizable in the darkness. The chief of staff realized that in just a few seconds, these two men could quickly disappear into their turret and slam shut their hatches. And then it would be no easy task to capture them. They could communicate with their own by radio, a simple task for them in this situation. This could not be permitted!

The task of utmost importance was to lure the enemy artillerymen out of their turret. Nikolay Bogdanov loudly stated his name: "I am Captain Grossman, a liaison officer of 6th *Panzer* Division Headquarters. I have an order for all of our troops." And he pulled some kind of paper out of his pocket and illuminated it with his flashlight. He turned to the artillerymen and, in a distinct voice, commanded: "Come here!" He gave the same order to his own driver-mechanic.

The striking figure of the 'German captain' Bogdanov (about 5' 11") and his commanding voice, his stated duty position, and some kind of paper in the hands of this officer - all taken together had their effect. In seconds, the artillerymen were standing at attention in front of the chief of staff. A third 'German' - Mikhail Bolotin - ran up and quietly sidled up to the left of the "captain," opposite one of the enemy soldiers.

Events unfolded with kaleidoscopic speed. Nikolay turned on the large beam of the flashlight, handed one of the artillerymen the paper, and at the same instant shone the light into both of their eyes, blinding them for seconds. "*Berem!*" (Take them), the 'captain' commanded. And then "*Ruki vverkh!*" (Hands up); not "*Hende hoch!*" but in Russian. This was a greater shock; it froze them; it decisively suppressed their will to resist. On this signal, two more *gvardeytsi* flew like bullets from the *Emcha*. The dumbstruck Germans were tied up in minutes and deposited inside the Sherman. And so the first part of this difficult mission was quickly and successfully accomplished.

The second half of the reconnaissance mission was no less complex. The chief of staff announced his decision to the *Emchisti*: 'We will take the self-propelled gun in tow! We have to get off the road quickly, hide in the darkness, and get lost in the field. We have to get back to our own lines by the shortest route. We will strictly follow the main precept of the scouts: 'Never take the same road into and out of the enemy's rear!'

A few minutes later, a tow cable connected the enemy's self-propelled gun to the Sherman. The loader sat behind the controls of the trophy machine. Bogdanov, his gunner, and the two 'tongues' were in the turret of the *Emcha*. The duties had

been specified in the event of a combat engagement: the 'captain' would fire the main gun, and the gunner would serve as the loader.

When he considered towing the captive back to his own position, the chief of staff was taking an enormous risk. He well knew the ground pressure of his own *Emcha*. From the indistinct responses of the Germans, he understood that the self-propelled gun had a somewhat higher ground pressure.

Simply stated, he began to sweat freely. They could not turn on their head-lights. This task would demand enormous effort, skill, and dexterity from the driver-mechanic. He could not drive the Sherman into a hole or pile the German vehicle into a ditch or trench.

The first one hundred metres was the most difficult for the pair. They tried to pull the German vehicle straight in the tracks of the Sherman to conceal their direction of travel (it was almost impossible to recognize the signs of its track). The ruts were deep to the point that the *Emcha* had to use every ounce of its power. They changed the towing method and held the towed vehicle to the side of the Sherman's track. This was less strain on the engines. Thus they proceeded back to their own lines.

They began to approach the area where the forward edge might be. Nikolay Nikolayevich began to be concerned with how they might cross the front line. His own troops might fire on them, taking them for an enemy. He had to break radio silence. He quickly encoded a message: "I am returning accompanied. I am crossing the front line at (he gave the coordinates). Cover me by fire."

This daring night raid into the near enemy rear was safely concluded. Two weeks later, an Order of the Red Banner adorned the chest of Guards Captain Nikolay Bogdanov.

Erik Wallin represents a very different kind of soldier to Armin Scheiderbauer. Both shared many personal characteristics, including bravery and a certain sang-froid that allowed them to continue carrying out their duties even in the face of the most appalling adversities. Such traits would serve each of them well in the aftermath of the war. However, their attitudes to the continuing fighting by late 1944 are indicative of the fact that no single stereotype representing the late war 'the German soldier' existed. Men fought on for different reasons, no less steadfastly than the other. Certainly an anti-Communist ideology featured much more prominently in Erik Wallin's motivation than Armin Scheiderbauer's.

By the end of 1944 Wallin had served for some time in 'the Swedish Company' of the 11th SS Panzer Aufklärungs Abteilung, 11th SS Panzergrenadier Division 'Nordland'. The 3rd Company was so known because a high proportion of its members were Swedish volunteers, who saw themselves as participating in a 'crusade against Bolshevism'. Its parent unit, the Panzer Aufklärungs Abteilung or armoured reconnaissance battalion, was one of the Division's most potent combat units, well-equipped – even in late 1944 - with armoured personnel carriers, other vehicles, and veteran soldiers.

The 11th SS Division 'Nordland' was itself a notable formation. Although the 5th SS Panzer Division 'Wiking' contained a large number of non-German volunteers, its officer corps remained principally German. The 11th SS Division was created with the intention of becoming a truly 'international' SS Division utilising non-German officers. On this basis, it should be judged successful, for by the end of the war its ranks had contained not only Swedes but also Danes, Dutch, Norwegians, Estonians, Finns, French and Swiss.

By the end of 1944 Erik Wallin and his comrades were in Kurland, their Division part of Army Group North. The past summer and autumn had seen them participate in a number of fierce engagements with the advancing Red Army. Now, on New Year's Eve, it was time to draw breath, even if only for a short while.

We sat round the roughly-made bunker table playing cards, and listening to the front's New Year radio appeals from the highest commanders of the different services. We could also tune in to Christmas music. The bunker had been decorated, as well as we could, on Christmas Eve. There was a Christmas tree, fresh spruce-twigs, tinsel, and small items we had received in the recent field-post parcels. By New Year's Eve it was still looking as homely as it could in a temporary underground bunker. Soldiers' rough, chapped and frozen hands had tenderly and carefully conjured up this Christmas treasure for all to share. We still cared for such in the days between Christmas and New Year.

On the stove were some canteens with steaming *Glogg*, our Nordic version of English mulled and spiced wine. Every now and then each man took a mouthful from one of the canteens, for once carefully cleaned. We had enjoyed smoking lots of the generously distributed Christmas cigarettes, from field-post parcels that had also contained sweets and biscuits. The playing cards regularly slammed down on the rough table. Quiet humming to the melodies on the radio was only occasionally interrupted by some racy comment on the game, or by a violent snore from one of the comrades of the relief guard sleeping on the floor, the exhausted sleep of a frontline soldier.

There was a jarring signal from the field-telephone. It was the company commander. He wanted to speak to me about a planned fire correction for the next day. Our mortar fire was to be aimed at a new target in the enemy positions. He ordered me to go to our outpost closest to the enemy, outside the village, to try to get a general view of the area that my mortars would fire on in the morning.

One of my comrades took over my cards. I put on the snow camouflage overall, took the ammo-pouch for the submachine-gun and put the white-painted steel helmet on my head. On the way out, I took a generous swig of *Glogg* from my canteen on the stove as I looked around the bunker. Suddenly, it seemed so warm, cosy and full of comfort, even with its stamped-down earth floor. On the partially-boarded, black-brown, damp walls fluttered the shadows of the men around the radio, in the light of the Christmas candles. With my trusty MP40 submachine-gun under my arm, I nodded to the men at the table, shoved the white-frosted door open with my foot, and went out into the night.

The moon appeared from behind a silver-edged cloud and covered the entire surroundings in a dazzling bright light. In the reflected whiteness of the cold sparkling snow, all outlines appeared razor sharp. A group of trees, riddled by bullets and shells, with their splintered trunks and twisted network of branches, reminded me of grotesque figures in a fairy-tale about brownies and hobgoblins.

The village, or small town, or what once had been something like that, looked more ghostlike than usual. Out of the snow-covered piles of stone and rubble, where houses used to stand and where there were now neither houses nor streets, only solitary chimneys blackened by fire rose up here and there, missed by the Russian artillery and mortar-fire. In the snow-covered dead village, black holes irregularly dotted the ground among the ruins. They were the only traces of the day's Russian shelling. The artillery shells had made furrows, but where the rounds from the big 12cm mortars had hit, there were big round spots, with black splashes around them, spread out on the frozen ground.

No life was visible in the ruins. But if the alarm should go, warning of an enemy attack, swarms of 'creatures' would leap up among them, because under the ground, in the cellars of the damaged houses, there were soldiers everywhere. They were ready to run out into the trenches to meet the Bolsheviks with a deadly fire.

Such was the New Year's Eve of 1944–45 in Bunkas, the little 'nest' in Courland that had given us protection among its ruins from death out in the wide-open spaces of this vast landscape. Because of that it had become a link in the defence line that we soldiers called the HKL – *Hauptkampflinie*, or main line of defence - in the Courland bridgehead. Cut off from every connection with mainland

Sven Olov Lindholm, founder of the "Lindholm movement" and leader of *Svensk Socialistik Samling* (Swedish Socialist Union), the organisation from which many of the Swedish Waffen-SS volunteers were drawn. Erik Wallin was also a member. (Erik Norling)

Germany, we stood there ready to try to stop the violent assault from the east, from Asia.

After more than 3 years of struggle in the east, and 2 years of almost continuous retreat, our fighting spirit was still unbroken. We persevered under the hardest conditions. Every day, comrades faced death and destruction. The last physical energy and mental force was almost drained out of the common soldier, but our fighting spirit was still there. Our faith lay firmly in the final victory of the superior power of our weapons. Our trust in our own combat skill, against the barbaric masses from the east, was as strong as ever.

It was true that every day we heard on the radio, of the British and Americans pushing our comrades in the west ever harder and harder. Giant bomber 'armadas' every day and night threw their murderous cargo over German cities, obliterating lives and homes. But we knew that a significant part of the most vital German industries had gone below ground and were therefore invulnerable from the air. We knew that even better weapons would soon be mass-produced, and that the German forces in the west, just a few days before, had started a successful offensive in Belgium and Luxembourg. Soon, the terrible pressure of numerically superior forces would have to ease. We just needed some months of breathing space!

Then we would hit back with annihilating power, especially here in Kurland. The 11th SS *Panzergrenadier* Division Nordland and the other troops in this isolated island of resistance had an extremely important mission. With our toughness and persistence against the furious assaults of the Red Army, we could offer a breathing space to the reserves, who were now being organised and freshly equipped in Germany.

I put out my dangerously gleaming cigarette against the doorway. The bunker with the mortar crew was situated about 300 metres behind the actual front line. The company commander's bunker was in the cellar of what once was the railway station. He had told me to come to him first, to get further instructions. In fact it was quite a distance to get there, but on the other hand I could feel safe from enemy observation almost all the way. I moved the ammo-pouch to the side, gripped the submachine-gun harder and went off. In passing, I kicked a dead, stiff, frozen rat that had disgustingly exposed front teeth. There were plenty of big, fat rats in Bunkas.

Many rude words had been spoken in Swedish, German, Danish, Norwegian, and later, most likely, in Russian and Mongolian tongues too, over the ruins in Bunkas. I did the same, as I made my way to the CO's bunker, stumbling over frozen bricks. Fortunately, I did not have to bother about the Russian snipers, who otherwise were very numerous in our sector. We only had to watch out for the artillery and the mortars! However, they seemed to be celebrating New Year's Eve in peace and quiet at that moment. With aching knees I approached a protecting wall, about 20 metres from the CO's bunker. Between the wall and the bunker entrance the distance was open and unprotected. During the previous day, Ivan had managed to take a small hillock on the other side of a low railway embankment. From there he could cover the open distance with his machine-gun fire. Crouching, I ran over the open space and reached the bunker door just as I heard machine-guns 'rattle'. With a nasty singing and whirring they hit the walls and piles of bricks. Further back in the ruins the bullets ricocheted up in the air.

Officers from the *Panzer Aufklärungs-Abteilung* of the 'Nordland' Division, Narva, 1944.
SS-Untersturmführer Hans-Gösta Pehrsson (3rd Company) is far right, wearing greatcoat
and binoculars. At far left is *SS-Untersturmführer* Georg Eriksen, adjutant to the unit's
commander *SS-Hauptsturmführer* Rudolf Saalbach, who is standing second from left.
Eriksen was killed in action in Kurland in January 1945. The figure second from right, at
the rear, is *SS-Obersturmführer* Siegfried Lorenz (1st Company). (Erik Norling)

Reporting to the company commander, who was playing chess at that moment, I was permitted to take a short rest in the welcome warmth. The company
commander was my fellow countryman *SS-Obersturmführer* Hans-Gösta
Pehrsson, 'GP'. The strong discipline, even in the daily work at the front, which
only genuine comradeship between superior officers and their subordinates managed to maintain, gave the Waffen-SS part of its fighting power. Down here the
men had made it, if possible, even more homely than in the mortar crew's bunker.
A wall-runner saying „Egen härd är guld värd" ('Our hearth is worth gold'), which
in some strange way had found its way out here to the furthest outpost in the east,
contributed to the cosiness.

Without interrupting the chess game the commander gave me the orders.
They concerned just that 'troublesome' machine-gun nest out there, which had to
be wiped out. Our mortars had to make it a grave for any Red Army soldier who
dared to go there. The company commander served me a drink from a bottle of
Steinhäger schnapps – "for its good warmth," he said – and I went out to make my
observations. A connecting trench led me to the two soldiers by their machine-gun
in the outpost. Wild shooting was going on and I naturally, wondered what was
happening.

"Oh, they are just firing in the sky over there, to celebrate New Year's Eve, and we have to answer."

By then the insane shooting-party had spread to the whole sector. Everywhere firearms crackled on both sides.

"Seems they are totally drunk on the other side," the machine-gunner said. "Listen to their brawling!"

On the other side of the railway embankment, only about 50 metres from our machine-gun nest, the Bolsheviks had their most advanced position, which was manned only at night. Sometimes they used to attack our guards by crawling across and throwing hand-grenades. In the daytime the position was empty.

Some sounds were heard that were rather unusual for ordinary nights at the front. Someone played a mouth organ, and we could hear the others talking quite loudly. After a while the firing became less intense and soon it ceased completely. Even the exhilarated Bolsheviks over there became silent. In peace and quiet I could make my observations and calculations for the next day.

The weather was on my side, because the clouds, which occasionally swept over the front line, covered me as I went to take a look at surroundings that were usually lit by the moon. The violently battered area was silent. The silence was only occasionally broken by the metallic sound of a weapon that hit some object, or by a hushed mumble from the enemy side. Not even the usual sounds of engines from supply columns, so common at night, nor the clattering sounds from tanks, could be heard. Only now and then a flare rose into the sky and for some moments threw a sharp light over the deserted and lacerated landscape. New Year's Eve at the front!

The beautiful scene kept me out there after I had carried out my orders. Generated by the stillness and the meaning of the Eve, a mood caught me as I was standing there in the trench, together with my two comrades. My thoughts began to wander. They were suddenly interrupted when from the Russian trench on the other side of the railway track I heard a raucous guttural Mongolian voice:

"Comrade, why are you so melancholy? Did you get cabbage soup for dinner today, again?"

The words came slowly, in terribly broken German, but in a conversational tone. In the calm, bright night they reached us as clearly as if the Russian were here, among us three, in the machine-gun nest. The machine-gunner grabbed my arm and we all looked at each other in amazement. For the first time, in three and a half years of war, we experienced a Bolshevik talking to us over no-man's-land. So bitter had been this struggle that it had never happened, as it had during the First World War, that the soldiers fighting each other had spoken across the trenches during a pause in the fighting.

As we recovered from the surprise, we started to laugh out loud, and the laughing spread to the other posts in the guard line, where they too had heard the Russian. The slow tone, the heavy accent and the mutual point about soldiers' food always having recurrent cabbage soup, had given a perfect comic effect. The machine-gunner beside me fired a joyful burst up into the sky and, for a few moments, the rattle of all automatic weapons in the neighbourhood rolled out over the wide-open spaces. Then it became quiet. We waited excitedly for what might come next.

"Why do you shoot, comrade?" asked the same voice from the Russian side.

"If you come over here and play the mouth organ for us, I will not shoot any more," said the machine-gunner.

We peered cautiously over. It could be a trick to make us feel safe. You never knew. The shrewdness of the Bolsheviks had often caused us inconvenience.

The night sky was now completely cloudless, and the intense, cold moonlight, strengthened by the reflective light of the gleaming snow, made the surroundings almost like daylight. All the guards nearby had heard what the two had said, and were now waiting for the Russian's answer, without relaxing their attention. From the other side an eager mumble was heard. It was obvious that the proposal from this side has been taken under consideration. Then it became quiet on the other side. Through the wide open doors of a freight car that had fallen over on the railway track between us and their 'nest,' I saw a head come up and stand out clearly against the gleaming white background. Then a pair of shoulders emerged and indeed, there came a Red Army soldier, in full view, struggling towards the railway embankment. Another two followed.

Having reached the car, the first one blew a few tunes on the mouth organ to convince us that the asked for music session had come. They made some completely unsuccessful attempts to climb the wrecked car. Obviously there was a lot of vodka splashing around in their stomachs. But after all, it was New Year's Eve only once a year. Even on our side the mood was quite good, thanks to the generous bestowal of Steinhäger, Korn, Stargarder Kümmelschnapps and wine, which we had received in the Christmas parcels. The drunken (to put it mildly) Bolsheviks gave up their attempts to climb into the car amid general laughter, and instead lined up in front of it, on our side.

The first tune was burdensome and melancholy, with capricious Russian twists and turns. Their faces were in the shadows, but I could clearly see the seams in their thickly padded tunics, which swelled over their broad, stocky figures. There was a sudden change to a more vivacious tune. It sounded like a Cossack dance. The second man at our machine-gun started to jump to the music, with both feet together, to get the cold out of his feet, but had to give it up because of the quickly increasing speed of the rhythm. In a wild crescendo the music stopped.

The Russian in the middle made an attempt at a deep bow and fell headlong. A howl of laughter was heard from the guards on both sides. With difficulty he worked his way up on to his feet again, apparently hurt by the heartless laughter. When the laughter had somewhat subsided, there came from the fourth soldier, in the Bolshevik outpost on the other side of the embankment, a dirty joke about private parts, that every veteran on our side understood without any problem. Then the snorting laughter rose like a surge over the open space again, and echoed back from the ruins behind us. It followed the three New Year's Eve musicians, as they arm-in-arm started their staggering retreat to the nest on the other side.

The company commander who had heard the jollification as he was standing outside his bunker, philosophising, came into the connecting trench with us to find out what was going on. Excited by the remarkable experience, all three of us started to tell him simultaneously about the Bolsheviks' New Year's idea. As he heard the astonishing story, he said, laughing and holding up his hands, "I have heard about such things, but that it should happen here, in a war with such a fanatical enemy and in front of us, the Waffen-SS, whom every faithful Bolshevik hates, sounds like a Scandinavian sailor's yarn." He shook his head thoughtfully. "I wonder what Ivan is up to. There must be something else behind this sudden cosiness."

He looked in the trench-mirror, turned it slowly in different directions, studied the terrain just in front of us and the ground closest behind the nearest enemy positions, and deliberated. "Damn it, men! Just keep your eyes and ears wide open!" He returned to his bunker.

The conversation over no-man's-land started again. We chatted about this and that. The subject of Christmas gifts came up. It was obvious that the Red Army soldiers had got some extra fare, too, despite the Soviet godlessness. Then an eager overbidding about the excellence of the received gifts started. When they enthusiastically described the fine contents of their parcels, we laughed, mildly indulgent, and knocked them flat with a full list of our own Christmas gifts, but we carefully improved a few grades of quality above what was real. The effect was noticeable.

But the Bolsheviks were tough. We had noticed that, during earlier engagements over the past three years. Even this time it seemed they did not want to give up, without trying a 'counter-attack.' After some mumbling they raised their voices over there and came again with renewed strength. But we saw through them. They went too far with their violent exaggerations, but it cannot be denied that they had improved their position. It began to seem like a 'dead heat!'

Then the final decision came fast and unexpectedly. An old lady from Westphalia had put the victorious 'weapon' in our hands – a pair of slippers, which she had sent in the Christmas parcel to one of the guards to the left of us, whatever use he could have made of them out here. He let the Bolsheviks hear what a nice Christmas gift he had received.

Astonishment on the other side and then the question:

"What are slippers?"

A comrade who understood a little bit more of the Russian language than the rest of us, explained to Ivan what they are.

" *Tufli, tufli,*" he shouted in 'fluent' Russian, in a class of its own, and added a description.

But the Red Army soldiers were still as struck with wonder as before. They had never seen any *tufli.* Poor devils! They would neither have the money, nor the chance, to get a pair of slippers in the Soviet 'paradise' of workers and farmers, even if they ever came home from the war at all, and still had their feet!

The triumph was complete. You could almost talk about total destruction, because over there they seemed absolutely struck dumb. Imagine how warm inside that old woman over there in Westphalia would be as she, in the next field-post letter, read what a great moral victory she had helped us to win.

They were bad losers, those Red Army soldiers. They completely lost their fighting spirit and then they began to get indecent and insolent. They asked for addresses of girls in Berlin, who they said they would soon visit, and promised us a fairly acceptable existence in Siberia. The machine-gunner in our trench found it to be the last straw, as one of them said:

"Hitler soon kaput!"

"Hey, send a New Year's card to that bandit from Georgia, in the Kremlin, and tell him from us that we soon will come eastwards with our King Tigers again, and then he'll shut up for a while," he answered, shouting.

That 'dig' about King Tigers, the new 69-ton heavy tanks, that neither Russian, British nor American weapons could hurt, seemed to have an effect, because the Bolsheviks went 'soft' again. They suggested swapping Christmas gifts. They seemed especially eager to swap tobacco and cigarettes. But their *mahorka*, some sort of pipe-tobacco, a terrible brown stuff that you perhaps took when you had no moss, and that we already had come to know, with disgust, in Russia ... we didn't want that!

"Very good *papirossij*, fine brand Aviatik ," said one of the voices appealingly, from the other side of the railway embankment. Aviatik is one of the better cigarette brands among the Russians.

"All right! You get a packet of fine German tobacco for four packets of Aviatik," said one of our comrades, who already had vainly tried to swap a packet of tobacco, dry as dust, among us in the company. The tobacco, under all circumstances, was better than the Russian *mahorka*, so he was not unfair to the Bolshevik.

They both climbed out of their trenches and approached each other. It was a strange meeting between east and west. The tall SS man was in a white snow-suit, with his assured, half nonchalant and death-defying bearing – *morituri te salutant*. The stocky Red Army soldier, like an Eskimo, was in a quilted uniform with a rolling, splashing walk. Just as they were within reach of each other, a bullet whistled past from a guard further away, who did not know the situation, and had seen the two figures. They ran away from each other with giant leaps and disappeared under cover, as flashes came from different directions.

"Now you've pissed in your trousers!" someone shouted at the hastily returned exchanger who, annoyed and embarrassed after the first fright, only muttered something incomprehensible and undoubtedly very indecorous.

While we had been associating in this 'civil' way with the deadly enemy, the Division's staff had received reports about the events occurring here. Suspecting mischief, the Divisional commander had given orders to aim all available weapons at the terrain in front of our sector, ready to fire if something should happen. But all remained peaceful. Gradually it went silent. Soon dawn would come and then it would be time for the Bolsheviks to move back, if they wanted to avoid getting shovelled into the hard frozen ground of Courland as corpses.

Zoya Alexandrova was something of a rarity even amongst Soviet women who participated in the Great Patriotic War. To a greater extent than any other armed forces, the Soviets employed women on the frontline. However, in the ground forces at least, this tended to be in a non-combatant role, for example, as medics. Zoya was an exception to this rule, albeit by chance!

Prior to her service as a scout with the 65th Tank Brigade during 1944-45, she had served as a frontline medic. However, she found her independent character caused resentment amongst many of the male officers in the units to which she was attached; it seems they were used to having things their own way with their female comrades. Her restless nature and desire for action soon caused her to move much nearer the sharp end of the war.

Soviet scouts dressed in summer camouflage. (Artem Drabkin)

I didn't return to the Regiment after my illness for I wanted to stay away from this scumbag Popukin.[2] Not far from the hospital there was a drill regiment, to which the former commander of our 251st Tank Regiment, Bordyukov, had been appointed. I requested to be sent to his unit. All that spring and summer I served as a military nurse in this regiment but in the autumn I felt like going ... Where to? I didn't know ...

At that time tank crewmen were being sent to frontline units. How could I go? Who would send me away from a drill regiment? I arranged with a doctor that he would give me an assignment to a hospital in a Polish town, the name of which I don't remember. He wrote it in such a way that I could cut off the heading and only the name of the town remained. Then I found the headquarters of the 69th Army in which Masha Sabitova worked. Her new boyfriend had a high rank. I lived with them for a month and put some weight on. I felt that I could not live this way anymore and wanted to go to the front. I asked Masha's boyfriend to send me to a tank brigade. It turned out that by that time Bordyukov had been appointed as a tank brigade commander in the 11th Tank Corps, which fought as part of the 69th Army. I travelled to him, found his dugout. I was standing next to it when his wife came out and said: "Zoya, Petya will not take you to his brigade." – "Why?" – "Because you used to correspond with Masha." And then I was directed to the neighboring 65th Tank Brigade commanded by Lukyanov. I would fight in its ranks till the end of the war. The first I heard from the commander when I had arrived was: "Stay with me." – "And what's going to happen to your girlfriend Zina?" – "She's on holiday, in Moscow." – "No way, you'd better send me back to the Army Headquarters or send me to the scouts." And I was sent to the scouts!

---

2   Commissar in Zoya Alexandrova's previous unit, whose advances she had consistently rejected.

The boys from the scout platoon I'd been led to by the Scout Company commander greeted me very guardedly. The platoon commander Alexandrov, my future husband, seated me at the table in a bath-hut. He himself sat down imposingly, one leg on another, with a cigarette in his long fingers. He began to ask me, who was I, where from: "Do you have any medals?" – "Yes." -"Which one?" – "For Battle Merits." – "Aha…" This medal, 'For Battle Merits' or as it was called at the front 'For Sexual Exploits'[3] was usually given to PPZh's, or wives in the field. Masha had such a medal too. I had been put forward for the decoration with the Order of Glory for the Kursk campaign, but Popukin had arranged a useless reference for me. How much I hated this platoon commander back then! Later on I rejoiced when he had a car accident and got smashed so badly that he barely survived. After the war Alexandrov told me "At first we thought that you'd sinned a lot and come to our platoon to pray for forgiveness!" This kind of attitude to me didn't last long and soon I became 'one of them' for the guys, who just looked out for me.

The Scout Company was located on the Pulawy bridgehead. I hadn't told them that I was a nurse and became an ordinary scout – I was trained to position myself in the field with the rest, I navigated by compass and used a gun.

---

3   The award 'For Battle Merits' was the lowest kind of award for soldiers and officers in the Red Army. Both names – original and humorously renamed – sound similar.

Part V

North-West Europe

The *Reich* border, the Ardennes and Alsace
(December 1944-January 1945)

Part V

North-West Europe

The *Reich* border, the Ardennes and Alsace
(December 1944-January 1945)

Operation Market Garden had demonstrated to the Allies that victory in the West could not be taken for granted. The remainder of 1944, and particularly the winter months of that year, provided further evidence that the war was far from over. This was a period of virtual stalemate, when most fighting was confined to a narrow strip of territory between ten and twenty miles deep. Allied advances were small, and achieved at a fearful cost. One reason for the slowness of the Allied advance in these months was the German army's effectiveness, as at Arnhem, in regrouping its depleted forces, in order to resist even surprise attacks. The hesitancy of Allied armies to press home their advantage when they did force the Germans to retreat, as at Falaise, was repeatedly punished by their opponents.

Three other factors were also of importance in this particular phase of the war. The first of these was that the rapid advances of August had overextended meant supply lines, creating shortages at the front. In September, General Patton's 3rd Army, which had advanced nearly 500 miles in twenty-six days, was forced to halt before reaching its objective because it had simply run out of fuel. Further south, 12th Army Group traced its fragile supply line all the way down to Marseilles, along a single railway line. The Germans, by contrast, were now closer than ever to the factories on which they depended for their supplies. Despite Allied bombardment, these factories were actually able to increase their production in 1944.

The second factor was the terrain on which the Allies were now fighting. In the centre, the Allies were now driving towards the Siegfried Line, or West Wall, as the Germans called it. This was a system of fortifications running for 300 miles from Basle to Cleves. In this sector the Allies were facing troops who could take refuge in forts and pillboxes in certain areas, and behind barbed wire and cement anti-tank defences in others. In the Vosges, and the area south-east of Aachen known to the Americans as the Hürtgen Forest, the terrain was of a type naturally suited to defence rather than attack. These were wooded areas, with narrow, impassable roads, in which rapid advance was difficult, and day-to-day living conditions extremely testing. The Germans, who were able to take shelter in their defensive bastions, enjoyed a clear advantage in these sectors.

The third problem for the Allies, which compounded the difficulties of the terrain, was the hostility of the weather conditions in late 1944. In October, twice as much rain fell in Lorraine as in an average year, while the winter which followed was one of the coldest of the century to that point. Mud, snow, and ice made progress by tank virtually impossible, even in sectors which were not too wooded or mountainous for heavy infantry. At the same time the area in which the Allies enjoyed a clear advantage - airpower - was effectively neutralized by atmospheric con-

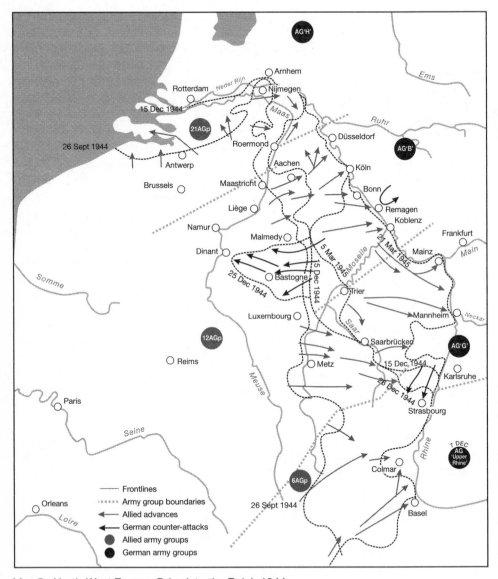

Map 5   North-West Europe: Drive into the Reich 1944

ditions: between 15 October 1944 and 15 January 1945 there were only twenty-three 'flyable' days in total. The result was a period in which, for most combatants, the experience of battle was one of small encounters and skirmishes in woodlands and villages, with only small gains being made, and day-to-day living conditions wet and miserable.

When Frank Gurley arrived at the front line near St Remy in the high Vosges on 1 November, these difficult conditions were all too plain to see:

As darkness settled into the forest clearing, a shadowy convoy of two-and-a-half ton trucks rumbled quietly into the area. We clambered aboard and stacked our horseshoe roll packs on the floor between our knees. As soon as we were ready, the trucks rolled quietly forward again, the drivers straining to see in the scant cones of faint light emitted by the blackout drive lights. Normally driven in a noisy and undisciplined fashion, tonight the drivers kept their vehicles under strict control, shifting gears quietly under their weighty human cargoes, and idling the truck motors as softly as cats purring in the gathering gloom.

If the trucks were quiet, their helmeted human cargoes were even quieter. For once, like the trucks themselves, we were neither noisy nor undisciplined. Most of us were lost in thought, asking ourselves questions for which we had no answers.

"What will it be like?"

"How will I act under fire?"

"Will I still be around tomorrow night?"

"Will I chicken out like Sergeant Lollander and shoot myself in the foot?"

"Will I see my girl and my parents again?"

"Will I screw up and let Captain Young and the others down?"

"Will the experience we're about to go through change my personality and outlook?"

I did some silent praying and could feel that others were doing the same. Scotty Kyle and I stood upright behind the truck cab and warned the others whenever a low-hanging evergreen branch came along. The road was unpaved, very narrow, and bordered by thick evergreen walls.

"Duck! Branch!" I whispered loudly a dozen times. Everyone lowered their heads as the branches slapped across the truck's ribs. Fate seemed to be drawing us along on long invisible ropes in the darkness. The trees wouldn't tell us anything but seemed to be whispering among themselves. The trees must know the answers, for hadn't the war gone right through here? They knew; now it was our turn to learn.

If this truck movement had taken place back in training at Fort Bragg, the truck drivers would have gunned the motors loudly or forgotten to turn off the lights or smashed into trees or driven off a cliff into a lake or through some farmer's chicken coop roof. But here in the real world of war, there was no unauthorized noise or light, and no collisions, confusion, or screw-ups. The trucks rolled inexorably forward toward the unseen front line that lay somewhere ahead in the black night.

Finally, the ride ended and we dragged our horseshoe packs off the truck. Beyond this point, it was feared that our truck motors might give away our presence to listening enemy ears. We were led up a forest path through the evergreens. Beside the path we could make out ghostly silhouettes of tanks and tank destroyers parked under camouflage nets. Their guns were pointed toward where the enemy must be. Others were fighting in the war too and nobody seemed too excited about it. So why should we be afraid?

During a short rest break, an artillery major came out of a small net-draped bunker beside the road to chat with us. "We have two ways of delivering counter battery fire," the Major explained. "One way is to get a sound ranging of the enemy guns, unless the wind is blowing toward the enemy, which it often does in the Vosges. Another even better way is to line up the position of the enemy gun from its muzzle flash unless the gun has flash defilade behind a steep hill. Despite the large number of hills here, we can usually see enough of the flash to be able to apply the triangulation technique."

"What's that, sir?" I asked.

"Once we get two or more different fixes where the gun's flash is coming from, we can calculate its location and wipe it out promptly. It's that simple."

Through the major's triangulation technique, I supposed, it would be only a question of time before the enemy's artillery would be completely eliminated. Without their artillery, how long could the Germans hold out? It was a comforting prospect. American technology was a wonderful thing, in war as in peace. I half wondered why their artillery hadn't been knocked out already if it was so easy. But basically I hadn't the slightest doubt about the Major's story.

The climb continued. We were perspiring heavily. Men began to go down under the weight of their loads. "It's Smith. Somebody stay with him until a medic can get here." The man who folded was always somebody else. Nothing could happen to ME. Other guys might get killed, although I hoped they wouldn't, but not ME.

In the Army, and especially in the Vosges, the hills seemed to go up but not down. When finally we reached what seemed to be the top of the long ascent, we were led off the road among the trees. After the squad leaders conferred with Lieutenant Mueller, Jim Gardner gave us the straight poop. "We're not going to relieve the other outfit till morning." This brought murmurs of approval. "There's a little town about a mile down in front of us," Jim Gardner went on. "If it was daylight youse could see it from here. The Fifteent' Infantry of the Toid Division is going to take the town tonight. In about fifteen minutes, you'll hear the most tremendous artillery barrage you ever hoid in your life. After they take the town, we'll relieve 'em and move into the houses." We dug shallow slit trenches in the pliant Vosges soil. Then we rolled up in our shelter halves and blankets and were soon asleep.

When we were awakened at 0500, I asked if anyone had heard the "tremendous artillery barrage" Jim Gardner had promised. No one had.

Sergeant Gardner had sold some product or service back in the Bronx before being drafted. In the Army, he continued 'selling' whatever he came in contact with, which at the present moment happened to be his side of the war. He probably could have sold the enemy on laying down their arms if he had had a safe conduct pass through the lines and a little basic German grammar.

It was drizzling slightly in the High Vosges forest where we had spend the night. It was Thursday, 2 November. We kicked dirt into the slit trenches that had served as our beds, honoring the training principle of "leaving the area in the condition we found it in."

Somehow the company's kitchen jeeps managed to come forward up the narrow trail we had marched along the previous night and served us hot dehydrated eggs and real bacon before we continued moving up. Hot chow undoubtedly lifted our morale, but to some of us, the meal had overtones of the favor done a prisoner before taking 'the long walk'. The final leg of our trek to the front led along a winding mountain road, past camouflaged tanks. Tall evergreens stood high and mighty over our heads.

This morning there was hustle and wisecracking, but no special fears or heavy thinking or questioning. The fear, thinking and questioning had apparently been creatures of the night. It was now raining steadily and the woods were full of mist. During the rest break, Jim Gardner explained that the 3d, 36th, and 45th Infantry Divisions of VI Corps were holding the front lines in our sector. He said the 45th had been squeezed out by the others, and that while they were still out of contact with the enemy, it was decided to insert our division to relieve them.

Finally we reached the front lines and met the men we were to relieve. They were friendly, rugged-looking guys, with beards and camouflage netting on their helmets. We stood around chatting beside their foxholes while they awaited the order to move to the rear. The rain seemed to run off their helmets onto their raincoats and onto the ground without getting them the least bit wet. It was our first look at combat men and we were duly impressed.

"We waited seventy-nine days since the Riviera invasion for you guys," one of them said with a grin. "Where you been?"

"We got here as fast as we could," I said. "We only left New York October 6th."

"That's pretty fast", he acknowledged.

"Twenty-five days from Manhattan to the front," I added. "We were the first convoy to come direct to France from the US"

"Are you guys from the 100th?" he asked.

"Er, yes," I admitted, fearing this might be a punishable breach of security. But I feared even more that this authentic combat man would consider me an idiot if I didn't reply.

"Where are the front lines?" I asked my new friend.

"Front lines? You're them," was the answer.

"Then where are the Germans?"

"Jerry? Oh he's out there somewhere, don't know for sure where."

"You mean there's nobody between us and them?"

"That's roger."

"My squad leader said your division got squeezed out," I said.

"Not that I know of," he replied. "Say," he said, "what do you plan on doing with those fancy full field packs and those horseshoe rolls? I even saw one of your boys with an extra pair of shoes dangling from his pack."

"But that's all standard equipment," I said. "We lugged that stuff all the way from Fort Bragg. Where are yours?"

"Threw 'em away long ago," he replied with a grin. "How do you expect to chase a Jerry when you're loaded down like a Penn Station Red Cap?"

"But how can you sleep without blankets?" I asked.

"We have small sleeping bags which the kitchen carries around and hands out at the end of the day's fighting."

"But what about towels, washcloths, underwear, soap, razor, toilet articles, stationery?"

"This isn't a beauty contest," he replied, "If we take a town or get relieved like today, we wash up and shave. Otherwise, no."

"Have you got a toothbrush?" I asked.

"Nope."

"What about pup tents?" I said.

"I pack the shelter half in with the bedroll, but I haven't seen a tentpeg since I forget when."

"Did you ever get a bayonet charge by the Germans?" I asked him.

"In Sicily one day we did," he replied. "Some gung-ho Kraut outfit came out of a gully waving bayonets at us like we were a bunch of rookies. I let 'em get close, about seventy-five yards maybe, and then I really creamed them with my BAR."

"Not bad," I said.

"You know," he said, "seeing dead Krauts lying around don't make any more impression on me than leaves laying under the trees. But when I see one GI lying there cold, it really busts me up inside."

"Have you had many casualties?" I asked.

"We've been pretty lucky coming up the Rhône Valley," he replied. "Since the invasion we only lost ten men from the platoon." A platoon at full strength normally had forty men including one officer, so these "lucky" guys had already lost about twenty-five percent of their strength in less than three months.

He explained that the rhythmic artillery sounds we were hearing overhead that ended in distant explosions far off were "our stuff." The occasional ear-splitting crashing sounds we heard behind us were enemy shells, landing in our rear areas. German artillery smoke was black and American artillery smoke was white. In the small arms category, the enemy weapon that was fired in nervous short bursts was called a "Burp gun." The German machine gun also fired very rapidly, while our machine guns made a slower, pounding sound.

I noticed that their rifles were 'preserved' under a coating of what appeared to be rust.

"Do they fire?" I asked timidly.

"Sure they fire," was the reply. "We run a patch through the bore once in a while and keep the chamber clean. The M-1 is a good gun and doesn't need too much maintenance."

He pointed to a young soldier walking past the foxhole. His only equipment seemed to be a rifle and a single bandolier of ammo slung on the outside of his raincoat. The young soldier had landed in France as a Pfc. and was now up for a battlefield commission.

"He's our new Platoon Leader," my friend said. "He's still nineteen."

Another 45th man observed cheerfully, "If Jerry pulled a counterattack right now, we'd really be laying for them. We've got double strength all along the line." They chuckled at the delicious thought of the enemy falling into such a trap.

"Hey you guys, keep it down to a low roar, will you?" their youthful platoon leader said. The men complied, lowering their voices respectfully.

"He's right," one said. "The Kraut forward observers can hear a pin drop sometimes."

One of the 45th guys reminisced about the advance up from the Riviera. "Over on our right at night we could see the lights of Switzerland," he said. "It was a beautiful sight."

I raised the question of the best way to fight a tank. I said we had been taught that when a German tank bore down upon you, you first tried to stop it with anti-tank grenades or a "bazooka." If this failed, you scrunched down in the bottom of your foxhole while the tank rumbled over the hole. The tank's weight would usually cave in the sides of your foxhole but not deeply enough to crush you in the bottom. Then, as soon as the tank had passed beyond your hole, you were supposed to stand up quickly and hurl a "Molotov Cocktail" (a gasoline-filled bottle with a fuse) onto the tank's rear deck. If all went according to plan, the Molotov Cocktail would explode upon impact and the enemy crew would burn to death as their tank was enveloped in flames.

"Is that what they're teaching back at Benning?" one of them asked.

"At Benning and Bragg and everywhere else," I replied.

"Here's how it actually works," he said. "It won't be a one-on-one duel between you and that tank, because the tank will usually be accompanied by *Panzer grenadiers* (armored infantrymen). Those babies will do everything in their power to prevent anyone from firing a bazooka or tank grenade. As far as hiding in the bottom of your hole while the tank goes over you, the first problem is those *Panzer grenadier* boys who'll flush you out of there like an old possum. Even if they don't, the top soil here in the Vosges is very soft. A tank running over your foxhole will crush in the sides so deep that it'll finish you off ninety-nine times out of a hundred."

"So what's the right solution?" I asked.

"There's no solution," he said. "When we see a tank bearing down on us, we drop everything but our rifle and head for the hills like big-ass birds. Those *Panzers* will chase one lonely GI through the trees, so you have to outwit them the way a rabbit does on a rabbit hunt."

"So who stops them?" I asked.

"Stronger medicine than you," he replied. "57mm anti-tank guns, M-4 Sherman tanks or maybe tank destroyers with a three-inch gun or 90 millimeter. But never an M-1 rifle like you got."

That was enough to remould completely my ideas on how to fight tanks. A year of training in the States had taught us the Ft. Benning solution, but a few sentences from a real fighting man was enough to wipe out every false preconception.

Finally the order came for the unit we were relieving to move out. With much well wishing on both sides, they saddled up their modest belongings and left the Germans exclusively to us. Their farewells could not have been warmer if we had known them for several years instead of only two or three hours. There was, it seemed, no cause or room in the combat infantrymen's world for jealousy, selfishness, or other vices of the spirit.

"I wonder if the Krauts know we're here?" Doc Emmons, the erstwhile Company Barber, asked Robert E. Jones. Now that we had reached the front lines, Doc Emmons was no longer the barber, but was engaged full time as assistant BAR man to Robert E. Jones.

"Naw, doubt it," Jones replied. "They'da pulled a counterattack already if they know'd a bunch of 4-Fs is now agin 'em."

Like the rest of us, Captain Young had mostly listened during a lengthy meeting with the CO of the company we were relieving.

"We started with 187 men and we're now down to 90," Captain Young was told. "You can't afford to be too discouraged if the same thing happens to you." Captain Young pondered the numbers and said nothing.

"Another thing to remember," the other CO said, "is that it isn't your fault if men are wounded or killed. You have objectives to take, and it's your job to take 'em. Casualties are unavoidable, but if you put the blame on yourself, you won't be able to do your job any more."

Captain Young pondered the other man's words. Then he said, "You saw us come up to relieve you this morning. What were your impressions of our discipline, deportment, equipment, and morale generally?"

"I'll be frank," the other CO said. "When my men first saw your boys hunched under those horseshoe packs, they said, "'Boy, those poor lambs are going to get slaughtered!'"

"I suppose we've got a lot to learn," Captain Young said. "My Division and Regimental commanders were over here in the First World War and my Battalion CO is a West Pointer. You'd think somebody would have clued them in about how much equipment is reasonable and necessary up here."

"The School of Hard Knocks is the only reliable teacher," the other CO said. "There's always a wide gap between garrison doctrine and actual combat conditions."

They shook hands and the other CO moved off through the woods toward the rear. Captain Young told his Communications Sergeant, Sergeant Lou Nemeseck, to get in touch with Battalion on their newly installed telephone wire.

"Lou, we've got to find out what the situation is, and what's to happen next," Captain Young said. "Try to find out from Battalion what we should be doing."

"Yes sir," Nemeseck said quietly. This was the first time he had seen Captain Young in less than full control of a particular situation. It was also the first time the Captain had called him "Lou" during the year they had been working together.

Peter Hall, serving further north with the 1st Worcesters, near Nijmegen, recalls similarly difficult conditions:

On 6 October, most British troops on the 'Island' - that was the piece of ground between the rivers Waal, Neder Rijn and the North Sea - had handed over to the US 82nd Airborne Division. We moved south-east to an area called the Dekkers Wald. The 'Winter War' had started. We were being kept for the assault on the formidable Siegfried Line! Both the Germans and ourselves, inhibited by the weather from mobile warfare, indulged in a period of probing reconnaissance; patrolling against each other's forward positions. The aim - to find out where were

A dramatic photo of British infantry clearing houses, autumn 1944. The men are equipped for close-quarters fighting; the figure in centre with his back to the camera carries a PIAT anti-tank projector. (Imperial War Museum BU1335)

respective strong points and weaknesses. This - before we engaged in the next big 'punch-up'.

Because of the snow, both British and German patrols covered their traditional uniforms with white camouflage suits. This made us indistinguishable friend from foe! This resulted in a number of ludicrous incidents. I will describe one such incident - in which I was personally involved. I think it appropriate to give this story the not original heading - 'Ill Met by Moonlight!'

Sometime in November 1944, the Commanding Officer ordered me to select a patrol partner and investigate a group of farm buildings - which, if occupied by the enemy, could threaten the defences of our present position, or cause embarrassment to our future offensive plans. The Commanding Officer was observing the time-honoured maxim: 'Time spent in reconnaissance is never wasted'.

At about 2300 hours on the appointed day - or rather, night - my patrol partner and I moved through our own forward defensive positions into the snowy waste, camouflaged, very effectively, by our snow-suits. I have to confess that such patrols as this, gave me a lift. I did not enjoy squatting in a slit trench by day - whilst the powerful guns of the Siegfried Line shelled us. It was greatly preferable to do something active. As usual, I digress! Let me remind you that our patrol task was to investigate a group of tactically-placed farm buildings between our lines and the enemy positions.

The night was clear and frosty, with a full moon: good for navigation, not so good for concealment.

Brigadier H. Essame (left; commanding officer 214th Brigade) and Lieut-Col R. Osborne-Smith (1st Battalion, Worcestershire Regiment). (Imperial War Museum BU1448)

We moved to a small ridge overlooking the buildings - about 40 yards away - about half a mile from our own forward positions. I ordered my patrol partner to take up a covering fire position while I went down to take a closer look. Cautiously, I moved to the buildings - comforted by the thought that, should I run into trouble, I could expect a burst of covering fire from my partner to get me out of it. To my great relief, I found that the buildings had been abandoned by the enemy. There was evidence of recent occupation - opened German ration tins, recent cooking, etc. I guessed that the buildings had been recently occupied by a German section (about 10 men) - probably supporting a Spandau machine-gun.

This was valuable information. It meant that the enemy did not intend to attack us in our present, rather precarious positions, but were pulling back to regroup further east. Well pleased with the result of my reconnaissance, I made my way back to where I had left my partner. HE WAS NOT THERE! I saw in the snow the imprint of his body where he had lain as he covered me forward. I also saw footprints in the snow coming from the east (the German position). I further saw footprints going east and west. It was also apparent that the second spoor had been made by people who were running. The indentations in the snow had a deeper impression on the front of the foot - rather than on the flat of the whole foot.

Puzzled - and rather perturbed - I made my way back to Company base to deliver my report. The first person I met on re-entering our own lines was my erstwhile partner.

I roared at him, "Where the bloody hell have you been!" He looked very shamefaced:

"Sir, I was covering you down to the farm. I was concentrating on what you were doing. Suddenly, I felt a tap on my shoulder. I heard a voice whisper 'Hans! Hans!' I looked round and saw a young blue-eyed bloke dressed in a white snow suit bending over me. We both realised, Sir, that we weren't on the same side - and scarpered in opposite directions! I'm sorry, Sir, I let you down!"

I suppose that I should have put him on a charge - but I didn't! Thus, adding yet another to my many military misdemeanours! The thought of those two young men, in the middle of nowhere, giving each other the fright of their lives made me laugh. I couldn't charge him after that! The soldier in question (obviously I won't name him!) subsequently distinguished himself in action. He achieved the rank of corporal and earned himself a well-merited 'mention in dispatches'. I did, however, choose a different partner for subsequent patrols!

Throughout the late autumn and early winter, the Allies continued to make progress, albeit slowly, and at a heavy cost. On 21 October Aachen was finally captured, after a long and bitter struggle. Strasbourg was liberated just over a month later, on 24 November. Then suddenly, in mid-December, the situation changed completely, as offensive operations within 12th Army Group were brought to almost a complete halt. The reason was a sudden counteroffensive launched by the Germans in the Ardennes, an operation codenamed Wacht am Rhein. *On 16 December the German troops of Army Group B surged out of the forests of the German-Belgian border. Their aim was to capture Antwerp, and thus split US 12th Army Group from the Anglo-Canadian 21st Army group in the north. As Hitler and his strategists had foreseen, the winter weather prevented the Allies from deploying tactical air support. This, combined with the surprise element of the attack, meant that the German offensive was initially highly successful, inflicting heavy losses on Allied forces. Major Sam Carter remembers the Allies' disarray in the face of this attack:*

Cold and snowing. When 3rd Battalion, 18th Infantry, left Langerwehe for a rest and relaxation period, it returned to the town at the Belgium, Holland, Germany border. Our men were enjoying this respite from battle. Quite a few of our officers and men took a little break in Brussels, including Colonel Peckham, leaving me the Battalion Commander.

Early 16th December 1944 we got orders to move out. The R'N'R was suddenly over. It seemed as though the Germans had attacked in the Ardennes and kicked the hell out the 99th Division, the 2nd Division, and part of the 28th Division. No-one had expected such an attack in that area. We were to move down to Eupen, to cross the Elsenborn Plain, and stop any move towards the north. I organised to move the 3rd Battalion out. As we got near Eupen, all the roads leading to this area were jammed with artillery, support units and engineers. We had a difficult time getting through this traffic jam. It extended for miles. Some newsmen managed to find me and wanted to know what we were going to do. I said that as long as this mass of material and people blocked roads that the Germans also had to use, we were not going to worry. But as soon as the roads were clear of Americans and their equipment we would then act.

It had been reported that the Germans had dropped a large force of paratroopers south and east of Eupen. The 3rd Battalion was to screen the area and clear them out. Finally, the roads were cleared and our troops were spread out on each side of the road and moving south. Shortly, we started running into a few German paratroopers. They had been scattered all over the forest and Elsenborn Plain.

No two plane-loads were even close together. A paratrooper said that they were to follow up white discs hanging on trees that led them to a meeting-place in a large building in the forest. They were quite despondent. The German POWs were young men, well-fed, new uniforms, good weapons, and some good survival items.

We had been fighting Germans who were older, thinner, and worn from so much battle. They wore old, unkempt uniforms, and had very poor rations. Further items, worn under the clothing of the POWs, were nice rabbit-fur jackets. We decided they would no longer need these jackets. So we took them for our own use.

We swapped some of their emergency field rations for some of our emergency C Rations. The half pound packet of bacon was really good. By the end of the second day we had collected all the German paratroopers and moved out on the Elsenborn Plain. Now we started collecting US soldiers from the 99th Division and the 2nd Division. We were getting enough men from the 2nd Division to be of some use. Men from the 99th Division were told to move away from the road, dig themselves in foxholes, 5 yards apart, and wait for some of their officers. We moved through a road on the Elsenborn Plain and had to collect a great quantity of snow-drifts. The dozers had kept the corridor through the area that had ice-walls 10 to 12 feet high, on each side. Our final area was the 1st Division right flank between Lyons and Melmerdien.

The US Army was not equipped for the damp or winter fighting, but we survived. We had some Mickey Mouse boots which kept your feet warm but soaked with water. Twice a day men had to take their shoes off and massage their feet and put on dry socks. To dry their wet socks, that were removed, they were to wring them out and put them near their stomach, under the clothing they had on, and they would dry. Foxholes in the snow, with a little straw on the bottom and a candle, would keep a man real warm. In fact, he might have a hole at the top, to prevent the person from getting too sweaty or get too hot.

The Battalion had one Weasel, a tracked jeep, that we used to carry hot food to the men. In our area, the snow was about waist-deep and our other vehicles could not make the run. The company in reserve was kept in a village with enough houses to contain them. There was heat and hot meals. They cleaned up back in this area. Companies were rotated, so that every third day the men would be back in the warm area. Captain Dino Roncanio was our Battalion S4, and he had busied himself to see that the Battalion had everything it needed, if he could possibly find it. He made sure that the warm area was always warm, and that there was plenty of hot food.

Captain Leonard B. Andy, S4 of 1st Battalion. Major Frank Dupree was Regimental S4. A load of stiffs was being hauled to the rear and waited to get the word to move. In the meantime, a truck load of new arrivals had pulled up to get ready to go to the Units. Major Dupree gave the word for the truck with the stiffs to move off. He did not notice that replacements had arrived. Then he noticed the dead men still had on their Mickey Mouse boots. He yelled to the truck driver: "Hold it!". Then to some S4 men, "Get those boots off the stiffs, we need them for the new men coming in".

While we waited to be welcomed to the 1st Division, we had no camouflage white dress. So white sheets and any other white material that could be found was fashioned into some sort of a camouflage cover. At times it was real cold, especially for the patrols going out at night. Some men had their hands so cold, they could not hold their weapons. The weapons would fall. Then they could not pick the weapons up or hold to them. We would just hope and pray the men would get back while the weather was so cold.

We were moved back to the right flank of the 1st Division, after we had our turn in Buchenwald. From this position the 3rd Battalion, 18th Infantry was on the right edge of the 1st Division hinge to close the door on the Bulge. The night we started the attack, a raging blizzard was in progress. The movement for the attack was over a large open flat field within half a mile of the German positions. Then there was some steep ground to climb to avoid an area where the Germans had their positions and bunkers. Once up in the wooded area the ground was again rather flat. Our patrols had finally located their position and the bunkers. Once Company L, 18th Infantry, started to attack in the early morning. But they got caught in the open field at daylight, and suffered heavy casualties. The snow was simply too deep and movement was very slow. From this we learned a bitter lesson.

The leading element of the battalion were on the extreme right flank where our patrol had been able to penetrate to some extent. Units reached a steep rise in the ground without opposition. It was dark, and the blizzard was unmerciful. To climb to the top of the hill, our men had to pull themselves from tree to tree, and then use the trees as blocks to push with their feet. Once on top to the flat ground our troops found that the German positions were empty. Our men moved rapidly through the bunkers and started rounding up the Germans. They insisted we were crazy to be out fighting in such terrible weather. You know they were sent to the rear and the war was over for them! We had a long way to go and keep on fighting.

At first the German's daring attack was successful, forming a seventy-mile salient into Allied lines. Allied losses were high, totalling around 80,000 men, most of them American troops. After eight days, however, the tide began to turn. The Allies were able to hold the encircled Bastogne, one of the Germans' key objectives. At the same time the Germans, whose supply lines had been cut, began to run short of fuel and equipment, while casualty levels amongst their ranks were devastatingly high. By Christmas, the Allies were once again in the ascendant, but they were to suffer a second unpleasant surprise, however. In order to concentrate the Allied attack on the German salient, General Eisenhower had to redeploy troops from other parts of the front, with the result that Allied lines had to be thinned in the Low Vosges and the Alsatian Plain. Hitler was quick to spot this new weak point, and rapidly launched a second counteroffensive to capitalize upon it, codenamed Operation Nordwind. Where Wacht am Rhein was designed to divide the Americans from the Anglo-Canadians, Nordwind was intended to force a withdrawal from the Alsatian Plain, an action which, it was hoped, might cause a breach between the Americans and the French, for whom the concession of the newly captured Strasbourg would be unacceptable. This, it would hoped, might prepare the way for a peace in the West, which would allow the Reich *to focus all its military re-sources on the Eastern front.*

It was in this second 'Battle of the Bulge' that Johann Voss found himself involved in early January 1945. Voss, a twenty-year-old machine gunner in SS Mountain Infan-try Regiment 11, 6th SS Mountain Division 'Nord', had served in Karelia and Fin-land. After dramatic retreat southwards, following the surrender of Finland in September 1944, he had spent a quite and restful Christmas in Denmark. Yet, as he headed towards his new posting in early January, he and his companions were in a gloomy frame of mind:

The train rumbled very slowly over the bridge across the Rhine on its approach to the main station in Cologne. Despite the cold outside, Schmidtchen, our sunny comrade from that city, had opened the door of the wagon a bit to catch a glimpse of the river. In the moonless night and total blackout, however, no lights along the river banks were visible and no sparkling reflection on the water marked its course. We were staring into complete darkness.

I didn't care. The river had never stirred the patriotic feelings in me that it did in others, nor could I understand its much celebrated romance. My first impression from a rail trip along the river years before had been a scenery of hills that in the monotony of their endless vineyards seemed deprived of their natural beauty. There was another crossing of the Rhine that came back to my mind—December 1939, the war being in a lull, our family was on the way to see my father over Christmas at his station near the Belgian border.

This was the same setting, the same thick air of foreboding. In these first days of 1945 on the way to the Western Front, though, it was the river's historical signif-icance that prevailed in my mind. The river had been a symbol of Germany's asser-tion of her western territory from the days of ancient Rome to the Napoleonic Wars and even to the present. Now the front was getting closer and the battle for the *Reich* had begun.

"Germany's 'River of Fate'," I said to Heinrich; "it prefers to stay in hiding. Just the way we are kept in the dark about our next mission."

"Well, at least we know by now that it'll be the Western Front and not the East," Heinrich said.

"That's right, and aren't we lucky? I hated the idea of being back in the East. Still, where are we going?"

"Whatever, to me, it's all the same. The East or the West, what difference does it make anyway?" Heinrich said ruefully. "We won't hold them up."

The train had now come to a halt in the main station. With the door still slightly open, we could see people hurrying about, if only in the short moments of their crossing one of the dim circles thrown on the ground from the darkened lamps above.

"Listening to you," I said, "one could think of throwing away our arms just as well. Don't you think that with one more great effort, maybe this front can be sta-bilized or even pushed back? Wouldn't things look quite different then?"

"Yeah, sure, just the way we stopped them on their way down from Normandy. My dear Johann, if you had taken some time to read a paper instead of ogling that

Danish girl, you'd know better. This great effort of yours took place only a month ago in the Ardennes. It didn't get us far."

"Sure, I know, but the Ardennes is woodland, ill-suited for a *Panzer* army, and there's more wood-land down south. Now if all the mountain divisions coming from the North were employed in the woods, thrown into an-other real big thrust, it could work, don't you think so?"

"I envy your opti-mism," Heinrich said, ending our talk.

The train moved on and was going now slowly through the city of Co-

Johann Voss and his father photographed during a rare one-day pass during *Gebirgsjäger* training in Bavaria, 1943. (Johann Voss)

logne. Schmidtchen stood at the door. We heard him groan in his funny Cologne dialect, "Oh my God! Look! See that? I didn't know it was as bad as that!"

I went to the door and looked out. I remembered towering rear walls of the business and housing districts on both sides of the thoroughfare, but there was total emptiness now. Sometimes a ragged structure glared out from the dark flat, ex-panse. The city of Cologne was gone. Even in the dark we could see that much. Schmidtchen was shocked beyond words at what he saw. We stood there, not knowing what to say. As the train slowly took up speed, Schmidtchen jerked the door shut.

Some days later, we were back in combat again. Our area of operations was the Low Vosges.

We stood in a small circle, the men of my gun and Heinrich with a few of his men. We were freezing, our hands shoved deeply in the pockets of our anoraks, caps and shoulders under the hoods of our canvas sheets for protection from the sleet that swept through the forest. As always, we had dug in, but it was too cold to remain in our foxholes. We shifted and stomped our feet to keep warm. Other groups stood around, scattered over the area, the wood full of them. All three *Jäger* battalions of our regiment were assembled, waiting for the attack to begin early next morning. Our objective was to retake the hills that were lost by some infantry division only one day after they had moved into the positions we had held before—two hills near the village of Reipertsweiler.

The hours in the assembly area before an attack are among the most miserable moments in a soldier's life. The thought of one's own death cannot be chased away, nor can the nagging certainty that one's own luck cannot be permanent. This waiting, I think, is the most sombre experience of being up front in a war which seems endless; sooner or later, it is bound to be my turn. Death is no shared or communal experience; it is utterly individual. In those moments, one is quite alone in the middle of his comrades. No one talked, our faces were concealed in the dark; only now and then a face under the peak of a mountain cap would light up from the red glow of a cigarette.

American artillery had already claimed casualties in our ranks during the days before. In the afternoon, heavy artillery fire fell on our assembly area. It seemed as if our new enemy's resources in barrels and ammunition were without limit. From the day we disembarked from the train, the Americans kept hammering our supply and approach routes without surcease. On our march up to the front, we had seen the results: dead horses, destroyed carts, and a dead mule skinner spread-eagled in the middle of the road. Again and again, we sought shelter from bursting shells. We observed a gruesome sight when we walked a forest trail and passed a bunker: a Red Cross flag sticking out and a heap of dead bodies next to it, piled up like firewood. We'd get to know the special way of the Americans with their artillery even more cruelly during the months to come.

The Americans would not send their infantry forward until they had done their absolute utmost to destroy their enemies with awesome displays of artillery firepower, which often lasted for hours. This was a luxury which we, unfortunately, could not even hope for at this stage of the war.

Our SS Mountain Infantry Regiment 12 had been part of Operation *Nordwind* from its start on New Year's Eve. When we reached the area, the rumour was that the regiment had suffered heavy casualties in their first action at Wingen. There were wild stories of the regiment breaking through the American lines, of a great number of prisoners taken and of a deep penetration into Alsace—good news, good for our morale. The bad news, however, was that only a few days later they had had to withdraw because, somehow, the units on both flanks had lagged behind. Our sister regiment had lost too many dead, missing, and wounded. One of them had his testicles shot off, they said. It was hard to shake off all that misery as we gathered on that night in the assembly area for our first encounter with the *Amis,* as we referred to the Americans.

I had seen our new opponents only through my binoculars. On our first day in the line, we repelled a probe they had started, inflicting casualties on them. Their action hadn't ended yet when they sent their medics and an ambulance right onto the battlefield to rescue their wounded. I couldn't believe my eyes. What kind of a war was this? Nothing like that would have happened at the Eastern Front, but here, some of the rules of war seemed still to be in force, valid for both sides. In the background, I saw their officers racing around in their compact little cars—as if we were on manoeuvres! This first encounter seemed to support our general feeling that these Amis couldn't be regarded as mortal enemies.

Yet, our first real clash with them was to result in one of the great ordeals we were destined to go through.

"Goddamn!" Heinrich suddenly burst out. "Why are we standing around here the whole goddamned night doing nothing, getting soaked and stiff in the knees? Come on, let's put up a tent, keep the wet out, and try to get some sleep?"

Bing and Stricker went for some brushwood to lie on while Heinrich and I buttoned four triangular canvas sheets together. Others didn't bother that much and just pitched a square sheet for two. A little later, the four of us lay down in our tent, huddling together. The comfort we gained from it was imaginary rather than real. Shivering all over, I felt the sleet trickling down from the canvas upon the moss right beside my head.

I must have slept for quite a while because it was only at dawn that I noticed that the sleet had turned to snow. Outside the woods, the white-covered terrain shimmered through the tree trunks. We removed the tent, took up our gear, and put on our white-covered helmets, ready to go. We then hung around for hours. For some reason the attack was postponed until noon.

When our artillery preparatory fire began, we rushed out and swept in a skirmishing line down the slope that lay between us and the hills beyond. The resistance was feeble; the few advanced posts were soon eliminated or overrun. The *Amis'* main force was on the wooded slopes of the hills. As soon as we arrived at the foot of one hill, the American mortars and howitzers began firing. The rifle companies continued to advance uphill and disappeared into the wood where they now met stiff resistance. All over the steep terrain more and more duels of infantry weapons flared up. Our attack grew into a fierce, uphill fight.

My squad dug in at the foot of the hill, ready for action, while Heinrich's gun was already up there on the slope. The American artillery fire was precise and brutal; the shells bursting around us tore up the white cover of snow, leaving behind large craters of brown dirt. Our comrades in the rifle companies further up in the wood bore the brunt. During pauses in the artillery firing, we listened, trying to discern their progress. In the late afternoon, it seemed our men were stuck near the

Johann Voss (left) and some of his comrades prepare for alpine training outside their lodge, 1943. (Johann Voss)

hilltop. We wondered how long they could hold on up there under the continuous mortar and small arms fire from the American positions located on higher ground.

It was a relief when, finally, our artillery sent some rounds over to the enemy's positions on the hilltop; our *Nebelwerfer* joined in, their rounds whizzing overhead with a terrible hiss and rapid rate of fire. We were in a full-scale battle.

The weather worsened. The temperature fell below zero; a light blizzard slowly enveloped the battle in a muffled and weird atmosphere. Then it was our turn. We were assigned to another rifle company and climbed diagonally up the wooded hill. As it turned out, our destination was the enemy's rear. Their present front line was unknown, but it was evident that the mass of them had withdrawn towards the hilltops. So we sneaked round the combat noise while the battle raged on. It was impossible to make out whether our original assault was being continued or whether the Amis had started a counterattack and our *Jäger* were fighting it off. There was no doubt, however, that the enemy was determined to hold his ground.

Only by great luck were we spared becoming victims of our own manoeuvre, which was to encircle the American position on the hilltop. We were just around the hill, already stalking downward across a wide glade, when we were barely missed by one of our own *Nebelwerfer* rounds. Sent down flat into the snow by the horrible noise of the rockets, we lay there scared to death for a few seconds when the rapid sequence of rockets detonated in the glade no more than 30 meters from us.

Eventually, under cover of darkness and unnoticed by the enemy, we reached the rear of the American force—a reinforced infantry battalion as we learned later. My gun's position was on a steep forward slope, a clearing which fell down toward a trail on the bottom of a ravine leading up to a saddle between two hilltops, one of which we had passed. We emplaced our gun under a rocky outcropping and, without delay, started digging into the frozen ground.

At dawn, it stopped snowing and the temperature dropped further. For a short time, there was a lull all over the battleground. Surveying the terrain, it became evident to me that our slope was dominating what must be a vital supply route line to the American battalion on the hill. I searched the ravine with my binoculars. Down to the left was a small bridge; somewhere up along the trail, a detachment of our anti-tank gunners were said to be lying in ambush with *Panzerfausts,* but I could not see them. We, it seemed, were an inconspicuous part of the snow cover spread over the hillside overnight.

Suddenly, further up the saddle, we heard the engine of a vehicle coming down fast. A dark-green tracked vehicle came into our sight as it was rumbling down from the upper end of the ravine. A big gun stuck out from a turret. Bing opened fire right away. The tracer bullets whizzed home, but they didn't do too much harm to the tank's armor. A minute or two and the thing would be right in front of us, but this wasn't to be. Some distance further up, fate caught up with it. *Whamm!* A fireball! The tank stopped cold and jerked off the road. A *Panzerfaust,* fired from the whiteness, had knocked it out. The crew piled out and our men, emerging from the snow, captured them, and that was that. We, up on the slope, were jubilant for a moment. Never before had we 'Indians' seen a tank being destroyed. We also realized, however, how much we were exposed to more tanks once they managed to force their way up the ravine and were not intercepted by our anti-tank gunners in time.

It wasn't long before the Americans launched their first massive action to rescue their battalion on the hilltops. They started with an artillery barrage. It was the worst I ever endured. It lasted for at least an hour and a half. Shells rained upon us like hail in a thunderstorm. There must have been tens of thousands of shells scattered over our regiment's positions. How on earth could the Americans mass such artillery in such a small sector? On our slope, we were to some extent protected by the rocks above our position, but the fire was so dense that we thought it unlikely that we would come out of there alive.

I don't know what was going on elsewhere; I only witnessed what happened within my sight. When the barrage ended, the Americans moved two anti-tank guns in. One of them appeared down at the bend of the trail, took up position, and started blasting away, apparently unharmed by our small arms fire farther down. Eventually, under the cover of gun fire, the first American infantrymen came forward round the bend, leapfrogging between the trees along the trail. We opened fire on them at a fairly great distance, more or less at random, but they forged ahead until they came under our more precise fire and were stopped not far from the bridge. There they disappeared in a hollow, seeking shelter from the fire.

After the shelling, a messenger arrived to learn about the situation. It seemed all our men on the slope had remained unhurt, certainly because we formed only a thin skirmish line, widely spread over the terrain, and because we knew how to take advantage of the cover available in a woodland like this. The messenger told us the casualties among the rifle companies were heavy, and Schaper had fallen, he said, up there at the hilltop, a direct hit, tearing him to pieces. It was only later that I felt the loss of an NCO to whom I had grown close. His good-natured features and his rolling gait as he trudged through our position at the Kiestinki front had been one of the human aspects which made me feel at home with our battalion.

Down the ravine, the American guns kept firing, and more of their infantry came forward. If this assault didn't stop, our thin circle would break and the ravine would be open for the rescue of the American battalion. Finally, some rounds of our *Nebelwerfer* came hissing and screaming right over our heads. The first clearly missed its target, the second and third must have totally knocked out the two guns and their crews. The attack collapsed soon thereafter, at least as far as we could see. The forward American squad remained invisible somewhere near the bridge, afraid to come out into the open, trapped in their shelter. We figured they had some wounded among them.

Behind us the battle raged on. The worst area was on the summit of the hill, where, according to a messenger, the now-encircled American battalion was being pressed back into an ever-smaller perimeter. It was obvious they were desperate to find an exit, supported by their howitzers somewhere outside which did not stop firing round after round on our positions in a fierce attempt to crush the besiegers. Listening to the continuous bursting of shells up there, I thought of Heinrich being in the midst of it. We dared not imagine the casualties among our comrades. We never had experienced such massive shelling in the North.

Sometime later on, the inferno burned out and silence descended on this tormented piece of earth. It seemed, and we direly hoped, that we had held the ground around the hills. With the tension easing off, we began to feel our exhaustion. The total lack of food, of sleep, and of protection from the cold for the last thirty hours was written all over our faces. What brought back some life into our worn-out limbs during those lulls—aside from the hope that this matter would soon be over—were the cigarettes which lasted far longer than our food. Nonetheless, there were still duties; we had to keep an eye on the trapped squad down by the bridge and, whether we liked it or not, we had to improve, deepen, and camouflage our foxholes, and fortify our gun emplacement with rocks and timber. Somehow, though, we managed brief moments of relaxation, ordinarily remaining upright in our foxholes and dropping off into a ten-second sleep.

In the afternoon, the Americans made another attempt to get through to the hilltop. It was only a matter of half an hour, but the attack told us something about our new opponents. This time, we saw them dashing up the road with two tanks, their roaring engines announcing their approach long before they appeared round the bend. The gunner of the lead tank continuously banged away with his machine gun. We had expected something like that. If they could pass the bridge unharmed, we, up on the bare slope, only had a slim chance in a duel with them. Our bullets would only scratch their armour while, in turn, they would have us at point-blank range as soon as we started firing.

The trail, however, was steep, especially downward towards the bridge, and the ground was frozen. So, as they rumbled up to the bridge the first tank spun on the ground, slid sideways and offered her right flank to our men in ambush by the bridge. The next moment, the tank was hit. Smoke poured out. The turret opened and the crew climbed out, obviously wounded, and sought cover behind the second tank. The second tank was blocked by the lead tank, and so, in turn, were our men with their *Panzerfausts*. There was a brief moment of hesitation on both sides. Then, suddenly, the turret of the second tank opened and out jumped a single man. Watching through my binoculars, I thought him to be an officer. Ignoring the danger he was exposing himself to, he hurried over to the hollow where the infantry squad was trapped, helped some wounded men to reach the tank and loaded them on the deck, one after the other. Stunned, we followed this extraordinary rescue action without firing a single shot. The officer jumped back into the tank, spun around on his tracks, and dashed back to the rear. Those of us witnessing the scene, whether nearby or more distant, instinctively felt there was no honour to be won by firing upon this death-defying act of comradeship.

At nightfall, we still were without provisions. Hunger isn't good for morale. There was a growing grumbling among my men. Stricker pointed his chin to the trail below. "What's on your mind," I asked, being sure I was reading his thoughts.

"I think I'll have a closer look at that tank down there," he said.

"Alright, go ahead. I'll give you half an hour. Make sure you don't get shot at by our own people." Cautiously, he made his way down the hill toward the tank that had come down the day before.

He was back in time and brought a few C-Rations, cookies, and cigarettes; the first provisions we appropriated from the enemy.

My memory of the next two days is blurred, probably the result of the continuing frost, hunger, lack of sleep, and the nagging doubt all of us had about coming out of there alive. Nature, or rather the weather conditions, as well as our physical and mental state, became our primary enemy during the rest of our time on the slope. The weather worsened and the battle raged on. The Americans didn't attempt another breakthrough at our ravine, but again and again, there were nerve-racking exchanges of small-arms fire in our neighbourhood, indicating assaults from inside and outside the perimeter. Meanwhile, the American artillery continued firing on our positions around the hill as, in turn, our howitzers kept shelling the summit. Snow had started to fall again, and when the wind sprang up, it turned into a blizzard that swept in gusts over the snow-bound hills. I see myself standing in the foxhole next to our emplacement—in the bottom, frozen water around my feet as I wake up with a start from a short spell of abysmal sleep—and I see Bing's and Stricker's profiles next to me, hard and grim under the rim of their helmets, their hoods on top and their anoraks covered with snow.

I'll never forget my own secret thoughts during the nights. They were about dying and surviving, promises that if I ever got out of there I would never in my life complain about anything on earth as long as there was shelter and warmth and a regular meal. I thought of becoming a farmer, which seemed to guarantee such vital needs—something which never before had entered my mind.

The American battalion gave up on the fifth day after our regiment's attack had begun. That morning, they had made a last attempt to break through, only to suffer more casualties. On that day, efforts from outside had already ceased. They surrendered in the late afternoon at the request of our regimental commander and our battalion commander, who had led the fighting around the hilltop. Their losses were terrible. Of the original five companies, only about 450 went into captivity, most of them casualties. They left their positions toward our rear echelon so that, much to our regret, we had no opportunity to have a look at our gallant opponents; I am sure, though, that our comrades behind the hill were forming something of a guard of honour watching the captured GIs passing through their lines. Their officers, some twenty-five of them, were received with all honours at our regimental headquarters. Rumour had it that all of the men were handed a box of *Schoka-Kola* each, a fine gesture by our commander, although I heard some grumbling that there weren't any boxes left for us.

At daylight, we had a closer look at each other. We couldn't help laughing at the five-day-old beards on our pale, emaciated faces. For me, it was a mild shock to see my comrades' utter exhaustion. How long, I asked myself, could this go on? To return, we took the shortcut over the hilltop. We walked across the centre of the stage, and saw the bodies still lying about in the devastated woodland, most of them separately, some already laid in rows by their comrades; they made peculiar bundles, easily recognized even under the snow.

Battalion headquarters was just around the last bend on the road north. We passed our mule station set up in a small stand of spruce. As we trudged by, the mule skinners watched us as if we had just risen from the dead. In the rear, they said our own casualties were lower than the enemy's, but they were still heavy. Much to my relief, I found Heinrich safe and sound. His number two gunner had fallen, though, shot in the neck when they brought an American attack to a stop thirty metres from their holes, the bullet ripping up the gunner's carotid artery and killing him instantly. One of his South Tyroleans had also been killed. Moreover, I learned that another platoon leader of the 12th Company had also been killed. Later in the day, I had our medic take a look at my feet; he said I had two frostbitten toes; I was lucky.

The regiment had pushed the door wide open. The Americans were in retreat.

The very next day, we began our pursuit south, which meant stalking in skirmish lines through the hilly woodland and mopping up the area. For us, it was quite a new experience. The region had not been evacuated and we were bringing the war back to the people living there in their bleak settlements. They closed their window shutters at our approach, their faces speaking volumes. Certainly, we weren't welcome here.

In a small hamlet on our way, we met some resistance from American troops, but it was quickly broken. We found their remnants, signs of abundance as it seemed to us: cigarettes and candies. It was then that my squad picked up an American heavy machine gun, complete with tripod, cart, and ammunition. We reckoned that sooner or later the enemy would start a massive counterattack, and that we would need all the fire power we could get. So we took the 'extra' equipment. Stricker was 'promoted' to this gun's number two gunner.

We reached the village at the foot of the hillside by nightfall. Our advance platoon discovered that the *Amis* hadn't yet withdrawn; at least they had left a rear party there. It was a short fight. Bypassing the village lying in a deep valley, we blocked their withdrawal, seized the place, and picked up the rear party together with their equipment. There were short bursts of submachine guns from our men swarming in from all sides, vehicles with roaring engines stopped in their wild flight. No casualties on either side were reported. Loot was seized, PX goods and lots and lots of oranges—luxuries we hadn't enjoyed for years. All that greatly contributed to our rising spirits.

Mopping up the village took us another hour or so, then all was quiet again. The American main force showed no inclination to come to their comrades' help, although they couldn't have failed to notice what had happened.

We moved our gun into an emplacement south of the village, right beside our anti-tank gunners. Bing was at the gun. I noticed he had become taciturn. I knew he was Alsatian and that somewhere on the plain extending in front of us was his home.

"You must feel funny, coming home under these circumstances. Where is your home town, anyway?" I asked.

"About twenty-five kilometres from here, half the distance to Strasbourg. It's a small village," he replied quietly.

I tried to cheer him up. "Just the right distance for a bicycle ride on a Sunday afternoon."

He remained silent.

"Maybe, on a clear day, you could see it from these hills?" I prompted.

"Yeah, I guess so," he said curtly.

I saw I had missed the right tone, and I felt my own ignorance about Alsace. I knew it was borderland, taken from us under the Versailles Treaty, and in dispute between France and Germany for hundreds of years. I tried again, "It's still French territory, Alsace, isn't it?"

"That's correct."

"Is your family entirely German or Franco-Allemand?" I asked.

"We're German all right; my mother tongue is German" he confirmed.

"But you speak French fluently, don't you?"

Bing responded, exasperatedly, "You know I do."

I remembered him singing a French song in our bunker east of Kiestinki, with Bäumler accompanying him on his harmonica, something he only descended to on our firm request and when he was drunk:

Pour qu'je finisse mon service	*To put an end to my service*
au Tonquin je suis parti,	*I departed for Tonquin,*
à quel beau pays, mes dames,	*for the beautiful country, my ladies*
quel paradis des petite femmes.	*what a paradise of little women.*
Elles sont belles et fidèles,	*They are beautiful and faithful,*
et je suis d'venu un mari	*and I became the husband*
d'une petite femme du pays,	*of a little women of the land*
qui s'appelle Mélaolie.	*called Mélaolie.*
(Refrain)	
Je suis gobé d'une petite,	*I'm husband of a little woman,*
c'est une Ana-, c'est une Ana-	*she is an Annamite.*
une Anamite	
Elle est vif, elle est charmante . . .	*She is vital, she is charming.*

I had always wondered where he had picked up that song; it was a serviceman's song, after all. After a pause he continued, "At any rate, I didn't join the *Waffen-SS* to prove I'm a German, if that is what you mean."

"No, not at all, don't get me wrong," I protested. "It's just that I'm trying to put myself in your position, fighting to win back your homeland, which actually has remained foreign."

"Foreign or not foreign—I don't think borderlines are that important. I once thought it was about Europe against Bolshevism. Then it went all wrong. Now I find myself in a kind of civil war. It's more and more confusing and drives me crazy!" he confessed, frustrated.

Surprised, I blurted, "Now, come on. Civil war! We're fighting the Americans, aren't we?"

"From my view it's not that much different. Besides, do you know who are our opponents down at Colmar?" he asked, expectantly.

"No, I don't," I confessed.

"I learned it only recently: French troops under the command of General Leclerc."

"So what?" I said, still mystified. "They aren't more than *'une quantité négligeable.'* Nothing to be afraid of."

He didn't reply for a while. When I glanced at him, he was looking over the sight of his gun, his chin resting on the butt, a far-away look in his eyes.

"I thought you knew," he said eventually. "If they got me alive, I would be shot right away for defection."

The issue was never pressed. Bing was killed two months later. He was only one of the European volunteers, the ones who set out to fight Bolshevism and in the end became victims of their idealism, either on the battlefield or in the chauvinistic pitfalls of inter-European borders. I cannot believe that their idealism is dead, their vision of some greater zone where the common interest will prevail and where borders, as Bing said, are not that important anymore.

As with the Wacht am Rhein, *the early successes of* Nordwind *could not be sustained; the German forces were unable to exploit their initial gains, and the operation was officially called to a halt after a few weeks. On 16 January, Allied counterattacks finally erased the Ardennes salient, pushing the Germans back to the line they had held in early December. On 20 January, the French 1st Army attacked the German units remaining in Alsace. The Germans retreated to the east bank of the Rhine, once again sustaining heavy casualties. As a whole German losses in this period actions were devastating; estimates suggest that casualties in the Ardennes offensive alone exceeded 100,000. The Germans had also used up a large quantity of arms and munitions in these operations, resources which were irreplaceable at this late stage in the war. These heavy losses of men and materiél guaranteed that the German army would not be able to muster any further military operations on this scale for the remainder of the war in the West.*

Part VI

Eastern Front

The Soviet drive through Europe (January-March 1945)

Part VI

Eastern Front

The Soviet drive through Europe (January-March 1945)

By the start of 1945 all soldiers on the Eastern Front knew that events of the past few months – even in Hungary – had been little more than a prelude to the great Soviet offensive that would be imminently unleashed on the very heart of the *Reich*, an effort known to history as the Vistula-Oder Operation.

Unfortunately for the German military and civilian population this was a view not shared by their supreme leader, as Hitler confidently asserted that the Red Army's build-up in the central sector of the front was "the greatest bluff since Genghis Khan". Once again, tactical flexibility was thrown out of the window as Hitler refused to countenance giving up any territory, or to transfer some of the hundreds of thousands of troops in Norway, North-West Europe or cut off in Kurland to the East.

The *Stavka* planned a vast effort in the centre, aiming to end the war in about 45 days by a series of hammer blows involving 1st, 2nd and 3rd Byelorussian and 1st Ukrainian Fronts, supported by 4th Ukrainian Front. The keys to victory were the three principal bridgeheads over the Vistula held by the Red Army, at Pulawy, Magnuszew and Baranow, out of which a great mass of men and material were to erupt when the offensive was launched. In the Magnuszew bridgehead alone the Soviets had crammed 400,000 men, 1,700 tanks and a mind-numbing 8,700 guns, heavy mortars and rocket launchers supplied with 2½ million shells – more than 2.5 times the total Soviet artillery expenditure at Stalingrad. The artillery was arrayed wheel-to-wheel at a density of more than 300 guns per kilometre. Armoured units were to maintain as rapid a tempo of forward movement as was logistically possible.

The storm broke forth in the early hours of 12 January when 1st Ukrainian Front opened the offensive. All the efforts of senior German commanders to wrest some degree of tactical initiative for themselves came to naught in the face of Hitler's intransigence and the sheer power of the Soviet effort. Two days later 1st Byelorussian Front joined in, followed soon after by the other Soviet Fronts involved in the offensives. Within a matter of days the German frontlines had been utterly shattered, and the troops were in full retreat, verging on panic in places. Amidst blinding snowstorms the Red Army's armoured forces set a cracking pace, such that by 3 February the Soviets were on the line of the Oder river, in some places only 35 miles from Berlin.

During February the tempo of the Soviet advance slowed. In the north the Red Army fought its way through East Prussia, slowly and meeting dogged resistance, the German defenders aided by many natural obstacles. By the end of the month, the *Stavka* could be pleased with its forces' progress – huge gains had been made,

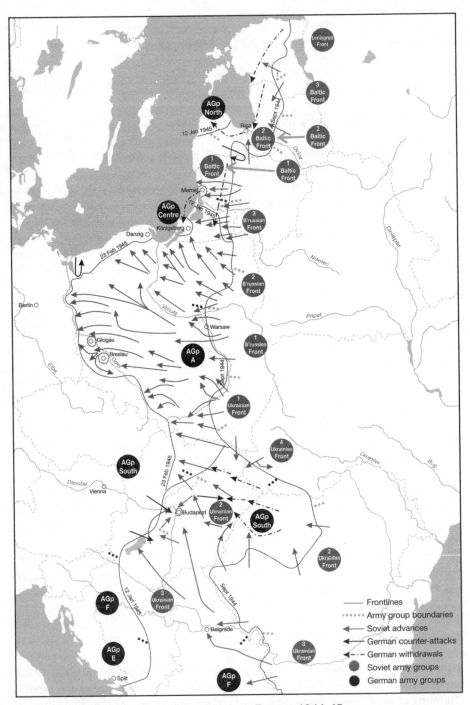

Map 6   Eastern Front: Soviet drive through Europe 1944-45

and after much bloody fighting only isolated pockets of resistance remained in East Prussia, West Prussia and Silesia.

Further to the south, the fighting for Budapest had raged fiercely. The Soviets had temporarily halted their offensive on 28 December. Before it could be resumed the Germans launched a major effort aimed at relieving the city. Amidst desperate fighting conducted by some of the most élite *Panzer* formations the counter-attack came close to succeeding. However, displaying their habitual prowess at cobbling together desperate defence themselves when required, the Red Army held tenaciously onto their positions around the city. By early February German efforts had been halted for good. The fighting within Budapest raged unabated until 13 February. The garrison attempted a breakout, but of the 30,000 men who began it, less than 700 reached German lines.

During March the Soviets continued their efforts to clean-up those parts of East and West Prussia, Silesia and Pomerania remaining in German hands. Amidst much hard fighting, they succeeded except for a few exceptions, notably Breslau (Lower Silesia) and Königsberg (East Prussia). In the centre of the Eastern Front efforts intensified to develop bridgeheads over the Oder in preparation for the final battle for the very heart of the *Reich*. In particular, severe fighting took place for Küstrin, directly east of Berlin.

Hitler was reluctant to concede complete defeat in Hungary, and on 5 March the last major German offensive of World War II was launched – Operation *Frühlingserwachen* or 'Spring Awakening', aimed at recapturing Budapest. With a spring thaw making the ground very heavy going for armoured forces, the attack stalled after promising gains had initially been made. With perfect timing the Soviets launched an immediate counter-attack, throwing back the German and Hungarian forces they encountered, and clearing virtually all of western Hungary by the end of the month.

Thus by the end of March the Eastern Front had again reached another critical stage. Having cleared much of the eastern territories of the *Reich*, the Soviets now prepared to launch their final offensive on Berlin itself.

The thoughts going through Armin Scheiderbauer's mind in the build-up to the Soviet onslaught that was the Vistula-Oder Offensive must be representative of hundreds of thousands of his comrades. Certainly, a fatalism took hold of many men during those final months of the war. His account is certainly remarkable – he had already come through Operation Bagration and lived to tell the tale. To be able to tell of being caught in the very maelstrom of the opening of the Soviet Vistula offensive and come through to the other side makes him a fortunate man indeed.

In the dark New Year's night my thoughts raced ahead into the New Year and what it might bring. The *Reich* was gripped by its enemies on its Eastern and Western borders. In East Prussia the Soviets had touched the soil of the *Reich* and committed unimaginable atrocities. During my leave, almost daily, hundreds of American bombers had flown over our small town, down the Danube, towards Vienna. Standing at the doors of their houses, many inhabitants had watched the great aircraft taking their course, unopposed, with imposing equanimity.

There was some compensation in the fact that I was back with the '7th'. I looked up Klaus Nicolai. We had a quick welcome nip and went to the bunker of the regimental commander. *Oberst* Dorn, the *Grand Seigneur* from the Rhineland, welcomed me to the regiment and informed me that I was to get the 1st Company. The company was at the moment in reserve in the so-called second trench of the extended trench system. The next day it would move back into the frontline. At the 1st Battalion, *Hauptmann* Fitz and *Oberleutnant* Küllenberg, the *Hauptmann* and the Adjutant, welcomed me with a loud 'hello'. I knew them from the previous summer. Then a runner took me forward and at the Company I was welcomed by *Leutnant* Martin Lechner who was to take over command of the battalion's heavy weapons company.

I had become friends with Lechner in spring 1944 in Schweidnitz. At that time he had come from the war school to which he had been sent as an active *Unteroffizier* with above average potential. He had good manners and you could not see the '12-Ender' in him, even if at the Ersatz battalion he had not had any comrades. I had put myself out a bit for him for which, I noticed, he had been grateful. But we celebrated our reunion with the appropriate drop of the hard stuff. Before that of course we had done another tour of the bunker. I had to see and greet the men. They should get a look at their new 'boss' straight away. After that we sturdily went on to have a few jars, because that was still the best tried-and-tested way of getting things off to a good start. Finally Lechner got up and made a speech on the theme that the 1st Company must be the 'first' not only in name but also in achievement, something it was now and also must remain in the future. Not quite so awkwardly and seriously as Lechner, I also said a few words to him and to the men of the company. I stressed my pride at now being commander of the 1st Company of our old regiment, and that was the truth.

The next night we moved into position in the *Nase*, or salient, at Poweilin. It was extremely unfavourable, because the main line of resistance ran at a right angle, one arm pointed in a westerly and the other arm in a southerly direction. The Soviets could come from two sides, in the intersection of the angle enemy fire was possible from three sides. Our neighbour on the right was the 2nd Company, on the left was the Divisional *Füsilierbataillon*. Only a hundred metres of the trench had been dug out to knee depth, so that during the daytime you could only move through it by crawling.

Because of the way the trenches ran in the entire *Nase*, the men of the company regarded themselves, in the event of the expected large-scale enemy offensive, as 'written off'. With almost complete certainty, those in the *Nase* could expect to be overrun or cut off. As far as anyone could see, there was no way of escape. Fire could come from three sides, attacks from two sides, and to the rear in front of the second line were our own minefields only passable in narrow channels. Whoever survived the heavy barrage before the attack had to face the attack itself. Scarcely anybody would be able to survive that. Because of the minefields and the completely open, gently rising terrain, to retreat did not offer the slightest prospect of getting through in one piece. Thoughts like this I had to keep to myself, and particularly the thought that, if the worst came to the worst, I had only my own pistol to keep me out of the Soviet captivity that I viewed with such fear and horror.

During those days, or rather nights, I was continually moving around the trench from post to post and bunker to bunker, in order to get to know every one of the men under my charge. Many knew me by sight, many by name. Actions like Upolosy, Nemers and Raseinen and many others, bound us together. Also I spoke the language of the Silesians, who still formed the majority of the regiment. I was able to converse with them in their local dialect, so that none of them felt that I was a stranger. Soon after I joined the regiment I had learned to speak Lower Silesian and Upper Silesian. Once, on an exercise march in the vicinity of the garrison, an old dear had said to me that I was certainly a Schweidnitzer. Telling her that I was not, I had laughed at her, and she had got angry.

My company troop leader was the young Berlin *Unteroffizier* Ulrich Lamprecht. He was a student of Protestant theology with the Iron Cross First Class on his narrow chest. Every day he read the book of proverbs of the Herrenhut Brethren. In the days that remained until the offensive, I read the proverbs with him and also the corresponding references from the New Testament, which I had in my pack. Among the runners Walter Buck stood out, He was a thirty-five year old businessman from Hamburg. He matched the type of the intelligent soldier, who has long since passed normal military age, and who lacked the ambition of youth. He was reliable and did his duty well, as did the other runner Reinalter, a farmer from Swabia.

The company command post lay on slightly rising ground, in the middle of the bridge of the *Nase*. The linking stretch leading to the main trench could be seen by the enemy, during the daytime. Therefore, if at all possible, we had to remain in the bunker.

On 9 January I received orders to prepare an assault unit to bring in prisoners. It was to be led by me because I was the most experienced of the company commanders. The order, and above all the fact that I was to lead the assault unit, did not comfort me at all. I still did not feel myself to be sufficiently familiar with the terrain. I would also be responsible for the operation. There were others who had not yet had the opportunity to win a decoration. I spoke about it openly with Martin Lechner, who agreed with me entirely. But the assault unit was called off, on 12 January, after it had been announced that the Soviets had begun their large-scale offensive. With 3,000 tanks they moved up from the Vistula bridgeheads of Baranov and Warka.

Those were the omens as I faced my 21st birthday the next day. I celebrated it, therefore, on the evening of the 12th in the expectation that from 12 midnight on the 13th a special feeling of 'consecration' would set in, befitting the significance of the fact that I had attained my 'coming-of-age' as a citizen.

On 13 January the enemy's major offensive in East Prussia began. It was still quiet where we were. There was harassing fire of varying strength and noise, and from time to time snatches of songs from the enemy trenches. With the field kitchen came 'best wishes' and the usual bottles as presents. The General, the Divisional Adjutant, the commander and the commanders of the Artillery regiment whom I knew, *Oberst* Dorn and the battalion commanders all sent their congratulations. I was touched by the expressions in them of the respect and esteem in which my achievements were held. In the light of what faced us, the wishes were of particular warmth and sincerity. Unfortunately, the mail that I used to send them all home was lost. Unexpressed, but certainly honourably meant, was the wish that *Leutnant* Roberts had expressed to me in the summer in Raseinen. When we were saying goodbye to each other, as we were changing positions, he squeezed my hand and, smiling sadly, no doubt with the premonition that he was to die soon, said 'stay alive'. He had been killed in action in October on the Narev.

At 6pm the company commanders received their orders at the Battalion. Since *Hauptmann* Fitz had left in the night after he had been wounded, *Oberleutnant* Husénett, wearing the Knight's Cross, had taken over command of the battalion. I had gone off with the runner, Buck, and the dog. At the battalion command post we had learned more about the serious situation in the Vistula bridgeheads and in East Prussia. There was no longer any doubt about the fate that awaited us.

On the way back, I went with the runner into the completely destroyed village church of Powielin. It had been a quite simple little old wooden church, but the tower had been shot off during the recent fighting. One single token remained to remind you of its religious purpose, namely a large cross on the side of the altar. 'Thy will be done', I could have no better prayer. When I got back to the company I strode once again from bunker to bunker, and went from post to post, to give everyone one more word of confidence.

On the morning of 14 January, as we had since the morning of the 12th, we were expecting from hour to hour the beginning of the heavy barrage. According to the custom of the Soviets recently, the thunderclap was to be expected on the hour, i.e. at 6am, 7am or 8am. After we had been spared the unavoidable event on the 12th and the 13th, the beginning had to be today, because the long-observed preparations of the enemy allowed for no other possibility. They would have to get as far as possible in daylight after the effect of their devastating fire. It would last several hours and would land on our positions. Their attack would necessarily have to be as early as possible. Thus the preparatory fire would also have to begin very early in the morning.

I was with the men of my company in the bunker. We were lying or sitting on bunkers or at small tables, weapons and steel helmets ready to hand. An all-consuming nervousness, that no one let show, dominated us. A cold feeling crept over me, that trembling in the stomach that used to affect me in school before exams. But when at 7am the fire did not erupt, I hoped that the Soviets would today be sparing us once again. The feeling was reinforced because even on the dot of 8am, by my service watch, nothing happened.

But just as I was about to say what I was thinking, there began the dreadful crashing, the familiar noise of 'Stalin organs' firing. Several of them must have been firing in sequence, because the crashing went on for what seemed an eternity. Only within the detonations of the organ shells did the barking reports of cannons and those of howitzers, mortars, and the *Ratschbum* sound out. The earth was literally shaking and the air was thudding. An uninterrupted grumbling thunder descended upon the German lines. Obviously the enemy were trying to destroy the minefields of our trench system, extended fourfold, and to flatten trenches and shatter bunkers.

The only things dangerous to us in the company bunker were the shells dropping very close by, of which there were not a few. The whistling, rushing and crashing of shells round about indeed almost drugged the senses. But we were lucky and along the whole 'bridge of the nose' we only received a few direct hits in the trench and none on the bunker. I got the impression that the Soviets were sparing the *Nase*. Even the advanced observers of the artillery and our heavy weapons company beside my command post remained untouched.

After exactly two hours the bombardment suddenly broke off. A paralysing calm fell over the front. It meant that the Soviets were moving their fire forward, in order not to endanger their attacking infantry. *Raus*, I ordered, and that meant going into position in the small trench system around the company command post. All nervousness had fallen away from me. The patient waiting in the bunker was at an end, we could see and deal with the enemy. Outside there was fog, but it was the powder smoke from the massive amount of exploded shells that had dropped on our positions. I thought that I could not believe my eyes when on the right I saw that the second company had already retreated a long way. I then saw the enemy rapidly advancing in battalion strength on to the second trench. The Soviets went round my company and cut us off. But from the left, charging at the company command post, there came the left wing of a confused brown wave, approaching unstoppably with cries of *Urrah*.

But the most shattering thing about the picture was the fact that individual German soldiers were running away in front of the assaulting Red Army troops. They were wobbling with exhaustion, without weapons and equipment, plainly at the end of their strength. But we had to fire, even at the risk of our comrades thinking that we were firing at them. So I carefully took aim at the Soviets storming up behind them. They had in the meantime approached to within 100 metres of us. In the feeling of desperation that there was no way that we could escape from that dire position, other than dead or as prisoners, an uncanny calm came over me.

As I had learned as a recruit in our much vilified drill, I took aim and fired, disappeared behind the parapet after firing, then quick as a flash popped up again a little to one side and got the next enemy in the sights of my *Sturmgewehr*. I succeeded in hitting enemy officers and machine-gunners. They were clearly recognisable, especially the officers, by the arm movements with which they accompanied their already audible orders. Thus, as one after the other fell, hit by my bullets, I was seized by a triumphant savage pleasure and by the hope of escaping once more. I watched one of the men I shot, stepping on persistently with his head lowered. Then, he was hit by my bullet. Slowly he struck his chest with his hand and finally fell forward. That picture will never leave me as long as I live.

The miracle happened. The targeted fire from my rifle, and those of the runners, brought the attack to a standstill. The Red Army troops went to ground. Then, pursued by our bullets, they drew back far to the rear and sought to connect up again to the forces on their right. We had lost our connections both to the right and to the left because the Soviets had already pushed forward a long way, Meanwhile, my platoons had left the trench. They gathered in a line, one man behind another, in the secondary trench leading to the command post. I gave orders immediately to go back into position. There was no more immediate danger just then, for the very reason that the enemy was not at all concerned about us. However, the longer-term situation seemed hopeless. Sooner or later we would certainly fall into enemy hands.

I was still considering how we could get out of that wretched situation when, on the right from the sector of the 3rd Battalion infantry fire could be heard. It could mean nothing other than that our battalion had held its position. It must therefore be possible to connect up to the 3rd Battalion via the abandoned sector of the 2nd Company. There was no longer any wireless contact with our own battalion. Even the advanced observers had evidently been able to withdraw in time. So I had to make the decision to remain in the position or to connect up on the right to the 3rd Battalion.

I decided on the latter course because it seemed to me to be unlikely that the position could be held. It could also be assumed that orders would be given during the night to evacuate the main line of resistance, insofar as it was still occupied by our people. In the light of that it seemed unimportant from which point the company should begin its withdrawal. Since the waves of the enemy had rolled past us on the right and on the left, I gave orders to withdraw along the main trench to the right towards the 3rd Battalion. The *Oberfähnrich* took the lead and I myself remained at the rear. Like the captain of a sinking ship, I was the last to leave my company sector.

An enemy reserve company spotted our withdrawal, changed its direction and made moves to attack us. A particularly dashing group was storming up at a run outside the trenches while my company was withdrawing hurriedly along the trench to the right. To make the withdrawal easier, I formed a rearguard with a machine-gun and the two runners. With care I picked out again the nearest of the attackers. When they felt our resistance, they left off their pursuit. It was doubtless not part of their immediate task. Eventually there only remained a short length of trench to overcome, in which there were Soviets. We managed it with a few shouts and a short *Huura!* It was easy because for the most part they were wounded and the group had no leader. We even took prisoner some slightly wounded troops and chased others away. Those who were seriously wounded we left alone. Soon we had connected up with the 3rd Battalion. The men took a breath, and I went to the battalion command post. The commander, *Hauptmann* Dolansky, greeted me with words of recognition for our achievement. He immediately reported our arrival to the Regiment through the still intact telephone line. All that remained of my strength deserted me and I could almost have fallen asleep. I really had to 'pull myself together' so as not to give in to exhaustion.

Towards dusk a captive Soviet captain was brought into the bunker. An active officer, about 25 years old, he said he had never been in action before. He had only arrived a few days previously with an entire division from Siberia. Through this and other information we slowly formed a proper idea of the inexhaustible reserves of the enemy.

The third line of trenches, to which we had had to withdraw during the night, ran along the back of a slope. In front of us was some woodland. On the right of it about 600 metres away there was a single farmhouse surrounded by fruit trees. As we could see from their movements, the Soviets had already reached the edge of the woodland. Our trench was continuous and well constructed and excellently camouflaged with snow. We ourselves, as we moved into it from the edge of the woodland, had only noticed it when it was a few metres away.

We must have only settled down in it for an hour, when out of the woodland came two Soviets who briskly and unconcernedly walked towards our trench. They had machine-pistols slung around their necks and were walking comfortably side by side almost as if they were whistling a little song. They came to within 200 metres, to within 100 metres and even nearer, without having noticed our trench in front of them. I quietly gave the order to let them approach and to take them prisoner. Fifty metres away from us they slowed their steps. Twenty German voices shouted *Stoi!* Whereupon they turned round and ran back, weaving as they went. In the hail of bullets they collapsed. I had not anticipated that. They must have been riddled with bullets.

Some time after that period of cruelty and bitterness there was movement at the farm. As a result of it the enemy artillery opened up and obediently dropped shells on us. I scanned the farm with my binoculars and discovered the advanced observers. There were two men with wireless sets, whose heads, shoulders and equipment could be seen behind low cover. I asked to be handed a rifle with a tele-scopic sight and for a runner to observe through the binoculars. Then I pushed my-self carefully over the parapet of the trench and calmly took aim. There was a soft pressure as I fired. The observer's head sank on to the cover and that of the second man disappeared. My runner saw through the binoculars the dead man being dragged back into cover. An hour later came the order to evacuate the position. In the meantime another Soviet artillery observer had taken over directing the fire, which unfortunately was so accurate that we had some casualties.

A position as well constructed as the fourth line, in which we spent the night of 17 January, I had never seen. The bunkers were as much as three metres below ground level. The trench had been dug out to the height of a man. It was provided with secondary trenches, and in places with rails. The rifle positions and machine-gun nests were tactically in the correct places. It could not have been better in the trench warfare of the First World War. So this was the so-called *Gauleiterstellung*, which led over 1,000 kilometres along the eastern border of the *Reich*. It had been built in autumn 1944 by women and girls who were either volunteers or on war ser-vice, under the direction of officers who had been injured in the war. On the Oder, even Gisela had participated with pickaxe and shovel in that massive project.

From my perspective in the trenches, the position, apart from some buildings that should have been blown up, was an ideal one in which to spend the winter. Not a spadeful more could be dug out of the frozen ground. The Powielin position, with its trenches in places only knee deep, bore no comparison to this one. But I had no feeling of confidence. Even though I had no overview of the wider situa-tion, I did not reckon on staying there long.

My feeling had not deceived me. After sleeping for a few hours in deep exhaus-tion I had woken up. At dawn I emerged from the bunker. The houses in front of the position, 50 metres away, made me nervous. As it came light, movement could be seen. It turned out that there were some individual Soviets in the houses and that more were moving in. In ones and twos they came running over the bridge which led over a stream on the other side of the farmyard. I had the machine-gun spray the bridge, whereupon in the background a movement to the left, along the stream, could be seen. After quite a long time, individual rifle fire sounded from the neighbouring sector to our left. The direction of it moved more and more obliquely to the rear in our direction of retreat. While it was gradually becoming light, the enemy were also advancing on the right about one kilometre away. We were threatened with encirclement. Our neighbours on both sides crumbled. They left their trenches and withdrew, widely separated.

The battalion commander, *Hauptmann* Wild, could not decide to evacuate that magnificent position without orders. There was neither telephone nor wireless connection to our Regiment. In view of the threatened encirclement it seemed crazy to stay in the position. Behind it stretched several kilometres of open plain, offering no kind of protection. To withdraw across it in daylight would involve heavy casualties. No runner came from the Regiment who might have brought the order we were waiting for. The pale day brightened and the rifle fire behind us to the left became more concentrated.

Hauptmann Wild waited and brooded. To surrender the position without the enemy attacking was a decision with far-reaching consequences. Even apart from the possibility of court martial proceedings, the order to evacuate meant giving up trenches and bunkers of such good quality as we had never had before. Even if the enemy had dug in on the other slope of the bank only 100 or 150 metres away, this would still not have been any 'close-quarters corner' such as we had in October in the Budy-Obrebski position. At the company commanders' meeting I pressed for the order to withdraw to be given. I pointed out that otherwise, if there were any further delay, the battalion of nearly 150 men would be lost. *Hauptmann* Wild came to his decision. We climbed out of the trenches and moved off over the wide, snow-covered field.

While the battalion was retreating in open order, suddenly bursts of fire from machine-guns and machine-pistols hit the right flank. There were Soviets in a small trench system, not 30 metres away from me. Men hit by the bullets were collapsing all around. One cried out that we should take him with us. Who could have done that? Everybody was running, and in long jumping strides I ran along with them. Then suddenly there was a blow against my head. As I was running, I was spun round. I fell, and pulled myself together again. My head was thumping, but I felt that I was not wounded. Stumbling, I ran on, zig-zagging across the expanse when there was no cover.

After some 100 metres the commanders were able to bring their units under control and to change the running flight into an orderly retreat. At the end of the fields lay the next settlement. A machine-pistol barked out from there and a voice, going haywire, was shouting out. Both weapon and voice belonged to *Oberst* Dorn, who was firing in the air over our heads in order to halt the retreating troops and bring them into their positions. 'You *Schweinehünde*, will you stand still!' he roared, although this was not necessary. I had never seen the *Oberst*, this quiet and kindly man, so excited. Clearly he had not seen and did not know anything of the retreat of our neighbouring units and nothing of the enemy machine-gun fire that had hit us from the flank as we were retreating. But the *Oberst* was fair and experienced enough to immediately grasp the situation and not to hold us responsible for it. He knew that in the sixth year of the war the troops were already too worn out to be able to make anything of a situation such as this.

Lengthy retreats demoralise any troops, as had been seen in the summer of 1944. There on the Soviet front was added a massive momentum not present on the other fronts, apart perhaps from the partisan war in the Balkans. It was the fear of being taken prisoner, the fear of falling into the hands of an inhuman enemy.

Goebbels' propaganda had a boomerang effect. The bitterness with which the war was waged against Bolshevik Russia marked it out as a struggle between personal deadly enemies. The disregard of the Red Cross, the news of the atrocities carried out by the advancing Red Army, all this had long since extinguished the chivalry practised in earlier wars. However, it seemed to be still present on the other fronts in the West and South. Two ideologies were battling it out. The protagonists knew that the conflict would only end with the destruction of one or the other. In the East it had never been a decent war.

One notable thing was that on the evening of 17 January 1945, quite against my usual careless custom, I had put on my steel helmet instead of my field service cap. An indeterminate but compelling feeling had made me do it. When I was at last able to take off my steel helmet I saw the reason for it. The bludgeoning blow, that had thrown me to the ground, came from an infantry gun. It had very nearly penetrated the helmet, but the inserts of sheet steel and leather had stopped it from going right through.

From the beginning of the large-scale offensive on the 14th until the 20th January we had carried out a fighting withdrawal of almost 70 kilometres. On 23 January *Oberleutnant* Küllenberg was shot in the stomach. Apart from the commander, I was then the last officer in the battalion.

The following night brought me the craziest experience of that winter retreat. I had received orders to take over command of the rearguard. Who else could have done this, since there was no other officer there anyway. I had bent over the *Hauptmann's* map, the only one in the battalion, and with clammy fingers had dug out of the map case a pencil and a little slip of paper. Out loud to myself I had spelled out the unpronounceable Polish place names and written them on the slip of paper. A few lines, an arrow pointing north, and the sketch was ready. The runner Buck had similarly had to look at the sketch and then I reported my departure. '*Auf Weidersehen, Herr Hauptmann, Leutnant* Scheiderbauer reporting his departure', I had said, in a fairly unmilitary fashion, and Wild had replied 'Go with God, my boy, go!'

The company of only 14 remaining men, sat in the overheated room of a farmhouse warming themselves before the 20 kilometre night march, or rather, journey. The 14 chaps comfortably fitted on the vehicles, so that it was clear that their feet could be protected. The entire battalion was 'motorised' in this way with the help of 10 such 'combat vehicles'. The head of the column set off, and I remained behind with two vehicles as rearguard. It was a dark, almost mild night, and we were not freezing to any great extent. No wonder that the men dozed and dropped off, and seemingly the horses did too.

Then suddenly the penultimate vehicle had driven into a ditch and the men on it, woken up with a shock, were only just able to jump down from the vehicle as it tipped over. 'Dopey sod!' they cursed the driver, and 'wretched nag' was how he cursed his horse. Of course the men pushed the vehicle back out of the ditch again, loaded the ammunition boxes back on to it, pulled up their hoods and sat back on it. They were annoyed about the 10 minutes the accident had lost, and the fact that by then they had lost touch with the battalion.

We drove on and the men dozed on. But I stayed awake, lit up my sketch with the glowing tip of my cigarette, took compass bearings, and waited for the left-hand fork in the road leading westwards. But it didn't come. We drove past a brightly-lit farmhouse in front of which a lorry was standing. 'So we're not last', said one of the men. The situation slowly began to seem suspicious to me, because we had already gone too far northwards. But suddenly we heard vehicles in front of us that must come from the battalion. Out of the darkness the outlines of houses emerged. It was doubtless a village in which the battalion was waiting for its rearguard. The distance became less and less, and the outlines of buildings, trees and vehicles became clearer and clearer. These must also come from other units. We overtook some, until an obstacle brought us to a halt. I jumped down in order to look with the runner for *Hauptmann* Wild.

We passed figures shrouded in white and were suddenly asked, in Soviet, 'Well, who are you?' I assumed that the man asking the question was a Soviet *Hilfswilliger*, many of whom served with our baggage-train, and had paid no more attention to him. But then the chap had moved his hand in a suspicious way and was holding a weapon in it. My runner, the medic, suddenly planted one on his chin. Bellowing loudly and falling backwards he shouted '*Germanski, Germanski!*' Shots cracked out and shouts rang out.

There was complete confusion in the Soviet baggage-train into which we had stumbled. No one could recognise anyone else in the darkness. I shouted 'Out! Into the fields!' We had to get away from the village street and the vehicles. The only option open to us was the field to the left of the road, because on the right the road was blocked. Franz stuck close to me. The other men were swallowed up in the snow and the night. After an hour of strenuous searching and muffled shouting we had only found seven of the fourteen. Then we set off, without vehicles and without machine-guns. I could not hold up any longer if I wanted to avoid being seen when it got light.

It was the only time during my time as a soldier that I lost my bearings at night. The sky was cloudy and the Pole Star could not be seen, and my sense of direction let me down. I was convinced that the west was in the east, but my compass showed the opposite. I wavered between which I should trust, my instinct that had never yet let me down, or the compass. Then reason and drill, which were the stronger, won through and trust in the compass saved us. We were stamping through the snow in the direction my compass showed as west. From time to time we had to wade up to our knees through the snow. At last a farmstead came in sight. There we had to ask the way. Fortunately I had written down the place names along our retreat. I could not send any of the men still shocked by the experience to the farm, so I went again with Franz.

While the rest of the group waited near a tree that we hoped to be able to find later, Franz and I, with the safety catches off our weapons, crept closer. A dog set off barking, but from the house there was neither light nor any sound to be heard. We knocked on the window and on the door until an anxious farmer opened up. Were there any Soviets here yet, the Upper Silesian Franz asked him in Soviet, to which the Pole replied: 'No, you are the first'. Smiling to ourselves we got him to tell us the way to the road and the names of the next villages.

Soon we had found the road again. Just as it was becoming light, we at last found the battalion in the third village. With the help of *Hauptmann* Wild's map I had to establish that we had missed the fork in the road by five kilometres. At the regiment and at the Division they were agitated when they found out, on the basis of my report, that enemy baggage-trains were already in the village where we had had our adventure.

On 25 January we had come to within 10 kilometres of the Vistula to the south of the town of Graudenz. From midnight there was a two-hour halt. After three hours' slow night march we crossed the frozen Vistula. Pioneers had reinforced it to form an ice bridge so that tanks and heavy artillery could also get across it. At 5am in the area of Deutsch-Westfalen, I set my foot on the western bank. The positions ran along the riverbank on the Vistula embankment. On the western bank a strip of meadows about one to three kilometres wide then ran along the river, ending in a steeply climbing hill. About 10 kilometres north-eastwards was the town of Graudenz with the visible silhouette of its fortress. Called after the Prussian General, Courbiere, it stood high above the Vistula.

Far to the south of Armin Scheiderbauer, Dmitriy Loza and his comrades in the 46th Guards Tank Brigade were again at the forefront of the Red Army's efforts to wrest control of Budapest from the Germans and Hungarians.

January 1945. We were fighting round-the-clock fierce battles with a surrounded enemy force in the Hungarian capital. The enemy had made three desperate attempts to break through to his forces that had fallen into the ring of encirclement. On 2 January, he launched the first unexpected strike from the area southeast of Komárom (on the Danube River, seventy-five kilometres northwest of Budapest) on the general Bicske-Budapest axis. The enemy had a superiority over the Soviet forces of 1.7:1 in troops and 2.4:1 in tanks and self-propelled guns. Despite sustaining serious losses during the five-day offensive, the Germans were able to advance to a depth of twenty-five to thirty-seven kilometres on this axis.

The offensive of the Second Ukrainian Front played a significant role in halting this first enemy strike. In accordance with a 4 January *Stavka* order, the 6th Guards Tank Army, in conjunction with the 7th Guards Combined Arms Army, launched an attack from the area of Kamenitsa (on the east side of the Gron River in Czechoslovakia, forty-five kilometres northwest of Budapest) along the northern bank of the Danube to Komárno (on the Czechoslovakian side of the Danube River from Komárom), with the mission to capture nearby river crossing sites. Our offensive would thus threaten the German formations that were straining toward encircled Budapest.

The combat actions in this operation were characterized by a series of peculiarities that did not have analogues in the past. The offensive of the units of the 9th Guards (formerly the 5th) Mechanized Corps of the tank army commenced without an artillery preparation. The breakthrough of the enemy defence was accomplished at night, in a snowstorm. The rapid penetration of our tanks into the depth of the enemy's dispositions in such complicated weather conditions was made possible by the skilful employment of gyrocompasses mounted in each *Emcha*. Before this, we simply paid no attention to them, regarding them as superfluous. "Their turn arrived to lead us forward!" They enabled us accurately to maintain the specified direction of the offensive in practically zero visibility conditions. The T-34 did not have such remarkable navigational instruments.

Before the beginning of this operation, we were ordered to leave gyrocompasses only on the Shermans of the battalion and company commanders. The remainder were to be removed and given to the 5th Guards Tank Corps of our tank army. Help was needed: "As brother to brother!"

An intact bridge and a small bridgehead on the west bank of the river had been captured as a result of the actions of the forces in December 1944 on the Gron River (in Czechoslovakia) west of Kamenitsa. It was from this bridgehead that the 46th Guards Tank Brigade, the first echelon of the 9th Guards Mechanized Corps, was to attack.

The great difficulty in preparing the attack toward Komárno was that it required concentrating the forces in their start position in an extremely limited period of time and, of course, secretly. On the night of 4 to 5 January, the brigade executed an eighty-kilometre road march and concentrated some twenty kilometres from the forward edge of the enemy's defences, somewhat offset from the intended breakthrough sector. This facilitated masking the axis of our intended strike from the enemy. The brigade had the mission to move into its start position (western outskirts of Kamenitsa), deploy in pre-battle formation in the bridgehead with the *tankodesantniki* aboard, launch a sudden night attack to break through the enemy defences in front of the Gron bridgehead, and, by the night of 7 January, capture crossings on the Danube.

The brigade commander, Guards Lieutenant Colonel Nikolay Mikhno, an energetic and experienced officer, conducted commanders' reconnaissance of the march route and starting positions with the commanders of subordinate and attached units. During the course of this work, they determined the quantity of engineer effort required to maintain the unhindered movement of combat and logistic vehicles. In a short period the assigned group of sappers prepared the march route. Traffic regulators were posted at isolated difficult sectors and markers that could easily be seen at night at the remaining route segments.

Important issues were also resolved at the bridgehead: the sequence in which units were to cross the bridge and the passage of our tanks through the combat formation of the defending forces. Particular attention was given to the problem of attacking at night. The forecast was for very bad weather. An azimuth was determined from the Gron bridgehead. The order was issued to the squad commanders of the *desantniki* and officers of all ranks: "Everyone must know the azimuth!" Tankers were to write this azimuth on the inside walls of their turrets; artillerymen, on the shields of their field and anti-aircraft guns; *tankodesantniki*, on the stocks of their submachine guns.

The work that was conducted to prepare for the offensive permitted the brigade's units to reach Kamenitsa without delays and subsequently to accomplish, for the most part, their difficult combat mission.

I - deputy commander of the 1st Tank Battalion - was designated commander of the forward detachment. It consisted of a tank company, two platoons of *tankodesantniki*, and a battery of large-calibre anti-aircraft machine guns on American armoured half-tracks. The detachment's orders were to slam into the enemy's defence and, rapidly penetrating into the depth of the enemy's disposition, lead the brigade onto the designated axis. And this was at night, on unfamiliar terrain. In sum, we had to resolve an equation with many unknowns.

All this in continuing stormy winter weather. The forecasters predicted no quick letup in the storm.

The hands of our watches approached 0200 on 7 January. The brigade commander arrived in the 1st Tank Battalion. He assembled all the officers and conducted a brief meeting. We received the latest intelligence data on the situation. He expressed confidence in the successful accomplishment of our mission in the abnormal weather conditions. And bade me farewell with the words, "I know there will be difficulties. I have faith that you will not be driven off your course. Forward, and only forward! Do not be looking to the flanks!"

The snowstorm howled. We were glad for this. Snow and a cold, gusty wind drove the Germans into their shelters and deep dugouts. The *Emchas*, painted white, blended into the white background and were hardly distinguishable in the gusty snowy swirls.

At 0300, Nikolay Mikhno issued the detachment the order, '200' (commence the attack). With muffled engines, the tanks moved to the forward edge. The sappers guided us through the passage lanes in our own minefields. They directed us precisely through the narrow lane prepared in the enemy's explosive obstacle belt. Our artillery was silent, prepared at any moment (upon signal) to open fire. Because of the weather conditions, the use of close air support was totally out of the question. We were counting on surprise.

The column of the forward detachment crushed the enemy in his first position on a narrow sector of the front. The brigade's main body crashed into the enemy's position behind us while still in march formation. The distance between tanks was twenty to twenty-five metres. In such a column formation, each Sherman could fire only in one direction, with hardly a deflection to the left or right. Only the lead tank had a full sector of frontal fire. The *Emchas* machine-gun fire was supplemented by submachine-gun bursts from the *tankodesantniki*. When necessary, the motorised riflemen also hurled their grenades.

The detachment's stunning strike, and that of the brigade main body, in the middle of the night, in such crazy weather, turned out to be a complete surprise to the enemy. There was practically no resistance along the forward edge and in the near depth of the defences. Our attack had begun well! Now the main thing was not to be delayed, to break rapidly toward the subsequent nodes of resistance. The detachment hurried: "Speed, speed!" We had to take maximum advantage of the surprise of our attack and the bad weather. And, of course, maintain the correct heading. There were three navigational instruments in the detachment. This was ordered by Lieutenant Colonel Mikhno. I and two additional tank commanders (at the head and rear of the column) followed the azimuth. Such duplication was necessary not only for control but also in the event one of the vehicles that had a gyrocompass broke down.

The snowfall stopped. How fortunate that the weather change found us in the depth of the defence and not at the forward edge. Here the density of enemy forces and means was less. I stared into the darkness. Ahead, slightly to the right, I saw a light. And then the muzzle flash of a shot. I reported this by radio to the brigade commander. His precise instruction was, "Attack from the march! Do not permit the enemy to come to his senses!" Since all the radios in all the *Emchas* were operating on a single frequency, each platoon and tank commander heard the brigade commander's order. I did not have to repeat it.

We were headed for an important objective of the defenders. The light there had gone out. But we knew the direction to it. The tracks of the lead Shermans threw up whitish vortexes. The light flakes of the just fallen snow covered the vision blocks and gunsights with a thick shroud. We had to clean them frequently.

We came upon a brick factory, the location of an enemy artillery firing position. The appearance of Russian tanks was like a bolt out of the blue. It was our last easy victory. Having worked over the Germans with main guns and machine guns (the *tankodesantniki* helped), the forward detachment surged forward. The brigade's main body was behind us about one and one-half kilometres, attacking on our heels. So far, the detachment had not managed to break away from them. Again I demanded, "Increase speed!" The diesels were working at full throttle.

Artillery struck from the direction of the village of Bela. Several illumination rounds burst over our heads. And immediately fountains of earth, mixed with snow, landed in front of the Shermans. The enemy was laying down barrier fires in an effort to intersect our path of subsequent movement. To attack straight into artillery is to swim against the tide. It would lead to unjustified losses. I made the decision to go around the brick factory from the southeast and come in on the enemy guns in Bela from the flank. The enemy had managed to force us off our azimuth. Anything can happen in battle!

Maneuvering along a snow-covered field and opening in the woods, the Shermans came out somewhat south of Bela. The strong gusts of wind were insufficient to cover the noise of our engines. And this permitted the Germans to determine our approximate location. They quickly calculated our coordinates precisely. True, the white paint of the tanks essentially concealed them on the snow-covered field. At high points under enemy observation, our tanks left clearly visible tracks. With each minute, the enemy fire strengthened. One of the Shermans, which had stumbled upon some invisible obstacle, stopped. It was immediately enveloped by thick black smoke. The gusts of wind blew the smoke in various directions, at times clearing it from the engine compartment. New clouds of smoke billowed from the vehicle.

Immense fountains of explosions cut up the field to the left and right of us. The enemy was firing with heavy guns. The salvation of the tanks was in the most rapid closing with the enemy and in increasing the interval between the attacking vehicles. I ordered: "Increase speed! Disperse!" Motors roared. Finally, we drove out of the illuminated zone. Darkness swallowed the *Emchas*. We left the subsequent series of enemy shell explosions behind us. The Shermans were scattered along a snow-covered steppe. They surged forward. Dismounted submachine gunners ran bent over behind the tanks. Nearby shell explosions sent them sprawling flat in the snow. They immediately jumped up and chased after the still moving 'Americans'.

The crews conducted volley fire from the march. Even if its effects at night were lower than in the day, it constrained the actions of the artillery crews. It affected them psychologically. We approached the enemy artillery position. The tank of Guards Senior Lieutenant Kibarev was set afire by a direct hit. Driven by the wind, the flames blazed behind the turret, near the auxiliary fuel drums. They should have been dropped off before the attack. But we were breaking into the enemy's rear. It was difficult to foresee how the situation would develop. Therefore, we were forced to ignore the strict requirements of the regulations. Risking his life, the loader, Mikhail Parfenov, climbed out of the tank and put out the fire with a piece of tarpaulin, burning his hands in the process. The gun commander, Guards Sergeant Nasibulin, continued to fire the main gun at the enemy, with the tank commander acting as his loader.

In the end, the Shermans finished off the enemy with their tracks. In an instant, everyone and everything in the position was crushed or flattened. The tanks stopped on my command. Motors were turned off. We needed a breather, and so did our diesels. Most important, we had to set the necessary azimuth for our subsequent movement to Muzhla.

The remaining units of the 1st Battalion arrived. I reported the results of the battle and our losses to Ivan Yakushkin.

Again we set off into the night. We carefully followed our gyrocompass. The detachment captured the Muzhla railway station practically without a fight. At this time we received a reconnaissance report that Kebel'kut (three kilometres northwest of the station) was defended by infantry, reinforced by tanks, self-propelled guns, and anti-tank guns. The enemy had managed to activate his closest reserves. Now, we would have to take each village by storm. The brigade commander ordered the forward detachment to go all the way to Kebel'kut, pin down its garrison with fire, then await the approach of the brigade main body.

We fought an intense battle all night for this enemy defensive strongpoint. And by morning it was in our hands. A direct road to Komárno was opened. But I had to go in the opposite direction. I received a new mission from Guards Lieutenant Colonel Mikhno: to take two tanks (with *tankodesantniki* on board) and return along the route we had just fought to Salka, where our night raid had begun, and there pick up fuel and ammunition trucks.

The pressure of such Soviet offensives as the one Dmitriy Loza describes participating in above were forcing the Germans to juggle with their few remaining well-equipped formations. In late January the 11th SS Panzergrenadier Division 'Nordland', with Erik Wallin amongst its ranks, was withdrawn from Kurland and transferred by ship over the Baltic to Stettin in Pomerania. Now part of the 11th SS Panzer Army, it was earmarked to participate in a limited German counter-offensive named Operation Sonnenwende ('Solstice'). In the event, the offensive achieved more psychological than material success, in that although the territory regained was small, the sheer fact that the Germans had been able to launch a surprise counter-offensive at all shook the confidence of the Stavka, causing it to concentrate on clearing operations to the north of the Berlin axis of advance, at the expense of the capital of the Reich itself.

In the second week of February we were once again face to face with the Bolsheviks.

Since the Vistula position had been broken through, the situation at the front had changed radically. A great proportion of the heavy equipment and weapons had been lost, for instance much artillery. At the same time it had become more difficult to get replacements from Germany, as the never-ending bombings put the traffic into chaos. The Red Army could throw forward brand new corps of artillery, and immense numbers of tanks, without interruption. Especially effective was the new Stalin tank with its enormous 122mm calibre gun.

... It was just east of Massow. The main frontline followed the edge of a forest. I was ordered to take up a forward position with seven men. From a slight depression in the field we were to stop Soviet infantry attacks with two machine guns, model MG 42. We had arrived at night in our section to take over from a *Wehrmacht* unit. Barely arrived, I had to go forward with my men and our MGs. In pouring rain and pitch black darkness we groped our way to our three pits. I took the middle one with Gebauer, a German farmer's son from Rumania, and brought the MG in position, hoping that we would have some cover when day broke. The second MG was to our left with three boys and the remaining three crawled into the pit to the right with assault rifles and MPi's (the German version of 'tommy guns').

In case of an attack this position was hopeless! There was no connecting trench back to the main line. Only at night could one crawl back to 'safety'. We could only hope that the Reds would keep quiet. They did, but only 'til early morning. First came an overture by the Soviet artillery. As they kept up their fire for hours, with increasing intensity, we little mice hiding in our holes began to understand that this was not any little artillery softening up. The avalanche of shrapnel raged back and forth over our whole sector as far as we could hear and guess. Mercilessly it ploughed the field from one end to the other. As darkness again fell, the fire from the muzzles lit up the horrible landscape almost like searchlights in an air attack on a city. We huddled as best we could to survive this ordeal. The weather changed and the rain turned into a drizzle but steady and grey in small droplets, gradually becoming hazy. The muddy soil in and around our pits dissolved into a porridge-like muddle that oozed up over our boots, smearing our weapons and making us miserable. Within a couple of hours our uniforms were soaked. The coat, heavy even under normal conditions, had absorbed so much water that it felt heavy as lead. The mud in our boots made a sucking noise. Luckily most of the fire went over our heads, because the men before us had made a good job of hiding our position. Only occasional shells burst in our immediate vicinity. The main line behind us bore the brunt of the hail of steel and fire.

For three days and three nights we had to lie in these godforsaken pits, waiting, waiting, waiting ... The rain started pouring again. No food reached us, any connection backwards was unthinkable as long as the fire raged between us and the company. In the morning twilight of the fourth day Gebauer had the watch. The rest of us were lying half asleep and starved in the mud totally exhausted. Suddenly Gebauer shook me violently: "They are coming!"

A quick glance through the camouflage. There, only thirty metres away, a drove of Bolsheviks were approaching - no time to panic! They were well on the way to try to overrun our company. It seems that they had not yet discovered our well-hidden position. In spite of the foggy air I could already see a second wave of infantry emerging from the haze, only fifty metres behind the first one. I got the machine gun going and fired for all I was worth. My fire and the screams of the wounded woke up the other boys, and our weapons spat fire and death on the brown masses.

The wild firing soon got a reaction from the surviving attackers, who had gone to ground and discovered us. I happened to look to the left and saw a Bolshevik working his way through a depression towards us, to get at us from behind. In the same instant he saw me and disappeared. There he was again! He aimed a burst from his sub-machine gun at me. The lead whistled around my ears. The duel was on! The distance was hardly twenty metres. I got hold of an assault rifle and waited for him. Gebauer had to handle the MG alone. We took turns shooting at each other - head up, head down, up, down. Martin, the *Rottenführer* with the other MG in my group, could have touched the Soviet if he had looked in that direction but he did not notice our duel. Finally the Soviet made a mistake. Either because he was too lazy or in order to fire more quickly, he let his machine-gun stay up, visible to me, while he ducked down to wait for my next shot. I squeezed the trigger then stayed up with my finger on the trigger. There! His head was up again behind his weapon, and before he could react he had a hole between the eyes. The head was thrown back, then sank, disappeared and his limp hand dropped his weapon.

Furious, the Bolsheviks threw themselves against this unexpected little obstacle that our position became. The situation was hopeless but the boys fought formidably. The circle around us became ever tighter. In the heat of the battle one of the boys in the pit to the right straightened up with his machine-pistol and let it make a sweep that killed maybe ten of the enemy, giving us some breathing space, but he soon sank down, shot through the belly. There was less pressure but we had lost one of our brave men. We would not be able to hold much longer, but the enemy lay in lifeless heaps around our position. I sent up a red signal rocket: "Enemy attacking!" No sign of life behind us. Maybe they had got so used to the artillery fire that had rushed over our heads that they were now asleep, while we up front were fighting for our lives? Another red rocket. No reaction. I got boiling mad at our men back there and could have cried with fury. While I helped Gebauer to feed the machine gun with new ammunition I could hear myself swearing non stop, wishing them the worst possible tortures in hell.

I let Gebauer handle the machine gun alone while I fired alternatively with the assault rifle and with my machine-pistol. He forgot the danger, pushing his chest above the parapet in order to fire better. "Down!" I screamed through the hellish noise. He reacted with a reckless laugh, just nineteen years old ... and continue to send a devastating fire into the attackers.

Another Red Army wave came rolling forward to smash us. They were totally unprotected in the open field. Gebauer lifted his head to see better. "Head down!" I screamed. Too late! Gebauer suddenly jerked backwards and sank to one side. I turned him around towards me. He was hit under the left eye, the bullet passing through his neck. He was still alive, blood flowing down from cheek and neck. He embraced me, his fading eyes looking at me desperately. He begged, "Write to my mother ..." His embrace slackened, the arms sank while he whispered, "Just a few lines ..." And then I was alone, so alone and miserably small in my fox-hole. Something like panic tried to get hold of me. I made an effort to think, "Calm, just calm, take it easy ...", but my whole body was shaking.

Martin was now also alone. I called out to him to take his weapon and come over. He came rushing with wild leaps. To the right also one boy was left. All the others had died with a bullet through their head. We got him over to us. I implored them to try and keep their heads down. Of course, Martin in his eagerness forgot my advice. That was enough and he broke down seconds later with a bullet just above the nose ridge. With our machine guns (the MG42 was unsurpassed, the fastest of its kind in the whole war) we two survivors managed to keep the enemy down and away. For some inexplicable reason we didn't receive any incoming mortar or artillery fire. Maybe the fighting units were too mixed, too confused. Suddenly we heard from behind the roars of "urraaa". They had broken through!

"Grab the gun and run!" I bellowed to my comrade, as I got hold of my own MG, hooked some ammunition belts around my neck, and carrying an ammunition box was soon out of my position. Zig-zagging over the field in a crazy run, we reached what was left of the 'protective' edge of the wood. My comrade was a few leaps behind me. As I threw a quick glance behind me, I saw him grab his chest, then fall forward. From the cover of the trees, I looked up once more and saw him lying there, weakly waving at me. Too late, nothing doing - the Soviets were already there! I kept running and reached a glade among the trees. Four Bolsheviks come rushing from one side with their tommy guns spitting lead at me. I dropped my gun, all the ammunition, and flew more than ran, with the bullets whistling around me and ploughing into the ground around my legs. Theoretically I was already a dead *Unterscharführer*, but a soldier must have luck! That is what I had that day. I dived in among the trees further on, and all of a sudden I found myself in the midst of our company - now numbering only a handful ... there was our Swedish commander smoking a cigarette. He looked me up and down and said, "It's not that bad! Could be worse." With his calmness I felt embarrassed, standing in front of him short of breath (my chest could have burst!) - shaking and sweating after the tremendous tension. (Much later I found out that his calmness was a fake to avoid panic amongst the few men he still had in his company. In the course of a few hours it had lost more than half its strength. In the midst of this cauldron of death, screams, groans, and mutilated, blooded bodies, his pretended nonchalance and complete calmness saved the lives of our surviving men. Such an officer one could follow all the way to hell and back!)

The company commander sent out a couple of men to re-establish the connection with the neighbouring units. One man was sent back with a report on the dangerous situation. An *Oberscharführer* received the order to make a counter-attack with three men. I was one of those so 'privileged'. Some counter-attack! Four men against an enemy force of probably more than a company's size! And these four totally exhausted, physically and mentally gone following the last four hours of shocking happenings. It did not make sense, this promise of certain death, but discipline and the feeling of duty urged us on.

Death surrounded us from all sides, pushing us on and seeming to give us wings. With wild roars of "Hurrah" we push on through thickets and bushes and fired madly against the swarm of brown figures rising everywhere and turning to flee our impetuous attack.

Suddenly, a Bolshevik stood before me, barely three or four metres away, his face a rigid scared stare. My short burst of bullets before he had time to squeeze the trigger made him keel over with a harsh groan as I rushed past him. We recaptured the whole wooded sector in a matter of minutes that to us seemed an eternity, encompassing our whole lives. We reached the edge and threw ourselves into the previous position of the company and continued firing furiously at the stream of enemy infantry now fleeing from the wood towards a low ridge beyond the field that offered them protection. Two stragglers jumped blindly over us and dropped just a few steps beyond our trench with perforated backs. The whole field was covered with fallen enemy soldiers. And all four of us alive! Incredible, inconceivable! We looked at each other, radiant in this bloody mess and mass of death – we could have cheered. What a counter-attack! But my heart thundered ready to burst. We were totally exhausted, and a reaction of fatigue set in.

By and by the rest of the company drifted back to the recovered positions. My commander ordered me back to the death trap of my fox-hole, where I had already lost seven boys. All alone with my MG, surrounded by fallen SS men and enemies! Never before had I felt so miserable , forlorn. I would rather have thrown away my MG and run far, far away, but there it was again, that damned feeling of duty. It held me in a steely grip. I become aware of a steady groan nearby. Peering cautiously I saw that it was one of our boys. He had a bullet through both hips and the underbelly. I made him roll over on my back, then crawled slowly towards our defensive line with this heavy burden. The risk of being seen by the Soviets was better not thought of, but we made it! The same *Oberscharführer* who led our 'counter-attack' saw us and came crawling to help me. Once in safety we get hold of a stretcher and carried him to the rear. Here we found a big barn, where the floor was covered with dead, dying, and seriously wounded, some of them our close comrades. We hurried out of this place of groans, screams and death rattles - back again to my lonely foxhole! I noticed in the two o'clock direction some vague movements in the vegetation. A glance through my binoculars - Soviets! A quick report to my commander. Already as I glided down into my MG pit, the first 10.5 cm shells came whooshing over my head, ploughing through the terrain and smashing a Red Army attack before it could get going.

Twilight sank over the torn battlefield. Soon it was completely dark. It became cold and my teeth chattered as I sat there behind my weapon in the scary darkness. Pictures passed through my feverish head, grotesque pictures of wounded comrades and the slowly fading eyes of the dying Gebauer. Now and then I got a fright hearing the faint noises of some Soviet night patrol. All night they came, testing and prying, their wheezing whispers so near.

The contrast could not be greater between the desperation felt by Erik Wallin during his experiences in Pomerania and the exuberant confidence – despite war-weariness – displayed by Vsevolod Olimpiev as the 1st Guards Cavalry Corps went over to the offensive in Poland. His account is also significant for the mention he makes of war booty or 'trophies'.

It was in the middle of January 1945. The Sandomierz bridgehead situated on the western bank of Vistula south of Warsaw was filled with experienced Red army troops battle-hardened by four years of war and armed with the latest materiel. Everyone was waiting for the order to advance. We were at the peak of our military might. Morale was high, everybody felt that our victory was drawing nearer but there was a bit of sadness as you felt one might not live till that day. One would unwillingly recall the alarmed and depressed mood of the Army and people in the autumn of 1941 when a real danger of foreign enslavement had hung over the country and the bled-white infantry had nearly forgotten what our tanks and aircraft looked like.

A Soviet 45mm gun crew crossing a small river. Shell carriers with ammunition boxes are behind the gun. (Artem Drabkin)

At last the order to advance was given. The German defence lines were broken through and the tank corps raced westwards to the borders of the hated *Reich*. The 1st Guards Cavalry Corps, which included our 143rd Guards Anti-tank Artillery Regiment was moving straight after the tanks along with the infantry and motorized units. All five batteries of the Regiment were armed with new 76mm ZiS-3 guns towed by powerful Studebakers, the crews consisted of experienced fighters seasoned in many battles.

Here it's necessary to explain what kind of role the cavalry had back then. No doubt, in some ways it remained an antiquated form of troops built on traditions of the horse-mounted armies of the Civil War of 1918-21. Nearly everything was like during the Civil War: cavalry squadrons armed with carbines (later with submachine-guns) on their backs and sabres at their sides, carts drawn by four horses each with obsolete Maxim machine-guns on them, all war supplies in wagons and carts drawn by two horses or one each. But no one would gallop into a cavalry charge with drawn sabres. The latter were mostly used for chopping brushwood and opening tins. The squadrons would dismount in a combat and operate as a common rifle unit. In the meantime the high maneuverability and cross-country ability of the cavalry remained and it allowed its use in advance operations and especially in raiding the enemy's rear. In 1943 the firepower of the cavalry corps had grown significantly during the modernization of the armed forces of the country. Each of them was strengthened with mechanized units: a regiment of rocket launchers (*Katyushas*), an artillery-mortar regiment, an anti-tank artillery regiment and also a tank regiment.

On moving forward we were liberating one town after another in south-western Poland tearing down banners with spidery swastikas everywhere. The population hung out their red-and-white flags immediately.

As in all major battles since Stalingrad the most difficult job in the battle for Silesia lay on the shoulders of the armoured troops. Our tank brigades and corps comprised a formidable force, armed with T34s with long-barreled 85mm guns and supported by self-propelled guns of various calibres up to 152mm. But their losses were not small either. One could see burnt or inverted T-34s, often without their turrets, which had been blown off by exploding ammunition and lying nearby near almost every centre of defense. It was better for a novice not to glance into a hatch so as not to see what was left of a burnt-alive crew...

The advancing troops had to overcome the eastern sector of the defensive ring of the whole of Germany. Large calibre flak guns were a serious threat for the tanks. The following picture was typical: a lone destroyed T34, sometimes two of them and 200-300 metres further away - a crushed German flak gun surrounded by the corpses of enemy soldiers.

However we rarely had to set up our guns for point-blank shooting. The enemy had few new tanks, and the German Command had been throwing into combat everything that could move and shoot. I remember a destroyed antiquated German tank with a round turret and a small gun beside a small Silesian village. A crewman naked to the waist and with his head torn off by a shell was hanging out of an open hatch on the turret side.

The Regiment was crossing the *Reich* frontier in a dull February morning. A General - commander of a Cavalry Division - standing on the roadside saluted the passing column and urged us to avenge for our ruined cities and villages and for the suffering of our people. We had already been preparing to avenge the Fascists for three years. Now a question was being asked: who and how? The regiment had entered its first town in Silesia. A small town around a factory - all the Germans had fled and only few Polish workers stayed. The soldiers wandered off to empty houses looking at the rich quarters with a great interest. Many of them were asking naively why the Germans with all their wealth had wanted to conquer Russia, poverty-stricken compared to them? In the night we had to use cigarette lighters and candles to light up the houses and as a result of that many of them caught fire. I don't remember a case of anyone setting houses on fire deliberately. The same was typical in other towns of Silesia, most of which were taken by us with practically no fighting.

The fast breakthrough of our tanks was unexpected for the German Command, and it had failed to organise evacuation of the population. People had been leaving behind all their possessions and fleeing in panic with no luggage, using mostly bicycles as for transport. There were so many abandoned bicycles on the road that they created obstacles for the army vehicles and they were simply crushed by tank treads and trucks' wheels. When the German civilians had failed to flee they would hang out white flags in windows. It was a strange and uncommon sight for our soldiers. Nobody had surrendered to the conquerors mercy in Russia.

The issue of revenge ceased to have significance itself. It was not our national tradition to take revenge on women, children and elderly people. And I didn't come across any unarmed but combat-fit German men either in Silesia or, later in

April, in Saxony. The Soviet soldiers' relations with the German population where it had stayed may be called indifferent and neutral. Nobody, at least from our Regiment, harassed or touched them. Moreover, when we came across an obviously starving German family with many kids we would share our food with them with no unnecessary words.

The problem of trophies was quite serious. It was impossible to ban a soldier from the country devastated by the Fascists from taking a watch, a camera or even an accordion from an empty enemy town. What else could he put into his only 'trunk' - his backpack with its strange soldierly name *sidor*? I have to say that our soldiers stuck to an unwritten rule: to take trophies only from abandoned houses and not to touch the Germans who stayed. More serious trophies which fell into our hands would be shared between all of us. In one town we came across an abandoned haberdashery, whose shelves were full of men's silky underwear. Laundry was a problem for us and we put on those shirts and underpants. And we changed them, and changed them again. It turned out that lice don't stay on silk clothing and thus seemingly the insurmountable problem of lice had been eliminated. Food trophies, which helped to expand significantly our rations, were quite uncommon. Once the soldiers found in an abandoned candy store a huge amount of round boxes with plates of *choco-cola* chocolate apparently assigned for *Luftwaffe* airmen. At first we feared that the chocolate had been poisoned but then we checked it out and the Regiment ate this tasty stuff for a month.

The trophy issue was soon put on a legal base by an order from the Commander according to which every serviceman was allowed to collect and send home a parcel. Officers were allowed to send ten kilos a month, soldiers five. One of the Regimental batteries managed to fill a whole Studebaker with their parcels! But then a dramatic episode occurred and after it no one would busy himself with parcels. That battery was set on the banks of the Oder in an open position for point-blank shooting, on its own with no infantry or cavalry support. No one knew for sure where the enemy was. The battery commander was warned that our infantry would come around, probably in the night. One had to be on full alert under those uncertain conditions. But the seasoned commander - the only one in the Regiment awarded with the Order of Lenin - had taken no special measures for reasons known only to himself. He had set out two sentries to guard the firing position (one of them immediately made himself comfortable for a sleep in a nearby cutting) and went for a rest to into the basement of a nearby house with the men from the battery. As one of the survivors told us, later in the night a group of skiers in white camouflage arrived. When hailed by the sentry they answered in Russian: "No strangers here". The sentry who was expecting the arrival of friendly troops raised no alarm and was captured immediately. The skiers, who turned out to be German seamen brought in from ships, threw a hand grenade into the basement and began to machine-gun the artillery men running out of there. The battery commander was amongst the first killed but part of the soldiers made their way out through the side windows. The commander of the second platoon which had been placed in a separate position four hundred metres away was alerted by the noise and shooting and ran to the battery commander to find out what was happening. He saw a line of skiers and their commander saying something to them in the darkness near the guns of the first platoon and then understood what was happening. But it was too late - the Germans jumped on him and tried to tie him up. The tall Siberian threw off the enemy soldiers and, having torn off and left in the enemy's hands his map-case and mittens, disappeared into the darkness. When he came back to his guns he didn't dare to open fire for fear of hitting his comrades. In the morning our self-propelled guns came around and restored the situation. The human loss amongst the battery men was not small. Two guns and their tractors had been put out of action and a Studebaker truck loaded with trophies had been burnt out with *Panzerfausts.*

Having survived the bombardment and opening phase of the Vistula-Oder Operation, Armin Scheiderbauer was now involved in what the Red Army regarded as 'clearing operations' in Prussia. Possibly better than any other account in this book, the following extract illustrates the dire situation in which the German soldier found himself by the spring of 1945.

The main line of resistance had been maintained for two or three days in front of Schwenten. After the departure of General Meltzer, the Divisional commander was *Generalleutnant* Drekmann. At noon he visited my command post. In broad daylight he came driving up to the forester's house, along the road, in full view of the enemy, with the red flashes on his overcoat. Outside the house he stopped. It was only with difficulty that he could be persuaded to come down into the cellar. At first I thought, because of the grand way in which he had arrived, that he was overexcited. But the reason for his behaviour soon became clear. He had obviously been knocking back too much cognac. His initial briskness soon passed over into joviality. Then he adopted a patronising and encouraging tone as far as the situation was concerned. When the opportunity presented itself, I mentioned that I was the Regiment's 'last horse in the stable', namely the last *Schützenkompanie* commander to have survived from 14 January. That made no impression on him and he soon drove off again.

Walter shouted loudly after him the wish that a *Ratschbum* would get him. That would teach him the meaning of fear. But luckily for all of us that did not happen. On the contrary, the same afternoon a similarly careless attitude had the result that little *Hauptmann* Hein was not so lucky. He had been called *Freund* Hein, in 1943, by *Oberst* von Eisenhart. Like many others he had also been a friend to me. It was said that, in the school of the neighbouring village, the Divisional commander had held a large officers' meeting. The Soviets must have noticed. They radioed to their firing position with the result that there were several dead and wounded including *Hauptmann* Hein. The careless General, however, had remained uninjured.

On 7 February the Soviets had pushed us out of the village. I had given up the command post in the forester's house and withdrawn 500 metres up the road to the Maierhof. There a man from the 14th *Panzerabwehrkompanie,* had put paid to a 'Stalin' tank with a *Panzerschreck*. The main line of resistance then ran along the front of a brick-red so-called *Insthaus*. At the rear were the entrances to the living quarters of the estate workers, the Instleute. I lived in the kitchen of that squalid dwelling. Facing the doors to those dwellings was a ramp a metre high, to which I owed my life.

To get some air I stepped through the door on to the ramp, leaving the door open. Every now and then a mortar shell exploded close by. But the ramp was in the blind corner of the building. It seemed to give cover against shell splinters that came from above and also against the dangerous splinters from mortar shells that flew out horizontally. Then, suddenly, a shell exploded very close by. A blow on my chest flung me through the open door back into the room. The men leapt up and surrounded me, helped me up and asked if I was wounded. At first I did not know. Then I saw and could feel that my limbs were in one piece, I could move them and I was not bleeding anywhere.

What had happened? A shell splinter, just the size of a fingernail, had gone through my winter overcoat. It then bored through the thirty-two page map, which had been folded sixteen times, stuck between my winter clothing and my field tunic. The paper of the map, folded many times, had so reduced the momentum of the shell splinter that it had been slowed down before it went through my field tunic. The shell, as it fell, had passed within 20 centimetres of me and the slope of the ramp. The ramp had caught all the shrapnel flying in my direction apart from the one shell splinter that I pulled out of my coat. However, my intention to send home, as war mementoes, the shell splinter and the map that saved my life was fruitless. At that time the post was no longer functioning properly.

The following night I was ordered to lead an attack in order to move the main line of resistance forward a little. Nobody knew where the enemy was. A Soviet Maxim machine-gun was popping at us from the rising ground to the east of the forester's house. However, there was to be no preparatory barrage. We were to report and then to drive out the enemy with a shout of *Hurra*. It was a well-known fact that the Soviets avoided fighting at night. But the high-ups had evidently forgotten that we too were no longer the heroes of the first years of the war. In spite of everything we went forward.

There was impenetrable darkness. Soon it took all our efforts to keep the leading man in sight. We were shadows and outlines creeping over the snow-covered terrain towards the chattering machine-gun. Every one of the soldiers no doubt felt, as I did, the pounding of his own heart. After a while the enemy machine-gun ceased firing. We got as far as the forester's house, but it too had been abandoned. The enemy had evidently withdrawn of their own accord. We had by then reached the southern edge of the Tucheler Heide. With differing degrees of intensity, the enemy went about driving us out of the wooded terrain.

By 11 February we had spent three days and three nights in the woodland and in the snow. We had been without a roof over our heads and without sleep. On the first day the Soviets were still trying to advance into the woodland, but then had given up. I had not heard for quite some time the rattling and twittering of infantry weapons in the woodland. Sometimes, when a ricochet whistled into a certain corner of the woodland, it sounded just like singing. 'The little birds in the wood, they sing so wonder-wonderfully' was the line that occurred to me, in romantic longing. But it was not at all romantic just very serious when one of the 'singing' bullets slashed open the flapping leg of my winter trousers. In snowy hollows we tried to snatch a quarter or half an hour of sleep. We did not manage to sleep for longer because, as time passed, the cold, 10 degrees below zero, penetrated our ragged uniforms. In my case there was the added misery that my feet, which had otherwise been warm with walking, threatened to freeze to the soles of my boots. They had turned to ice.

On the evening of 12 February we crept into the Mischke forester's house. It was the only house for miles around. At night it was packed full of soldiers from various units. Following *Hauptmann* Wild's orders I tried to get my people, insofar as they were not outside on sentry duty, together in one room alone. My attempt failed. So I had to go round trying to free up at least a few corners of rooms for us. It was important, because the forester's house was on the front line in our sector. At any moment an enemy assault unit could attack. To be able to repulse it, the unit commander had to have his people together at all times ready for combat at the shortest notice. That, however, was not guaranteed if the members of a large number of different units were lying about, mixed up in the numerous rooms.

In the very first room I met resistance from a *Feldwebel*. The men around him, apparently his people, made room to a certain extent willingly, but he on the other hand remained lying down. I spoke to him sharply and gave him 'as an officer the direct order' to get up immediately and to leave the room with his people. He remained unaffected. 'I will give you two minutes. If you have not obeyed my order by then I shall shoot you!' I did not wait to see the effect of my words, but went to *Hauptmann* Wild, to report the incident to him. Wild sat in the light of my tallow candle, not looking up, and said drily: 'Do what you want'. '*Herr Hauptmann*, I just can't simply shoot the man!' I exclaimed. But *Hauptmann* Wild, the brave man, the fatherly comrade and the pastor, seemed to be at the end of his strength. He did not express an opinion and he took no part in what was agitating me. He shifted on to my shoulders the responsibility for deciding and acting, and once again replied tonelessly and apathetically, 'Do what you want'.

Irresolute and uncertain I turned back, fearing that the chap would still be lying in his corner. That was in fact the case. I could no longer restrain myself. Stirred up to the highest degree, I shouted at him: 'Get up immediately and leave this room, or I shall shoot you on the spot!' Inwardly I was trembling. I wondered whether the chap would obey this order. While my trembling fingers were reaching for my holster, another *Feldwebel*, one of his comrades, intervened to calm and to placate me. Even his words, that the man who was refusing to obey my orders was a tried and tested and excellent soldier, I turned against him, saying that in that case he should know all the better that he had to carry out my orders like any others. But even as I was saying this, and as the *Feldwebel* had pointed out to me, I felt that the behaviour of the man refusing to obey my order could not have any rational cause. He was completely exhausted and at the end of his strength.

What would have happened, if I had shot the man? Nothing would have happened. As in earlier retreats and crisis situations, it had become the duty of senior officers to use weapons in cases of refusals to obey orders. They could shoot the offender immediately and without a court martial. I was therefore, formally, completely within my rights. The facts of the case clearly attested to a refusal to obey orders. Moreover, my commander had expressly given me a free hand. The order was in fact completely well founded. But what were those men doing in our sector? Were they men who had been scattered or were they deserters? To establish which it was, I was much too agitated and did not have the time. I had only time for the shot that would re-establish discipline and order.

But I did not fire it! The man was almost as exhausted as I. Probably, just like me, he had not slept during the previous days and nights. He had most likely been overwhelmed by a physical, mental, and spiritual exhaustion that left him no longer in control of his actions. It would have been the same for me, if I had not been an officer, if I had not had to be a leader and if the enormous agitation about the inconceivability of this refusal to obey orders had not then overwhelmed me. A remnant of common sense within me restored my sense of proportion. I gained enough control over myself to be able to ponder whether the insignificance of the case was worth his death. Was it right that my order should be carried out by that man? So I came to the conclusion that I should not allow myself to be guilty of his death, even if I was in every respect justified in doing so, even if it was my duty to do so.

I walked out into the dark of the February night. I was oppressed by the dichotomy of feelings of defeat that my formalistic spirit had suffered. But I was also glad of my victory over that spirit. For one trembling moment, I had held the life of that man in my hand and nearly destroyed it. Outside, the *Feldwebel* comrade of the mutineer joined me and said that I was 'a fine man'. He seemed suddenly to trust me, because he had recognised me as a fellow countryman. Then, in all seriousness, he proposed that I should travel to Vienna with him. He had, he said, a motorcycle and sidecar, his unit had been wiped out and he had had 'enough'. With me as an officer, he said, we would easily get through the *Feldgendarmerie* checkpoint and through the *Heldenklaus*. I was speechless. Should I now have this man arrested, taken away, and shot? I shook my head, uncomprehendingly, without saying a word. He disappeared.

Such events could not be allowed to seriously affect a soldier's actions – to have done so would have resulted in a complete breakdown or worse. There was to be not let-up in the Soviet pressure in Armin's sector.

At the northern edge of the Tucheler Heide, a little beyond the wood, the battalion had moved in to a wide sector. We could only hold on at key points. On the morning of 26 February we had repulsed an enemy patrol. Since then the enemy had not pushed on after us. They were obviously exhausted and needed a breather. They stayed in the wood, preparing for another assault. Because of that, we hoped that a few days' rest would be granted to us. Almost overnight the snow had disappeared. The warm March sun had sucked it up, and a mild wind was blowing over the fields, all newly brown. In the open meadow, tiny shoots of green seemed to be sprouting. My imagination seized on to an illusion of reawakening life. Our winter clothing was handed back to the baggage-train.

The railway station at Gross-Wollental was the battalion key point. It lay furthest to the left. It was occupied by the remnants of 'my' 1st Company. There were still 15 of them, commanded by a *Leutnant* who had just come from Germany. They had installed themselves in the railway buildings and had a good field of fire. Within the solid, thick walls they felt themselves to be protected, for the time being. It was the typical brick station of a smaller town, such as could be found in a good 1,000 stations in northern Germany. A little while before it had still been in operation. The air still smelled just like a railway station.

The small farmhouse that housed the command post had thin walls. The only room was on the southern side facing the enemy. Since we had already grown apathetic as a result of our exertions, comfort had won the day over the regulation efforts to provide security. Instead of taking up our quarters in the stable on the southern side of the house, we used the room facing the enemy. There were two beds. Men and officers slept in them, in shifts, of course without being able to take off their boots or clothes. We had not been used to such peace for a long time. I could count on my fingers the days and nights that I had not slept without my boots. That continued during the war of movement, the trench warfare, or whenever else, in that campaign.

In my dreams I heard the hiss of a hand-grenade and the nasty quiet fizzing of the fuse before it exploded. I was dreaming that an enemy assault unit was in the process of digging us out, and had thrown a hand-grenade into the room. Still half asleep I jumped out of bed and the laughter of my comrades brought me fully awake. But there was an element of truth in the dream. An infantry gun shell had come through the wall over my head and the headboard of the bed. It had stuck into the opposite wall of the room. Mortar was still crumbling down from the wall.

On 4 March 1945 at 8.05am, a forward observer reported heavy enemy movements from Gross-Wollental moving northwards. At 8.15am, accompanied by intense aircraft activity, there began a heavy enemy preparatory barrage, particularly on the sector of our left-hand neighbour, Grenadier Regiment 7. Following that, the enemy, supported by strong armoured forces, attacked from the direction of Gross-Wollental and Neubuchen towards the railway line.

That was how the regimental history described the start of the day. As I recall, the neighbouring sector on the left was under heavy fire. The commanding high ground to the north of Gross-Wollental lay behind us to the left, and fell into enemy hands. The battalion, that is, our 15 men, received orders to re-take the high ground. First we had to pull back a little to strike. Then we moved up to where the artillery positions were, in order to be able to move in a semi-circle round the high ground that had been lost. In the meantime the enemy were giving the terrain a vigorous pounding with heavy weapons. In particular they fired on the farmhouses that lay on their own. They rightly suspected firing positions to be there. They had also spotted our movement while we were approaching the open heights. At the last farm at the foot of the heights there were field howitzers under trees that were firing on them.

From the enemy positions came the thumping of the mortars. All round we could hear shells whistling towards us and exploding. From early morning I had felt, 'in my water', a sense of apprehension. So I was almost relieved when what I had dreaded actually happened. I had thrown myself to the ground. But I jumped up too soon, in order to move towards the house, thinking there might be better cover there. I must obviously not have heard the mortars fire because of the sound of the explosions. The severe pain of a considerable flesh wound in my left buttock forced me to the ground. I painfully crawled towards the house. I felt a lack of air that worried me. I knew I must have been shot through the lungs. One of my runners dragged me into the house where I was laid down on a bundle of straw. A medic from the artillery bandaged me up. I was taking shallow breaths, gasping and struggling for air.

The best chance of getting to the rear and to a dressing station was to go on the artillery food vehicle. It had just arrived at the firing position. It was to take me with it. But it took another quarter of an hour that seemed like an eternity, until it was ready. Then I was lifted up on to the little wagon. The loading area was too small to lie down, so I had to sit up with the driver. But I hung rather than sat on the driver's seat, at the same time clinging on to the driver and to an iron armrest. A wild drive began. Enemy aircraft flew over us. The driver could not risk using roads and lanes. The horse was galloping in terror. The wagon bumped and tossed across country over meadows and fields, furrows and trenches. It was sheer torture. At the staff of another unit the driver unloaded me. A doctor gave me a tetanus injection. Sometime later I was loaded up into a *Sanka* i.e. a medical vehicle. After an absolutely endless journey I arrived at the field hospital section of the 35th Division, our neighbouring division.

There, in a small village school, the wounded as they arrived were laid on bundles of straw. A medical officer sorted us out according to urgency, not according to rank. All men are equal before God and before the court, but also before the surgeon's knife. Of the two schoolrooms, one served as an operating room, the other as a preparation room. In the latter I was undressed and, by means of injections, somehow stabilised. Scarcely had the surgeon finished with one man, than he got to work on me. Half on my belly and half on my right side, I lay on the operating table. It was only a local anaesthetic under which the operation was carried out. The doctors asked me questions and forced me to answer them. Meanwhile, I could hear my breath bubbling out of the entrance wound, and could feel them working to close it. How long that lasted I have no idea. According to what they said, they were doing plastic surgery on my skin. The effect of the anaesthetic had already begun to wear off by the time the larger shell splinter from my behind and another lodged immediately next to my spine, were taken out. The Staff Medical Officer, Dr Brunn, asked whether I wanted to throw the shell splinters away. I replied, 'Too bloody true'. The scars would be mementoes enough for me. The shell splinter in my lungs I would carry for the rest of my life.

During the Soviet drive into the heart of the Reich *it was units such as the scouts, to which Zoya Alexandrova belonged, that were at the very forefront of the advance, riding on the tanks, and making gains into German territory of some seventy kilometres a day at times. Throughout the period covered by this book Zoya's parent unit, 11th Tank Corps, was attached to 1st Byelorussian Front, operating on the central axis of the advance through Poland and into Germany. The following account by Zoya demonstrates superbly well what it was like to form part of these armoured spearheads.*

They used to send a tank platoon on reconnaissance with a platoon of scouts seated on the armour. I was always on the front tank. The guys who manned it had called me over and only then did it emerge that I was not from their section. Nevertheless, I stayed with them. The most brave and courageous blokes were on that tank. Five men: Khramov, Volkov, Bitnik, Groshev and Shekin. The latter was as cute as anything - we all thought that he was virgin but after he had died a letter came from a place the brigade had been placed for regrouping. There were pictures in it: a child's foot in one and a hand in another... They were all 20-25 years old and nearly all of them had been criminals who had done time for stealing. Foolhardy blokes they were! Anatoliy Andreev, a former burglar aged about 40 was their

Soviet scouts along a river bank. Note the camouflage pattern on the figure nearest to the camera. (Artem Drabkin)

leader. There were other soldiers, but these guys were cocky, strong and, most likely, good thieves. They had been transferred to our company after a conflict with the commander of the submachine-gun company they had been fighting in. He kept collecting trophies even after the end of the war. And these guys took revenge and cleaned him out of everything!

Every scout had his own place on the tank. Mine was the third on the left hand side from the front. Khramov was the first, Volkov the second, myself the third, then Groshev and so on. We would go to the enemy's rear to reconnoiter the integrity of bridges, their guards, distribution of enemy troops, firing positions, and to draw the enemy's forces to us. We hadn't been told to take prisoners for interrogation... Once we were back from duty we would get a new one. We had not even been given rations to take with us! We had to switch to 'green fodder'. Polish villages were so poor, even in Russia there was no poverty like that. Well, we were careful to go into richer-looking houses. All credit to the Poles, they met us well, fed us, gave us drinks and smokes. We slept mostly on the tanks, on the move. Now and then we slept in Polish houses but dressed and shod, unlike the Germans who usually slept in underwear.

Once in the night we were moving on our tanks very slowly and carefully because we knew that the enemy was all over the place. We were approaching a village when a chap in an unbuttoned overcoat and with no hat shot out of a side street yelling and pointing at a two-storey house: "The fascists are there!" He refused to climb up on the tank and ran away. The scouts discussed it with the tank crews and decided to fire on the enemy. We lay down in the snow in front of the tanks. One salvo, then another one. Germans poured out of the house, most of them undressed, and we began to machine-gun them. One scout was badly wounded and we had to send one tank back. We laid the man on the transmission and Anatoliy Andreev and I lay on either side on our bellies. The tank raced at a full speed. It was dreadful and it seemed that we were as one with the armour, but I couldn't get rid of a feeling of terrible loneliness for we were rushing across the land occupied by the enemy. We left the wounded guy in a village together with tank crews and machine-gunners wounded earlier in the morning and returned to our comrades. As it was found out later on, the Germans had occupied this village again. Then those poor fellows were never heard of again.

At a place called Mniszek on the Radom River, the German aviation was seriously impeding the advance of our brigade, but there were no heavy losses. Andrey Chupinin and I fell behind our tanks after another air raid. We didn't retreat from the road during an aerial attack and began to run from one tank to another until we saw our tank already moving onto a bridge. But we failed to catch up with it as it accelerated and we climbed on the following one. As soon as the first tank had approached the opposite bank it was hit and exploded. Chupinin and I were thrown off the second tank by the shockwave. We leaped up, ran behind a building and then another shell exploded nearby. Andrey said: "Well, Zoya, we have escaped two deaths today!" We found our guys and for some reason Chupinin went back with one of his mates. Then I saw somebody was waving his hand: "Come over here!" I ran up and saw Andrey lying with his side torn apart and his lips whispering: "What a fool I am... I know what I'm dying of." He had put two 'lemon' hand grenades into his pocket and forgot about them. Then he slipped his hand into the pocket for something and accidentally tore out a firing pin.

Once we dropped into a Polish village before Tomaszow on the Pilica River. There was a German commandant's office in it. The scouts surrounded the office straightaway, shot the guards and the commandant himself. Next night we came to another Polish village beyond Tomaszow and decided to send a group to reconnoiter while the rest were looking for overnight accommodation. One poor family called us to stay overnight at their place. The Poles were friendly and well-disposed but they had nothing to feed us with. We had called at a store before but it was empty. There was a tin in there and we picked it up, then jumped on our tank and headed further across a field. Wind, blizzard, cold. After we'd stopped in the village we felt hungry and decided to open the tin. I was given some of its content to taste – it turned out to be liquid soap. So we slept hungry till morning. The scouts came back upset from their duty – their job had been done but Petya Khokhlov - a modest good bloke - had been badly wounded. They put him on a tank and drove away. He returned to the unit after treatment at the end of the war.

In the morning an elderly Polish woman told us how to find the village headman's house. Three of us went there. We glanced into a window of his house and saw two Germans having their breakfast. The guys got angry, entered the house, grabbed them and killed one on the spot, in the yard. The other one tried to flee but Sasha the motorcycle rider caught him up and finished him off. The guys did their best not to kill anybody in front of me since I found it hard to take, would become sullen and take a long time to get over such cruelty... And now the guys demanded food and spirits from the headman as if nothing had happened. The headman didn't put out enough, far less than for the Germans. The guys threatened him and soon the table was crammed with good food.

Another time we headed into the enemy's rear on 10 tanks with the Scout Company commander Captain Melnikov. Somewhere in the forest we found out from a forester that the road ahead of us had been mined. While they were searching for contact with the Brigade via radio I nestled down on the transmission. Then I heard somebody running and calling near each tank: "Zoya, Zoya! The Captain needs you." It was hard to leave the warm spot but I had no choice for I was on service. And it turned out the Captain had merely wanted to brag in front of the Poles that he had a girl amongst his scouts!

Once we were directed to drive explosives to a neighboring brigade on a motorbike. And believe it or not – the engine began to play up. We were barely dragging along and due to be caught up by an artillery column. The road was narrow and we huddled over to the side of the road. One 'hero'-driver caught up with us, swore a lot and then turned his steering wheel so that the gun swung, hooked our motorbike and threw it off the road. I was struck and thrown into the air, I made an overhead somersault and flew somewhere downward, already unconscious. When I had come to myself I was in the snow and wherever I gazed everything was white. I leaped up and crashed down: my left leg was disabled. The guys rolled down the slope, lifted me, pulled up onto the road and got into the motorbike's sidecar, right on the tolite blocks. I don't remember what happened then.

Next day we changed for an armoured carrier, which turned over on a steep turn and covered me. I lost consciousness again and when I had recovered I 'heard' a funereal silence. From under the vehicle I saw the boots of the guys standing in a mournful semicircle. I squeaked faintly: "Get me out of here!" The guys cried out, righted the vehicle or, maybe, simply pulled me out and carried to the nearest house. I lost consciousness again and woke up from cold water being poured on my face. The house was full of women evacuated from Warsaw who didn't expect to see a girl like me amongst the scouts. How astonished they were – they were grasping their heads, swaying and exclaiming: "Woman! Woman!" Generally I had been dressing like a man, trying to stay unnoticed.

In the night we were directed to break through the frontline and go deep into the Hitlerites' rear to draw off a part of the enemy's forces. I still couldn't walk well but the guys were very keen on taking me with them. They were saying: "Such an interesting assignment - a raid through the enemy's rear! We'll seat you on the transmission and escort you". Around midnight we raced through the frontline. Local civilians told us the Germans were hastily preparing to evacuate from the town of Grec, the nearest to the frontline. Two Poles volunteered to be our guides. We stopped about a couple of kilometres before the town. Our tank moved forward to reconnoiter the situation. We rolled up to a high wall and suddenly heard a *Panzerfaust* shot at the tank. The guys jumped off the armour and ran in all directions. One more shot and the tank was hit but didn't catch fire. I landed on my sore leg and fell as if mowed down. Vitya Groshev was yelling "Zo-ya!" constantly and heart-rendingly. But for some reason there were no more shots. My hair was standing up on end for fear that any second now I'd be taken prisoner. I saw tank crewmen crawling out of the machine through the lower hatch. I leaped up and my leg began to walk, as they say, from fear. We managed to crawl out of the trap through a roadside ditch with the loss of the tank gunner-signaller Nikolaev and one Polish guide.

After the war I lived with my husband in Germany, learned to speak reasonable German and then understood why the Germans hadn't shot at the running scouts. Apparently the Germans had been confused by my name: 'Z-o' means 'so' and 'Ya' means 'yes' in German.

In the morning we got an order via radio to advance towards Tomaszow-Mazowiecky. There was no bridge across the river and we had to ford it, getting our

Zoya Alexandrova: "Several of our scouts had been surrounded in the town of Srem. When we arrived on a motorbike to help them out, they had got out of it themselves but one of them, Kolya Maksimov, had been badly wounded in the stomach and died on the way to hospital. The Germans retreated over a bridge beyond a river. We – Sasha the motorbike driver, Alesha Zinchenko, Pukanov and I, still very lame, raced after them to the opposite side of the town on our three-wheel 'horse'. The streets were completely deserted. We had ridden up to the very end of it and found no Germans. We rode back and couldn't understand anything: the streets were full of people, we were cheered, invited inside the houses. We stopped in a small square near the bridge. Some Poles ran up to us and a cameraman took a few shots of the first liberators. Again there were astounded shouts: "Woman!" and one Polish gentleman tipped on me a full pack of sweets… I got a photograph of this when we were already on the Küstrin bridgehead via the Commandant of Srem." (Zoya Alexandrova)

boots full of cold water. We barely managed to drag our motorbike across. The tanks fell behind us and it was impossible to move further without them in wet boots and with no idea where the enemy was. That's why we listened to everything and picked up a rooster's crowing not far off, which meant that there was some habitation nearby. Soon we approached a silent village with neither Germans nor hosts in the houses. But there was smoke over the chimney on each hut, which meant that the stoves were stoked. We took off our boots, wet foot-wraps and socks in one hut (we always had clean underwear, for the Germans had it in abundance and we hadn't been taking anything else as we had even no backpacks) and hung all that around the Holland stove. The hostess came in noiselessly, glancing at as uneasily. But, seeing that we were friendly disposed she felt comfortable and began to stir up the stove with a poker to make the fire burn better and let us dry our socks faster. We were very hungry but for some reason we were seized by such shyness that we asked for nothing, only thanked her for the favours given and took off to catch up with our guys.

Our motorbike broke down on the road, so we threw it away and jumped on a passing armoured carrier. The enemy was snapping feebly in Tomaszow and our tanks broke through it straightaway. We caught up with them only in the fields beyond the town. It was in the night, a blizzard broke out and fierce snow was lashing our faces, beating out tears from our eyes. We sat on our tank and I, hungry and shivering from cold, was seated on the warm transmission. It was gracious of them, since my permanent place was on cold armour on the left side of the tank.

Whilst Zoya Alexandrova and the 1st Byelorussian Front continued their advance into central Germany, further north Erik Wallin was involved in the desperate defence of the Stettin bridgehead. His narrative gives ample evidence of the power of the Soviet artillery, or Stalin's 'God of War'.

Stettin had to be held at all costs, so that the forces at Küstrin and Frankfurt-ander-Oder, that were blocking the road to Berlin, could not be attacked in their flank. The Soviets, as well as our senior command, had realised the vital importance of this bridgehead to the German defence. Because of that, they had sent forward everything they could manage to scrape together from other fronts. On the Kurland front the fighting faded, because many of their artillery corps, armoured divisions, mortar battalions and infantry divisions, among them some of their élite troops, had been moved to the sector at Stettin-Altdamm. They were to force us back over the river.

Day and night an annihilating rain of shells of all calibres, from the heaviest howitzers, heavy Stalin organs, 120mm mortars and infantry guns, down to 37mm anti-tank-guns, beat against our positions in that narrow area. It was full of soldiers, weapons, ammunition, and supply depots. Our casualties were heavy. Pehrsson, our company commander, was wounded and brought back over the bridge to Stettin.

Under the unbroken Red assaults the bridgehead had been squeezed smaller and smaller. It now looked like a 'hedgehog-position' of the same sort that we had experienced, numerous times before, over the two years of retreat from Russia. Only one way back remained - the bridge over the Oder to Stettin. Already the frontlines ran only some 100 metres outside the city limit of Altdamm. Day and night the Soviet artillery hammered on our positions and Altdamm itself, where everything lay in ruins under a dense black-brown veil of smoke over the whole area.

To get some sleep was unthinkable with the ground shaking all the time as in an earthquake, and the air thundered and vibrated with the howling and exploding shells. Pained, dirty and unshaven soldiers' faces were wherever we looked. Supplies came irregularly, although there was plenty, both in Stettin and in Altdamm. More than once the food patrols were swept away by shells on their way to the forward positions.

We could stand the hunger. Exhaustion was worse. Our eyes smarted and our faces were stiff. There was no quiet place in this burning and exploding inferno, where the groaning of the wounded filled every little pause between the shell impacts. Everywhere the shells fell with their devastating and lacerating rain of shrap-

Hans-Gösta Pehrsson, the Swedish commander of the 3rd Company, *SS Panzer Aufklärungs-Abteilung* 11, 'Nordland' Division, known to Erik Wallin and many others as 'GP'. Most of the Swedish SS volunteers served in this company. He ended the war with the rank of *SS-Hauptsturmführer*, and was the most decorated Swedish volunteer, having been awarded the Iron Cross 1st and 2nd class and *Ehrenblattspange*.
(Erik Norling)

nel. Walls fell down over advancing troops, or over wounded on their way to the first-aid stations. Concrete cellars tumbled inwards like boxes of toy bricks. Our underground bunkers became death traps. Rounds with delayed release from the Soviet 120mm mortars penetrated the roofs before they exploded. Trapped there, the men were struck down by the razor-sharp splinters.

With six mortars, my platoon had taken position in the yard of a house that had been completely riddled with bullets and shells. It lay a short distance outside the actual residential area of Altdamm. Among piles of broken bricks from fallen walls, twisted iron beams, radiators, and remains of furniture that had been thrown out of the windows by the explosions, the men worked with admirable calm and precision in the midst of the rain of shells. Our fire-controller, an *Unterscharführer*, was in a cellar in an advanced position. As long as the field telephone worked, the rounds rose in a continuous stream against the sky from our barrels.

No other mortar platoon could have kept up their firing, better, at least not under such conditions. But, after all, they were staunch guys, all of them. Several had been in the thick of it ever since the engagements at Narva and Dorpat. Even the newcomers stood up to prove themselves, inspired by their older comrades' calm and presence of mind. All had been hardened by the last few weeks of purgatory. They had been running the gauntlet among the Bolsheviks. After such experiences we either fell down or got stronger.

But hanging in the balance was the telephone connection. Time after time the cables were cut by shells and I had to send out two assigned signalmen to locate and repair them. Every time made my heart heavy. Hardly any soldiers had a more dangerous task than these *Strippenzieher*, and the numbers of their fallen were among the highest of all soldiers. The line breakdowns were innumerable, and then they had to go out and make repairs. I had already lost three signalmen during the few days that we had been here. They were three magnificent men. What courage, what death defiance in the rain of shrapnel!

In the evening I was ordered by the new company commander to go over myself to relieve our observer. He had had a nervous breakdown. That told me quite a lot about what was waiting for me over there. I left the command post to calm and reliable Kraus, a promising NCO, and then I was off.

The storm of artillery had decreased considerably and did not worry me too much as I went on my way. Much more violent, on the other hand, was the rattle of the infantry fire. I guessed there was close combat going on right then, somewhere over there. Explosive bullets whistled fiercely in the dark. For most of my comrades the artillery fire was the most unpleasant, but I preferred that to these damned explosive bullets, of which I was scared to death. By then they whined closer than ever around me. They hit twisted and charred branches, tree trunks, and then exploded. It was nasty, and I felt like a child afraid of ghosts when passing a dark graveyard.

It was not a long way I had to dash, just a couple of hundred metres. But it felt like an eternity. Through the dark, now and then lit up by a flare or two, or by sudden muzzle flashes, I found my way to the observation position and slid down the remains of stone stairs. As I quickly opened the door and as promptly closed it behind me, a disgusting, musty smell of old perspiration, blood and engine oil hit me.

A burning piece of cotton waste, drenched in oil in a tin can, stood beside the field radio and our observation telephone, on an elegant Chippendale table of the sort often found in northern Germany. It was the only source of light down there. It smelt and stank terribly. On a small gracefully elegant chair was an *Untersturmführer* from the staff. He was sitting there controlling the radio connections. A submachine-gun was hanging over the fine back of the chair and muddy boots scratched its fragile legs.

Moaning wheezes came from two unbelievably mutilated bodies that had been laid on the floor, with a pair of shredded and bloody overcoats as the only protection against its hard and cold cement. A medical orderly pattered to and fro between them, in hopeless attempts to ease their pain. Neither of them could live much longer. One of them had no face. Where eyes, nose, mouth and chin used to be, was only a hollowed- out, bloody mass, out of which the death wheeze pressed, squeaking and snuffling. Out of the other's left corner of the mouth ran a stream of blood. The man I had to relieve sat shrunken on the edge of a camp bed with his head buried in his hands, which nervously ploughed back and forth through his hair. At every shell's explosion that came close to us, he jumped up with fear in his eyes. In contrast to this terrible scene there sat *Untersturmführer* Schwarz, tough and unperturbed, without equal in the company.

He sat on a sugar-box beside the stinking piece of cotton waste, seemingly untouched by everything and everyone around him. He was squeezing lice! He had just finished with his shirt, and was checking the wisps of hair in his armpits and the hair on his chest once more, to be sure, so that no little parasite should get away. Then with obvious pleasure he pulled the shirt over his head. He opened his trousers and started to search every seam, thoroughly, and calmly. All the while dispatch riders ran in and out, the wheezes of the dying continued, and heavy shells detonated so close to us that big pieces of cement fell from ceiling and walls. The noises trembled and sang in the head with the thunder and atmospheric pressure. Each time Schwarz found a louse, and there were plenty of them (here at the front we never got rid of them), he lifted it with a pleased grin against the weak light, snapped it with his nails, then let it fall down in the hot oil in the tin can. He did everything with calm, almost lazy movements.

Now and then Schwarz glanced furtively at the two dying men on the floor. He shook his head compassionately. Without any particularly dramatic accent, he turned and said to the officer by the radio "Do you see now that it's going to be hell for us?" Then he continued his raid among the lice.

Our new company commander came down to us. Schwarz rose to attention, with his trousers down. The newcomer, a sympathetic *Obersturmführer*, straight from Berlin, had not yet had time to become acquainted with Schwarz, a somewhat unusual officer. He was clearly surprised but received his report with a very straight face. It was clear that he had difficulty staying serious.

Then he caught sight of the bloody figures on the floor and knelt between them. He spoke in a low voice to them but got no other answer than the moaning, irregular wheezes. He whispered a question to the medical orderly and got a shake of the head as an answer. Then he stood up and gave a short, stiff salute to the two dying men.

Schwarz, with one hand holding up his trousers, went on reporting to the company commander. The *Unterscharführer* whom I had just relieved, went out to urinate. A roaring explosion was heard just outside the door. Covered with chalk dust, with his combat tunic in shreds, and scratches on his face and hands, he came rushing down again. His eyes were staring with fright and his body was shaking. From his stammering, disconnected and slurred speech, we understood that the shell had penetrated and destroyed the wall, a few metres from the entrance to the cellar, against which he had just urinated. He was completely finished. The company commander took him out and sent him to the rear as, together with his orderly, he left the cellar.

All night the Soviet artillery heaved thousands of shells over our positions. My section of our company got its share, and it now seemed to me a wonder that our cellar had not collapsed from a direct hit and buried us. Towards morning the artillery fire increased even more, so that it sounded like an endlessly lengthy drum-roll, from which it was impossible to discern the single rounds. Trenches, bunkers and foxholes were ploughed apart by heavy shells that tore the crews to pieces. The firing was moved forward to make way for the advancing infantry forces. After bloody and close combat, hand-to-hand, in the ruined positions, they managed to break through in a couple of places. Our own side lacked the strength to force back the enemy, so we were ordered to disengage, and withdraw to new positions on the outskirts of Altdamm.

The retreat and occupation of the new positions was not followed by the combat pause we so badly needed. In an unchangeable, implacable onslaught the Soviet artillery hammered on with its shells. Explosive bullets whistled uninterruptedly with devastating results. The struggle had changed character. Previously it had raged over fields and groves and through separate small villages. But now it rolled from house to house, from street to street.

The circle around the defenders of Altdamm was increasingly tightened. Everywhere Red Army soldiers swarmed forward and were shot to pieces. But they were followed by new waves. This yellow-brown throng was like a lemming migration. They fell in drifts. But over the corpses came new masses that raged without interruption, and without any sign of weakening. They waited around corners while the artillery, or the tanks, shot a defence 'nest' in a house to pieces. Then they rushed forth over the street, down into cellars, upstairs, and took the whole house, then on to the next. Was there no limit to their numbers?

Against this avalanche stood a fragile wall of completely exhausted men who were in mortal danger. They were SS men whose numbers shrank alarmingly day by day, even minute by minute. With the bitterness that characterised house-to-house fighting every man held out to the uttermost. The lightly wounded only gave themselves time to get a bandage at the nearest first-aid station, before returning to their combat positions. Every single man who still had the strength to keep himself up and handle a weapon fought with a fury that I had never seen before.

But our fighting strength grew weaker and weaker. More and more men were brought back bloody and torn, never to return, and no reserves came to fill the ranks. Only a thin line of hardened, determined veterans remained. They were hungry, deathly tired, bloody, many with bandaged arms or heads, unshaven, black from soot and smoke, mud and lime-dust, with uniforms torn to pieces. They felt their strength weaken but still determinedly clung to their weapons and aimed them with devastating effect against the seemingly endless assaulting forces.

After three days of furious fighting from house to house, orders finally came, on 20 March, to retreat over the Oder bridge. The situation had become very dangerous. The Red Army brought their main forces from the south, up along the banks of the Oder, to reach the bridge and with that, catch us in the bridgehead, as in a sack. In the afternoon, as the order reached us, we had managed to advance to a distance of only 300 metres, from the street that continued out on the bridge, our only way back. With superhuman effort the rest of our Division managed to stop their advance for some hours, and as darkness fell, the retreat started. By then the Bolsheviks had had time to correct the fire of their anti-tank guns against this most important street.

It became a case of 'running the gauntlet,' because their observers could see the flames from the exhaust pipes of our vehicles, as we clattered and rumbled at full speed towards the bridge. They aimed their guns at the flashes. For the crews in our vehicles it was many minutes of unbearable stress, driving through the danger area and over the bridge, until they reached the slightly safer Stettin side. But everything went comparatively well and the bridge was not blown up until the last men of the rearguard had crossed over.

The bridgehead at Stettin was a piece of German land drenched with blood, where some of the German fighting forces' best divisions desperately defended themselves against a wild assault by whole armies. But they had completed the task. The bridgehead had disappeared. Where the fighting had raged, fallen Soviets were lying by the thousands.

The *Panzer Aufklärungs Abteilung* of Division Nordland, its armoured reconnaissance battalion, was now in poor condition. For the second time in six weeks, we rolled through Stettin, this time westward. In the city, ravaged by bombs, the Soviet artillery had already started to complete the destruction that had been started by the British and American bomber armadas. Only very few civilians could be seen on the streets, but soldiers on the other hand were many. The preparations to meet the Red assault against the city itself were in full activity. Positions for the artillery were dug in the parks, and foxholes in the streets. Heavy trucks were positioned at street crossings, so that at the appropriate moment they would be used as barricades. Assault guns were dug in, and *Nebelwerfer* and mortars were brought into positions among the ruins. Above all this hung a black-yellow veil of smoke, coming from the violently burning Altdamm. Fires had also now started in Stettin and were spreading further and further.

All this we observed only mechanically. Neither eagerness nor energy lit up our eyes. We did not have the strength. Certainly we had felt terribly tired many times there at the front, but the tension, and the ever-present danger of death, had kept us up and going. It had worked as a stimulating drug, at a time when tiredness should have claimed its due long before.

As we now, temporarily, had managed to pull out of the 'jaws of death,' nerves relaxed again. Now we really became aware of how extremely tired and exhausted we were. Arms and legs felt heavy as lead, face and body ached. The mental tiredness made itself even more noticeable. It was impossible to complete a train of thought, to make a clear observation or a sober reflection. The exhaustion took the form of total apathy. The crews in the half-tracks sat slumped on their seats, thrown to and fro by sudden swervings. Even though they were thrown against the hard sides, they sank into a trance-like sleep. Everyone, chiefly the drivers and commanders of the vehicles, had to exert all their strength to take the long column to safety.

The fighting on the Eastern Front throughout this period was bitter and brutal. However, as Vsevolod Olimpiev relates, it was not always the enemy that was doing the killing.

In early March near Breslau, which was surrounded by our troops, the Regiment was set up for anti-tank defence next to an *Autobahn* running from Berlin across the whole of Silesia. There was about fifteen kilometres to the frontline and we ended up resting there till the middle of April. I, as a Sergeant Major and a former student who had been in combat since 1941, was appointed Commander of the Control Platoon of the 1st Battery. I had to give away my faithful PPSh submachine gun and received instead a Nagant revolver with fifteen cartridges, which I would have cause to regret later on.

Just at that time one would notice odd losses when people were dying not from the enemy's but from friendly fire. One sunny March morning the Regiment's officers led by the Commander - Guards Lieutenant-Colonel Boldyrev - took off for a field drill. Having crossed the *Autobahn* the group strode in loose order down a footpath. Then a group of our ground attack planes took off from an aerodrome situated several kilometers from us and as usual shot a test cannon burst into the air. We had been seeing it on a daily basis, already paying no attention to it. But then the ears of seasoned soldiers got a feeling from the sound that a burst of shells was heading towards us. Our reaction was instantaneous and we threw ourselves on the ground. Nearby explosions sounded and it began to smell of tolite. In a few seconds we got up, shaking the dust off, but one of us who had been the last in our file stayed on the ground with his legs crossed under his body. When he was lifted up blood splashed out of his solar plexus. Two hours later the Senior Lieutenant, my comrade from the battery, died, opening the chain of non-combat losses in the Regiment. Unfortunately it was not the last one of this kind.

In early April intense traffic of tanks and other materiel was unleashed westwards on the *Autobahn*. We got wind that a new advance was coming.

Part VII

North-West Europe

The final push to the River Elbe (February-May 1945)

Part VII

North-West Europe

The final push to the River Elbe (February-May 1945)

With the failure of operations Nordwind *and* Wacht am Rhein *at the end of January 1945, the end of the war in the North-West finally came into sight. In the words of Major Sam Carter: "It was quite obvious that the Germans had shot their wad and we had a big mopping-up job to do prior to the Rhine River. Then, if we could get across the Rhine River, the War would rapidly come to an end."*

The task was not a trivial one, however. The order to reach the Rhine, Allied forces had to advance across a front of 250 miles. Though the distance between the front line and the river was not great – a mere eighty miles at the widest point - in many sectors troops had yet to penetrate the defences of the Siegfried Line (or West Wall), which promised to pose a formidable final obstacle.

The first significant operation of this period was US 1st Army's attack south of the Hürtgen and Roer dams. The attack encountered only weak German resistance; by 4 February a position several miles inside the West Wall had been reached, and by 9 February the dams were finally secured. For the British and Canadians progress proved was more difficult. On 8 February 21st Army Group launched Operation Veritable, an attack south-east of Nijmegen into the Reichswald. Several weeks of difficult fighting followed, in conditions similar to those encountered by the Americans in the Hürtgen forest in late 1944. In his diary Robert Boscawen recorded the frustrations of this period. He also reflected on the new challenges posed by contact between Allied troops and German civilians:

Friday, 23 February. Did not move off till about ten in the morning. A damp and rainy day, but everyone was in extremely good form at breakfast. I don't quite know why. Rather a chaotic start in my troop, as they were not all present at the time, so we went off without them only to find them running down the street after us. Teach them a lesson. We drove out of Nijmegen down the familiar main road to Mook passing the billets we lived in last November. The roads and streets are packed with vehicles bearing all the div. signs I know, showing that nearly all the British and Canadian troops were in this sector. The rain made things miserable; however, I had an excellent haversack ration of duck given me by Ian. Down as far as Gennep, and from there we drove along the railway to Goch.

All the way the road and fields around were covered with shell craters, showing the size of our opening barrage. We passed over several lines of trenches, part of the Siegfried Line, camouflaged in places but they seemed little affected by the shelling. In the whole way I only saw one dead German, which was rather disappointing from what we had been led to believe. The railway was poor going even for tanks, and we bounced about over the sleepers. It was creditable that only one broke its

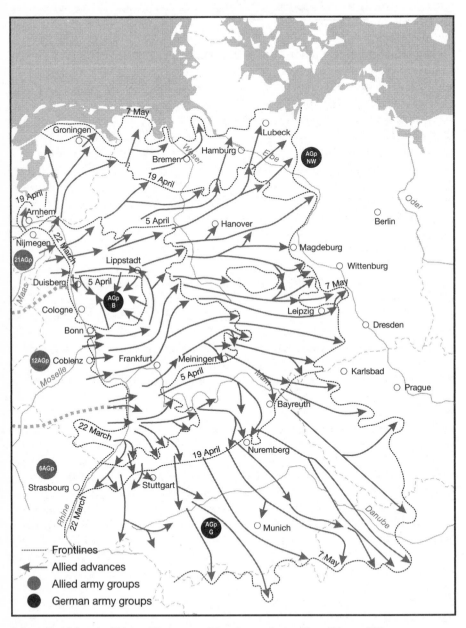

Map 7   North-West Europe: Final push to the River Elbe

track. Passed John Yerburgh and Henty Smith. John was working away with a broken-down tank. I believe he is now the Mick Technical Adjutant.

We crossed the German frontier at Hassum and entered Goch, a badly battered small town, mainly shellfire, but few houses left un-damaged except the water tower, well camouflaged like a church. Desultory white flags were hanging out of a few of the windows. 6th Guards Brigade HQ was in Goch. We turn north of Goch for two miles and the Battalion harboured in a field around two battlestruck farms, a rather dismal place. The luxury of billets is now over once and for all, I'm afraid, and we have to sleep out again under our bivouacs. There was a German POW cage in a field over the hedge from the Squadron that caused considerable interest. Several people went to listen to the interrogation of the prisoners, stupidly I did not. One who refused to talk was being made to dig his own grave alongside some other graves. However, at the sight of our Padre, he at once started to talk.

I saw the Commander this evening and he came up about my MC. Brown produced some dinner for us in our cowshed, – very welcome. I went to bed in the bivouac with my crew; fortunately the weather is mild for February.

Saturday, 24 February. Brown managed to find an excellent egg for my breakfast, after which Ian and I walked to the Reichswald Forest for our daily duty. The end of it was about a mile away, but it was an exceedingly uninteresting pine forest, little signs of German equipment, only some heavy stonking. Dermot did tremendous stuff by building a wonderful fireplace in a cattle shed that made things much better. Guardsmen were rushing in and out collecting the chickens putting them in a pen, and of course the inevitable problem of a number of cattle and pigs left behind, poor things.

Continuous stonking going on all the time from our guns situated all round. The 4.5s in the next field making a beastly row. In the distance we could see the Typhies were stonking away having a good day. The Canadian attack was going well and the 11th Armoured Division were attacking Udem and trying to go as far as the last Siegfried defences. This morning the great American attack towards Cologne started. Already they had several bridgeheads across the Roer.

I tried to polish off some of my letters this afternoon. I had one from Sergeant Brough's sister thanking me for a photograph I sent of my troop in Normandy. She always writes a very nice letter. George also wrote, just back from a weeks leave in Rome. It is strange to see two letters after one's name on the envelope.

Sunday, 25 February. Still in our field at Goch. Rained hard in the night, but fortunately our bivouac held water. A dull day no good for flying, a pity. Saw Drill-Sergeant Robertson this morning, a great friend of mine, and I was pleased he had got a decoration. He had won the C-in-C's Certificate for Conspicuous Service. Church parade was held this morning, but I missed. Walked through part of the forest with Dermot this afternoon, though saw little signs of warfare and only two dead Germans. A letter from Basil convalescing at home now and will not be coming out again, also one from Val at Pirbright. Went to bed early, but a noisy night due, I think, to an enemy counter-attack quite close, anyhow four hours of continuous stonking on both sides.

Monday, 26 February. No sign of moving yet. Morning routine of maintenance, guncleaning and PT. This afternoon walked with Jimmy and Dermot to Brigade about three miles away, a long and hard walk. We saw Peter Chance, but he was not very informative except that we should be flung in soon. The German Para Divs seem to be fighting well still. We passed several colossal 7.2 inch howitzers banging away somewhere. 11th Armoured was due to attack this afternoon.

27 and 28 February. There is excitement in the air. The attack on our front is going well. Udem has fallen and Canadian troops have reached the last Siegfried defences. The Guards Armoured is expected to be thrown in as the final *coup de grâce*. Rumours came in the Americans were advancing on Cologne. Everyone is optimistic about the war. It is rather like last August.

Rather restless that we are not yet called upon. Camouflaged my tanks with a new wire netting. After lunch had a short walk with Ian, and then a bath in a bucket in a cowshed, and felt much better for it. Another heavy lot of stonking this evening.

Thursday, 1 March. After a bad night I retired to bed again for the morning. My inside was extremely ill. I must have one of the bugs flying around, most unlike me, and in the afternoon Johnny Thompson packed me off to hospital. Much to my disgust I was driven off in an ambulance to the Advanced Dressing Station, and from there to the Field Dressing Station, typical Army. I was put in a staff car for Nijmegen and then to bed in a Dutch house. There I remained comfortable and undisturbed save for the drone and thud of the V-1s as they dealt their blows on the town. On the way back we had passed through Cleve, now reminiscent in its destruction of a Norman town, battered beyond recognition.

I spent the next morning in bed, feeling much better and recovered, but stayed in all day as it was trying to snow.

The Yanks have reached the Rhine near Düsseldorf and are shelling Cologne, while only a few miles from our troops moving south. This must be well out of date too, as I only heard it on the nine o'clock news.

I foresee a long and difficult day tomorrow. I am going to get back to the Battalion, somehow or other, and everyone will try and prevent me.

Saturday, 3 March. Set off early from the Doctor's grip, picked up a jeep from the Battalion's 'B' Echelon, most fortuitously just next door, and drove off at great speed to Schaijk, fourteen miles behind to the reinforcement unit. I had to obtain a piece of paper with my name on it just to show I had passed through. A mile or two out of the front line and the real thing, the battle of the red tape, begins. They had no -notification I was required by the battalion and, if they had, they would have sent someone up. Until then anyone discharged from hospital must stay put there. One of the reinforcement officers would show me to the mess. I was clearly getting nowhere with the Duty Officer and asked to see the CO. He was in the mess too, so off we went to a small hut, my driver tailing me close behind. There were a crowd of intensely bored-looking officers sitting round the walls and a stuffy, elderly looking Welsh Guards Major. It was all too much like Anthony Armstrong. I just wanted a piece of paper so that I could get on my way without delay; the Battalion were moving any moment now, could he help me? No, he was sorry he could not. I must join them in the mess; where was my kit?

That was with the Battalion, I said. I was going there in the Squadron jeep and had to pick up another officer on the way. I was sorry I couldn't stay and it was too bad about the piece of paper. He looked at me hard and saw he wasn't going to win. Grumpily he caved in. The others round the walls beamed with delight. Into the

Robert Boscawen (far right) near Goch: waiting to join battle to clear the Germans from the west bank of the Rhine. The others in the photo are Dermot Musker (left) and Jimmy Priestly (centre). (Robert Boscawen)

jeep outside at the double, my driver couldn't wait to let the clutch in and with a bang, we shot away. Back then to Nijmegen, picked up the 'Colonel', as we called Timmy Smyth-Osbourne, from 'B' Echelon and on up to the Battalion, through the Reichswald and on to Goch, where I found them in precisely the same position. They were at two hours' notice to move. I'd made it.

The Division was to move due south to Kapellen to close in on the diminishing German bridgehead this side of the Rhine opposite Wesel. The Germans were pulling out of the Rhineland as fast as they could.

Sunday, 4 March. Was a cold and wet day. Remained at Goch. A small church service in the evening. Warning came to move at one a.m., so early to bed. 5th Brigade had already moved. We are again in 32nd Brigade, forming with the 5th Battalion the Coldstream Group, fighting as one command, and we would remain thus for the rest of the war, two Groups to each Brigade.

Monday, 5 March. At one a.m. moved south through Goch and Weeze, not too bad a night drive. The road was lit by the reflection from violet-coloured searchlights, 'Monty's moonlight'. Arrived just short of Kapellen village at dawn, cooked breakfast at the side of the road, and expected to have a battle later in the day. The General drove past and took up his Tac HQ in a farmhouse just ahead of my troop. We had moved a few yards off the road into this field shared with two batteries of twenty-five pounders. The noise was terrific. Firing at short range, the low angle shells whistled a few feet only above our heads. Beyond Kapellen 5th Brigade were having trouble in some woods, held up by SPs and a SS Para Battalion, and the gunners solemnly stonked these woods. We were going to attack, Jimmy gave out preliminary orders and we stood to, but the plan failed to come off; other objectives had not yet been reached. Remained in the field with morale steadily sinking. The Wesel bridgehead is quite small by now, the Canadians are closing in from the north at Xanten, but the para boys are making a stiff fight for it. The Micks had lost about five tanks.

During the morning the Corps Commander, General Horrocks, arrived in a scout-car to visit our General. Carrying a map case, he leapt out of the top of the scout-car and hurried into the farmhouse. All was a bustle at Div. HQ and he was there for some while before he left. One of the Div. staff told me that with the battle for the Rhineland virtually over he was now going back to plan the next move, the breakout across the Rhine. Shortly afterwards Div. HQ upped stakes and moved off too.

Tuesday, 6 March. Stayed all day in this muddy field at Kapellen, expecting to attack, but by bad luck that caused some ill-feeling afterwards, we were not wanted. The 5th Battalion did a good small attack on the woods beyond Kapellen, after a terrific barrage from some nine field and medium batteries, – two of them in our field. It made a colossal row. They put down fifty rounds 'of gun'. Unfortunately some of these fell short on to our Guardsmen and killed and wounded several of them, I'm afraid. The attack was limited, but went well, though the para boys held out strongly.

My Guardsmen amused themselves by boating on a small lake by our field in punts and canoes. Dermot, of course, fell in, so did most of my crew. I survived, fortunately. Good fun, and helped to keep morale high.

Wednesday, 7 March. Still in this gloomy field, now about two or three miles behind the line, waiting to attack beyond Kapellen. Waiting, always waiting, that's what war is about. Clear day and the 'Typhies' are out and make a good sight. Walked round with Ian and a gun after some duck in the nearby pond. Letters from Edward and Mary arrived this evening. I must write to them soon.

The German civilians round about seem wretches, and mostly Russian labourers, whilst the houses of course have been looted by the Germans themselves. Masses of food, eggs etc. to be had. Earlier two of my crew had been across the fields to obtain eggs from a farmhouse. To their surprise they were well received by an attractive German girl. Later a rumour went around that someone from elsewhere in the Battalion had been there too, supposedly found her willing, and 'had her down'. My troop were shocked and I had heard them discussing this in lowered voices. Later that night it became the topic of our bivouac. Would there be such easy lures amongst the vanquished maidens when we had crossed the Rhine, the dreams of licentious soldiery no doubt since history began? My hopeful crew began to cheer up no end as such vistas opened before them. I had to keep to myself my recurrent forebodings these last few days about the occupation of a hostile, sullen nation, whose hatred of England would have been compounded by years of RAF bombing. Among the white flags I had seen was a tattered sheet strung beneath the windows of a German hovel. It bore crudely written words, '*Nie wieder Krieg.*' Perhaps such weariness would prevail.

Boscawen and his companions were beginning to look to the future with hope. For German soldiers, by contrast, the early months of 1945 were ones of growing despondency. Now fighting on German soil, soldiers saw at first hand the devastation which had been wrought by the conflict. Increasingly too, soldiers feared for the safety of friends and family, many of whom were now caught in combat zones. Johann Voss, who had retreated from the Vosges after the failure of Nordwind, recalls the darkening mood:

When we turned over our positions to the unit moving in and spent some days assembling in the rear, it was inevitable that we were confronted with the grim reality of the general war situation. Back from the woods and moving along the roads in the open, we instantly saw that 'Fortress Germany', as it was called in our propaganda, was a bastion without a roof, open and exposed to Allied bombers. In daylight, except in bad weather, we lay low lest the American fighter planes fall upon us like hornets. Troop movement had become practically impossible in daylight.

One day, we heard on the radio that something terrible had happened at Dresden, of some terror strike of a level and cruelty unknown until then; no details were given. Worse yet, the Red Army had entered the *Reich* and was already west of the Oder. Here on the Western Front, but further north, the US Army already held two bridgeheads on the east bank of the Saar and was pushing toward Saarburg.

This stage of the war, increasing in ferocity, appeared all the more frightening as apparently there was nothing we could do about it. In hindsight, one could say that it had been obvious all along how things were bound to go. Until then, though, the general thinking among us had been that our High Command was capable of organizing an effective and lasting defence line along the borders of the *Reich* and that some way to end the war could be worked out. Even if it came to the worst, our leadership would know best when to give up to avoid total disaster and the needless sacrifice of human lives. As we listened to the radio, however, we heard little more than the call on the German people to persevere, and the invocations of Providence, for that matter. Oddly enough, we weren't deaf to those appeals. Wasn't this the time for the Waffen-SS to show its unwavering loyalty? Yet, at the same time, there was a growing sentiment of doom and an end to hope.

It was also at that time that I learned about Christina's death. The letter I had written her from Denmark came back unopened together with a letter from a friend of hers. Christina had been killed in an air raid while on duty at her hospital in Hannover early in January. So, in the gloomy atmosphere of those days, this news came as another blow, a personal one, but, all the same, fitting into the general pattern. It hurt; the pain with all the other pains went deep into my heart.

Heinrich helped me to get over that dark hour. When I had put back the letter into the envelope, I had seen his questioning glance and told him. A while after I had left the shack to be by myself, he had followed me and appeared by my side. "I know how you feel," he said. "I know it hurts. But believe me, it'll pass."

"You know, I'm wondering what in the end will be left that is worth the sacrifices," I said, leaving out my more personal feelings. "I mean, this war isn't for its own sake. It's for keeping something dear to us, people we love, some part of our own life. Am I right? But if all these things are going to be ruined, what is all the suffering for?"

"Yes, I understand," he said sympathetically. "Don't worry, it's only a weak moment. Three weeks ago, I had my own dark hour when I got my week's leave and had no place to go because Königsberg was under siege. And there've been other dark moments before, I can assure you. I still haven't any idea of my parents' whereabouts. But we can't afford that kind of worrying. It won't make you feel better, anyway."

"How can one stop thinking what it is all for?" I protested.

"By facing the truth that things do happen to us, all sorts of things and all the time, and that there's little we can do about it." He continued, musing, "You see, in general there isn't too much you can do about the course of your life. Most things just happen to you. Having volunteered for our unit was just an exception. But the next moment you were part of the system, no more choices. So you have to put up with things as they happen and play your role, play it as well as you can. No use worrying about what you can't change."

"But you can't stop thinking."

"I didn't say you should. On the contrary, you must think to draw conclusions. If you can't change the course of events, you've got to take it."

"I don't think I can live with that."

"Oh yes, you can."

"I don't know if I want to."

"It'll make you stronger. Once you come to that conclusion, your mind will be free for more important things than worrying."

"Such as?"

"Your duty."

"Point is, I can't help thinking about what our duty is in this state of the war."

"Well, call it loyalty if you have to call it something. Have we fought in Lapland, at the Volga, and in Africa to throw away our arms the moment the enemy enters the *Reich*?"

He had spoken in a low and composed voice. What he said was another invitation to his world of stoicism in which I knew he felt at home. Besides, he was right. Hadn't we sworn to be the most faithful of the faithful? This moment was his hour. There was an air of serenity about him. Hope was no longer needed to outweigh the fear of loss.

A few nights later, we left for a new sector to the north and west. It turned out only later that the division, acting on special orders from the Führer's headquarters, was to launch an attack across the Ruwer River, south of Trier. At first, our transport by truck appeared to be an aimless drive about the region rather than part of a planned operation. Driving by night and resting during the day in obscure places we, the plain soldiers, lost all orientation. We went along winding roads through wooded hill country, sometimes passing through vineyards on steep slopes high above deep river valleys, the Moselle or the Saar perhaps; we didn't know. Somehow the journey seemed to be a blunder. The forlorn villages in the hills, still inhabited, seemed to turn their backs on the troops rushing through the night, as if seeking cover against the war closing in. At last, our tour ended in a little town called Hermeskeil. From there we marched west.

The attack was set for 0400 on 7 March. We prepared as if going on a raid. We didn't take all our MGs with us and left all our heavy equipment behind. Heinrich's gun and my own were combined in one squad, Heinrich acting as gunner. Waiting for our departure time, we stood around in silence and tried to keep warm. For several days, the temperature had dropped below freezing again. A thin cover of snow was spread over the country. The night was pitch dark. You couldn't see the man next to you except for the glow of his cigarette. Suddenly, there was a stir. An officer passed near by, some words in a soft deep voice to the men he brushed with his greatcoat; there was the faint gleam of a Knight's Cross. The battalion commander was on a last tour of inspection before we moved. It was good to know that he would be with us behind the American lines. For that was where we were going to operate: in the rear of the enemy's front line, south of the city of Trier.

We started in single file, clambered quickly over a footbridge our engineers had built, and then set off cross-country. I had no idea where our position was to be, nor how we were to get there. Someone somewhere ahead was supposed to know. To not to get lost in the total darkness, each one in the line was tied to the man in front of him by a rope.

First, the path ran parallel to the valley and then upwards toward our main objective: a road which ran along the ridge of the hills from north to south, a main supply route for the US Army. We walked for about one and a half hours, with many interruptions for orientation. About halfway up we walked parallel to the ridge. Then we halted. So far, we had remained undetected. The night was still. Our platoon leader appeared, groping his way along our line, and ordered us to dig in on the forward slope that fell gently down to a village. However, in our jet-black surroundings, it was impossible to make out a proper spot for our machine gun to be emplaced. We just knew that we were standing in a bare field and that the ground was frozen.

"Listen," I said, "this must be a mistake. You don't really expect us to emplace our MG on this ground? What are we supposed to do here, anyway?"

"Secure our men up on the road against the village down there," the platoon leader said. "By the way, the *Amis* have some tanks in there."

"What do you mean? You think we'll fight the tanks with my MG?"

"Don't blame me. The order is clear. We have to hold this ground until further orders. About the tanks, don't worry. The battalion has positioned an anti-tank platoon by the exit of the village; they'll take care of them with their *Ofenrohre*. There won't be more than two or three, anyway."

"But we can't even dig in. This field is frozen hard as rock."

"We've still got far more than an hour before dawn. That should be enough. If you can't dig, tell your men to scratch themselves into the ground, no matter how, and for heaven's sake, don't make any noise."

"Why the hell don't we attack as long as it's dark and the tanks aren't out in the open?" I demanded to know, but he had already vanished into the blackness. I was desperate.

"This is going to be a fiasco," Heinrich said, scratching the surface of the ground with his spade. "It's pointless to establish an emplacement here. We should try to get out of here as soon as possible."

I told him what the platoon leader had said.

"Oh, shit! What goddamn shit!" was all he said and carried on working the ground. I went around looking after the others of our squad.

All of us feverishly worked with our spades, heedless of the noise, and managed to excavate flat hollows for cover, Heinrich and I even made a small embrasure, but still had no more than a sham of a machine gun emplacement. In between, I lost my sub-machine gun; working the ground I had laid it aside and then was unable to find it again in the pitch dark. So, in expectation of the enemy, I found myself crouching on all fours and groping for my weapon, cursing and feeling panic rise, until I finally touched the treasured piece of metal. Down in the village there was a constant noise of what must have been the idling engines of the American tanks.

Dawn came an hour later. Suddenly, behind us, some two kilometres up on the hill, there were submachine gun bursts, explosions, more small arms fire. Obviously, the battalion had its first contact with the enemy on the road. Then, at various other places, automatic weapons fire flared up, first on the right, then the left. Our artillery sent over their first rounds for support. In no time, a battle was underway behind the American lines.

On our slope and down in the village nothing moved. All of us felt the rising tension. For a moment, we cherished the hope we would still be ordered to attack the village before it was too late; we were prepared for any desperate action if only we could get off this field. This hope was not fulfilled, however. For now, down in the village, we could hear the roar of the tanks' engines being revved up, one after another, each roar soon turning into a dark drone. There were more than two or three of them, perhaps many more. We could hear them moving about and preparing for action. All our hope now rested on the engineers and their *Ofenrohre*.

Then, in the grey light of the early morning, the Shermans slowly appeared from the near edge of our rounded slope. Our anti-tank weapons, on which all our hopes rested, remained silent. What had gone wrong down there? Were they employed elsewhere? Slowly, the tanks rolled upward: two ... three ... then more, six, or seven, I forget. First, we saw the lead tank with its turret open and the machine gunner opening fire on our foxholes from further down the field. The tank was still too far away from us to open fire. Then we saw American infantry in a skirmish line, cautiously taking cover behind the metal giants. Our men further down the slope had offered no resistance, or were there any? What could be done, anyway, without anti-tank weapons?

While the lead tank was slowly going on and the gunner kept firing away, Heinrich had him his sight. We couldn't take that any longer. In an act of despair, we opened fire, a couple of bursts only, no tracers. Immediately, the gunner disappeared, the lid slammed down, the machine gun pivoting awkwardly on top. The tank stopped, went on and stopped again, and so did the others. Their infantry hit the dirt. Moving forward in a somewhat oblique direction, the tank's crew now had discovered our conspicuous position. The vehicle jerked around on its tracks and came directly toward us while the others moved on, deploying in a dispersed formation. With turrets closed, the tank crews began their deadly work of eliminating each of the foxholes scattered over the field, slowly and without mercy.

The lead tank rolled ahead another length toward our emplacement, stopped, and aimed its big gun at us. Faced with the black hole of the gun's muzzle, we had just enough time, a fraction of a second, to press ourselves with all our might down into our hollow. Then the first shot was fired. It missed entirely. From that moment, though, we were silenced all the same. Just the incredible noise and concus-

With the 'garbage gang', the detail to which the author was assigned as punishment for being insubordinate to an American officer. Johann Voss is on the far left, standing.
(Johann Voss)

sion of the shot at such close range is something no man can take. Waiting for the second shot, head pressed to the ground, I was eye to eye with Heinrich. His complexion had turned pale white, his eyes were wide open and full of terror, just the way I must have looked to him. The second shot hit the ground right behind us but did no harm either.

A short pause. We remained tightly flattened on the bottom of our insufficient cover, completely still. The other tanks passed by and worked their way up the hill. Bing was hit and we heard his terrible wail, "My leg! My leg!"

Then the third shell went off, again meant as a direct hit. It was another miss! It was unbelievable. Were they playing cat and mouse with us? Was it a prolonged execution? A kind of torture? Whatever, we didn't reckon to get out of there alive. Next time they wouldn't miss.

Then, the Sherman's crew had another try. There was another terrible blast, lifting the ground and making our bodies jump, but this time the shot came too short, exploding directly before our embrasure, hurling our machine gun up in the air and throwing up the dirt of the embrasure down on us. It was the last shot.

All the time, I had been fully conscious of what was happening. The firing came to an end. We heard the excited voices of the infantrymen closing in from behind the Sherman. I realized it was over. Miraculously, we had survived and remained unhurt—thanks to the fidgety nerves of an American tank gunner. Slowly, with our hands up, we rose from our hollow. The infantrymen approached, slowly and nervously, constantly aiming their rifles at us. I heard Bing moaning from his hole behind me and looked back. He lay there still seeking cover, one leg strangely twisted and bleeding profusely. "Get up, Bing!" I shouted. "It's over!" But instead of putting up his hands first he grabbed his rifle with both hands, probably to prop himself up. It was a terrible mistake. The same moment, one of the GIs hurled a hand-grenade over into his hole. We hit the dirt, and the explosion followed instantly.

I was deeply shocked and still on my knees when someone jerked at my helmet, choking me violently with my chin-strap until it came off. It was my first and painful lesson as a prisoner who is not supposed to wear a helmet. Standing upright again, we were quickly searched for weapons. We looked around, and what we saw was the saddest sight we ever faced. Wherever we looked, none of our men remaining on the field was alive. Bing's body was torn apart. Stricker was dead, and so was one of our replacements. In the foxholes farther away, the men were lying motionless in the awkward positions of the dead.

For a while, we kept staring at the ghastly scene, before one of the infantrymen was ordered to take the two of us away.

On 7 March, the same day that Voss was engaged at Lampaden, an event took place which had important implications for the course of the wider war in north-western theatre. On this date US 1st Army had the good fortune to come upon a railway bridge which had been unsuccessfully destroyed by the retreating Germans. This enabled them to cross the Rhine and form a bridgehead at Remagen, Shortly afterwards, on 13 March 3rd Army launched an attack across the Moselle. This was followed by a swift advance across Saarland, culminating in a crossing of the Rhine near Frankfurt on 22 March.

Two days later, on 24 March, the British and Canadians of 21st Army Group, along with the US 9th Army, finally crossed the Rhine at Rees and Wesel. The crossing itself was achieved with minimal casualties. However, the accompanying airborne attack, designed to secure the high ground beyond the river, encountered fierce resistance. British Paratrooper Denis Edwards was once again in the thick of the action:

Operation 'Varsity' began on 24 March, 1945. The target for our battalion was the railway station at Hamminkeln, together with the Ringenberg road bridge over the River Issel, the railway bridge slightly to the north of the road bridge, and the road running westwards from Hamminkeln and Ringenberg.

The strategic aim was to capture these bridges and other objectives that would deny the enemy the opportunity to counter the assault across the Rhine by Montgomery's Second Army. The airborne bridgehead was then to be held until the Second Army broke through to relieve it.

The airfield of departure for our battalion was at Birch, in Essex, from where the take-off began at 0630 hours. About sixty aircraft, gliders and tugs, were queued for take-off.

A strange event occurred at this time. One of the corporals who had been with us in the Normandy campaign had by this time been promoted to sergeant of his Platoon. While waiting to enplane he had a premonition that the aircraft was fated and doomed. He ran off, only to be later detained, tried, stripped of his rank and sentenced to military detention. He might well have received a more severe sentence than a few months' detention had it not been for the fact that his premonition was justified. The glider in which he would have travelled took a direct hit and was destroyed with no survivors.

I have been told, although I have no personal recollection of the matter, that our Horsa was in fifth place in the queue for the runway. I do remember, however, that we were the last to get airborne, as our tow-rope snapped while we were on our take-off run, this being a not uncommon occurrence, since the tension in the rope was at its greatest as the glider accelerated while being dragged along the runway. A tractor was quickly sent down the runway to drag us back to the start line and eventually we were ready to go again, but now at the back of the queue. We were thus the last combination to leave, travelling toward Europe in grand isolation.

Our tug pilot, however – Wing Commander, later Group Captain, Alex Blythe – did not follow in the wake of the airborne armada. After a chat on the intercom with Stan Jarvis, our glider pilot, he had a new course plotted by his navigator in order to reduce the journey by a few miles and thus to arrive earlier. He intercepted the other aircraft exactly where he expected, close to the destination, and reinstated us close to our correct position in the formation. He was later full of admiration and praise for the precision navigation demonstrated by his colleagues.

Regrettably, the Germans knew only too well that we were on our way and they were ready and waiting. Following the British glider-borne landings in Normandy and Arnhem in 1944 the Germans had certainly realized that the most effective way to deal with the British troop-carrying Horsa, and the equally large and flimsy Hamilcar gliders was to hit them with incendiary bullets. Perhaps even tracer bullets were sufficient to set these large and slow gliders aflame long before they reached the ground.

Bullets zipped through one side of the flimsy plywood fuselage and out of the other as we approached our landing zone, and as we came in to land part of one wing, an aileron, and the tail section were shot to pieces by shellfire. Listening to the bullets ripping through woodwork around us was none too pleasant, but amazingly none of us was hit by them. Even more miraculously, unlike most of our comrades in other gliders and those paratroops who jumped, we suffered no casualties at all during the actual landing.

Stan Jarvis, our young RAF glider pilot, had been trained as an RAF pilot, but was hurriedly transferred to flying gliders for the airborne forces because of the heavy loss of Army pilots at Arnhem. He put our Horsa down as close to the railway station as we could have wished. Many years later Stan recounted how, after we had all fled the wrecked glider, taking cover wherever we could amid a hail of incoming missiles and bullets, one of the lads said to him, "I know that before you left the airfield we asked you to get us as close as possible to the railway station, but if you had landed any closer we would have been in the ruddy booking office."

From the River Rhine to the landing zone the surface was already clouded by smoke from the guns and bombs and smoke-laying equipment used by the ground forces in preparation for crossing the Rhine. Stan Jarvis recalls how he cast off from Alex Blythe's Dakota tug aircraft while in dense smoke, with no sight of the ground whatsoever.

While he and his co-pilot, Peter Geddes, were looking desperately for clues as to our exact whereabouts, pieces of our glider were literally being shot away. As they identified a stretch of *autobahn* to the east of Hamminkeln, they steered towards where they would expect the railway station to be, while four feet of the starboard wing, together with most of the aileron, were blown off by a flak burst. He put us into a fairly steep dive as the tracer and machine-gun fire intensified and became more accurate. Then he saw the railway lines and the station, levelled off at about fifty feet and went in for his landing, skimming the fields and the posts and snag-wires that had been erected to discourage glider landings. The tail section was shot away just as we landed, but the cargo of men was intact, with no injuries whatsoever.

The official record shows that between 24 and 25 March, 1945, the regiment suffered one hundred and three killed. A normal company consisted of six officers and one hundred other ranks. At the end of 25 March our position was: 'A' Company, four officers and fifty-six other ranks; 'B' Company, two officers and forty-five other ranks; 'C' Company, four officers and fifty-two other ranks, and 'D' Company, three officers and fifty-eight other ranks. This was a truly awful rate of loss.

In total the British 6th Airborne Division had 1100 casualties and the American 17th Airborne Division suffered similar heavy losses. Many of the gliders were literally shot out of the sky and 100 members of the Glider Pilot Regiment and RAF men who flew the gliders also lost their lives. This was the price that had to be paid to overwhelm the German defenders and ensure the success of the land-based Rhine crossing.

Unlike Denis Edwards, Peter Hall's Rhine crossing was a straightforward, if memorable, experience. Once on the east bank of the river, however, he found himself engaged in one of the most difficult and costly battles of his military career.

The *autobahn* was not, really an *autobahn* at all. It was still under construction. It was a heaped-up embankment which offered superb fields of fire against an assaulting force. Furthermore, this excellent defensive position was occupied by elite and determined parachutists and backed by skilled enemy artillery. The enemy had had time to site machine-gun positions forward of the *autobahn*. The 27th March was going to prove, for both sides, a very hairy day!

The Brigade plan was that there should be a 2 battalion attack on the *autobahn*, 7th Somerset Light Infantry on the left and 1st Worcestershires on the right. It was also planned that on the right of the Worcesters, that 51st (Highland) Division should attack at the same time. The Battalion plan for our allocated objective was that we should advance with two companies in the assault. These were 'D' Company on the left, (Bryan Elder) and 'A' on the right (mine). Each assault company had, under command, a troop of tanks from the 13th/18th Hussars. 'B' and 'C' Companies were held in reserve to pass through the assault when we had achieved our objective and, also, to secure the woodland beyond.

A Battalion Orders Group was held at approx. 1100 hours and H-hour was fixed, if I remember correctly, for 1145 hours. This gave little time for reconnaissance, company and platoon orders, and marrying up with our supporting tanks. Thanks to

Major Bryan Elder with men of D Company, 1st Worcesters. Left to right are: unknown Private; Company Sergeant Major C. W. Bryant; unknown Private; Major Bryan Elder; Private Dick Pigneguey (signaller attached to D Company); Captain Percy Huxter (second in command of D Company). This photo was taken in Germany in April 1945 just prior to the battle at Ahlhorn crossroads, where Bryan Elder was wounded.
(Louis M. Scully)

established battle-drills, good training, and practical experience, all the preliminaries went well. It was a miracle of military efficiency that, in spite of incredible logistical difficulties, we crossed the start line on time, and with the correct groupings.

Then, things started to go wrong. From start line to the objective for the assault the distance was about 1000 yards. We, the infantry, had to advance over flat, open country, with practically no cover from the enemy's machine-gun fire. And this was intense! We had to rely, solely, on the principle of fire and movement (which I have described earlier) and close with the enemy as quickly as we could.

An additional complication was that, although the actual day of our assault was sunny, the ground was sodden and muddy. It eventually proved impossible for tank movement. Although this was a major disadvantage, it did not detract from the ferocious firepower that my supporting troop of tanks were able to bear onto the enemy. This was a contributing factor to our final success in this particular, hard-fought engagement.

'A' Company had advanced to within about 200 yards of our objective when our supporting tanks bogged down. Stuck in the mud. I went forward to the troop leader's tank and pressed the button on the rear of the vehicle. This should have made it possible for voice communication between us by telephone. For some reason it was not working! The tank just sat there like an enormous iron elephant's turd. No response from the crew inside. Their machine gunner continued to pour hot lead into the heaped-up *autobahn* - but not where I wanted it!

It was vital that I talk to the troop leader, and so I clambered up onto the tank and banged, with the butt of my machine pistol, onto the closed-down lid of his turret.

An age seemed to pass. I felt like Long John Silver's parrot, perched on his shoulder when he was leading the pirate charge against the stockade in Treasure Island. I was 10 feet off the ground and there was a lot of 'rubbish' roaring about. Under these circumstances, an infantryman finds that the ground would be a very pleasant place to be! Eventually, the turret trap opened. The troop leader's head appeared.

"What the bloody," he started to say.

"Shut up and listen!" I snarled. "You're stuck and can't move. We can and we're going to. I'm going to do a shallow right-flanking movement onto the objective so that we won't mask your fire. You will concentrate everything you've got onto the following specific areas."

I indicated them by pointing.

"Keep an eye on our movement. It won't be text-book pretty but we will go split-arse. When you see a red verey light, you will stop firing AT ONCE! Got that?"

"Wilco," he said. "Wilco" means I hear and will comply.

Whilst I was giving him his orders, I saw 'D' Company on my left. They were in deep trouble and could not move forward. I could not expect a co-ordinated attack with mine from my old friends, but I could enjoy their fire support. I felt that I had to tell Bryan Elder what I was going to do. If we succeeded, we would turn the enemy's flank and he (Fritz) would have to withdraw, thus enabling 'D' Company to advance and secure their objective. Bryan could also help by concentrating on the same fire targets which I had given to the 'tankies'. The more lead was thumping into our objective, the better our chances of making it.

There was no wireless communication between Bryan and me, and so I had to 'run the gauntlet' in order to speak to him personally. This necessitated a sprint in the open of about 150 yards under heavy fire. I SPRINTED! I got to Bryan intact. I told him of my intentions. He agreed. "Good luck you bloody crazy Mick!" he shouted. I sprinted back noticing little splashes of mud exploding around me. I was being targeted by a Spandau machine-gun. I managed, somehow, to step up a gear or two! I made it back to Peter Wade's platoon.

"Peter" I gasped, "We've got masses of covering fire. We're going to attack in echelons of platoons. That's your objective. Get going!"

"Right," he answered. "Nice day, isn't it?"

Off he went, but unfortunately, not very far. An undetected Spandau machine-gun, immediately on the right flank of his advance and forward of the main enemy positions, opened fire. Peter was severely wounded in the leg and a number of his guys were killed. Although wounded, Peter threw a smoke grenade to his right which obscured the view of the enemy from our advance. A vital factor in our eventual success.

"'A' Company," I yelled, "Follow me!"

We dashed forward, rather like a bunch of Fuzzie-Wuzzies in the battle of Omdurman. I would not have scored any 'Brownie points' for this manoeuvre had it been an exercise on Salisbury Plain, but we made it. As we hit the objective what I knew would happen, did! The enemy hit the position which we, minutes ago, had occupied, with a most ferocious Artillery Hate. Fritz was employing his normal defensive tactic: slow down the assault with small arms fire and then, hit it with all the big stuff at your command. In this battle there was lots of it; our speed of advance frustrated the enemy by seconds!

I was sorry for the tankies but, not unduly concerned. Cocooned as they were in their iron contraptions, the worst that they could expect was a headache, unless a tank sustained a direct hit in its petrol tank. I was much more concerned with my own wounded and about 'D' Company who had no such protection.

However, we had turned the enemy's flank. 'A' Company had kicked open the door and the eventual success of the battalion attack was assured. I had three immediate priorities. First, to report our success to Battalion Tactical HQ over the WT net. (Thankfully, our wireless was still intact.) Second, to turn the enemy trenches round the other way, in case there was a physical counter-attack by Fritz. I did not consider this to be likely. He would be too preoccupied in withdrawing his surviving soldiers to fight another day, but – Be Prepared! Third, to get our own wounded into the comparative safety of our newly won territory – the excellently prepared defensive dug-outs that Fritz had constructed.

The first two priorities were fairly easily accomplished. The third took a little longer. Tactical HQ had promised me help in casualty evacuation. This was generously, courageously, and efficiently forthcoming, but we did not get all our wounded evacuated till after nightfall. I had to do something from my own resources. I organised a party of volunteers to come out with me to bring back as many wounded as possible, to the shelter of our newly won positions.

Although Fritz had abandoned his first ferocious artillery hate, there was still intermittent shelling from him over the ground where we had advanced, but, he could not see his target any more because his OP's had either been killed, captured or had scarpered. He was firing 'hit or miss' - happily, in this case, it was mostly miss. My own efforts were a bit pathetic. I and my 'oppo' only managed to bring in one wounded. He was very cheerful and grateful, although we must have hurt him like hell with our inexperienced handling.

'A' Company took its objective by 1700 hours. Bryan Elder and my old comrades in 'D' Company did not succeed in attaining theirs until after dark (about an hour later).

During the night, 'B' and 'C' Companies passed through us as planned, and we were, temporarily, out of the battle. We did, however, see the results of our endeavours. There were, approx 30 German dead, and about the same number, some of them badly wounded, surrendered to us. It had been a triumphant but sad day. We in 'A' Company had lost good comrades. But - against formidable odds - we had achieved what we had been required to do. I felt that this battle was a bonding between my new command and me. Some five weeks later, in another battle, my instinct proved to be right.

Despite such fierce and costly encounters, for Allied troops, the mood among the Allied troops in this period was one of optimism, and even exhilaration. Peter Hall noted of the aftermath of "the battle of the autobahn":

This battle seemed to have a marked and adverse effect on Fritz's will to fight… He had had the initial advantage, but had lost it to us. To use a boxing simile – it was as if Fritz was punch-drunk and hanging onto the ropes for dear life.

On 28 March, a day after Peter Hall's encounter at the autobahn, *Robert Boscawen noted in his diary:*

I cannot believe if can last much longer, the whole front is crumbling and the armour is on the move. We are keen to be flung in, so as to race across Germany. Lead on. It is a terrific feeling. Really after six years it is coming to an end. My God how wonderful.

In the remaining six weeks of the war, the Allies had three major objectives. The first of these was the clearance of Army Group B, the opponents of the Americans in the Ardennes offensive, from the Ruhr. The fortuitous capture of the bridge at Remagen has suggested a daring plan to Allied strategists. The idea was that as US 1st Army broke out from their bridgehead at Remagen, US 9th Army would strike out south-west of Wesel. The two armies would link up, encircling the German troops. The operation, which was launched on 25 March, was a success: by 1 April the Ruhr, which had been the target of the Arnhem offensive six months earlier, was had been encircled. Realizing the importance of this industrial area, Hitler ordered that the Ruhr be declared a 'fortress'; German troops were to stand and fight, rather than attempting either to retreat or escape. Nevertheless, the encircled troops could not withstand Allied pressure for long, and eventually the encircled troops surrendered on 18 April. Around 317,000 German soldiers were taken prisoner.

From April, a substantial portion of American forces were concerned with a second objective – a drive through southern Germany, with the aim of suppressing the so-called 'National Redoubt'. This latter was an area in the Bavarian and Austrian Alps in which the Allies believed a large force, comprising a substantial number of committed Nazi troops, were gathering. Fortunately for the Americans, such fears proved ill-founded; even areas of difficult terrain, such as the Thuringian forest, barely slowed the Allied advance in this sector. Indeed, it was in this region that Georg Grossjohann, the survivor of so many battles, was finally to forced to admit defeat:

At the end of March 1945, I was finally transferred to the course for regimental commanders. Just two years before this writing, the Federal German archives in Cornelimünster discovered that there were two copies of my orders for the course from March 1945 in the their records, so they were kind enough to relinquish one for me to keep. Unbeknownst to me, the orders included an order of merit list drawn up by Army Group G headquarters, which indicated that I had been slated to command a Grenadier regiment.

Even in March 1945, I took care that my Joseph was allowed to accompany me to the course. Once there, Joseph was highly welcomed, because soldiers of his rank were in perilously short supply. Now, however, he worked not only for me, but also for a major from the general staff.

Originally, the course was planned to begin at the Army Communication School #1, in Halle-on-the-Saale, but that was quickly cancelled. Next, I was to proceed to the tactical training facility at Grafenwöhr. Upon my arrival there, a huge Allied bomber squadron was just flattening the last walls of the camp. In spite of the now hopeless situation, the course was continued, though quite sporadically, until the end of the war. Somehow, I was still impressed by this unperturbed muddle.

Among other things in the orders to report to the course was a directive that "Army Group G is to provide a final evaluation of *Major* Grossjohann no later than 1 May 1945! I am almost sure that it was sent out, but got stuck somewhere at the war's end.

The last stop for the course was the garrison for mountain infantry in Mittenwald, and Krün and Wallgau, two quaint mountain villages that were nearby.

The news announced on 30 April that Hitler had been killed during the defence of Berlin was received in different ways by the participants in the course. Astonishingly, the numerous SS officers working in this area reacted especially coolly, a phenomenon which *Bundeswehr-General* Gerd Schmückle later mentioned in his book *Ohne Pauken und Trompeten*. We all understood that this was the beginning of a very difficult time for the German people. After Hitler's death became known, the course director, *Generalmajor* von Larisch, assembled the attendees one more time in the schoolhouse of Krün. "What you have learned in the past weeks was certainly not in vain, for just a few years from now, there will be a new German army!" These were the general's words of farewell.

In my reveries, I thought of the statement of my little *Oberst* after the victorious French campaign. He, too, was correct then by portraying the end of that campaign only as the end of outpost skirmishing. . . .

Only a few years later, of course, the words of *General* von Larisch also became reality. As early as 1948–49, the Western allies are said to have debated a military contribution by Germany and to have inquired under what conditions the Germans would be willing to establish a new army. . . .

In any case, after his speech, *General* von Larisch declared the course dissolved. Every participant received several weeks' pay and, if they desired, a rucksack, clothes, and heavy mountain boots from the stock of the mountain infantry.

A few days earlier, I asked that my Joseph be discharged with his papers completely in order. Without difficulties, he reached his hometown and his especially friendly and big family. His old mother became a dear friend to me in the difficult post-war period. "If it wasn't for the *Major,* our Joseph might not be alive anymore," she said. Being the owner of a farm in Lower Bavaria, she supported me occasionally with plenty of food.

Shortly before the Americans moved into Krün, I withdrew to a comfortable ski lodge in the Karwendel Mountains, accompanied by two SS officers and a Major iG. The lodge was owned by Christian Weber, a well-placed Party member, and president of the Bavarian Motor Racing Club. In the higher mountains, well hidden by the deep snow, the SS men stashed away large stocks of food. Thus we didn't suffer, but actually enjoyed the beautiful start of springtime. Soon, we learned that some female SS auxiliaries had 'fraternised' with the Americans right after their arrival. I tried in vain to stop one of the SS officers from visiting his girlfriend in Krün. He left anyway, but he was expected! In the darkness of night, the well-informed victors shot him on sight, in a meadow in front of the farmhouse in which his girlfriend had found shelter. With certainty, one of her colleagues gave him away to the Americans and, in turn, received considerable stocks of groceries and luxury items that had been in storage.

The girlfriend of the SS officer was sentenced to a long prison term by an American military court for abetting a fugitive. She served her term in the women's prison in Aichach. I later once paid her a visit in prison.

I don't have to talk about the attitude of a large part of German people, specifically in my case, the Bavarian population, towards soldiers just before and after the war. Everybody must have had his own experiences. It happened that when soldiers wanted to take a rest with the farmers, those would cry out "the Americans are coming," which would cause the soldiers to flee into the mountains. Then, the farmers would loot the luggage that was left behind. Regarding the willingness of our population to collaborate with the victors, we don't, by God, have to look down on the French in their days past.

One day at breakfast in our lodge, we were discovered by some armed foreigners and they took us away. Fortunately, one of us had gone up to where the butter was kept in the ice and observed our capture. Armed with an automatic pistol, he followed us through thick brush, fired a few rounds into the blue sky, and our paths and the paths of our escorts separated surprisingly quickly. After this, we went back to our hut. It seemed now, however, appropriate to abandon our comfortable shelter at once. We separated and left the lodge by different routes. I had all unnecessary ballast removed from my rucksack and, except for a couple of pairs of socks, filled it to the top with thousands of cigarettes from the SS depot. Later on this proved exceedingly useful.

In the beginning, I hiked along lonely mountain trails until I arrived at Kochel am See, where I deposited all my medals, as well as pertinent documents, with a home owner whom I trusted.

Afterwards, I crossed much of southern Germany, where I could easily evade the Americans, whose checkpoints were only on major roads. I had no problems with food. All I needed to do was to take a pack of cigarettes from my rucksack, which I guarded with my life, and soon I could enjoy a healthy meal at a farmhouse of my choice. Then, I arrived in Betzgau near Kempten im Allgäu at the house of the mayor, who was until now also the local farmers' leader. I offered my help with harvesting hay, which had already begun. Since I grew up out in the country in my East Prussian homeland, I still had profound knowledge of all types of work related to agriculture. Therefore, I was soon entrusted with activities requiring higher qualifications. Together with the two nice daughters of the house, I took care of the milk cows, including my part of the milking.

As eventually happened with all leaders, great and small, from any Nazi Party organization, my mayor and ex-farmers' leader was one day arrested and imprisoned. What his crime may have been, I don't know. Maybe one could suppose that he indoctrinated National Socialism into the cattle of Betzgau—and I don't mean just the bovine ones!

General George S. Patton, Jr. opened the camp doors soon after the war's end, and sent all the little fish home, and in many cases, back to work. He paid for that by losing his post as Commanding General of the US 3rd Army.

The mayor's nice wife asked me if I could not at least stay until her husband would come home. In view of subsequent events, maybe this is what I should have done.

One late afternoon I went for a swim at a nearby pond. There, I was approached by an American officer, who assumed I had been a soldier. He asked for my papers. A German-speaking Dutch woman, probably a souvenir the American got in the Netherlands, translated. He was quite a nice young man and said I must be very exhausted after wandering around so much without sufficient food and shelter for such a long time. Of course I did not tell him that I had been quite well cared for by a local farmer. The American called his driver and ordered him to take me to the Army hospital in Kempten. As always, I took my well-stocked rucksack with me, sort of like a beach bag. I picked up my ski-pants and the good hiking boots from Mittenwald from my mayor's lady a few days later. In all truth, I could inform her that I now had been "taken prisoner."

The final, and in many ways most significant Allied objective, at this late stage of the war, was the closure of the eastern and western fronts. In late march Eisenhower sent his famous message to Stalin, suggesting that the Allied armies should meet on an Erfurt-Leipzig-Dresden axis. The final military objective for the western armies was not, therefore, to be Berlin, as Roosevelt had originally suggested in 1943, but the Elbe. According to Eisenhower's plan, General Bradley's 12th US Army Group would lead the main thrust towards the Soviet lines. Montgomery's 21st Army Group would protect Bradley's group on its northern flank. The Elbe was reached by the U.S. 67th Armored Regiment on 11 April. The British reached the river just over a week later, shortly after the capture of Arnhem by Canadian troops on 14 April. On 25 April US forces encountered their Soviet counterparts for the first time at Torgau on the Elbe. In the media, this historic encounter was presented as an uncomplicated triumph: a long awaited meeting of friends and allies. The reality on the ground, as Denis Edwards was soon to find out, was rather more complicated.

On 28 April we learned that we were to move up to Suttorf on the River Elbe. This was about ten miles east of Lauenburg where the British forces had formed a bridgehead, and we marched there the following day with no major incidents.

Leaving Suttorf in the early evening of the 30th we marched to the crossing point on the River Elbe. The crossing was carried out at midnight, using a temporary bridge put across the river by our sappers. Moving off eastwards immediately, we swung north a little later to attack the hamlet of Nosdorf.

Before dawn on 1 May we took the village of Nosdorf, moving on five miles or so immediately afterwards to Schwartow soon after first light.

On 2 May we encountered a stream of liberated prisoners of war, and a little later substantial units of a German army, complete with long columns of tanks and artillery. This huge German force was travelling westwards along the same routes that we were using to advance to the east. They outnumbered us many times over but fortunately they were no longer interested in fighting. It caused a very considerable traffic jam as their long lines of fully equipped, heavy, medium and light tanks, troop carriers, heavy artillery, large lorries and an assortment of smaller vehicles blocked the narrow roads.

Denis Edwards (far right, swimming trunks) on the Baltic coast, May 1945.
(Denis Edwards)

This fleeing army, intent only on escaping from the Russians, considerably impeded our progress towards our next objective, Gladebusch. We took advantage of the situation to rest at the roadside, watching the enemy drive past us in full battle order. It was a very odd state of affairs, but certainly a sign that serious German resistance was almost ended.

The Germans were virtually indifferent to our presence. One high-ranking German officer, however, immaculately dressed and with a stiffly arrogant Prussian manner, left his staff car and crossed over to where we were resting at the roadside. In perfect English he told us that the German and British people had a great deal in common, whereas the Russians were nothing but savage barbarians. He suggested that if we were wise we would join forces with the Germans, attack the Russians and drive them all the way back to Siberia. He said that the Russians were desperately short of food, supplies and ammunition. They could neither feed nor guard prisoners, he maintained, nor did they have the spare bullets to shoot them. What they did to anyone that they caught was to hack off their hands, or sometimes their feet to prevent them from running away or taking up arms against Russia in the future.

With the liberated German concentration camp still fresh in our minds, and still with the nightmare memories of living skeletons and piles of dead bodies, we were not too impressed with his stories of Russian atrocities. We were also far from being persuaded by his suggestion that we should start a new war just as the present one was ending.

At that time we knew nothing about German concentration camps, or their purpose of systematic extermination, but we told him about the death camp that we had liberated a week earlier. It was quite obvious from his baffled expression that he simply did not know what we were talking about.

The next day we moved up to Lutterstorf village, and then on to Bad Kleinen. There, on 3 May, 1945, at Bad Kleinen, midway between Wismar and Schwerin, on the banks of a river that linked the Baltic Sea with the great inland lake of Schwerin, and not many days' march from the Polish border, the victorious British and Russian armies met.

For us it was the end of a 280-mile advance across northern Germany that had begun on 24 March with the Airborne landing at Hamminkeln. We had been marching almost flat out day and night for what seemed like an eternity. Now we were camped on the western bank of the river, looking across at our Russian comrades-in-arms camped on the opposite side. They crossed over a wide bridge in considerable numbers from their side of the river and invited us to drink vodka with them; whatever else may have been in short supply they appeared to have an almost unlimited amount of their favourite tipple.

They obviously used their visit to have a good look round our tented camp, for when darkness fell a large band of them paid us another visit, this time uninvited. They entered our main supply tent and, at gunpoint, tied up the Quartermaster and his staff and made off to their side of the river with most of our rations!

When the theft was discovered we immediately placed an armed guard at our end of the bridge and refused to allow any more Russians to cross to our side. They did likewise. This may well have been one of the first acts of what was to be called the 'cold war' and which was to endure for half a century thereafter.

The morning after their raid on our supplies one of the lads from the Quartermaster's staff thought that he recognized one of the Russians who had been in their raiding party. A group of us crossed the bridge and were met at the other side by a Russian officer. We assumed that he was an officer as he wore some kind of uniform, while most of the others, Mongol types from their appearance, were dressed like peasants in scruffy smocks.

As best we could, by sign language, we pointed out the man who we believed had been a member of the gang who had stolen our food. The Russian seemed to understand what we meant; he nodded, then turned and strode across to the suspect that we had indicated. We assumed that he was going to question him, or bring him over to us for positive identification. Instead, he drew a revolver from its holster, put the barrel against the man's mouth and fired, blowing off half of his head. We were horrified as he returned to us, grinning from ear to ear, and indicating that, while the man may have stolen our food, he would certainly not be eating any more of it!

No offer was made to return our rations and as we retraced our steps to our side of the river I remembered the words of the German officer who, only a few days earlier, had told us that the Russians were different! Certainly they appeared to have been severely brutalized, but warfare is always a brutalizing experience and the Soviets had suffered more than most, particularly because the Nazis did not even acknowledge their right to the benefit of the Geneva Convention.

I doubt if the German officer would have recognized or understood that the war which brought about such brutality was his war, not theirs. He would not have been able to understand that the savagery and brutality of his own people, although just as horrific, or worse, could not be excused as resulting from years of suffering and privation. It was in evidence from the beginning, as they sought to make themselves masters of Europe.

Five days after the meeting at Torgau, Hitler was dead. One week later, on 7 May 1945, German troops surrendered unconditionally. The war in Europe was at an end. Peter Hall recalls this, and also his first encounter with the Soviets, which occurred shortly thereafter.

A week after my return to the Battalion, Field-Marshal Montgomery met the representatives of the German Armed Forces in a tent on Luneberg Heath. The war in Europe was over! Germany had surrendered, unconditionally.

It was a memorable moment and, I'm afraid, I got very drunk. I was not the only one in 21 Army Group to overindulge on this occasion.

The next two weeks were wonderful. No more fighting; no more wondering if we would survive to see the sun come up on another day.

The 1st Worcestershires closed up on the west bank of the river Elbe. We could see, for the first time, our Allies - the Russians - on the east bank. Initially we waved to each other with great enthusiasm. But - when our soldiers started to swim in the river, warning shots were fired over our heads. We took the hint. Uncle 'Joe' Stalin did not want his troops to be contaminated by the decadent Western Democracies!

For the Allies, the final battles of the war had been among the easiest of the campaign. However, as both Edwards and Hall sensed, for the Russians, things had been very different.

Part VIII

Eastern Front

The Last Months (March-May 1945)

Part VIII

Eastern Front

The Last Months (March-May 1945)

By the end of March 1945 the Third *Reich* was in its death throes. On the Eastern Front, the German forces had been pressed back to within 30 miles of Berlin. To the east of the River Oder isolated pockets of Germans held out in an ever-decreasing number of fortified towns and cities. The majority of Hungary including the vital oilfields and the capital city Budapest had fallen.

Yet until this time it was not at all certain that a Red Army offensive against Berlin would follow imminently. The strategic situation was altered by the rapid gains made in North-West Europe by the Allies. After initial slow progress towards breaching the natural barrier of the Rhine, the second half of March had seen tremendous advances made deep into western Germany. Stalin, ever alert to ensuring the Soviet Union's premier position in Central and Eastern Europe in the post-war make-up, decided that it was imperative the Red Army conquer all German territory east of the Elbe – the Soviet zone of occupation decided at the Yalta conference. Above all, securing the jewel in the crown – Berlin, was vital.

The central sector of the front now witnessed a deceptive lull as the Soviets redeployed a huge mass of men and material away from the northern and southern sectors where they had been involved in clearing operations in preparation for the decisive strike against Berlin and central eastern Germany. The lengthening days and warmer weather could not, however, disguise the disparity in forces being massed for the coming battle. The defences along the Oder and in Berlin itself had been woefully neglected. Until virtually the last moment Hitler refused to acknowledge the need to prepare Berlin for defence, seemingly more intent upon discussing the recapture of Budapest. Armoured forces vital for the defence of the Oder line were withdrawn and transferred south. Zhukov, marshalling the Soviet forces, was encountering problems of a different kind, as he struggled to bring order the sheer size of the Soviet forces – over 2½ million men, more than 6,000 tanks, 7,500 aircraft and nearly 45,000 guns and rocket launchers.

Of course, action continued in the northern and southern sectors. During the end of March and early April remaining pockets of resistance in East Prussia, notably the city of Königsberg, were reduced. To the south, early April witnessed gains being made by the Red Army through Czechoslovakia and into Austria, where Vienna fell – much to Hitler's chagrin – on 13 April. Yet all were sideshows compared to the decision to be made in the centre.

The final offensive against Berlin was launched on 16 April. The key to the German defence was the Seelow Heights, a commanding position overlooking a nightmare terrain of small woods, marshes and rivulets. Both sides knew that if the Seelow Heights were taken, the battle could only have one outcome. Desperate defence and Soviet errors contributed to the Seelow line remaining unbroken for

227

three days. However, by 19 April it had been breached and the units of 1st Byelorussian Front were pushing towards the city itself. The following day the outskirts of Berlin were reached, and by 25 April the city was surrounded. The final outcome was now completely inevitable, and despite Hitler conjuring up images of relief efforts and counter-attacks, these barely existed outside of his own imagination. Using all of their experience gained in conquering countless other German towns and cities, the Red Army made remarkable progress, urged on in the knowledge that Stalin was desperate to see the Soviet flag hoisted on the Reichstag by 1 May. The Soviet troops were undoubtedly assisted by the fact that the best of the German defensive forces had been destroyed outside the city limits. The majority of the defenders of Berlin itself were Hitler Youth and *Volkssturm* units, and police and other *ad hoc* combat forces. On 30 April Hitler shot himself, and two days later the city surrendered.

Progress had been made elsewhere, principally in the south, where the second half of April saw much hard fighting in Czechoslovakia.

US forces had linked up with the Red Army near Torgau on 25 April. By 3 May the Soviets were at the River Elbe. Four days later the Germans surrendered to the Western Allies. The final German surrender – to the Soviets – came on 9 May, following the very last offensive of the war on the Eastern Front, when Prague was captured. The war on the Eastern Front, or Great Patriotic War as the Soviet people referred to it, was finally over.

Zoya Alexandrova, as a member of a scout company with the Red Army's 65th Tank Brigade, was once again in the forefront of the action during the crossing of the Oder.

Closer and closer to the Oder. We went for reconnaissance on ten tanks. We searched a village, woods, a cemetery, a field. We came across a line of houses in the outskirts of a big village and stole up to it in a small group. Not a single soul in the houses. Those who had not fled had hidden in cellars. A German self-propelled gun stood in the field not far off and opened fire on us. I ran to have a look at it and came across Fedor Avdyushin, killed. I ran back, led the guys to the spot and they quickly buried him.

Suddenly the enemy's aviation flew over and drove us into the basement of a large shed. We squatted down along the wall with submachine-guns on our knees, and surprisingly enough fell asleep instantaneously. We woke up to the alarmed whispering of Petya Groshev: "Guys! The Germans!"

I opened my eyes and saw that everybody had woken up but sat in the same pose – everybody was bolt-upright. The bright light from a nearby burning building lit our silhouettes. I didn't know how long we had slept. It was already night. We leaped towards the exit and turned left. A file of Germans was walking to the right from the shed. We moved up to the burning building through a side street. The Germans apparently took us for their own as the guys were dressed in German clothes of various kinds and only I was in my unfailing waterproof cape. We sharply turned right into the darkness beyond the right side of the burning house and then raced headlong towards the cemetery where we found the rest of the scouts together with Alexandrov.

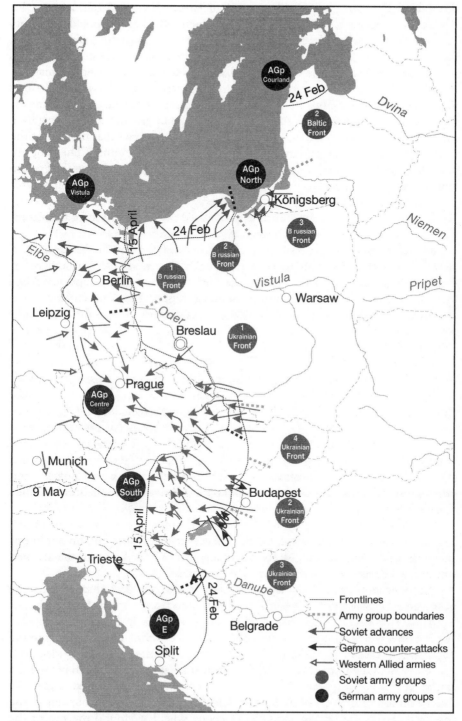

Map 8   Eastern Front: Berlin Offensive and final Soviet operations in the southern sector of the front

I remember the crossing of the Oder, which was not yet free of ice and the narrow strip of land of the Küstrin bridgehead where we had got a foothold. Nobody was bringing us food and we had lived on 'green fodder' until the bridgehead widened. Thirty years later I received a letter from our scout Ivan Masloid. He recalled in it those first days on the bridgehead: "You know, Zoya, I remember when we went out on this assignment you were the senior (this was near Frankfurt-an-der-Oder). It was spring, mud, I had boils on my bottom, we were moving along the frontline to communicate with some unit in order to update the data about the enemy. I couldn't walk fast then, was falling behind all the time, but couldn't admit to you why, and you kept swearing at me to make me catch up."

Having walked several kilometres and met no one on the way we found the unit, received the necessary information and quietly walked back. We were walking without haste, and, I'd say, quite light-heartedly, joking. And suddenly our group came across the Germans in a clearing still covered by snow. And surprisingly each of us immediately 'picked out' his enemy and aimed his weapon at 'his'. They'd spotted us too but we turned out to be faster. I fired from my TT pistol, the German fell, managed to get off a shot, but missed. My second bullet hit him on the forehead a bit above his left eyebrow; the Fritz lay in the snow, a spurt of blood gushed from his wound and he was obviously dying... My God, I killed a man! I clenched myself inside so as not to show the guys that I felt so uneasy. It's one thing when you shoot along with the others and don't know whose bullet makes someone fall, but face to face, eye to eye... I've remembered that moment to this day - I can see every second of it and hurt.

After a while we were withdrawn from the bridgehead and sent to clarify if a bridge across a tributary of the Oder was guarded. It was daylight. We covered our tanks in white. We entered a large German village and moved forward with a lot of caution. Suddenly a group of children ran out of a shabby house towards us. They were our girls taken away into slavery. There was no limit to the joy: they cried, hugged and kissed us and worried that we would go back and they would stay and be driven farther into the German rear. We reached the bridge and there we were met with such intense machine-gun fire that it tore the camouflage off all our tanks. We returned to the village and reported the situation via radio. They ordered us to stay in the village.

In the night the tanks of our Brigade came over, we returned to the bridgehead and lodged in a hut standing in the open: it was by a half-destroyed village street closer to the enemy lines and that's why no one had dared to occupy it. We boiled a big pot of water in the sheltered yard, the guys had a bath and when my turn had come the Fritzes began mortar shelling. I was not scared but I feared that if I got killed the guys would see me naked with a big bruise over my whole hip. Remember the time when I was thrown off the motorbike? I realised how bad was it only there, at the Küstrin bridgehead.

They were sending us only spirits and smokes from the rear. Whoever was distributing it didn't dare stay with us and we wouldn't try to talk him into that. We had to get food from any possible source. In the nearby village of Maschnow one side of the street was ours and another one – neutral. The guys found a way to go over there and bring back some delicacies. Once Masloid brought back a cow and Sasha Asulbaev – a chef by trade – cooked us some excellent meatballs.

Almost every day someone would go for orders to Valentin Pavlov - Commander of the 3rd Tank Battalion located nearby. The road to there was exposed to fire and that's why one had to run as if in a 100 metre race. Once I had darted out breathless next to Pavlov's tank followed by hammering submachine-gun bursts on the opposite side of the tank. And there on the spot one crewman began to outpour his feelings for me. I had to answer diplomatically that the war hadn't ended yet and no one knew who of us would survive... It was a second confession of love during that day. Many years after when meeting my comrades I often heard: "Zoya, I used to be in love with you". And a former scout Masloid told his former comrades, not me: "I used to love this woman and still do". He told me that the guys of our platoon used to chat: "Who will Zoya choose out of us after the war?" I chose the Platoon Commander Alexandrov. It's hard to write about him since he had not been on our tank in the raids.

Several people, including me, had been called back to the rear to receive awards. We reached the crossing. A bridge was being built across the Oder. When we were approaching the bank of our territory the enemy's aviation flew over. Oh God! What kind of hell was this! They were pounding the crossing without a break. It was incomprehensible how much the sappers and bridge-builders had to endure.

We ran up on the riverbank; the German flyers were strafing it and there was no place to hide. We threw ourselves on the ground but what was the use? We leaped up and ran... I was awarded the Orders of Glory 3rd Class and Red Star for the battles between the Pulawy and Küstrin bridgeheads. We were driven back to the river on an armoured carrier but the driver named Koch didn't go down, stopped and said: "They're already shooting – I'm not gonna drive further down". Khramov smacked his fist on the armour: "Drive on!" But we went down a bit more and the same happened again. The guys gave Koch a fair basting but decided not to rely on him anymore – that guy always had something 'broken' during combat.

In the northern part of the Eastern Front, Soviet efforts to clean up pockets of resistance continued. Armin Scheiderbauer had been badly wounded, and was soon being moved to Danzig, a major port on the West Prussian coast. The pressure of the Soviet advance had caused a huge number of people to flock to the area, so that by early March, when Armin arrived there, it was filled with over 200,000 troops (over 100,000 of them wounded), and more than 1½ million refugees, all alike desperately seeking to avoid falling into the hands of the Red Army.

After the operation I was moved into a small room. In one of the two beds was the man wounded in the stomach, who had been operated on before me. I was able to have a closer look at him and to recognise him. He was the commander of the reconnaissance battalion of the 35th Infantry Division. He was a Major and a holder of the Knight's Cross. From time to time we spoke to each other. But I had the strange thought almost immediately that there was little hope for him.

Even so, they also seemed to consider me to be a serious case. The Major and I were nursed by a particularly capable *Obergefreiter* medic. On his tunic was the *Kriegsverdienstkreuz* First Class, which testified to his quality. Every quarter of an hour, I estimated, he came back into the room and administered injections in my upper thigh. During the two days I spent there, I must have had, I estimated, getting on for 80 injections. For years afterwards, the area in which they had been administered above my knees was numb.

The following night the Major reached the end of the road. He was increasingly struggling for air. It seemed to me that he had a heart attack. The medic came with Dr Brunn and they brought an oxygen machine but could not help the poor man. I was then alone. But I was myself too weak to be significantly affected by the death struggle of my comrade. The following day the medic told me that the previous night an armoured breakthrough had been made. The enemy tanks, he said, had come very close, and they had feared that they would have to let us fall into Soviets hands. According to rumour, the two chaplains from our Division, the ESAK and the KASAK, i.e. the abbreviations for Protestant and Catholic 'anti-sin guns' had been 'snatched'.

On 8 March, after four days, I was at last transported away. A medical motor vehicle drove me and other wounded men to a station. It must have been the one at Preussisch-Stargard, where we were put in cattle trucks and laid down on straw. During the loading process some wretch of a medic stole my pistol. That filled me with the overpowering fury of the helpless. I was glad that immediately after I had been wounded I had, at his suggestion, handed over my watch to my runner Franz. In Danzig, *Sankas* took us to the Technical High School in Langfuhr. It had been set up as a military hospital. At first I lay with about 50 other seriously wounded men in a large hall. I was in a pitiful state, because I was getting no air. After a short examination, I was immediately taken by porters into the operating room. The porters were French prisoners of war obediently doing what was expected of them. From the map case, which had not been stolen from me, I brought out my remaining cigarettes, that I certainly no longer needed. Gratefully, I gave them to the Frenchmen.

The operating room resembled a gigantic human abattoir. A haze of vapours of blood, pus, sweat and filth, from the dressings and disinfectants filled the room. On several tables operations, amputations, and dressings were performed. A doctor had just finished the circular cut around an arm, then began an upper arm amputation. All that I saw, though only half-conscious. Acting as theatre nurses were Dutch medical students. Doubtless they were 'compulsory labour', and were getting some dreadful practical experience. I had to place my arm round the neck of one of these kindly and helpful nurses. Dizzy and weak, no longer used to sitting upright, I had my lungs tapped. An increasing lack of air, and the unbearable smell, had made me so apathetic that I scarcely noticed the short, severe pain when the doctor inserted the cannula. The intervention produced an aspiration of 700 cubic centimetres. It was no wonder that I had feared I was slowly suffocating. I was then able to breathe again during the following two weeks. The next aspiration produced another half-litre of fluid. After that there were only 20 cubic centimetres. Eventually the interventions were no longer necessary.

By then the hospital needed the room. So after about 10 days there was a great visitation headed by a General of the medical service. They sorted the wounded and had to empty some beds. In his numerous entourage there was one corpulent medic. He could have been a factory manager. He had doubtless only recently been caught by the *Heldenklau*, and had gone to ground in the medical service. When the swarm of doctors had passed my emergency bed, I asked that medic to hand me the inflatable pillow from the foot of the bed. He replied that I should ask someone else because he was not responsible for doing that.

I could scarcely believe my ears, and lost my temper. There I was, lying pale and hollow cheeked, hair on end from lying down, and uncut for four months, unshaven and generally run to seed, and obviously seriously wounded on a wooden bedstead. On the seat next to it was my field tunic with all its medals, including the silver wound insignia. In front of me was that fat man, with prosperity written all over him. He was all dressed up, his hair slicked down, and he had the nerve to say that he was not responsible for carrying out one small service consisting of handing over one small thing. Never before during my service as an officer had I lost control of myself before a subordinate, yelled at him, and pulled rank on him, as I had with this man.

With the last remnants of strength and breath remaining in my wretched body, bellowing, I unleashed the full fury of the frontline fighter against the 'damned' people behind the lines. 'We are letting ourselves get shot to pieces out there on the front line, and this swine, who has never heard the whistle of a bullet in his life, is not responsible for handing an inflatable pillow to a seriously wounded man!' I was going mad. Tears were choking my words. I was no longer in control of myself. Some gentlemen from the visitation at first were shocked and indignant. Then some staff came over to calm me down, while the travesty of a Samaritan hurriedly left the room.

Even more than the days, the nights in that room were full of dread. Every evening I was given morphine, but its numbing effect only lasted for a few hours. By one o'clock in the morning I would wake up in the stained bed and wait patiently for an unwilling nurse, who would get peevish having to clean things up. I had never experienced such an accumulation of misery as I had in that room. A boy near to me asked again and again for water. Shot in the stomach, he had recently been operated on and was not allowed to drink. Everybody tried to make him understand that, but failed. One moment when he was not being watched he opened his hot water bottle. I was too weak to be able to warn him as he greedily gulped down the contents. The following morning he was dead. Opposite me, another man had had both his legs shattered. Resigned and quiet, he lay on his bunk. That was the way he died.

On the other hand, those impressions, however depressing they were, gave me courage and I used them to pull myself together. I had no intention of dying. The hope of getting out was germinating in me. Certainly the town was encircled, and certainly I was not fit to be moved. In fact for days I had had a high fever, but that would pass, I hoped, and by ship or by aircraft I surely must be able to get away. I felt a hesitant joy at the fact that evidently I had got away with it again. With the greatest difficulty I managed to scribble some lines to Mother and to Gisela. Gisela received them, but Mother did not.

From there they carried me to a room on the second storey of the building. Six wooden bunks filled the room. My new comrades, all officers, were seriously wounded like me, but obviously over the hill. My right-hand neighbour was Franz Manhart, *Flak-Leutnant* from Grafenberg near Eggenburg in Lower Austria. (He had managed to reach the level of section head in the finance ministry in Vienna).

His left upper arm had been shattered but he could hobble. Opposite was the anti-tank *Oberleutnant* Nabert from Schweidnitz, whose left arm had been amputated. As it turned out, we had a whole series of common acquaintances in Schweidnitz, including an actress from the *Landestheater* whom I had seen in Sudermann's *Frau Sorge*. When his dressings were being changed, Nabert's stump gave out such a stench that we regularly felt sick. On the left next to me lay a *Panzer Hauptmann*, whose right upper thigh had been shattered. He tried in vain to move the toes on his foot. Then he was taken to be operated on, and came back without his right leg. After waking up from the anaesthetic he felt with both hands to where his knee had been. He could still feel it. The realisation that he was an amputee hit him like a bolt of lightning. Gasping, he drew the air through his teeth, then, without making a sound, he put his hands over his face in horror. On the evening of 25 March he was taken away by members of his unit. A destroyer had intended to make a run for it during the night, and was to take him along.

As I found out after the war from Herr von Garn, our Division also sent a detachment to remove wounded men from the hospital. Obviously the group could not have carried out the order properly, because they did not find me. No doubt they had only been on the ground floor. It is idle to speculate whether I might have been lucky and subsequently reached Denmark, with the regiment, on board a ship.

The frontline was approaching. The large pocket had shrunk to a beleaguered town, and declared a *Festung*. An old reserve officer, an invalid from the First World War and teacher by profession, went from room to room. He tried, as a 'NSFO' - National Socialist officer leader - to spread confidence in victory. Nobody took him seriously any more. But I still hoped that I might be transported away. Exactly three weeks after I had been wounded, my high fever fell overnight to normal. The crisis had passed. The euphoria of the convalescent came over me. The doctor declared me to be capable of being moved.

But by then it was too late. The harbour was blockaded. Two days before, it was said, one last hospital ship had sailed out. But it had been torpedoed and had sunk with hundreds of wounded men on board. In actual fact, it was the *Wilhelm Gustloff*. It was sunk by a Soviets submarine. There were several thousand refugees on board. Two days previously, when I was unable to be moved, I had struggled against my fate. Once again I had to learn my lesson and resign myself to the inevitable.

An elderly *Leutnant* from the supplies services, had been laid in the *Hauptmann's* bed. He was very drunk and had obviously been injured by a bomb splinter while in that state. Soon afterwards he died, still in the state of intoxication in which no doubt he had spent the last days and hours of his life. When he was taken out, I asked for his pistol. I still had the thought of making use of it.

In the meantime Soviet and British aircraft were bombing the town. Bombs fell day and night. Heavy artillery shells landed. In the park of the high school, artillery and flak went into position. The explosions of the impacts, very close by, and the sharp cracks of our own guns and cannons as they fired went on alternately. The front was right there. We lay helpless, stuck in bed, on the topmost floor of the building. On the doctors' rounds we asked if it was possible for us to be placed in the cellar. The station medical officer replied with the words: 'You're surely not just a bit afraid, gentlemen?' Saying that, he smiled, but at the same time remained for safety's sake under the cover of the lintel of the door.

He evidently considered us to be some of those guilty for the war. He perhaps believed that we should face our just punishment in the form of a bomb. He was not allowed to gainsay it, for instance by taking us down into the cellar. Even the ward medic no longer very often summoned up the courage to climb from the cellar to the upper ward. When it was absolutely necessary he brought up food. While butter and other provisions were supposedly stored in great quantities in food depots, they dished out only thin carrot soup to us. Sometimes there were a few slices of bread spread with cheese and marmalade. Right in front of our eyes, however, the medic would still be biting pieces off a block of chocolate. When taken to task about it, he declared shamelessly that none had been issued for the wounded.

All those symptoms indicated the end to be imminent. It was a collapse that was taking place around and within us. Had we deserved that fate? Should they leave us there to kick the bucket like miserable dogs? Should they leave us to the tender mercies of the Bolsheviks? Bitterness and disappointment came over me, and doubtless also over my comrades. There was silence in the room. Nobody spoke. Everyone, lying there so wretchedly on the floor, was alone at a turning point in his life.

On 27 March 1945, the Tuesday before Easter, a bright spring morning dawned. Neither doctor nor medic appeared. The enemy artillery fire had become more and more intense. A direct hit on the wall of the building sent window-frames and panes flying crackling into the room. Then rifle fire could be heard.

Thus it was finally clear that no one else was to get out. We would be consigned to an uncertain fate. But why, I thought, should they not leave me alone there? Who was I, to be able to claim that the course of my life should be only smooth and good? I realised that I had considered myself to be too important. I realised that I had been just a tiny interchangeable part in the massive German war machinery. But by then it was obviously grinding to a halt. I reached once again for the pistol. I took hold of it, but put it down again. The thought of suicide, was at first as strong and serious as it had been that time in Powielin. But by then it was done with.

Suddenly I knew that an important part of my life was certainly coming to an end, with us losing the war. However, life even if perhaps under completely different circumstances, would go on. It would still be worth continuing to live, but not to give in to oneself. A wonderful clarity came over me. Praying, I experienced the certainty that God would not leave me in the lurch, and that he would be with us, with me. I thought long and hard about my Mother. Lost in all those thoughts I detached myself more and more, finally completely, from the situation.

Then another medic appeared. He had orders to collect up pistols and medals. He announced that the hospital had been surrendered to the Soviets. He said that two doctors and ten medics had remained behind with 800 severely wounded men. 'The white flag', he said, 'had already been raised'.

Another hour passed. Franz Mahnart stood at the window and reported back on the situation. He saw our infantry retreating and the Soviets moving closer and closer. Meanwhile, again and again, there were moments of anxious quiet. Finally voices could be heard, announcing an approach from room to room. Andreyev shouted out several times. They were the same dull, throaty sounds that I had heard for the first time three years before in the woods at Upolosy. The voices had exactly the same effect on me as they had then. Both wings of the door were opened as the first Soviets entered. His machine-pistol at the ready, he stood at the doors and looked around. Meanwhile, outside, next to the house, German shells were still falling.

Armin Scheiderbauer recovered from his wounds, but was destined to spend over two years in Soviet prisoner-of-war camps.

Far to the south, Dmitriy Loza's 46th Guards Tank Brigade was about to play a vital role in the Soviet seizure of Vienna, a city Hitler had called "a pearl to which he would give a proper setting" during the Anschluss in 1938. This account also provides an excellent example of how the Soviets developed ad hoc *combat teams to make the most of opportunities presented to them during the last year of the war.*

Tanks are not made for cities! Their combat capabilities are sharply reduced there: manoeuvrability is limited; engagement ranges are, for the most part, extremely close; without adequate infantry support, these combat vehicles can be relatively easily destroyed by enemy anti-tank gunners from close ranges and from concealed positions. Tank units strive to bypass cities. There were, however, occasions when the order firmly stated, "Go in!"

Early April 1945. Formations of the 6th Guards Army had seized the cities of Sopron and Sombatkhey in north-west Hungary. Vienna was about sixty kilometres away. We had to interfere with the Germans' efforts to mine and destroy historical monuments and bridges, to move industrial equipment and cultural treasures out of Austria's capital. The army commander, Colonel-General A.G. Kravchenko, made the decision to send a detachment to Vienna. This detachment consisted of the 1st Tank Battalion, 46th Guards Tank Brigade (eighteen Shermans), three ISU-152 self-propelled guns, and a company of airborne troops - eighty men from the 1st Airborne Battalion of the 304th Airborne Regiment, commanded by Guards Lieutenant Nikolay Georgievich Petukhov. The detachment was ordered to function as a raiding detachment in the enemy's rear area, hurriedly reach Vienna, penetrate into the city centre from the south, and seize key objectives: the parliament building, art history museum, opera house, Belvedere Palace, and Academy of Sciences. We were to hold the captured buildings and surrounding blocks until the arrival of the main body of the 9th Guards Mechanized Corps. The crews were briefed that they would be operating in the enemy's backyard for twenty-four hours, possibly even longer.

The army commander cleverly included in the detachment the high manoeuvrability and firepower of tanks and self-propelled guns with the practiced ability of airborne troops to fight fierce and prolonged battles in the enemy's rear. It was ever so strictly ordered: "Except in the most extreme case, do not become engaged in combat on the way to the Austrian capital!"

We began our careful preparation for this unusual and, we understood, difficult raid on the evening of 8 April. Two crates of captured chocolate (one could live several days on them) were placed on each Sherman and, more important, the tanks and self-propelled guns were loaded with two norms of ammunition.

Shermans of the 1st Battalion, 46th Guards Tank Brigade, on the streets of Vienna, April 1945. On the side armour of the lead tank are written the words "For the Motherland!" (Dmitri Loza Archive)

The preparations and concerns took two hours. Everything was ready for the departure! The crews and paratroopers slept. How many hours would they have to combat the enemy without sleep or rest? No one knew.

Morning, 9 April. A thick fog blanketed the earth. The infantry at the forward edge did their uneasy work - they penetrated the enemy's defence. We received the signal, "go" ("Tanks, move out!").

As the detachment commander, I shared a single thought and emotion with each tanker - get to Vienna quickly. Two circumstances dictated such operations. First, the objectives designated for capture were located a significant distance from the front line. Their defence might still not be well organized. Second, the Germans were unlikely to conceive of the idea that the Russian command would take this unbelievably risky step - inserting tanks and infantry into such a large metropolitan area.

The battalion column approached the southern outskirts of Vienna, the area of Favoriten. From here lay the shortest path to the centre of the Austrian capital. An anti-tank gun fired from behind an earthen wall dating from the Middle Ages, setting one *Emcha* ablaze. Our hope for surprise on this axis had vanished. I ordered the unit to withdraw to the northern outskirts of Erla. The crews and paratroopers quickly ate their rations. I called a conference of the company commanders, and we discussed the developing situation. All the officers agreed: execute a manoeuvre, try our military luck at another spot. This was a normal course of action in such circumstances. But where should we make this effort?

The south-eastern sector of Vienna had several less dense built-up areas near the Danube canal. Honestly speaking, however, we did not have full confidence that the approach of Russian tanks to the city was not known here also. That is, on the new axis (if we went that way), we might not be able to achieve the necessary security for movement. One thing was sure. If we continued on our present course, we would suffer more losses.

We studied the layout of the south-western sector of the Austrian capital. We were looking for a route through Meydling to the city centre. There were substantial obstacles - hilly terrain covered by a forest and a winding road. The enemy would not need substantial forces to delay us. We decided upon a variant bypass Vienna from the south-west and break into the city in the sector of the Hutteldorf-Linz highway.

Austria's main highways were in excellent condition. The fires of war had not yet touched them. They were lined with tall, leafy trees. Their interarching green borders camouflaged the detachment well from the most dangerous threat in this situation - enemy aviation.

Darkness was approaching when the battalion reached the bridge west of Hutteldorf. Barricades blocked the streets and approaches to the bridge. Anti-tank fire struck the tank of Guards Senior Lieutenant Grigoriy Danil'chenko, commander of the 1st Tank Company. We were forced to withdraw a bit. We manoeuvred to the right and reached Hakking. Our mission was growing more difficult as time passed! Here a solid fortress wall of some length blocked our path. We could not go around it. Time was slipping away. We had to ram it with a tank. Guards Sergeant Nikolay Oseledkin, a driver-mechanic, executed this task masterfully. First he made a small breach. With several strikes of the tank's bow, he enlarged the breach until a Sherman could drive through it. The Guards tankers christened this breach the 'triumphal arch'.

Tanks with paratroopers clinging to them hurried along the railway embankment toward the western station. The city was going about its normal daily life - buses were plying the streets, trolley cars were clanging, and the Viennese people were scurrying about their business. Traffic policemen signalled our column forward without delay at three intersections. But this atmosphere did not last long. Soon the situation changed radically. They recognized us. One after the other, the canal bridges on our battalion's route of march went up in smoke. There were a lot of them.

Each *Emcha* commander had a map of the city. This permitted the detachment to continue closing on our designated objectives along multiple routes.

At 2300 on 9 April, I reported to the brigade commander by radio: "We have reached the centre of Vienna!" And so the first part of our combat mission was accomplished. The second - no less difficult - was to hold the captured area until the arrival of our own forces.

The principal concern of a commander in such situations is the organization in the briefest time of a defence and, in particular, its most important element - a system of fire. The tankers and paratroopers were arrayed so that each street, intersection, and passageway was under our constant observation. If an enemy appeared, he was destroyed by concentrated fires of all systems. The ISU-152s were our reserve for reinforcing the threatened axis or sector in the course of the battle.

On my order, Guards Lieutenant Nikolay Petukhov's paratroopers carefully began clearing the blocks adjoining the area occupied by our force. Their task was to clean out enemy soldiers. The fact that the electricity remained functioning in central Vienna until 0200 initially facilitated the accomplishment of this mission. As soon as the enemy realized the situation, he turned out the lights.

The night was uneasy. Knowing the city well, the Germans made several reconnaissance forays. They threw grenades at our tanks from the roofs and upper floors of houses. We had to park our Shermans under the archways of buildings. The paratroopers quickly liquidated this danger from above. The crews did not sleep. All were at their battle stations, prepared to defeat an enemy attack. Only near morning did the driver-mechanics and gun commanders manage to snatch a bit of rest. No one doubted that at dawn the enemy would launch his attack. And we were not mistaken. The enemy made his first strong attack in the morning.

Not long before this, the Germans had begun to fire with an anti-tank gun at an *Emcha* parked under an arch. During the night, they had dragged it to the upper floor of one of the houses north of Ratush'. The enemy managed to damage the tracks on two tanks. We quickly had to take appropriate measures to prevent the majority of our vehicles east of Ratush', the university, and parliament from being damaged. We wanted to leave them in those positions because from there they could better engage an attacking enemy.

I called the commander of ISU-152 battery and ordered him immediately to suppress the enemy firing point. The self-propelled gun, sliding along the asphalt on its broad tracks, took a position on one of the streets on the south-eastern side of the square.

All of us were curious. We wanted to watch the self-propelled gun blow the German gunners and their cannon to pieces. The tankers and paratroopers poured out into the street and began to wait. Now, recalling those minutes, I cannot excuse myself. As an inexperienced commander, I committed a serious error. At the time, I permitted these spectators to line the street. We paid a high price.

The Viennese lanes that ran in various directions from the central square were not wide. Beautiful houses with venetian blinds on their windows rose up on both sides of these lanes. Each soldier and officer would learn to his misfortune that these windows would end up on the street.

The shot of the self-propelled gun's large-calibre cannon roared forth. The air itself shook. One and one-half floors of the house, together with the enemy anti-tank gun and its crew, crashed to the ground. And in our own position? With a crash, the powerful shock wave of the shot broke the thin window glass in the houses near the self-propelled gun. Heavy shards of glass poured down on the heads of our spectators. The result was lamentable: scores of wounded arms and backs and two broken collarbones. Thankfully, the tankers were wearing their headgear and the paratroopers their helmets. Their heads remained intact. What now! We were fighting our tanks inside a large city for the first time. Bad experience is experience, just the same!

There was no time to moan or complain. Enemy tanks were already moving along several streets toward the university and the parliament. Infantry were attacking behind them, using the tanks for cover. The enemy was beginning an attack on a broad front. Very well, then, the hour had come to cross swords - armour with armour, fire with fire! We had the advantage. The battalion was deployed in combat formation. The Sherman fired more accurately from a stationary position.

A Panther, the thick armour of its turret and hull forming a shield, was leading the attackers on every street. The long-range cannons of the heavy tanks that stopped outside the direct fire range of our Shermans' 76mrn main guns enabled them to strike our combat vehicles from a significant distance. In this unfavourable situation, the *Emcha* crews, on general command, employed a minor but important deception. They backed their tanks deeper into the archways. They remained ready to reoccupy their position, on command, and spray the enemy with machine-gun fire.

Battles are decided in seconds. The driver-mechanic of Guards Junior Lieutenant Bessol'tsev's tank tarried a bit too long and was unable to reposition his vehicle immediately. This small lapse turned out to be fatal. The *Emcha* was hit. The commander and assistant driver-mechanic were wounded, but the main gun was undamaged. The crew bandaged themselves and remained at their stations on order of the junior lieutenant. The immobile Sherman was prepared for an unequal duel with an anti-tank round loaded in the main gun. The radio operator prepared a smoke pot; its dark grey screen at the right moment would effectively conceal the tank's position.

The rapid disappearance of our tanks, it seems, somewhat discouraged the enemy crews. The Panthers stopped. They hesitated, then slowly moved forward. One of the Panthers turned toward Bessol'tsev's tank, in all probability intending quickly to close the range in order to fire the killing shot. The junior lieutenant understood the enemy tank commander's intention. He ordered the radio operator to throw the smoke pot forward. The thick cloud of smoke began to obscure the archway and the street in front of it. Now let the enemy try to find the target.

At this time, assistance sent by the company commander, Guards Senior Lieutenant Ionov, came to Bessol'tsev by the rear courtyards. Knocking down the intervening fence, the Sherman of Lieutenant Abib Bakuridze approached Bessol'tsev's tank from the rear, quickly hooked a tow cable onto it, and towed it to a safe place.

The Panthers did finally reach the line where they could be destroyed by the fire of the *Emchas'* 76.2mm guns. The command went out over the radio: "Take your positions!" Ten seconds later, the archways of the houses on the eastern edge of the central square were bristling with the Shermans' long barrels. A cannon duel commenced at close range.

Combat in cities is a great number of violent isolated engagements, in which success depends on the quickness of actions, the coolness of commanders of all ranks, the mastery of each crew member, and the skill of the infantry support troops. Guards Lieutenant Konstantin Drozdovskiy's tank was in a very good position. The archway entrance into the courtyard was ten metres from the corner of the building. Adjoining the house was a small square. Earlier, Konstantin had prepared a good route for manoeuvre out from under the archway into the square and back. And not in vain.

Up to one and one-half platoons of enemy submachine gunners were advancing on Drozdovskiy's position. Behind them were two Panthers. The forces were unequal. But the Guards *Emchisti* did not flinch. They skilfully engaged in a one-on-one firefight. The lieutenant ordered the full weight of his main gun to rain upon the infantry, who represented a great danger to the tank. And then immediately to change positions. Volley fire with high explosive rounds cut through the enemy submachine gunners very well. Those who survived immediately turned back and took cover behind the tank and in a house. The sector of observation and fire was better from the new position. Konstantin saw two armoured vehicles approaching the square. They were almost in one line, in places shielding their vehicles behind house walls. There was deep thought shown in this combat formation. The Germans correctly figured that our tank could simultaneously knock out both targets with a single shot. An intact Panther managed to detect and hit an *Emcha* before the Sherman's crew was able to reload their main gun. In this single action, the enemy tank commanders demonstrated that they were not novices on the battlefield. Drozdovskiy accepted the enemy's challenge and turned out to be more clever than the Germans. The first anti-tank round struck the right flank Panther on its left track. The intact right track drove this tank to the left, pressing the adjacent tank into a wall. Both enemy tanks froze in place. At the same instant, a smoke pot flew from the turret of Drozdovskiy's tank. The thick cloud of smoke filled the square and street, depriving the Germans of any possibility of conducting aimed fire. Konstantin again changed his position. When the whitish shroud of smoke dissipated somewhat, the guards spotted a backward-moving Panther. A precision-fired anti-tank round forced it to stop in the middle of the street.

My command observation post was in the opera house. My reserve, the ISU-152 battery, was nearby. Radio reports were coming in from the company commanders. I was monitoring the conversations of platoon leaders with their subordinates, describing the axis of the enemy's main attack from a position north of Ratush' and the university to Belvedere Palace. The enemy's intentions were manifestly obvious: to divide our detachment's combat formation into two parts, press the larger (eastern) portion toward the Danube canal, and destroy it.

As a result of an almost forty-minute fight, the attacking tanks and infantry were halted at the approaches to the central square, three Panthers were destroyed, and we lost two Shermans. Not less than fifty enemy submachine gunners were killed or wounded. Our method of combating tanks- "hunting with Borzois" - that we had tested in past battles was not used in beating off the Germans' attack. Although I reminded everyone about it before the battle, I did not require its employment during our first encounter with the enemy. Drozdovskiy made one unsuccessful attempt, from out of a narrow alley. Not one Panther presented its flank to him, therefore he did not engage them. The damaged track of a heavy tank can be repaired in a short time. Meanwhile, this armoured pillbox is capable of conducting powerful fire with its long-range gun. The enemy, gathering up his forces, could once again launch his attack with the support of the immobilized Panther.

I had to turn the developing situation in our favour. And the quicker the better for our subsequent presence in Vienna. Our self-propelled guns were an effective means at my disposal. I discussed a plan of action with Senior Lieutenant Yakov Petrukhin, the battery commander of the big ISUs. We agreed on the following: the self-propelled guns, employing the long range and firepower of their 152mm guns, would strike first at the mobile Panthers. Their second priority was to fire on vehicles that had already been hit. This method would minimize the expenditure of ammunition. We faced many hours of combat before the arrival of our own troops.

The battery commander would pay special attention to concealing the movement of his self-propelled guns into firing positions. The Sherman crews would try at this time to distract the attention of the enemy tankers, conducting fire in order to blind them.

Yakov Petrukhin reported that he had selected two very suitable firing positions: they had good cover in front to defend the hull of his vehicles from enemy armour-piercing shells.

The firing intensity increased from our side along the entire eastern line. The *Emchisti* were attempting to solve two problems at once: to prevent the Germans from spilling out onto the central square by blocking them up in the surrounding streets and to cover the movement of the self-propelled guns to firing positions.

How slowly time passes when one awaits the decisive moments in a fight with the enemy. There was no doubt - the turning point was near. The long-awaited time had arrived. Two thundering shots assaulted our eardrums, blowing the glass out of the windows of nearby houses and rattling other windows some distance away. "Pardon us, beautiful city, that we cause you to tremble, and at times, we destroy parts of you! The laws of war are ruthless!" I wanted to cry out loudly, seeing the destruction we were causing.

The second Viennese spectacle turned out to be no less impressive. The strike of a large-calibre projectile (Yakov had ordered a concrete-breaking round loaded, for greater effect) knocked the turret off one of the Panthers that had already almost crawled into the square. The second heavy tank blazed up in an enormous fire. The ISU-152 immediately abandoned its position. It was as if they had poured boiling water on the enemy. The awkward armoured vehicles hurriedly began to withdraw rearward. The enemy infantry, now lacking tank support, ran away through courtyards and alleys.

And so the enemy's first attempt to divide the raiding detachment suffered defeat. The Shermans and paratroopers stubbornly held the centre of Vienna. I reported the battalion's situation to the brigade commander. He informed me that corps units were conducting a successful attack on the southern approaches to the Austrian capital.

Our chain of command took all necessary measures to provide air cover for the detachment. Thanks to their efforts, the battalion was not once subjected to German air attack during our entire time in the city. On the morning of 10 April, our fighters appeared in the sky above Vienna. We signalled our positions to the pilots with red rockets and sent them a radio password.

An air battle took place a bit later. One after the other, two Messerschmitts went down in flames. Trailing streamers of black smoke, they crashed into a forest. One of our aircraft was also shot down. A small speck separated from it, and several seconds later, the canopy of a parachute opened above it. The pilot was descending into the city. Suddenly, a Messerschmitt dove on him out of the clouds. An instant later, it was going after the defenceless pilot. Two Shermans simultaneously fired their anti-aircraft machine guns. The enemy fighter broke off without firing the deadly burst.

The parachutist was well oriented and, controlling his direction of descent with the risers, came down over us. It is quite risky to land in a city. He could land on the roof of a house, strike against a wall, or be hung up in a tree. He had to be extremely attentive. The 'sky ghost' failed to see a high-voltage line and caught his risers on its wires.

How could we get him down? It was dangerous for him to jurnp - the distance to the ground was too great. We stretched a tarpaulin between two Shermans, with the edges tied to the turret hatches. The pilot unbuckled his parachute harness and dropped like a rock. The strong canvas net cushioned the heavy blow. Giving way slightly, the tarpaulin threw the pilot upward. He quickly found himself in the tankers' embrace.

The detachment's personnel had not eaten hot food in more than a day. They were eating dry rations. If my memory serves me correctly, in the centre of Vienna was a restaurant that went by the name Astoria. I decided to order dinner for 180 people at this establishment. I delegated the battalion chief of staff, Guards Senior Lieutenant Nikolay Bogdanov (who spoke Gernian fluently) to reach an agreement with the restaurant owner. The desired meal time was 1200 (Moscow time). We had foreign currency - dollars, pounds sterling, and *schillings* - to pay for the dinner.

There was no doubt that the enemy's morning attempt to attack our positions would not be his last. Taking advantage of the coming lull, I headed for the area of the art history museum with a group of officers. It was possible that the Germans would again throw themselves at us from the Ottakring or Funfhaus sectors. We had to inspect the organization of the defences on the approach to the museum and make some adjustments to the system of fire based on the experience of the enemy attack we had just defeated. I repositioned the ISU-152 battery to an area south of the parliament.

After conducting the necessary work with the units, I decided to take a quick glance at the museum, to see its displays. We entered the building and were stunned. The halls were completely empty of paintings or sculptures. The walls showed only various sized dark rectangular and oval patches, signs that canvases hung here at one time. During the war years, each of us had seen the fascists' crimes more than once. And here was their latest crime: the theft of the artworks and historical artefacts that were the state property of Austria.

Passing through the labyrinth of large and small halls, we found ourselves in a cellar area. Immense joy flooded over us: here were stacked hundreds of latticed, reinforced crates. As it became clear, these crates contained the museum's displays - paintings, sculptures, and so on. It was obvious to everyone that the Germans were preparing to ship them. The hurried entrance of our raiding detachment into Vienna had disrupted the enemy's plans. These priceless treasures had not disappeared!

I returned to my command observation post in the left wing of the parliament. Nikolay Bogdanov and the restaurant owner were waiting there. The Austrian wanted to confirm one important detail of the upcoming meal. What kind of alcoholic beverages should be served? I thought about it for several seconds. This was not a minor issue. So I decided to allow the *Emchisti* and the paratroopers to drink a limited amount. They had earned it. "And what does the proprietor of the Astoria have?" I asked Bogdanov. "Cognac." I calculated that the troops had gone more than a day without sleep or rest. How strong a potion would not harm our mission? "And what else does he have, besides cognac?" "French champagne!" The restaurateur raised the thumb of his right hand and pronounced, "Gut!"

Who would have believed it! Where, and when, would we dirty-coveralled tankers get a chance to drink such nectar! I ordered champagne for the tables, one bottle for every two men. "Does the manager have an adequate supply?" I turned to Bogdanov. The Austrian made a mental calculation and replied affirmatively, "Ninety bottles is nothing!" We agreed on this quantity.

Thirty minutes before the appointed meal hour, the restaurant owner invited the battalion command to the covered tables. The table appointments were beyond criticism: snow-white table linens, nickel-plated utensils, and beautiful porcelain ware. In sum, everything was high class. Without a word from us, the owner and the chef walked around all the tables and sampled each prepared dish. This in itself guaranteed the quality of the meal.

The command went out to all the units: leave half the crews and paratroopers in the positions, and the remainder come to the Astoria for dinner! Thirty minutes was allocated for the meal, followed by a changeover of the personnel. Departure from and J return to the positions were to be conducted with the strictest observation of security measures.

The tankers, artillerymen, and paratroopers liked dinner. Yes! This was their first such feast along their wartime roads (for some, thousands of kilometres). No doubt, they would remember it for the rest of their lives. My deputies, chiefs of services, and I (seven persons altogether) began to discuss how much money to pay for this fare and with what currency. I will openly admit that we all were total novices in these matters. We made a 'Solomonic' decision, to let the restaurateur himself present us with a bill for the meal and specify the currency of payment.

The battalion chief of finance services placed three stacks of currency on the table: dollars, pounds sterling, and Austrian *schillings*. We called over the owner of the Astoria. Nikolay Bogdanov explained what was required of him. He hesitated a bit with his answer, and then expressed a preference for 'greenbacks'. He named a sum. I took the stack of dollars, the bank seal still affixed, and, saying '*Bitte!*' handed it to the Austrian. With a slight tilt of his head, he accepted the money and immediately secreted it in the inside pocket of his jacket. After several seconds, he pulled the money out of that location and hurriedly thrust it into his trouser pocket, not releasing it from his hand. With some trepidation in his eyes, he threw a hurried glance in our direction. The pupils of his eyes (I wasn't the only one who noticed) were greatly enlarged. What was bothering him? Unfortunately, we never found out. My tank commander, Guards Lieutenant Ivan Filin, came running in and exclaimed, "The Germans are attacking again!" We flew out from behind the table like the wind. Everyone hurried to his combat post.

We defeated this German attack, from the Funfhaus area in the direction of the art history museum and the opera house, easily and quickly. Having lost one tank and perhaps thirty soldiers and officers, the enemy withdrew to his starting positions. We had six wounded and two killed.

By the evening of 10 April, attacking units of the 9th Guards Mechanized Corps broke through toward the centre of Vienna through Meydling. The Shermans filled the streets and lanes of the Austrian capital. Our raiding detachment had accomplished its difficult combat mission! The battalion had fought in the enemy's rear, separated from the brigade and corps main bodies for twenty-four hours. The enemy had lost four tanks, two anti-tank guns, and approximately one hundred soldiers and officers. Our ranks were also depleted: four *Emchas* were destroyed, ten men were killed, and fifteen were wounded. In these most difficult conditions, the detachment's soldiers and commanders

displayed exceptional endurance, courage, and determination. They had mastered their experience of combat in a large city.

All the enlisted personnel of the 1st Tank Battalion, 46th Guards Brigade, the paratroopers, and the artillerymen were recommended for decorations. Later, I was awarded the esteemed rank of Hero of the Soviet Union.

On 13 April 1945, after stubborn street battles, our forces took full control of the city of Vienna. Many of our troops were awarded the medal 'For the Capture of Vienna'.

The first anniversary of Victory Day was being celebrated in our unit on 9 May 1946. At a ceremonial dinner on the occasion of this holiday, one of the officers said, "Hey, this is not even half the dinner we had in Vienna!" Those commanders who understood what he was talking about began to laugh. "What did you expect?"

I immediately questioned the chief of finance: "How much did we pay the owner of the Astoria for our meal?" "Comrade commander, do you remember the denomination of the bills in that packet of money?" "I think they were $100 bills." "Yes. And there were fifty of them." "Damn!" "We paid that hospitable Viennese $5,000 for that dinner."

That's what we thought at the time. Sometime not too long ago, I had a conversation with one of our Russian embassy officials. I told him about those long-ago April days of 1945 and about the dinner in Vienna and our settlement with the restaurateur. He corrected me. "There were not fifty, but one hundred $100 bills in that packet. This was the traditional bank packet!" This is why the Austrian's eyes got so big. It turns out that we, simple Russian soldiers, paid him generously! Probably no one had ever settled a bill so lavishly in this restaurant. So much so that it left him speechless.

As Dmitriy Loza and his fellow Guardsmen celebrated the capture of Vienna, Erik Wallin and the men of the 11th SS Panzergrenadier Division were being pressed ever further back towards the city of Berlin. If Dmitriy Loza's account is representative of a Red Army soldier fighting to capture a German (or Austrian) city during the last year of the war, Erik Wallin's is equally representative of the kind of fierce and confused actions that German soldiers found themselves fighting countless times, as they struggled to break free from the vice-like grip of the rapidly advancing enemy.

The forces from the east did not take any notice of our reborn fighting spirit! They just kept on moving forward in the same inexhaustible stream as before. They pressed us implacably back, closer and closer to Berlin. The forest belt grew thinner, and gradually gave way to smaller suburbs with grocery shops, newsstands, post offices, cinemas and gardens. Violent engagements raged around and through these residential suburbs that now were ruined without mercy. There was hardly any reason for us to evade and spare them for an enemy who only brought devastation and mass murder with him. That was why we clung tight, as long as possible, in every small village, until the Bolsheviks had reached the flank or even had come behind us. Then we had to be quick and fight our way out. Several times every day we fought our way out of real death-traps in this manner. Every time, some of us were left there, having fallen into the trap.

The residential suburbs were our base, where we tried to hold out as long as possible in order to give time for the defence further back to get organised. But in between, the struggle went on as violently, if not even faster, out in terrain that varied between dense forests and open fields.

The day before we reached the limits of Greater Berlin, it could have been about 21 April, my platoon with the half-tracks was sent forward. We had to act as support to infantry soldiers of the *Wehrmacht* out in the open, who tried to delay Ivan. Our comrades were well dug-in facing the edge of the wood, out of which the hollering brown-yellow masses attacked, time after time. Here we suddenly and unexpectedly had to deal with Bolshevik infantry who had no proper artillery or tank support. Under such circumstances their losses were sure to be heavy, but that did not bother their commanders who just sent forth their people, totally without mercy.

As our mortars went into action behind a rise in the terrain, their loss of men increased even more. We let them come out some distance on to the field, then the rounds exploded over them with annihilating effect. They did not knock down just one or two men, but five or six fell in the grass or tried, bleeding, to drag themselves back after each impact. Then the Soviets turned round and fled, as they thought, to the protecting edge of the wood. But they were met there by the same rain of steel, now even more effective because the rounds exploded against the tree trunks and so the shrapnel was given even more spread. Out in the field, in front of our positions, the number of fallen Soviets increased. They were no longer lying one here and one there, but in tight groups. Our own men over there became enthusiastic at the platoon's precision of aim and were lying hurrahing in their foxholes.

Our ammunition was finished and a half-track was sent back to the supply unit to get fresh rounds. As we, smoking, were waiting for new ammunition and the next Bolshevik attack, we suddenly heard an unmistakable clatter and the dull drone of tanks! Now our position was finished! The German commander there obviously had the same opinion, because the infantry retreated, past us. But three men stayed in their positions, volunteers with *Panzerfäuste*.

For us there was nothing else to do but to drive back. We could not resist though, driving up behind a group of trees and from there watching the final outcome in the field. Between the sparse trunks we had a good view. The thunder of engines grew and came ever closer. There, at the edge of the forest, the treetops floated to and fro, as if a violent storm raged or a giant advanced. With creaking from the broken trunks, a huge armoured giant pressed down the last impeding trees and rolled out into the field. Close to it, one on each side, two others heaved their way forward and in their tracks two more followed. Firing at the retreating infantry they drove out into the field.

In the foxholes over there, three small human beings lay crouching, with their hands clenched hard around their *Panzerfäuste*, with thumping hearts listening to the ever louder thunder from the tank engines. Man against machine! Now the whole ground over there was trembling from the enormous weight of the giants. Rigid with excitement we stared out. There could not be 50 metres between them. They had no nerves, those three. The tanks maintained very small distances between each other, 10–12 metres perhaps, as they rolled forward. They had seen our infantry retreating and hardly thought that death could be waiting for them in the abandoned positions. Soon they were quite close to the three, still shooting at the retreating infantry, and taking no notice of the foxholes. My cigarette burned, unnoticed, between my fingers that were shaking with excitement.

For God's sake get up, now, before it is too late! The tanks had driven into a perfect position for the three comrades in the holes. The small gaps between them became their destruction. When the first tank had come to a distance of 10 metres, three heads and *Panzerfäuste* came up like lightning, three short bangs, fire shot out of the *Panzerfäuste* and three tanks were hit. Two of them were burning. One of them exploded almost immediately. The third rotated round and round on its damaged tracks. The heads disappeared quickly with the empty tubes and came up again with three new *Panzerfäuste*. Before it had time to withdraw from the *Panzerfäuste's* short range of fire, the rotating tank received its death-blow and at the same time the two remaining were penetrated by annihilating tank mines.

Five heavy tanks were burning out on the field, destroyed by three unknown infantry soldiers who now rushed up from the holes and in a zigzag ran back over the field to get away from the advancing Soviet infantry. The bullets whistled around them and scratched up the earth around their feet. But before we rushed off to rejoin the company and avoid being surrounded, we could see our comrades disappear, unhurt, down into a dip in the ground.

The sun had been shining from a clear sky all morning. It was the hottest day of the whole spring so far. Summer was coming. In the gardens of the residential suburbs the fruit trees were blazing in the most wonderful blossom. Sprouting little buds had broken their covers and burst into fresh, light green leaves. How nice, just for an hour, to be allowed to forget the war, to forget the noise, to breathe the smells of nature, of fresh foliage and flowers, and to appreciate the coming of new life! But we could not take the peace and quiet for granted. Bloody events pushed us and chased us, from position to position. There was hardly time to take a few drags on a cigarette between the fights.

In the afternoon the company was ordered to dismount and go into action on foot. The drivers took the half-tracks back under cover from fighter planes. Under the command of Schwarck we went forward along the road that was to be blocked against the enemy tanks. Two other companies had the task of taking up frontal positions parallel to the road. To the left of the road, there was a belt of trees. We were given our positions, to keep the flank free. We had three machine-guns and a 7.5cm anti-tank gun as well as our usual small arms. We had a perfect shooting range against the open terrain, which separated us from the next belt of forest.

Tunics and shirts were taken off at once, and we started digging among tree-roots and stones. Thinking back, it is irresistible to make an amused comparison with the exercises in digging positions during the military training back home in Sweden. How idyllic that was! No exaggerated hurry, no unnecessary sweat, calmly and leisurely and with very little seriousness, the spades were turned. Who thought of the vitally important meaning of the ability to dig in rapidly? That ability, in war, meant as much for your life as handling your weapon the right way. Hundreds of thousands of lives had been wasted in this war, just because of laziness, and unwillingness to dig like moles.

But we, who now began to dig down in the stony ground of this forest belt, had seen enough of the war to know the meaning of the protection. Because of that we worked furiously, prized up stones, cut tree-roots and threw up earth with feverish speed. Our backs were bent like drawn bows, sinews and muscles were strained, sweat poured from our foreheads and flowed in streams down our naked backs. And you did not jeopardise your life for a smoke. The centimetres into the ground that you would lose could cost more than the taste of a cigarette.

The sun was blazing without mercy, and our throats ached from thirst. The Bolsheviks could turn up any moment. The sounds of battle were heard from all directions beyond the forest, and we redoubled our efforts to get deeper down. The blood pounded in the temples and the arm muscles quivered from the exertion.

Suddenly someone close to me 'hushed' and pointed at the edge of the forest on the other side. Everyone threw down the tools, put helmets on heads and jumped down into the holes with their weapons. Men came running fast over the field towards us. Our hands clutched the weapons harder and our eyes were screwed up, cool and calm, at the approaching soldiers. They were our *Fallschirmjäger!* Their characteristic helmets, that just in time told us their identity, saved them from being cut down by our machine-guns.

There were about 70 men, who came at top speed towards us. As they came closer, we stepped up from the holes. They were startled as they saw half-naked troops with submachine-guns in their hands, but Schwarck shouted to them. He called for their commander, a *Feldwebel* with the Knight's Cross, the Narvik shield and the *Kreta* cuffband, and let him give an overview of the situation over there. They had just been thrown out of their positions in the forest belt in front of us, but had only faced infantry. They had run out of ammunition, and then they had withdrawn. Their company commander had been killed, as well as the two men who had tried to bring back his body.

Schwarck decided that we should make a counter-attack. Since he had taken command over the *Fallschirmjäger*, we were a full company of more than a hundred men, just like in the old days. The newcomers got ammunition from our supply and then the entire force swarmed out into a firing line. I ran in the middle, beside Schwarck. Not a shot came as we crossed the field. In the forest belt it still remained peaceful, but as we came out in the open field again, it broke loose. Down! Schwarck turned panting to me "Shout like hell, as we rush up. The lads are almost finished, but we'll get them going if we shout altogether."

"Forward!" Schwarck shouted and I rushed up after him with a wild and husky "Hurrah!"

It was hard, because I was as tired and weary as the others, but it worked and the cry spread and echoed all over the narrow field, as we ran towards the violent infantry fire. As much as it stimulated us, it demoralised the enemy and in a flash we were over them. Like frightened rabbits they jumped out of their holes to get away, but our bursts reached their targets, no matter how they turned and twisted among the trees. We advanced and re-took some hundreds of metres as a defence sector for the *Fallschirmjäger*.

We promptly established a new defence of the contested forest belt. Ivan would not wait long before coming back. Schwarck, the *Feldwebel* and I went around and supervised the preparations. As I got furthest out on the right flank, it flashed into my mind that Schwarck had forgotten to connect with the companies by the road. In his eagerness to achieve a clever counter-attack, he had not thought of this important detail. Our position was unsupported.

By that time he was with the *Feldwebel,* away on the other flank, some hundreds of metres distant. It could be a matter of minutes. The last days' fights had brought so many sudden surprises and unexpected changes of situation that you had to be prepared for anything. A thundering clamour came suddenly from the blocking position by the road, where most likely Soviet tanks were involved. I did not waste time running over to Schwarck to inform him, but sent a man to report that with three men, I had gone to take up the connection again.

We ran over the fields and through the forest for all we were worth. Now the sound of gunfire could clearly be heard from a group of villas that I knew were within the blocking position. From there came the typical dull, muffled 'crack' of tank guns. My fears grew. They were confirmed as we came out of the edge of the forest and could see the road in front of us.

There, the last men of the two companies ran for their lives onto the road. Several were lying there already. One of the fleeing, with one trouser-leg ripped open and flapping, waved excitedly at us, that we should run backwards. It was his last deed in life. The next moment he disappeared in the explosion of a shell from the Stalin tank that with mounted infantry had just appeared from a bend about 100 metres from us. The men at the left rear anti-tank gun managed to shoot away some of the infantry from the tank, before they were torn to pieces by a shell from the giant tank.

We turned around at once. Now it was really only a matter of seconds! The whole would be lost if the Bolsheviks in front of us and behind us managed to make contact and realise our situation before we had had the time to withdraw from the trap. We had to get further back before they 'squeezed the pincers' around us. Like hunted hares we leapt away over the fields, through the forest, to the company. There they had just begun to get new combat contact with Ivan again. Short bursts of fire whirled in among the trees at the forest edge on the other side, where the attacking enemy lay. In an instant I had Schwarck informed about the situation. He cursed wildly as we had to abandon the position without getting the chance to give the Bolsheviks a new fight. But there was nothing else to do than order the company out of there immediately.

To fool the Bolsheviks the machine-guns first fired continuously towards the edge of the forest, while the rest of our men withdrew. Then, the machine-guns were pulled out of the trenches, and brought into the forest. All the SS-men and *Fallschirmjäger,* at full speed, ran up hill and down dale. We remained in the narrow forest, and ran close to, but parallel with the road. We dared not get too close to the road. The Bolsheviks had most likely advanced a long way with their tanks. We ran about two kilometres with the sweat dripping. All the time, with a hammering heart, I thanked my lucky star that had brought not only myself, but also the entire company out of a terrible situation.

Eventually we turned up beside a road leading into a residential suburb, and there met comrades from our *Aufklärungs Abteilung.* They were the survivors of the two companies that, along with us, had tried to hold the blocking position. *Sturmbannführer* Saalbach was there, giving orders about the preparations for defence of the village. For the first time in a long time we now met some civilians, who intended to stay to await the arrival of the Red Army.

The three of us had orders to advance and observe, so that we could give notice when Ivan was coming. It seemed they had been delayed in some way, otherwise they would have been there already. In a ditch, in the shadows from some oaks, we found a perfect place. It was a short way from the road out of the village, but still it was bordered by numerous, very nice family houses, away towards the direction of the enemy. We lay chattering about everything, especially about the shabby fellow in the shop, while we chewed his sausages and bread, and kept a sharp eye on the road. It was nice to be lying that way in peace and quiet for a while, and enjoying the warmth of the spring. There was rumbling, and crashing in the surroundings, but right there it was calm and pleasant.

Kraus was looking hard at the bend in the road about 400 metres from us. He blinked his eyes and looked again.

"What idiot is coming here on a bicycle?" he said.

All three of us stared in that direction, speechless with amazement. Someone was actually cycling along all by himself, heedless, with no thought that the road, any second, could be under artillery or machine-gun fire. The bicycle wobbled from one side of the road to the other. Either the man was a beginner or he was drunk, most likely the latter, as he seemed to ignore the danger. It was too grotesque! A Sunday cyclist in no-man's-land! He must be both drunk and crazy!

It was an Ivan! When he was only 60–70 metres away from us, we could clearly see him. No wonder he was cycling so badly. It was probably the first time he had sat on a bicycle. In Soviet Russia only the Stachanov heroes could afford such luxury. He swayed along on his lady's bike in the sun, with his submachine-gun on his back and a dispatch-case at his side. With pleasure he enjoyed the sight of the nice houses and the well-kept gardens, not seen at home in Russia It was a shame to destroy the idyll, but that dispatch-case interested us. It might contain important papers.

So a life was finished, to save others. A poor Soviet, like most of his fellow countrymen, harmless and kind when not incited to war by despots. With the mild nick-name of *Batjuschka* – little father – he was brutally interrupted on his life's first bicycle tour, that had taken him the wrong way in among the feared *Germanskij*. Riddled with bullets from a submachine-gun he tumbled over the bike. A figure turned up on the road in a flash, pulled the strap of the dispatch-case over his slack, dead arm and disappeared again. Fresh, young blood flowed over the asphalt.

Kraus ran back with the Soviet dispatch-case, to give it to the company commander, to be forwarded to the Divisional staff. Before he had time to return to us, the Bolsheviks launched their attack against the village. It came from the south, on the flank. Now it was safer for the two of us to get back to the company before we were cut off. We threw ourselves over the road, down into the ditch on the other side, where we were better protected from the shooting, which now started to spread in our direction, too. Then we ran along the ditch, back into the village, where the fighting had already started. We defended ourselves stubbornly, but in the long run we could not hold the position against their tanks and artillery and, despite heavy losses, more of their advancing storm-troops. Struggling from house to house, in highly dangerous steeplechases, through open gardens, and turning around the corners of the houses to riddle the Red Army soldiers with some final bursts, we retreated to the north-west where the forest once again hid our small unit. The Stalin tanks could drive a bit further westwards on the highway.

Orders came that we must, at all costs, recapture the village and close the road again. Three King Tigers came, as much needed support. If we had not had them, it was likely that the counter-attack would not have started. We had come close to being physically and mentally finished.

The expectation of being able to stop the Red Army in front of Berlin, and of having the co-operation of the western enemies, had faded. In fact we were already standing just outside Berlin, and could see yellow and blue-red trains of the metropolitan railway, standing there and being shot to pieces on demolished embankments. Time after time we saw railway-stations with names that are associated with Berlin. Over and over again we saw signs for *Commerz-Bank, Lokal-Anzeiger* and *Berliner Morgenpost.* This was all extremely depressing. From more and more gable walls the words *Berlin bleibt Deutsch!* stared down on us. But now we began to ask ourselves with despair in our hearts "Will Berlin really remain German?" The last hope was now with *Obergruppenführer* Steiner and his northern army which, we were told, was on its way to our rescue.

In the twilight we advanced towards the small residential suburb, now on fire. Before the Bolsheviks had time to organise an efficient resistance, we were over them with new-born, furious, attacking energy, which the presence of the King Tigers had given us. With murderous determination we let the weapons play among the surprised Soviets. They had felt secure for the night, and therefore had let the vodka flow. They fell in their drunkenness, and more than one enemy embraced his bottle in death. Those who managed to escape out into the darkness were easily picked off. Most were hit by a burst of gunfire or a hand grenade, when they showed up briefly as black shadows against the light from a burning house. We had recaptured the suburb.

We quickly organised our defence. After a short while, a smaller column of trucks, full of unsuspecting Soviets, came driving from the east. We let the cars through, and let them drive far in on the main street. Then, for several minutes our machine-guns and machine-pistols rattled against the cars. They swerved and skidded, crashed into house walls and fences, and overturned. We kept on firing until every movement in the chaos ceased, and the last cry of pain died out. With *Panzerfäuste* three Stalin tanks were knocked out the same way before the Bolsheviks became aware of the situation. During the night we had to defend ourselves almost uninterruptedly against their attacks, but now lacking the support from the Tiger tanks, we had to withdraw.

During the early hours of the morning orders came that our task was completed.

Towards the north-west, for the hundredth time, we fought our way out of a Soviet encirclement. Some comrades remained lying on the ground in the bursts of fire, but most of us escaped.

At the same time as Erik Wallin and his comrades were so busy fighting for their lives outside Berlin during those desperate days, Vsevolod Olimpiev and the 143rd Guards

Anti-tank Artillery Regiment were moving forward through Silesia. He has some very interesting observations to make from the point of view of an advancing Red Army unit, recording a number of sights and events that were indicative of the imploding Third Reich.

Our 143rd Guards Anti-tank Artillery Regiment of the 1st Guards Cavalry Corps crossed the narrow Neisse River before the dawn of 15 April via a pontoon bridge set up in advance. The river crossing was framed by beautiful 'firewalls' of tracer bullets but we found no enemy troops beyond the bridge. Our column was moving westwards without hindrance until 10am before we stopped to feed the troops. But we were punished for our carelessness straight away! Two Tiger tanks, which were apparently retreating from banks of Neisse, suddenly appeared from a forest five hundred metres away from us. The tanks opened fire on us without delay. We had no chance to unhook our guns from their tractors and set them up for combat. We were saved from serious losses only because among the pine trees there were many slit trenches previously dug by the Germans, in which we found shelter to await further developments. Fortunately the Tigers soon preferred to withdraw back into the forest, not knowing our real force. After that we really felt that we were in the enemy's rear. Later on up before the Elbe River the Germans didn't show any serious resistance. Our Corps was covering the left flank of the 1st Ukrainian Front, where the *Wehrmacht*, as far as we could see, had no large forces. The main thrust of the Front was targeted at Berlin from south-east and the main fighting broke out there. The guns of our regiment opened fire only rarely and only from indirect firing positions. The soldiers were saying: "At last we've given the Germans what they gave us in '41". Our advance was seriously hindered only by aerial attacks and so the Regiment switched to night marches resting in towns in the daytime. The enemy now used the Focke-Wulf 190 for ground attacks, replacing the Ju-87s too well familiar to us since 1941.

A guy of my age, *efreitor* (Lance-Corporal) Sasha Grigoriev, a peasant-hunter from near Tver, with whom I had been fighting since 1942, died in a regular aerial raid. He was a bit faint-hearted by nature and dreaded aircraft but had been thoroughly carrying out his duties of signalman. Sasha used to rush from hole to hole under any fire like a hare to reach a point where cable had been torn apart and fix it up. But this time his nerves let him down. Everybody knew a rule: during a dive-bomber raid you freeze in any hole or merely on the ground for a moving target is better seen from the air. Sasha had run and was mowed down by a machine-gun burst from a Focke-Wulf.

The scenes of the last winter came about again in regard to the local population. As in Silesia, the civilians intimidated by Fascist propaganda were on the run to the West leaving behind all their possessions. We were entering the same deserted villages and towns in which electric lights were sometimes still on. When the population had not been able to evacuate they would surrender to the victors' mercy before hanging out white flags out of all windows.

One morning the Regiment entered another town for a rest. Our Regimental cook unloaded the kitchen cauldron from a truck and went away to look for a place to set it up. Some Ukrainian girls, who had been working in the town, sent him to the owner of a nearby house. While the cook was walking up to his apartment on the fourth floor, the man jumped from a window and killed himself. He was an old German, a member of the Nazi Party. Soon after that the population had no place to flee to as the Elbe River was in their way and was being approached by the Americans from the West.

To all appearances the agony of the Hitler's regime was coming to a head. The Nazi bosses announced a total mobilisation and began to throw into the combat even old men and under-age boys. I remember an episode which occurred near the Elbe. Our column, moving down a forest road, stopped to let the vehicles which had fallen behind to catch up. I gave a command common for such a situation - to inspect the woods that were on the right hand side of the road. The soldier had not gone even ten metres when he yelled "Germans" and fired his PPsH. I leaped up, saw no enemy but defined the direction of shooting by the splinters of bark flying off the pine trees. We rushed into the woods and thirty metres away from the road found a wounded bloodstained boy 14-15 years old in German uniform. His mates had managed to escape into the woods having thrown their machine-gun nearby. The ambush had been organized manifestly unskillfully as their fire wouldn't have harmed us too much through the rows of pine trees. A machine-gun set up on the opposite side of the road to shoot across a clearing could have done a lot more damage to the column.

The private with a rare surname - Mershavka - who had discovered the ambush, was one of very few of ours who had been in the German captivity. Apparently he was not an ordinary man and used to be an officer before his captivity. The Order of the Red Banner on his soldier's blouse, which he had managed to save even in the Fascist POW camps, bore the evidence of it. A private soldier was rarely awarded with such an order. Another former POW - a photographer from Kazan in the past - served in the Regimental headquarters. This guy had been volunteering to shoot any captured Germans. I have to say that during our advance to Elbe we had already had an order to send all liberated POWs to the rear for a check-up. We came across this issue when the troops of our Corps had liberated a large POW camp in several kilometers before Elbe. An emaciated man came up to us and presented himself as an Artillery Captain who had been captured only recently - near the Oder in the winter. He requested us to take him on as a gun crewman for any position, even as a loader, but we had to reject him despite the shortage of people.

There were not only POWs from the Red Army but also people from the Allied armies, mostly Frenchmen. The latter were the most organized - they quickly lined themselves up on the camp parade ground and raised the French tricolor. All POWs were emaciated but our ones especially for they had not been receiving any Red Cross parcels unlike the French. Our POWs dragged themselves to the rear like ghosts, dressed in worn-out green German greatcoats with white letters 'SU' (Soviet Union) on their backs. The Frenchmen wore their own uniform.

In the morning I got an order to set up an observation point at a junction of two dirt roads near the camp. We hadn't even begun work when huge carts with inclined lattice boards harnessed to tandems of four horses in pairs turned out on the road from the west. These were the German farmers, who were fleeing from crossfire on the banks of Elbe. The carts were loaded up to the top with different goodies and foodstuffs. Our emaciated and starved POWs quickly guessed that there was a chance to profit by food. They began to search the carts taking away sausages, ham, cans with compote and other delicacies, not touching the owners, for all that. It was happening next to me and I didn't interfere. After all, it was a kind of justice. Then a minor but a characteristic episode occurred. A quite young French POW came up to me and addressed me in German. I managed to understand that he was an officer, very hungry and asked for some food. I waved my hand towards another cart, which was being ransacked by two Russian POWs thirty metres from us, thus giving him permission to take any food. He thanked me but didn't move to the cart and stood for a long while looking at all that in silence. It had become clear that this man, even being starved to death, wouldn't do what the Russians were doing, as another man's property - even that owned by his enemy - was inviolable. Finally we took pity on the Frenchman. He, nevertheless, decided not to refuse a piece of smoked ham just taken away from a farmer and offered to him. He took it with his trembling hands and kept thanking us with tears in his eyes for a long while.

Soon a battery of rocket launchers took up position next to the camp. A cloud of brick-red dust rose above the Elbe after their powerful salvo. The scared POWs began to run in all directions and the camp was quickly deserted.

Around mid-day I headed towards the Elbe to choose a place for a new observation point. On the way back I saw a terrifying scene in a lonely pine tree grove near the camp: a dead man dressed in ragged green greatcoat with the letters 'SU' on his back hanged from a tree. Apparently it was a Russian POW who used to collaborate with the camp administration and who had been subjected to a lynching court by his former inmates.

At the end of the same day I and two other soldiers had to go to the Corps headquarters with a packet. Driving down the street of a nearby town we noticed two tall men in civilian clothes, who were sacking an empty German house. It turned out that these two suspicious characters were Red Army officers from another POW camp situated nearby, who had been previously captured by the Germans. They spoke to each other in Russian calling each other 'Colonel' and 'Major'. As judged from the well-fed physiognomies of the 'Colonel' and the 'Major' there had been no problem with food there. People said that the personnel for Vlasov's Army were trained in this camp.

Back in the central sector of the front, the Battle of Berlin was in full swing, Erik Wallin finding himself in the epicentre of the inferno.

Gross-Berlin it said on a big yellow road sign that we passed as, in continuous fighting, we moved ever further westward that morning. It was a couple of days after 20 April, Hitler's birthday. We had left behind the wide belt of burning residential suburbs. Big factory blocks towered in front of us, and beyond them we could discern the sea of residential blocks of the giant city. A blue-grey haze lay like a veil over millions of inhabitants. It smothered everything with the dark smoke of vast conflagrations.

From Küstrin and onwards we had experienced only the prelude so far. Now the real battle of Berlin began! The final struggle against the giants in east and west, the 'Twilight of the Gods', had reached its peak and passed into its last phase. We found positions, already prepared, that the civilian population had dug and built ever since the Soviet breakthrough on the Vistula at the turn of the year.

At important road junctions the blockades against Soviet tanks were standing ready to be dragged into positions with tractors or tanks. There were trams, filled with paving stones, and big freight wagons with well-known names such as Knauer, Berliner Rollgesellschaft, Schmeling and others. Small foxholes, which had been dug in on almost every street crossing, were mostly already manned by some *Volkssturm* men armed with a couple of *Panzerfäuste*. Everywhere *Volkssturm* soldiers could be seen, most of them with just a helmet and a badge as identification.

Among them, were lots of young boys from the *Hitlerjugend*, aged between eight and twelve or thirteen years. After a mercilessly cruel war of bombs they were just as hardened as old frontline veterans. In the middle of the worst bombardments they showed a confidence and a balance of mind that scared us. We thought that these boys should be playing harmlessly in the schoolyard. As the enemy became visible or could be located by his firing, the faces of these small boys assumed the same grim, hard resolute look as those of hardened veterans.

Added to the confidence in battle of these warlike children, came a rancorous frenzy and a boundless contempt of death, which we grown-ups could not muster. With the agility and speed of weasels they climbed and struggled their way into completely impossible positions, to knock out a Soviet tank with a *Panzerfaust* or to finish off one or several advancing Red Army soldiers with a hand-grenade. There were quite a number of Soviet tanks put out of action by small boys in their early teens during the battle of Berlin.

We were constantly forced back. Out in Karlshorst lay the great racecourse, one of the largest in the world. During peacetime, it attracted like a magnet, tens of thousands of horse-racing, enthusiastic Berliners and foreigners several times a week. We held this securely until 23 April. Then a violent battle developed around the circuit and its closest surroundings. On the green lawn in the middle, our mortars were brought into position, together with those of the neighbouring companies. The remaining platoons fought as infantry outside.

Whistling and howling Soviet shells hit the stable-buildings and the platforms. Wooden benches and walls were splintered and whirled around in the air, and concrete walls were crushed. The artillery-fire grew into a rising crescendo from all sides. The great final bombardment of Berlin had begun. An impenetrable wall of gun-barrels closed, slowly but implacably, around the city. In the monotonously thumping thunder of the artillery and air bombs, the rattle of small-arms could only be heard at closer range. Amongst it all were the crashes of collapsing buildings.

The Bolsheviks had forced a barricade and broken through. Our own people were being chased over the track as we drove away. The Red Army soldiers were on our tail. Once again we were surrounded, and once again we managed to fight our way out.

Our next position of resistance became an enormous group of factories, crowned with the initials ASEA in giant letters. It became a fortress that temporarily held back the assault. The Soviets losses were horrible, because we could fire at them from all possible angles, thanks to the location of the factory buildings. Then they put in heavy artillery. It sang and thundered all around and the blast-waves threw us, half conscious, to and fro between the walls. The defenders who were killed by collapsing walls, ceilings and iron-girders numbered more than those who got a direct hit, or were hit by splinters. It became unendurable to stay in this inferno. Whirling stone, scrap iron and bloody body-parts made the air impossible to breathe, filled as it was with limestone-dust and gunpowder gasses. Once more we fought our way out with Death just an inch behind us.

All day we fought our way back in this way. Surrounded over and over again, we struggled on through narrow passages and back streets. Often we passed right through the middle of the fighting-line of other units. We always got through but with steadily growing losses. Sometimes we could take the wounded with us, some-times it was impossible, and they had to be left to await an enemy whose merciless brutality to SS men we knew only too well. The half-tracks had been sent back a long time before and we fought as infantry with our automatic weapons, *Panzerfäuste* and hand-grenades. We were hardly ever able to hold a position for more than an hour, then we were forced to run another race with Death, in the middle of Red Army soldiers.

It was unbelievable what masses they managed to throw at us. Constantly they advanced with their wild *urrää* yells, always supported by tanks. Many of their tanks were knocked out, but new ones constantly arrived. Despite that, their infan-try were lying in bloody mounds in the streets and backyards, or were hanging out from smoke-blackened window-openings. But no weakening in their attacking strength could be noticed. Their losses in this struggle must have been horrifying to any army commander at all, except for a Soviet Marshal, but the reservoir did not dry up. (After the war it became official that 300,000 Red Army soldiers had died in the battle of Berlin)

There were still civilians everywhere. It was almost too late for them to try to escape the attacking Soviets, who from the south had already advanced slightly west of Berlin and now were standing near Potsdam. Their assault had moved at such a breathtaking speed that the Berliners had had most escape-routes cut off be-fore they even knew the worst.

Still, though, the stream of refugees went wide towards Potsdam and towards the north-west, near Nauen. But even if tens of thousands, or hundreds of thou-sands of people managed to escape from the encirclement, there were still millions left, who lacked the possibility of getting out. Public transport was at a standstill. With only a wheelbarrow, or a rickety bicycle those poor people did not manage to get far with their children and their most necessary belongings. First they had to force themselves through the giant city's ruins, past blockages, over horse cadavers and human corpses that had already begun to pile up in the streets.

The people who decided, or had to stay, went down into the shelters. After all it was a life they had already got used to. They were cave-dwellers in the 20th Cen-tury! Down there they grouped together, waiting anxiously, agonising, listening to the constantly approaching sounds of battle. They felt the vibrations of the shell impacts and heard the houses collapsing above them.

Tens of thousands of these terrified people were crushed under the falling masses of stone. Or they were closed in from the outer world by a collapse, to face an agonising death by thirst and starvation that first drove them insane, before death came and relieved them. Those who survived had to save every drop of water and every piece of bread as long as possible. To run up from the cellar to bring water from the tap on the nearest street corner was like running to meet Death. In this city there hardly remained any silent spot. Merciless shells always seemed to find an unfortunate victim.

We had been forced as far back as into Berlin-Lichtenberg. One afternoon we were suddenly pulled out of the battle and were sent urgently southwards, down to Tempelhof and Mariendorf, where the Soviets had managed to make a dangerous penetration. It looked threatening for the aerodrome in Tempelhof. The half-tracks were driven forward at a raging speed along the burning Frankfurter Allee – Skalitzer Strasse – Gitschiner Strasse – Belle-Alliance-Strasse and directly south-wards.

Right in front of the gigantic administration buildings by Tempelhof airport, at the Flughafen underground station, one year earlier on leave, I had managed to miraculously escape death, together with a Swedish SS officer. It was during an American daylight attack, when a heavy bomb penetrated the metre thick concrete roof of the railway station and killed many people. It was now a petrol depot on an open field among barracks for Ukrainian workers. There the company stopped to refuel. Among other comrades from the other platoons that I met during this short pause was Ragnar 'the Giraffe' Johansson. During the hard fights of the previous weeks we had not seen each other even once. He was amazed to see me.

"Are you alive?" he asked, with audible doubt in his voice.

"Yes, as you can see."

"But the boys said that you got it at Küstrin," Ragge objected, obviously still not quite convinced. Then he smiled broadly, "Come, we must celebrate!"

He pulled me over to his half-track. From the inside he pulled a bottle, which he proudly showed off.

"*Danziger Goldwasser!* Good stuff. It's the company commander's, but we borrowed some. He can't take that much anyway," Ragge added with a tone which half excused, half intimated that we were doing a good deed by letting the commander be spared from drinking the whole bottle alone.

We took a big gulp each from the bottle of the noble drink, and then quietly and peacefully enjoyed a cigarette. It was the last time that I saw Ragge Johansson. A fine man and warrior, he was of a calibre that you do not find just anywhere. Ever since most of the Swedes in the Waffen-SS had gathered in our unit, he had been the connecting link. First as a motorcycle dispatch rider, then as the company commander's half-track driver, he had, thanks to his function in the company's staff, enjoyed greater opportunities for moving about than the rest of us. When the platoon was split up, he was the one who kept contact between the men, and he was a 'bringer of happiness,' who supplied us with rare newspapers and letters from back home.

As orders came to mount up, we just nodded, and cheered each other. We never thought that that could be the last time we saw each other. We had long since stopped worrying our heads about it. What would be, would be! But no oriental fatalism for us! Even if we had considered the possibility we still did not fall on each other, nor overdo our farewell. We knew each other so well! But a proper handshake would have been worthwhile and a simple but hearty "Thank you, Ragge! You were a strong soldier and a good comrade!" A high score for a good man!

The Bolsheviks had already reached Tempelhofer Hafen, 4-5 kilometres from the airport. In the residential suburbs of Lankwitz and Mariendorf we still held our positions, but in the open fields out to the east the Red Army soldiers had advanced like an avalanche and forced their way as far as the Teltow Canal. Right now the battle raged violently around the enormous group of printing and publishing company buildings at the south side of the canal, near the harbour. To prevent reinforcements getting through to our hard-pressed units on the other side of the canal the Bolsheviks laid a veritable barrage of bursting shells just over the blocks where we had to pass through.

The columns and masses of other troops that followed in our track were directed eastwards. Along Dorfstrasse and Germaniastrasse we drove down to Britz through a rain of shells. As we got there, we saw what was going to happen. The entire district was full of troops, infantry, artillery and several King Tigers. A heavy counter-attack was planned. Our entire Division was gathered.

As observer for a large number of mortars thrown together in a great hurry, I was lying with my field telephone in an advanced position in some ruins. It was quite peaceful there. Much worse was the sound of battle further away at the harbour. There everything was enveloped in an enormous column of smoke out of which fire sparked all the time. I could watch Soviet tanks rolling forwards, with flashes repeatedly shooting out from their barrels. Between and behind the infantry soldiers crawled and ran. In the middle of it all, smoke and geyser of earth spouted up from German shell-bursts. The buildings out there were burning sky high and around them raged hard fighting. I lay crouched there, having seldom had the chance to get such an overview of a battle.

Our own counter-attack started. From our artillery in Britz, Lankwitz and Tempelhofer Feld a threatening thunder rose, that quickly grew to a roaring hurricane. Like a scythe the artillery fire cut into the Bolsheviks' rear areas and isolated their foremost tank and infantry units. Then came the moment for our mortars. Like a hail-shower their projectiles struck down among the advancing Soviet masses of soldiers. The effect was increased by *Nebelwerfer* with their devastating explosive power. Regularly as clockwork the artillery fire thumped and thundered, and through its monotonous growling, howling *Nebelwerfer* projectiles cut their way forward to targets doomed to death. The area where the Bolsheviks had just pressed their way forward was transformed into a seething, smoking and fire-ridden maelstrom, where every second meant pain and death.

Behind me I heard engines growling. It was getting dark and in the fire-stained twilight our King Tigers, followed by infantry soldiers hardened by many assaults and close combats, rolled out of the ruins in Britz. They gushed forth in a powerful wave to crush what still remained of the Bolsheviks' bleeding spearhead. It was an immense and magnificent sight. For the last time I watched a tank battle. But it did not last long. Against our tanks the remaining Soviet tanks could do little. It was like using slingshots against stone walls.

The gap was closed, but all night long Ivan threw forward new masses to retake the lost terrain and open the way towards the airport and the heart of the city. It was a terrible, bitter struggle without mercy. Like confetti-ribbons against the red-violet night sky the tracer bullets drew their flashing lines in all directions, spraying mercilessly against each target. Behind us a boundless sea of fire spread over burning Berlin, over which cruel monsters without interruption poured a murderous cargo to keep the giant fire alive.

It was incredible that there was anything left of the city. Since the last days of November 1943 it had hardly been granted any rest at all between bombing raids. The flames in the heart of the city stretched enormous arms towards the sky and produced heat that drove up a violent firestorm. The American armadas came in daytime. At night, the British practised 'area bombing', a ruthless invention by Air Marshal 'Bomber' Harris.

Hundreds of thousands of soldiers were now struggling in a wide ring around the city, with despair in their hearts against overwhelming odds. Towards them rushed an endless stream of shells from tens of thousands of gaping gun-barrels. (Supposedly, 40,000 Red Army artillery pieces hammered on Berlin). What we had managed to re-conquer in an evening was step by step taken away from us again the following day. At dawn, a pale sun rose over the smoking ruins of the great dying city and with some weak beams penetrated the heavy smoke clouds, down to the fire-blackened house walls with their empty gaping windows. Corpses lay in the streets and among the rubble.

Exhausted but still fighting defenders kept up the battle that had once again regained the previous day's character. From house to house, from cellar to cellar, and from street to street we were forced backwards. We had the enemy on our eastern flank by that time. Via Köpenick and Baumschulenweg he had advanced far westwards and reached the eastern outskirts of Britz. Our command had to rush reinforcements to that area to try to stop the assault. At the same time the pressure from the south-west increased. The situation had become extraordinarily dangerous.

Around noon on 25 April, the position could not be held any longer and we were forced to give up Britz to the Bolsheviks. To get over to Neukölln we had to cross the Teltow Canal. There was only a rather narrow bridge. The sounds of battle came ever closer, when the Division, as usual the last to retreat, withdrew down towards the canal. The small detachments that covered the retreat were hard-pressed. Things became nerve-racking for those waiting for the vehicles, gathered tightly on the street that ran along the canal bank. People from the entire Division were standing there, almost a thousand men, tightly packed. They were the remains of the old well-tried regiments Norge and Danmark, and other units of our Division. They waited anxiously, but it was not easy for the vehicles to force their way through the ruins.

At last they drove down towards the canal street and the crossing could begin. At that moment a desperate cry was heard from the rear: "Two Stalin tanks have broken through!"

The tank panic hit everyone. Hundreds of SS men, who for years had faced death innumerable times without loosing their heads, were caught by wild panic. They fled rashly, trying to escape up on the half-tracks. The companies behind pressed on and everything was squeezed to a compact mass. Into this mountain of human beings the shells and machine-gun bursts came flying from the two Soviet tanks that had forced their way down the street. In front of me and behind me, to the right and to the left, bleeding and screaming soldiers fell to the ground.

What was left of the platoon I took with me to our half-tracks, which luckily were standing right at the front. As we got the vehicles started, hundreds of soldiers gathered around us desperately trying to climb up. The machine-gun fire and shell-splinters swept many of them away and the armoured sides of the half-tracks were turned red by their blood. As we moved down towards the bridge I saw that the fuse to the explosive charge under the bridge was already lit. In the panic someone had lit it too early. It squirted and sputtered from the fuse to the four rocket shells that were to blow the bridge into the air before the Bolsheviks could manage to get over. But how should we manage?

Behind us a volley from a Stalin organ hit the panic-stricken crowd with grue-some results. The men in the half-tracks did not know anything about the burning fuse under the bridge. They were already frightened enough. I stood with shaking knees while our vehicle slowly, slowly pressed its way over the bridge with the stream of fleeing men. Cold sweat came out on my forehead. Finally we were on the other side! Almost at the same moment as the half-track rolled off the bridge, the charge under the bridge exploded.

In the direction of Hermannstrasse the crew of an 88mm gun worked desper-ately to get the weapon in position, and to take the two Soviet tanks under fire. Be-fore they were ready, a new salvo from a Stalin organ came, hitting the north side of the canal and tearing to pieces the artillerymen.

What had happened to the other vehicles of my platoon? It was impossible to get a clear view of the situation on the other side. The iron construction of the bridge hung in the way and thick dust-clouds covered my sight. Had any of the half-tracks got up on the bridge as it was blown up or had the men jumped into the water? On the bridge, I had at a glance noticed that the remaining men started to jump into the water to swim over.

Filled with concern for the fate of our comrades, we drove along Hermannstrasse northwards. The gathering-point was U-Bahn Stadtmitte, where our Division Nordland's new command post was to be set up. For about an hour we zigzagged hither and thither on almost impassable streets. On a house wall we for the first time saw in hastily painted letters *SS-Verräter – Kriegsverlängerer!* ('SS traitors and extenders of war!') German communists had been at work. Was this the way it would be? Would they start to emerge from now on? Perhaps the civilian popula-tion's morale, which so far had stood up well under all the hard tests of the bombing war, had started to give way? Still we were saluted with "*Heil* Hitler!" when we some-times stopped on a street to ask some water-carrying civilian the way to Stadtmitte. But perhaps it was only because of fear of the 'death's-head' soldiers that they saluted that way. Were we going to be forced to fight an inner enemy, too?

We had hardly completed this thought when right in the middle of Hermannplatz we had bursts of bullets sweep over the half-track from a roof. There, German communists with red armbands were lying shooting, with ma-chine-guns that they had stolen from the *Volkssturm's* stocks. Soldiers from another SS unit came running, rushed up into a building on the other side of the square and put the roof over there under fire with their machine-guns, while some other men ran into the Communist house and set the upper floors on fire. Then they waited down by the front door, to see if the commies up there would prefer to die in the fire or try to get out, just to be caught and hanged from the nearest lamp-post.

We watched other depressing signs of disorganisation on our roving way to Stadtmitte. Numerous *Wehrmacht* soldiers were standing loitering, weapon-less, in doorways. As they caught sight of our half-track, they quickly stepped back into the dusk. The respect the *Wehrmacht* had for the Waffen-SS was without limit. How many times out at the front, had we been sent into action to get them out of trouble, trouble that only the SS could solve? We also met *Wehrmacht* soldiers who, helplessly drunk, staggered around in the streets, without caring about the howling shells or air bombs. On the opposite side of the street an old man and some women were just tearing large pieces from a swollen dead horse. A whistling shell approached. They threw themselves to the ground behind the horse for a moment, awaited the impact, stood up again and continued with bloody hands to tear, scratch and cut in the cadaver.

At last we reached Stadtmitte. There was not a single undamaged house along the entire Leipziger Strasse, one of the most famous streets in the world. Here, illuminated advertisements of all colours used to shine. Expensive luxuries in world famous companies' magnificent shop-windows used to tempt the eyes of the strolling elite and the hurrying financiers and businessmen. Now, everything was grey and dull with remains of rusty iron constructions like gnawed skeletons poised over smoking piles of gravel and bricks.

Down in the underground station, privates and SS generals crowded together. I managed to find an *Untersturmführer* from my division, who gave me orders to carry on with the half-track to Grunewald, where the supply unit was, and to await orders there. As fast as possible we drove westwards. We crossed the totally devastated Potsdamer Platz, the torn heart of Berlin, and the Tiergarten Strasse, that now with its naked, splintered and fallen oaks looked more like a fossilised forest. We went up the Kurfürstendamm. In pre-war days its boulevard cafés had drawn people from all over the world to stroll along its elegant pavements, past luxury shops, and nightclubs known for their beautiful women. All had been swept away by the war's brutal fist. Then we went on through Halensee out to Hundekehle in Grunewald. There, in the forest round the lake, we found the supply unit.

We arrived at twilight and not until evening the next day had we moved on to reconnect with our struggling comrades down in Neukölln. The fact was that I had been kept behind to gather people from mortar platoons of regiments that no longer existed, except on paper. With four half-tracks and 20 men we could drive into the city. Among them were my reliable veterans Kraus, Leisegang and Lindenau, who had managed to swim over the Teltow Canal the day before and during the night had found their way to the supply unit.

All that was left of the company was in action some streets south of Hermannplatz. We drove in on a side street to Hermannstrasse with our half-tracks and I went down into the cellar where Schwarz had his 'company staff'- just a signalman - to get my instructions. Schwarz was sitting on a sugar-box and studied a map of Neukölln in the light from a storm-lamp. His face was bright red. On another box in front of him, he had a bottle of *Danziger Goldwasser*. It was almost empty. Schwarz was drunk.

With an unsteady finger he pointed out a street crossing to me: "Here you take position with the mortars. Keep Hermannstrasse south of Steinmetzstrasse and this park in Rixdorf under fire."

"Yes, but it's impossible to be out there. Ivan holds the further part of Hermannstrasse and can shoot directly at us."

"Don't you come here refusing orders! I'm in charge now!" Schwarz sounded and looked murderous.

"OK, but come on out yourself, damn it, and take a look!"

He slouched after me up the stairs and out on to the half-dark street, where the shadows of the ruins fluttered irregularly in the light from the fires. Just as we reached the corner to Hermannstrasse, a shell whistled past us and with a boom tore up the asphalt about 20 metres from us. Quickly we pulled our noses back and Schwarz changed his opinion about the suitability of a mortar position on Hermannstrasse. We had to remain on our side street with the mortars mounted on the half-tracks. Schwarz took Walther Leisegang as orderly and returned to the cellar.

To prevent the muzzle-flashes from the mortars from being seen from the air, we now fired in the semi-darkness with *Salzvorladung*, a wadding containing salt that dampened the muzzle-flash. The telephone which connected us with our observer over there was handled by Erich Lindenau down in the cellar, where worried and excited civilians sat pressed against the walls and in the corners.

Up in the sky a familiar rattling engine noise came from a Soviet reconnaissance aircraft. It was of the type that the soldier's humour had given the name 'Iron Gustav' or 'Coffee-grinder.' The first name was because of this aircraft's custom, like an inspecting Sergeant-major, of turning up anywhere, and slowly, flying back and forth, even in the most violent anti-aircraft fire. The other name, because of the typical motor hum that mostly sounded like an old coffee-grinder's creaking. It swept back and forth, at hardly 100 metres height, and searched and searched, maybe for us?

Together with Kraus I was on my way down to Lindenau, on what errand I do not remember any more. We had just put our feet on the first step to the cellar, when suddenly the entire gable collapsed over us. A violent air pressure tore our helmets off and we were half buried in gravel and lumber. Kraus got on his feet right away. There had been an explosion close behind, right among the vehicles! Kraus went down again under the pressure, but was up again at once, unhurt. I tried to crawl to my feet, but failed.

From the half-tracks on the street cries and groans were heard and the sound of exploding ammunition, and down in the cellar the women cried hysterically.

Damn! What could this mean? It was quite impossible to get to my feet. At last, Kraus took my arm and helped me. My uniform was torn to shreds, and grey from limestone dust. My nice soft officers' boots, that I had been so happy about, were completely ripped. Staggering, I managed to get down the half-demolished stair to Lindenau. It hurt a bit in my left thigh and I touched the leg with my hand. It got quite wet. It was blood. And now the burning pain came. I was wounded. There was a large, wide-open hole all the way through the thigh. Out there the mortar ammunition continued to explode. The cries got fewer and weaker.

"Look! I'm wounded," I said and showed Kraus and Lindenau my bloody hand.

Erik Wallin's account of the brutal fighting for Berlin is quite remarkable, for incredibly few first-hand German accounts of this phase of the war exist.

If some thought that the end of April and the death of Hitler heralded a complete end to the fighting in the East, they were wrong, as Vsevolod Olimpiev discovered. Much of this fighting occurred when German troops attempted to break through the Soviet lines in order to surrender to the Western Allies.

At the end of April the bulk of the forces of the 1st Ukrainian Front came right up to the capital of *Reich*. Having crossed Elbe north of Dresden troops of the 1st Guards Cavalry Corps took up defensive positions facing south in order to prevent a possible enemy breakthrough towards Berlin.

Two batteries of our Regiment positioned themselves for point-blank shooting on the outskirts of a large settlement spread on the hills, which was defended by a cavalry Regiment. We had only one task - not to let the enemy through, which according to rumours, had been mustering forces for a strike. On 28 April I conducted reconnaissance of the nearby area with two soldiers, carrying out my duties of the 1st Battery Control Platoon Commander. What I saw didn't give rise to much optimism. There was no continuous line of defence due to the shortage of manpower, the cavalrymen were only in built-up places and wouldn't be able to hold out against large enemy forces.

Our fears came true at the dawn of the next day. It was still dark when the German infantry supported by two self-propelled guns began their advance. Our battery engaged them almost immediately, opening fire from three guns (the fourth was inoperative). To tell the truth, I was seeing an impressive picture of results of point-blank shooting at an attacking wave for the first time. But the enemy was stubbornly moving forward and soon the threat for the crewmen of being stricken by explosions from our own shells arose. The battery men kept shooting with submachine-guns in their hands. Finally the Germans were spent, and retreated. Suddenly our Battery Commander got a strange and incomprehensible order via radio from the regimental headquarters situated far in the rear - to send to the rear all vehicles including gun-towing tractors. Simultaneously the neighbouring 2nd Regimental Battery was ordered to leave its position. In practical terms it meant that our battery had been marked for sacrifice. Soon the enemy, having cancelled his frontal attack on the guns, increased pressure on the cavalry regiment, which had to give up one house after another. By mid-day the cavalrymen had practically left the whole village. The enemy submachine-gunners started running out of the houses in front of the three-storey hotel building occupied by the Battery Commander and the Control Platoon. The battery was in peril. The guns, which we had nothing to tow with, might be considered as good as lost. Any delay in retreat would threaten the loss of the crewmen. At that moment none of us knew that we had been surrounded for several hours. Our Commander - a blue-eyed sturdy Siberian fellow - Senior Lieutenant Fominykh, was a man of firm character and was not giving an order to retreat with no permission from above. It was given via radio only after noon. The artillerymen quickly began to leave the firing positions. I had not managed to climb on top of the stony parapet protecting the inner yard of the hotel when the German submachine-gunners began to run out of the houses shooting on the move. The situation became extremely acute. One had to run down about three hundred metres up a ploughed slope to the hillcrest in order to escape from fire. I could see in the corner of my eye the crewmen were running left and right from me throwing down everything hindering their run. I had to sacrifice my excellent trophy field glasses dangling on my chest. Having run up to kind of a pit on the crest of the hill I found a large group of battery soldiers and cavalrymen in this rather large hole. A tall young Uzbek, Seidov - Sergeant Major of our Battery - was the most senior amongst us in regard to rank and he took up the command with no hesitation. I had noticed him - a novice at the Battery - back during the fighting at dawn when he had brought round ammunition and food. Seemingly he could have gone to the rear (then there was such an opportunity) as any other would have done being in his shoes. But he lifted a heavy shell crate on his shoulders and ran to the guns under enemy fire, then took a submachine-gun and helped the crewmen to beat off the attack, having captured a German who had stolen up to our guns with a *Panzerfaust*. And now Seidov had helped us to get out of a really hard situation with his courage and promptness. The group under his command decided to break through to our positions after a short rest.

When we had gone down the other side of the hill we saw our truck, which had been sent to the rear at dawn with the Battery field kitchen, on the road. Two Germans in brown-orange *Volkssturm* jackets were trying to start its engine with a crank. We shot a volley at them from all the weapons we had, upon which they jumped into a trench and opened fire with a machine-gun. Our small detachment had to turn into a field in the middle of which, half a kilometre away, we saw some buildings surrounded by a stone wall. We entered through an open gate and the detachment found itself inside a large homestead yard the size of a football pitch. Another gate on the opposite side of the homestead yard was closed and we quickly understood that it was giving us a chance for salvation. I was among the first to run up to it. The picture my eyes captured through chinks between planks is still in my memory. A line of enemy soldiers - up to a platoon in number - was lying on the ground with their backs towards us. Most of them were in *Wehrmacht* uniforms, two or three of them in *Volkssturm* jackets and two of them even in our Russian greatcoats. Being taken aback, we recoiled behind some sheds. A thought flashed: we are in a trap - an enemy line in front of us and a machine-gun behind. Seidov, who had come to a decision first, gave a short order to break through. He quickly divided the group into those who would open the gate after his command, those who would fire from submachine guns and those who would throw hand grenades. Everything came out well. The enemy, dumbfounded by such a heavy fire, lost his mind. A group of the Germans tried to find cover in a shed's basement, into which we immediately threw hand grenades. That was when I felt sorry that I had only a Nagant revolver in my hands. After a short fight the way to our troops' position was clear. The enemy platoon paid dearly for the thoughtlessness of their commander, who had not set up an observer in the rear. It was not the same enemy who had advanced in 1941 and even not that one which was fighting on the banks of Oder in the winter.

At the end of that unforgettable day - 29 April 1945 - the remnants of the Battery crewmen gathered in our rear near a highway, on the outskirts of a large settlement spread along the Western bank of the Elbe. Our mood was depressed - we had lost our guns and some of us even our firearms. Suddenly a Willys jeep drove up to us with Colonel Mazin - the Corps Artillery Commander - next to the driver in his black felt cloak and red-topped astrakhan hat. "Where is the battery commander?" was his first question. He interrupted Fominykh's report and began to curse him in foul language in front of all of us: "You abandoned your guns, you let the Germans through, you will be court-martialed!" Our morale collapsed completely as we thought that the Battery would be disbanded. But as often occurs in war, exactly the opposite things happened. When the commanders had everything investigated it turned out that our Battery had held out longer than any other Corps unit and had left its position only by order. Many of the battery men were awarded medals.

The Germans had managed to advance for only several kilometers in our area. In three days our tanks came up to Berlin, quickly restored the situation and moved south-east to Czechoslovakia.

During the last days of April even the most die-hard of Hitler's supporters could sense that the end was near. As a member of the Waffen-SS, Erik Wallin could expect little mercy from the Red Army; as a non-German who had already volunteered to fight the Red Army with the Finns he could expect even less.

On 29 April the struggle raged very close to us and we lay listening anxiously to the violent exchanges of fire. Any moment shells could come whistling in among us. We felt miserably small. Like other wounded SS men I started to remove my SS insignia. The pay-book and my Swedish passport I got rid of, too. The passport was as much a death sentence to me, in the eyes of the Bolsheviks, as the Waffen-SS pay-book, because the photo showed me in Finnish uniform and there was also a stamp regarding my participation as a volunteer in Finland in 1941.

During the night of 30 April the firing outside started to move away and then we knew that the Soviets could be there at any moment. In the morning they came storming in, dirty, bad-smelling in a quite special, typical Red Army way, and with their submachine-guns up and ready. They started to snoop around everywhere, leering and sneering at the wounded, but otherwise they behaved correctly. Actually '*Berlin kaputt!*' was their stock phrase.

Then they started to examine every man. They went from bed to bed, pointing the submachine-gun at the chest of the wounded and asked: "You SS man?" There were several hundred SS men lying there with their hearts in their mouths, but all of them had removed their SS insignia and denied stubbornly. After all, they wanted to stay alive. A small bow-legged, flat-nosed half-Mongolian approached me. "Du SS?" he hissed out and forced the gun barrel deep into the pit of my stomach. I protested that I was an ordinary *Wehrmacht* soldier. "Da, da du SS?" he repeated and in my panic I thought I saw that everybody's eyes were on me. Then I managed to achieve something that reminded him of a smile and shook my head. Then he gave up. I was drenched in a cold sweat, but could now breathe more easily.

The Bolsheviks immediately started a careful clearance of the upper floors. Bricks and mortar were heaved away and we were moved up. Then we also got drinking water and a thin coffee. Soviet doctors came and helped care for the worst wounded. They started amputating, but without anaesthesia. I guess that about

The last known image of Swedish participation in the Battle of Berlin – a knocked-out armoured personnel carrier from the 'Nordland' Division (note sun wheel insignia), May 1945. The body lying to the right of the vehicle appears to be Swede Ragnar Johansson, the unit's last casualty, and a close comrade of Erik Wallin. (Erik Norling)

90% of the amputated bled to death. I got a new bandage. And it was just in time, because the old one was stiff with dried blood and pus and stank terribly.

In the afternoon of 1 May, Red Army soldiers came and told us, laughing, that Hitler was dead. "Chitler kaputt! Chitler kaputt! Bärrlin kaputt! Garmanija kaputt!" they roared. Heinau wept silently.

Quite remarkably, and after a number of close shaves, escapades and turns of fortune, Erik Wallin managed to make it to safety in the British zone of occupation. Few soldiers captured in the heart of Berlin were as lucky.

Dmitriy Loza has this to say about his fate during the final days of the war, and the legacy that it left to him.

I parted company with the Shermans long, long ago. But I have never forgotten them, not for a minute. Did I want to forget? Hardly!

Except for perhaps one month on a T-34, all of my time at the front was spent on foreign-made tanks. I saw it all: some were knocked out of action, some were blown up, and one burned. I avoided one misfortune - drowning. But I was 'chopped down', one can say, 'symmetrically'. My Matilda was hit in September 1943, and I was seriously wounded in the right leg. In April 1945, an anti-tank round fired from close range by a Tiger penetrated my attacking Sherman. Spalling from my own tank smashed into my left knee.

They discussed amputating my leg at the field hospital. Fortunately, the chief surgeon of the Second Ukrainian Front, Professor General Nikolay Nikolayevich

Shermans of the 1st Battalion, 46th Guards Tank Brigade in May 1945, after the end of the war. (Artem Drabkin)

Elanskiy, was at the hospital. This magician did the most complicated operation on me, reconstructing an almost primitive leg from shattered bone. I spent three months in recovery, more than half of it immobilized in a plaster cast. I left the hospital with all my parts. Such are the trials and tribulations of war.

Over my many years of service in the army, not once did I have to go to a doctor for help. But later, my wounds forced me to. It was 1948. I was a student at Frunze Academy. We were conducting marching practice for the parade on Red Square. It was physically very demanding and resulted in the opening of the wound on my right leg. Several tiny pieces of Matilda armour had worked their way out. And my left leg had swollen considerably. The medical conclusion was that I should be excused from all marching activity for the rest of my student time.

This was the first serious caution: "Remember your foreign-made shrapnel!" It was the beginning of almost forty years of wearing an elastic bandage on my left knee whenever I engaged in any strenuous physical activity.

During my annual officer's physical examination, the surgeon persistently recommmended that I undergo an operation to remove these fragments from my left leg. But they could not exclude the possibility of unforeseen complications. I had to laugh it off every time, saying: "These fragments are made of high-quality American armour plate. I think everything will be all right!"

And so I held them off for thirty years.

Something unbelievable happened sometime at the end of the 1970s. I was vacationing at a military rest area in Georgia. It was summer, an excellent time for swimming. A storm arose, lasting two days. When the sea had calmed, shifting sand and pebbles were obstructing the beach. Many of the vacationers, including myself, helped the staff of the sanitorium to clean the driftwood and debris from the beach. Before doing this, I should have gone back to my room for the elastic bandage. But I was lazy. Why bother?

While I was working, I did not forget about my wounded left leg. I tried to shift all the weight of the load to my right lower leg. The result was excruciating pain. The next day, I could not get my leg into my trousers. Three days of bed rest. This calamity befell me a week before the end of my vacation. I made it home with great difficulty. The doctors there decided to wait for the swelling to go, down, then discuss the issue of hospitalization and surgery.

As they say, "it's an ill wind that blows nobody good." The swelling went down, and I again refused to be hospitalized. I have not regretted that decision to this day.

Almost twenty years have passed without any recurrence, despite any stresses I put on my leg: I drive a car and work the garden at my *dacha*. I have thrown the elastic bandage away. I do not limit my physical activities. The doctors think that the large (Sherman) fragment under my left kneecap has displaced. I can dress and undress easier. And now, there is nothing pinching in my leg. It would be pointless to probe around. What a relief!

With the years, more and more often my wounds ache in bad weather. My fellow *Emchist* Gevorg Chobanyan, himself seriously wounded, calms me, and himself at the same time, with the words: "Can't sleep? Do your wounds bother you at night? They are your wounds. Accept your fate! These veteran pieces of foreign shrapnel will go with you to another world!"

The final account comes from Zoya Alexandrova, who describes her participation in the final drive on Berlin. Her closing comments must surely echo those of many thousands of her comrades.

Just before the advance on Berlin we were placed into armoured personnel carriers and kept a whole day on alert at an outskirt of the town of Gorgast. It was still dark when we headed off towards the enemy lines, slowly crossing a wide field. Artillery bombardment began. I looked back and was stunned! The line of fire took up the whole length of the horizon. I found out only after the war that searchlights had been used for illumination... Dawn was breaking. Our aviation was sweeping above us en echelon. The scene was awesome.

The frontline met us with a thick smokescreen... The enemy having retreated sent back a hurricane of fire on his former positions. We jumped off our armoured carrier and came across a trench covered by plywood. It was joy – a roof above our heads! Thunder and rattling outside and a paradise inside! Our chef Sasha treated us with pies – he had baked them beforehand with the intention of giving us a wonderful surprise during a short lull. After a short respite we moved along a railroad. The smokescreen began to dissipate and we could see traces of submachine-gun bursts through flying puffs of smoke.

Khamaev and Ekaterinchuk, left in reserve, ran away from the command post and tried to catch up with us on foot but were caught in an ambush and both died.

The advance stalled. The armoured carrier stopped near the railway. We quickly jumped off and the driver was wounded in the leg when leaving the vehicle. Khramov rushed up to it, turned on and drove behind a shed. The infantry began

Zoya Alexandrova: "After the war I was called up to a store full of captured material, and the Brigade Commander said: "Choose what you want." They opened a box and there was a dress in it. I am in that dress in this photo." (Zoya Alexandrova)

to catch up. An infantry captain was running across the road but suddenly collapsed, wounded by a sniper. I fell on my stomach and crawled towards him, some of the scouts followed me. We dragged the wounded man into a house and dressed his wound somehow. The scouts moved forward on foot. We got around a water tower and saw that the gun of Lieutenant Alekseev's tank was set against an enemy's tank and his gun against our tank. Basically they had shot each other from point blank range… Only two of our crew survived. Our scout Baranov drove the wounded away on a motorbike…

We were moving to the Seelow Heights along with tanks of the Kiselev's Company. We had to stop frequently because of shelling. A passage underneath the railway embankment was blocked up and most likely mined… Kiselev sent his machines across slantwise to the embankment. They crossed over it and carefully got down the opposite side. But met by dense enemy fire they stopped after a ten kilometre march. Then Khramov and Volkov talked the commander into letting them go to reconnoiter on one tank. They jumped on it and raced away.

They came back quite soon. Khramov was wounded in the side but his wide German belt saved him. The scout was doubling up in pain but stayed in action. The infantry caught up with us. The scouts' foray had been successful and now we knew the distribution of the enemy's firing positions. The platoon commander informed the battalion commander Spivak about it and he in turn asked the brigade commander via radio to "add some fire" onto ... our area. Soon something began to rustle and hiss above our heads. *Katyushas* had begun to play but struck us instead of the Germans. It was a nightmare. One of our scouts died, I was shellshocked... many, so many men died.

That light shellshock was reflected in my nervous condition – I couldn't bear the sound of *Katyushas* anymore. Unfortunately back then medicine didn't recognize light shellshock as illness and there were situations when people died not because they were afraid of something but because they couldn't control their nerves.

I was assigned to assist a surgeon at the first aid station of the Brigade. It was placed next to the position of the ill-fated Guards Mortars.[1] It's hard to express my feelings when I heard them 'playing'. Fortunately the guys had remembered about me and took me back. We fell under shrapnel fire on the way to Berlin and I nearly paid with my life trying to jump off the vehicle on the move.

We came back late at night. We entered a site in a Berlin suburb where the scouts had stayed for a rest. The snoring and moaning of sleeping men was resounding around the big room. Khramov, Volkov, Goutnik, Goroshko and Alexandrov sat at the table with a candle on it. When they saw me all of them stood up, except for Alexandrov, who had not been taking trophies. Then, as if under a command, they slipped their hands into their cherished pockets and – what a wonder – opened boxes and said "Choose!" I understood that if I refused they would be offended. And I took one piece from each. Generally we had been taking only underwear and food out of all possible trophies. The guys would sometimes take watches, trinkets. Truly, they would quickly squander them on sluts! I had not been taking anything because of the superstition: if you take you'll die. Only once I took a length of material in an abandoned German house.

In the morning we entered Berlin, where a ferocious and exhausting battle was raging. We came across Groshev, who had miraculously survived. He had found himself within the enemy's position and hidden in a cellar in which civilians were hiding. He had spent a whole day inside and no one gave him away!

The war for us ended on 2 May 1945. There was no limit to our joy. But we followed with our eyes the endless streams of prisoners trudging through the ruins of Berlin with a bitter feeling... Thus we had come to Berlin through thunder and fire, cheering victories and grieving over the loss of our comrades. I don't know how I had endured that prodigious and sweeping march, that farewell hurricane of fire. But one thing I know for sure – I was proud to leave my signature on the wall of the *Reichstag*!

---

1   Armed with *Katyushas*.

Further Reading

Further reading

The Campaign in North-West Europe 1944-45

There is a profusion of titles covering D-Day, Normandy and the subsequent drive through North-West Europe.

All of the official histories produced by the Allies are worthwhile. The first to appear was the British: *Victory in the West* by Lionel Frederic Ellis contained two volumes, *The Battle of Normandy* (1962) and *Defeat of Germany* (1969). The American official histories are even grander in scope, and overall more useful as they make a greater effort to tie in a range of sources, including making use of German material. The relevant volumes are: *Cross-Channel Attack* by Gordon A. Harrison (Washington DC, 1951), *Breakout and Pursuit* by Martin Blumenson (1961), *The Lorraine Campaign* by Hugh M. Cole (1950), *The Ardennes: The Battle of the Bulge* also by Hugh Cole (1965), *The Siegfried Line Campaign* by Charles B. MacDonald (1963) and *The Last Offensive*, again by Charles MacDonald (1973). The Canadian official history is an excellent piece of work: C.P. Stacey, *The Victory Campaign: The Operations in North-West Europe 1944-1945* (Ottawa, 1960). The German official history, published under the auspices of the *Militärgeschichtliches Forschungsamt* (MGFA) has not yet reached its coverage of the campaigns of 1944 and 1945.

Cherry picking some of the literally thousands of campaign histories is difficult. The latest study from Max Hastings, *Armageddon: The Battle for Germany 1944-45* (2004) is well up to that author's usual high standard. Even though it was published over forty years ago, *Caen: Anvil of Victory* by Alexander McKee (1964 and several later reprints) remains a classic. Two accessible series cover the fighting in Normandy, published by Osprey and Sutton. The former produce 4 volumes covering D-Day, all published in 2004: *D-Day 1944 (1): Omaha Beach* and *D-Day (2): Utah Beach and the US Airborne Landings*, both by Steven Zaloga; *D-Day (3): Sword Beach and the British Airborne Landings* and *D-Day (4): Gold & Juno Beaches*, both by Ken Ford, as well as *Caen 1944* (also by Ken Ford, 2004) and *Operation Cobra 1944* by Steven Zaloga (2001). During 2004 Sutton published the Battle Zone Normandy series: *Utah* (S. Badsey), *Omaha* (T. Bean), *Juno Beach* (K. Ford), *Gold Beach* (S. Trew), *Villers-Bocage* (G. Forty & S. Trew), *Battle for Caen* (S. Trew), *Operation Epsom* (L. Clark), *Battle for Cherbourg* (R. Havers & S. Trew), *Battle for St Lô* (P. Yates), *Falaise Pocket* (P. Latawski), *Operation Cobra* (C. Pugsley & S. Trew). A German view of the fighting for Normandy is provided by Paul Carell's *Invasion! They're Coming!* (1963). A more recent and very welcome study is *Normandy 1944: German Military Organization, Combat Power and Organizational Effectiveness* by Niklas Zetterling (2000).

Operation Market-Garden has also received blanket coverage. Cornelius Ryan's *A Bridge Too Far* (1974) remains a classic, but should be supplemented by Lloyd Clark's *Arnhem* (2002), Christopher Hibbert's *The Battle of Arnhem* (1962), and Robert Kershaw's *It Never Snows in September: The German View of Market Garden and the Battle of Arnhem September 1944* (1997).

The bitter fighting for the Siegfried Line and German borders has been the subject of a complete series from Spellmount Publishers, all penned by Charles Whiting. The best titles include *The Battle of Hurtgen Forest* (2000), *Bloody Aachen* (2000), *The Other Battle of the Bulge: Operation Northwind* (2001) and *West Wall: The Siegfried Line in World War II* (1999).

There is no definitive account of the Ardennes offensive. However, John S.D. Eisenhower's *The Bitter Woods* (1969) remains an excellent account. Jean-Paul Pallud's *The Battle of the Bulge Then and Now* (1984) is a bible-sized tome containing an adept text as well as over one thousand images. *A Blood-Dimmed Tide: The Battle of the Bulge by the Men who fought it* by Gerald Astor (1998) contains a large number of good firsthand accounts.

The final battles fought during and after the Rhine crossings are best covered by the official histories, but these can be supplemented by Peter Allen's *One More River: The Rhine Crossings of 1945* (1980), Hubert Essame's *The Battle for Germany* (1969), Kenneth W. Heckler's *The Bridge at Remagen* (1957) and John Toland's *The Last 100 Days* (1966). This last stage of the campaign in North-West Europe has received curiously little in-depth coverage from authors in the past twenty years.

Finally, some key biographies for this phase of the war include Nigel Hamilton's immense trilogy concerning Montgomery, *Monty* (1981-86), and Stephen Ambrose's *Eisenhower: Soldier and President* (1991).

The Eastern Front 1944-45

English-language coverage of the war on the Eastern Front in 1944-45 cannot be said to be comprehensive. To make full use of the sources available the reader must really have command of at least German and preferably Russian. However, for the purposes of utility, this section will restrict itself to English language works.

The best overviews of the campaign remain John Erickson's *The Road to Berlin* (1983) and Earl F. Ziemke's *Stalingrad to Berlin: The German Defeat in the East* (1968). Both are clearly written. However, an up-to-date study drawing on the most recently released Soviet records is required. Other interesting material is contained in Jürgen Thorwald's *Flight in Winter: Russia conquers January to May 1945* (1951).

The destruction of Army Group Centre has received disproportionately little coverage in English. The best is Gerd Niepold's *The Battle for White Russia* (1987), supplemented by *Belorussia 1944: The Soviet General Staff Study* (2002) edited by David Glantz, Steven Zaloga's *Bagration 1944* (1996), Rolf Hinze's *East Front Drama* (1996), and Paul Adair's *Hitler's Greatest Defeat* (1996). *The Battle for L'vov July 1944: The Soviet General Staff Study*, again edited by David Glantz (2002), is also instructive.

The battles in Kurland are described by Franz Kurowski in *Bridgehead Kurland* (2002). The other defensive battles during the autumn of 1944 have been virtually ignored in English.

Operations in 1945 are well summarised by the late Russ Schneider in *Gotterdammerung 1945: Germany's Last Stand in the East* (1998) and by Christopher

Duffy in *Red Storm on the Reich: The Soviet March on Germany, 1945* (1991). Alexander Solzhenitsyn's epic poem *Prussian Nights* (1977) adds much flavour.

The fighting in Hungary is best served by Krisztián Ungváry's majestic *Battle for Budapest: 100 Days in World War II* (2003), Perry Pierik's *Hungary 1944-1945: The Forgotten Tragedy* (1996) and Georg Maier's massive *Drama between Budapest and Vienna: The Final Fighting of the 6. Panzer-Armee 1945* (2004).

The final battles can still be followed in Cornelius Ryan's epic *The Last Battle* (1966). However, several studies by Tony Le Tissier are essential – *Zhukov at the Oder: The Decisive Battle for Berlin* (1996) and *Race for the Reichstag: The 1945 Battle for Berlin* (1999). His earlier *The Battle of Berlin 1945* (1988) is also still very much worthwhile. Vasili Chuikov's *The End of the Third Reich* (1967), penned by the commander of 8th Guards Army, which spearheaded the advance into Berlin, remains interesting. Antony Beevor's *Berlin: The Downfall, 1945* (2003) is the most recent account, and is the result of extensive research from Soviet and German sources.

Hugh Trevor-Roper's *The Last Days of Hitler* (1947) remains eminently readable. There have been two recent biographies of Marshal Zhukov: William J. Spahr's *Zhukov: The Rise and Fall of a Great Captain* and John Colvin's *Zhukov: The Conqueror of Berlin* (2004).

Index

Index of Persons

Alexandrova, Zoya, 20, 126-128, 186-191, 228-231, 268-270
Andy, Leonard B., 142
Asulbaev, Sasha, 230
Avdyushin, Fedor, 228

Baddeley, John, 100
Bakuridze, Abib, 240
Blythe, Alex, 213
Bogdanov, Nikolay, 115-118, 243-244
Bolotin, Mikhail, 116
Boscawen, Robert, 14, 55-60, 98-102, 201-206, 218
Braun, Christian, 87-88
Brotheridge, Den, 44, 47

Carter, Sam, 13, 50-51, 141-143, 201
Chance, Peter, 203
Chobonyan, Gevorg, 268
Churchill, Winston, 39

Danil'chenko, Grigoriy, 238
Denbigh, Billy, 100
Drozdovskiy, Konstantin, 240-241
Dupree, Frank, 142

Edwards, Denis, 14-15, 40-49, 212-214, 221-224
Ehrenburg, Ilya, 20
Eisenhower, Dwight, 83, 143, 221
Elanskiy, Nikolay, 266-267
Elder, Bryan, 214-217
Ellis, William, 96-97
Emmons, Ernie, 95, 138

Fox, Michael, 102

Gardner, Jim, 94, 134, 135
Geddes, Peter, 214
Gorodilov, Grigoriy, 75
Griffiths, Hugh, 100
Grigoriev, Sasha, 252
Groshev, Vitya, 189
Grossjohann, Georg, 16-17, 81-92, 218-221

Gurley, Franklin L., 13-14, 92-97, 133-138
Gutch, Johnny, 53
Gwatkin, Norman, 56

Hall, Peter, 15-16, 39-40, 49-50, 51-55, 138-141, 214-218, 224
Hershberg, Lennie, 95
Hitler, Adolf, 63, 141, 157-158, 224, 227-228
Hogberg, Hoggie, 95
Horrocks, Brian, 206
Horthy, Admiral, 108
Howard, John, 40, 43, 44, 47

Jarvis, Stan, 213
Johansson, Ragnar, 257, 266
Jones, Robert E., 94, 138

Khoklov, Petya, 188
Kravechenko, A.G., 236
Kyle, Scotty, 133

Lamprecht, Ulrich, 161
Lechner, Martin, 161
Leetham, Tony, 102
Lentz, Barney, 93
Loza, Dmitriy, 20-21, 74-76, 115-118, 169-173, 236-245, 266-268

Masloid, Ivan, 230, 231
Maxted, Stanley, 102
Middleton, Ririd, 55
Mikhno, Nikolay, 170-171, 173
Mulligan, Thomas, 93
Musker, Dermot, 203, 205, 206

Nemeseck, Lou, 138
Nicolai, Klaus, 73, 160

Ogden, Jack, 95
Olimpiev, Vsevelod, 22, 112-115, 177-181, 196-197, 251-254, 263-265
Oseledkin, Nikolay, 238

Parfenov, Mikhail, 173
Patton, George, 220
Pavlov, Valentin, 231
Pehrsson, Hans-Gösta, 122, 192
Petrukhin, Yakov, 242
Petukhov, Nikolay Georgievich, 236, 239
Priestly, Jimmy, 205

Rodney, John, 55
Rommel, Erwin, 42
Roncanio, Dino, 142
Ryder, David, 102

Scheiderbauer, Armin, 17-18, 65-74, 108-
112, 159-169, 181-186, 231-236
Schiel, Otto, 89
Smith, Henty, 101-102, 203
Smyth-Osbourne, Timmy, 205
Stalin, Josef, 39, 107, 221
Stepanov, Konstantin, 75

Szalasi, Ferenc, 108

Thompson, Johnny, 204
Thornton, 'Wagger', 49
Tychsen, Andrew, 96-97

Vedeneev, Sasha, 113
Voss, Johann, 17-18, 144-154, 207-212

Wade, Peter, 216
Wallin, Erik, 18-19, 118-126, 173-177,
191-196, 245-251, 254-262, 265-266
Wallwork, Jim, 46
Watkins, Tony, 101-102
Weber, Christian, 219

Yakushkin, Ivan, 75, 76, 116, 173
Yerburgh, John, 203

Zhukov, Georgi, 227

Index of Places

Aachen, 131, 141
Acsa, 115
Altdamm, 191, 194-196
Antwerp, 98, 141
Arnhem, 98, 131, 213

Bad Kleinen, 223
Baranow, 157, 161
Bastogne, 143
Bela, 172
Belgrade, 108
Bénouville, 41, 49
Beringen, 98
Berlin, 157, 159, 227, 228, 245-251, 254-
263, 268-270
Bernesebarat, 115, 116
Besançon, 90
Betzgau, 220
Birlad, 75
Boekel, 102
Bonlieu, 86
Breslau, 159, 196
Brussels, 98, 141
Brzoszuw, 114
Bucharest, 75
Buchenwald, 143
Budapest, 108, 115, 159, 169, 227
Bulford Camp, 40, 44

Bunkas, 120

Caen, 53, 55-57, 60, 98
Cagny, 55
Carentan, 40
Chalon-sur-Saône, 90, 92
Cologne, 144-145, 203, 204

Danzig, 231-236
Debrecen, 108
Dekkers Wald, 138
Deutsch-Eylau, 109
Deutsch-Westfalen, 169
Dole, 90
Dukla Pass, 113

Eindhoven, 98, 100, 101
Erdetarcha, 116
Eupen, 141, 142

Falaise, 56, 57, 98
Faubourg de Vaucelles, 60
Fort Benning, 137
Fort Bragg, 133, 137
Fort Devens, 13
Frankfurt-an-der-Oder, 191

Gennep, 201

Gladebusch, 222
Goch, 203, 205
Grafenwöhr, 219
Graudenz, 169
Grave, 102
Grenoble, 84, 85
Gross-Wollental, 184-185

Hamminkeln, 212, 214, 223
Hassum, 203
Hechtel, 98, 99
Heppen, 100
Hürtgen Forest, 131, 201

Kamenitsa, 169, 170
Kapellen, 205, 206
Kebel'kut, 173
Kemence, 115, 116
Kempten, 221
Khushi, 75
Kiev, 112
Kochel, 220
Komárno, 169, 170, 173
Komárom, 169
Königsberg, 159, 227
Krün, 219
Küstrin, 159, 191, 230-231, 254

La Courcourde, 89
Labeiki, 68-69
Lampaden, 212
Langerwehe, 141
Lauenburg, 221
Le Port, 49
Le Thillot, 92
Lowsha, 66
Lure, 92
Lutterstorf, 223
Lyon, 89

Magnuszew, 157
Marseilles, 84, 85, 86, 87, 92, 93, 131
Massow, 174
Minsk, 63
Mittenwald, 219
Mniszek, 188
Montélimar, 87
Moscow, 107
Mouen, 53-54
Muzhla, 173

Nasielsk, 108

Nauen, 256
Neubuchen, 185
Nice, 84
Nijmegen, 98, 102, 138, 201, 204, 205
Nijnsel, 101, 102
Nosdorf, 221

Overasselt, 102

Perpignan, 81, 82
Polozk, 67
Port Bou, 82
Potsdam, 256
Poweilin, 160, 162, 165
Prague, 228
Preussisch-Stargard, 232
Pulawy, 128, 231
Pultusk, 108

Raseinen, 72-73, 108
Reichswald Forest, 203
Reipertsweiler, 145
Remagen, 212, 218

Šahy, 115
Sandomierz, 115, 177
Schaijk, 204
Schaulen, 73
Schwartow, 221
Schwenten, 181
Seelow Heights, 227, 269
Septemes, 96
Serock, 108, 109
Sombatkhey, 236
Son, 98
Sopron, 236
St Remy, 133
Ste Mère Eglise, 40
Stalingrad, 65, 157
Stettin, 173, 191, 195-196
Suttorf, 221

Tarrant Rushton, 40, 44
Tomaszow, 188, 191
Torgau, 224, 228
Toulon, 84, 85, 86, 87
Tucheler Heide, 182, 184

Udem, 203, 204
Ulla, 69-70

Valence, 89

Vaslui, 75
Vienna, 227, 236-245
Vimont, 56
Vitebsk, 71
Volkel, 102

Wallgau, 219
Warka, 161

Weeze, 205
Werbali, 67
Wesel, 218

Xanten, 206

Zichenau, 108

Index of Military Formations

American
Army Groups: 12th, 131, 141, 221
Armies: 1st, 201, 212, 218; 3rd, 18, 131, 212, 220; 7th, 17, 18; 9th, 212, 218
Corps: VI, 83, 136
Divisions: 1st Infantry, 13, 50-51, 141-143, 201; 2nd Infantry, 141, 142; 3rd Infantry, 85, 92, 134, 135; 17th Airborne, 214; 28th Infantry, 141; 36th Infantry, 86, 92, 135; 45th Infantry, 85, 136, 137; 82nd Airborne, 138; 94th Infantry, 18; 99th Infantry, 141, 142; 100th Infantry, 13-14, 92-97, 133-138; 101st Airborne, 101
Regiments: 15th Infantry, 134; 18th Infantry, 13, 50-51, 141-143, 201; 67th Armored, 221; 141st Infantry, 86; 142nd Infantry, 86; 397th Infantry, 96; 398th Infantry, 96

British
Army Groups: 21st, 53, 141, 201, 212, 221
Armies: 2nd, 102
Corps: VIII, 55; XII, 55, 56; XXX, 55, 98, 100, 102
Divisions: Guards Armoured, 14, 55-60, 98-102, 201-206, 218; 1st Airborne, 102; 3rd Infantry, 55; 6th Airborne, 14-15, 40-49, 212-214, 221-224; 7th Armoured, 55, 56, 102; 11th Armoured, 55, 57, 203, 204; 15th Scottish, 53; 43rd Wessex, 15-16, 39-40, 49-50, 51-55, 138-141, 214-218, 224; 51st Highland, 55, 214
Brigades: 1st Malay, 16; 5th, 205; 6th Airlanding Infantry, 41; 6th Guards, 203; 32nd, 205
Regiments/Battalions: Coldstream Guards, 14, 55-60, 98-102, 201-206, 218; Glider Pilot, 42; Grenadier Guards, 56, 101; Household Cavalry, 98; 13th/18th Hussars, 214; Irish Guards, 56, 57, 98, 100, 206; 2nd Malaya, 16; 2nd Oxfordshire & Buckinghamshire Light Infantry, 41; 10th Oxfordshire & Buckinghamshire Light Infantry, 14-15, 40-49, 212-214, 221-224; 7th Somerset Light Infantry, 214; Welsh Guards, 100, 101; 1st Worcestershires, 15-16, 39-40, 49-50, 51-55, 138-141, 214-218, 224; 11th Worcestershires, 15

French
Armies: 1st, 17, 154
Divisions: 2nd Armoured, 95; 3rd Algerian, 92

German
Army Groups: B, 85, 141, 218; Centre, 63, 65, 71, 107; E, 107; G, 85; North, 71, 107
Armies: 2nd, 108; 6th, 81; 8th, 81; 11th SS *Panzer*, 173; 19th, 83, 87
Corps: Detachment D, 66, 68, 71; IX, 66, 71, 72; XX, 108
Divisions: 3rd *Panzer*, 109; 5th SS *Panzer* 'Wiking', 119; 6th SS Mountain 'Nord', 17-18, 144-154, 207-212; 7th *Panzer*, 72; 11th *Panzer*, 85, 87; 11th SS *Panzergrenadier* 'Nordland', 18-19, 118-126, 173-177, 191-196, 245-251, 254-262, 265-266; 12th SS *Panzer* 'Hitlerjugend', 43; 21st *Panzer*, 43, 56; 25th *Panzer*, 109; 35th Infantry, 186, 231; 95th Infantry, 108; 198th Infantry, 16-17, 81-92, 218-221; 252nd Infantry, 17-18, 65-74, 108-112, 159-169, 181-186, 231-236

Regiments/Battalions: 7th Grenadier, 65, 67, 71, 72, 73, 109-110, 160, 185; 11th SS Mountain, 17-18, 144-154, 207-212; 11th SS *Panzer Aufklärungs Abteilung*, 18-19, 118-126, 173-177, 191-196, 245-251, 254-262, 265-266; 12th SS Mountain, 146; 198th *Füsilier* Battalion, 85; 252nd *Artillerieregiment*, 72; 252nd *Füsilier* Battalion, 66, 71, 72, 160; *Panzerjäger Abteilung* 252, 72; *Pionierbataillon* 252, 72; 305th Grenadier, 85; 308th Grenadier, 85, 92; 326th Grenadier, 85, 89; 461st Grenadier, 67, 72, 109; 472nd Grenadier, 65, 67, 72, 109-110; SS *Fallschirmjäger* Battalion 500, 72

Soviet
Fronts: 1st Baltic, 107; 2nd Baltic, 107; 3rd Baltic, 107; 1st Byelorussian, 157, 186, 191, 228; 2nd Byelorussian, 157; 3rd Byelorussian, 157; Leningrad Front, 107; 1st Ukrainian, 65, 157, 252; 2nd Ukrainian, 108, 169; 4th Ukrainian, 108, 157

Armies: 6th Guards, 66, 169, 236; 7th Guards, 169; 43rd, 66; 69th, 127

Corps: 1st Guards Cavalry, 22, 112-115, 177-181, 196-197, 251-254, 263-265; 3rd Guards Tank, 72; 5th Guards Tank, 115, 170; 5th Mechanized, 20-21, 74-76; 9th Guards Mechanized, 20-21, 115-118, 169-173, 236-245, 266-268; 11th Tank, 20, 126-128, 186-191, 228-231, 268-270; 29th Tank, 72

Brigades: 65th Tank, 20, 126-128, 186-191, 228-231, 268-270; 46th Guards Tank, 20-21, 115-118, 169-173, 236-245, 266-268; 233rd Tank, 20-21, 74-76

Regiments: 143rd Guards Anti-tank Artillery, 22, 112-115, 177-181, 196-197, 251-254, 263-265; 251st Tank, 127

Related titles published by the Aberjona Press

Black Edelweiss: A Memoir of Combat
and Conscience by a Soldier of the
Waffen-SS
Johann Voss
240pp   Paperback
ISBN 0 9666389 8 0

Five Years Four Fronts: The War Years of
Georg Grossjohann. Memoirs of a
German Soldier 1939-45
Georg Grossjohann
204pp   Paperback
ISBN 0 9666 389 3 X

Some other available titles

Sledgehammers: Strengths and Flaws of Tiger Tank Battalions in World War II
Christopher Wilbeck   ISBN 0-9717650-2-2

Vanguard of the Crusade: The US 101st Airborne Division in WWII
Mark Bando   ISBN 0-9717650-0-6

From Normandy to the Ruhr with the 116th Panzer Division
Hans-Gunther Guderian   ISBN 0-9666389-7-2

Slaughterhouse: The Handbook of the Eastern Front 1941-45
Keith Bonn (ed.)   ISBN 0-9717650-9-X

Waffen-SS Encyclopedia
Marc J. Rikmenspoel   ISBN 0-9717650-8-1

Into the Mountains Dark: A WWII Odyssey from Harvard Crimson to Infantry Blue
Franklin L. Gurley   ISBN 0-9666389-4-8

THE ABERJONA PRESS
PO Box 629, Bedford, PA 15522, USA
Tel (814) 623 8308   Fax (814) 623 8668
Website: http://www.aberjonapress.com
Distributed exclusively in Europe by Helion & Company Ltd

Related titles published by Helion & Company

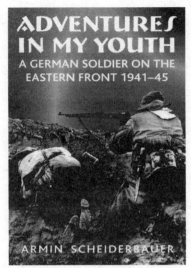

*Adventures in my Youth: A German
Soldier on the Eastern Front 1941-45*
Armin Scheiderbauer
224pp   Hardback
ISBN 1 874622 06 X

*Twilight of the Gods: A Swedish
Waffen-SS Volunteer's Experiences with
the 11th SS Panzergrenadier Division
'Nordland', Eastern Front 1944-45*
Thorolf Hillblad
144pp   Hardback
ISBN 1 874622 16 7

A selection of forthcoming titles

Diary of a Red Devil. By Glider to Arnhem with the 7th King's Own Scottish Borderers
Albert Blockwell   ISBN 1 874622 13 2

*To The Bitter End: The Final Battles of Army Groups North Ukraine, A, Centre,
Eastern Front 1944-45*
Rolf Hinze   ISBN 1 874622 36 1

Hitler's Last Levy. The Volkssturm 1944-45
Hans Kissel   ISBN 1 874622 51 5

Penalty Strike: The Memoirs of a Red Army Penal Company Commander 1943-45
Alexander V. Pyl'cyn   ISBN 1 874622 63 9

Red Star Airacobra. Memoirs of a Soviet Fighter Ace 1941-45
Evgeniy Mariinskiy ISBN 1 874622 78 7

HELION & COMPANY LIMITED
26 Willow Road, Solihull, West Midlands, B91 1UE, England
Tel 0121 705 3393   Fax 0121 711 4075
Website: http://www.helion.co.uk